THE DISABLED CO.

Social contract theories generally predicate the authority of rules that govern society on the idea that these rules are the product of a contractual agreement struck between members of society. These theories embody values, such as equality, reciprocity, and rationality, that are highly prized within our culture. Yet a closer inspection reveals that these features exclude other important values, relations, and even persons from the realm of contractual morality and justice, especially people with severe intellectual disabilities. Jonas-Sébastien Beaudry explores the moral status of intellectually disabled people in social contract thought and argues that this tradition needs to be revisited to include the most vulnerable. Addressing this problem will have concrete repercussions in law and policy because many issues that people with disabilities face are connected to deeply rooted assumptions about their status as full citizens or full members of our moral, political, and legal communities.

JONAS-SÉBASTIEN BEAUDRY is an Assistant Professor of Law at McGill University and a member of the Quebec Bar. His publications include articles in the areas of human rights, ethics, and disability theory, and a book on freedom of expression in Latin America. He has worked at the Supreme Court of Canada, the International Court of Justice, and has acted as a consultant on public policies for members of the Department of Justice, the Senate, and various disability organizations.

CAMBRIDGE DISABILITY LAW AND POLICY SERIES
Edited by Peter Blanck and Robin Paul Malloy

The Disability Law and Policy series examines these topics in interdisciplinary and comparative terms. The books in the series reflect the diversity of definitions, causes, and consequences of discrimination against persons with disabilities while illuminating fundamental themes that unite countries in their pursuit of human rights laws and policies to improve the social and economic status of persons with disabilities. The series contains historical, contemporary, and comparative scholarship crucial to identifying individual, organizational, cultural, attitudinal, and legal themes necessary for the advancement of disability law and policy.

The book topics covered in the series also are reflective of the new moral and political commitment by countries throughout the world toward equal opportunity for persons with disabilities in such areas as employment, housing, transportation, rehabilitation, and individual human rights. The series will thus play a significant role in informing policy makers, researchers, and citizens of issues central to disability rights and disability antidiscrimination policies. The series grounds the future of disability law and policy as a vehicle for ensuring that those living with disabilities participate as equal citizens of the world.

Books in the Series

Ruth Colker, *When Is Separate Unequal?: A Disability Perspective*, 2009

Larry M. Logue and Peter Blanck, *Race, Ethnicity, and Disability: Veterans and Benefits in Post–Civil War America*, 2010

Lisa Vanhala, *Making Rights a Reality? Disability Rights Activists and Legal Mobilization*, 2011

Eilionóir Flynn, *From Rhetoric to Action: Implementing the UN Convention on the Rights of Persons with Disabilities*, 2011

Isabel Karpin and Kristin Savell, *Perfecting Pregnancy: Law, Disability, and the Future of Reproduction*, 2012

Alicia Ouellette, *Bioethics and Disability: Toward a Disability-Conscious Bioethics*, 2013

Arie Rimmerman, *Social Inclusion of People with Disabilities: National and International Perspectives*, 2013

Andrew Power, Janet E. Lord and Allison S. DeFranco, *Active Citizenship and Disability: Implementing the Personalisation of Support*, 2013

Lisa Schur, Douglas Kruse and Peter Blanck, *People with Disabilities: Sidelined or Mainstreamed?*, 2013

Eliza Varney, *Disability and Information Technology: A Comparative Study in Media Regulation*, 2013

Jerome E. Bickenbach, Franziska Felder and Barbara Schmitz, *Disability and the Good Human Life*, 2014

Robin Paul Malloy, *Land Use Law and Disability: Planning and Zoning for Accessible Communities*, 2014

Arie Rimmerman, *Family Policy and Disability*, 2015

Peter Blanck, *eQuality: The Struggle for Web Accessibility by Persons with Cognitive Disabilities*, 2016

Anna Arstein-Kerslake, *Restoring Voice to People with Cognitive Disabilities: Realizing the Right to Equal Recognition Before the Law*, 2017

Arie Rimmerman, *Disability and Community Living Policies*, 2017

Paul Harpur, *Discrimination, Copyright and Equality: Opening the e-Book for the Print-Disabled*, 2017

Aisling de Paor, *Genetics, Disability and the Law: Towards an EU Legal Framework*, 2017

Piers Gooding, *A New Era for Mental Health Law and Policy: Supported Decision-Making and the UN Convention on the Rights of Persons with Disabilities*, 2017

Larry M. Logue and Peter Blanck, *Heavy Laden: Union Veterans, Psychological Illness, and Suicide*, 2018

Karrie A. Shogren, Michael L. Wehmeyer, Jonathan Martinis and Peter Blanck, *Supported Decision-Making: Theory, Research, and Practice to Enhance Self-Determination and Quality of Life*, 2018

Gauthier de Beco, Janet E. Lord and Shivaun Quinlivan, *The Right to Inclusive Education in International Human Rights Law*, 2019

Stephen Meyers, *Civilizing Disability Society: The Convention on the Rights of Persons with Disabilities Socializing Grassroots Disabled Persons' Organizations*, 2019

Paul David Harpur, *Ableism at Work: Law, Disability, and Hierarchies of Impairments*, 2020

The Disabled Contract

SEVERE INTELLECTUAL DISABILITY, JUSTICE AND MORALITY

JONAS-SÉBASTIEN BEAUDRY
McGill University

CAMBRIDGE
UNIVERSITY PRESS

University Printing House, Cambridge CB2 8BS, United Kingdom

One Liberty Plaza, 20th Floor, New York, NY 10006, USA

477 Williamstown Road, Port Melbourne, VIC 3207, Australia

314-321, 3rd Floor, Plot 3, Splendor Forum, Jasola District Centre, New Delhi - 110025, India

103 Penang Road, #05-06/07, Visioncrest Commercial, Singapore 238467

Cambridge University Press is part of the University of Cambridge.

It furthers the University's mission by disseminating knowledge in the pursuit of education, learning and research at the highest international levels of excellence.

www.cambridge.org
Information on this title: www.cambridge.org/9781316606681
DOI: 10.1017/9781316591482

© Jonas-Sébastien Beaudry 2021

This publication is in copyright. Subject to statutory exception and to the provisions of relevant collective licensing agreements, no reproduction of any part may take place without the written permission of Cambridge University Press.

First published 2021
First paperback edition 2022

A catalogue record for this publication is available from the British Library

ISBN 978-1-107-15285-4 Hardback
ISBN 978-1-316-60668-1 Paperback

Cambridge University Press has no responsibility for the persistence or accuracy of URLs for external or third-party internet websites referred to in this publication, and does not guarantee that any content on such websites is, or will remain, accurate or appropriate.

For Richard-Alexandre

Consider a birdcage. If you look very closely at just one wire in the cage, you cannot see the other wires. If your conception of what is before you is determined by this myopic focus, you would look at that one wire, up and down the length of it, and be unable to see why a bird would not just fly around the wire any time it wanted to go somewhere.
   Marilyn Frye, *The Politics of Reality: Essays in Feminist Theory*
         (Crossing Press, 1983)

Begin by imagining

a failure of will,

the boundaries of the body erased

like lines on a chalkboard.
  Sheila Black, "Playing Dead" (in *House of Bone*, Custom Words, 2007)

Contents

Foreword by Eva Feder Kittay		*page* xiii
Acknowledgments		xix
1	**Severe Intellectual Disability and the Social Contract**	1
	1.1 A Challenge to the Social Contract Tradition	1
	1.2 Who Are the "Persons with Severe Intellectual Disabilities"?	10
	1.3 Robust Moral Status	22
	1.4 Why Social Contract Theory?	28
	1.5 The Contractualism–Contractarianism Distinction	34
	1.6 Starting Points: Preservationists and Revisionists	39
	1.7 Structure and Summary of the Book	49
2	**Inclusive Contractarianism: Persons with Severe Intellectual Disabilities within a Society of Self-Interested Contractors**	53
	2.1 Generic Inclusivist Contractarianism	53
	2.2 Moralized Contractarianism	61
	2.3 When the "Tough Crowd" Rethinks Reciprocity	64
	2.4 Two Objections: Biting the Contractarian Bullet or Admitting an Unspoken Qualificatory Criterion	77
3	**The Capacity to Trust as a Contractual Basis for Robust Moral Status**	82
	3.1 A Trust-Based Conceptualization of the Social Contract	82
	3.2 The Nature of Trust	89
	3.3 Other-Regarding Trust and the Social Contract	105
	3.4 Can All PSID Take Part in Trusting Relationships?	114
	3.5 How Important Is Trust?	117
	3.6 Conclusion	124

4	**People with Severe Intellectual Disabilities as Active Citizens**	128
	4.1 Justice for Talents	131
	4.2 PSID's Capacity for Formulating and Realizing a Conception of the Good	144
	4.3 Conclusion	161
5	**People with Severe Intellectual Disabilities as Passive Citizens**	163
	5.1 PSID as Passive Citizens or Indirect Participants	163
	5.2 Dissociating the Concepts of Moral Legislators and Members of the Moral Community	164
	5.3 Problems with Being Represented by a Trustee in the Contractual Process	172
	5.4 Indirectly Acquiring Direct Moral Considerability Because the Contractors Make Provisions for It	177
	5.5 Extending Passive Citizenship to PSID in a Rawlsian Framework	187
	5.6 Conclusion	214
6	**Other-Regarding Concern and Exploitation**	216
	6.1 Situating the Chapter	216
	6.2 Hampton and Dimock's Feminist Contractarianism	217
	6.3 A Response	225
	6.4 Problematizing Contractarian Assessments of Costs and Benefits	249
	6.5 Noncontractarian Frameworks	255
	6.6 Other Failures in Accounting for the Special Value of "Outliers"	264
	6.7 Is Hampton's "Kantian Contractarianism" Not Other-Regarding?	268
	6.8 Conclusion	270
7	**Beyond Contractual Relations**	273
	7.1 Why Contractualism or Contractarianism Cannot Fully Integrate All People with Severe Intellectual Disabilities	273
	7.2 Taking Relations Seriously	278
	7.3 Taking Relations of Other-Regarding Concern Seriously	290
	7.4 A Relational Pluralist View: Care, Contract, and Beyond	292
Bibliography		297
Index		307

Foreword

Philosophical verities take hold and maintain a tight grip on the philosophical imagination. But there are times when we come to recognize that a putative philosophical verity is not veridical. This reveal takes more than vision; it also takes careful, rigorous, and systematic argumentation. This is what Beaudry gives us and in doing so allows us to drop old philosophical chestnuts and adopt a more adequate understanding of justice and contract theory. Such a chestnut is one with which mostly all professors of philosophy have experience.

Each semester, I would proclaim to my undergraduate students in introductory philosophy courses: "Man is a rational animal" (adding that "man" is the generic term meaning men and women). Inevitably some student would raise her hand and ask, "[B]ut what about people with serious mental illness or people with severe intellectual disabilities?" I can't recall how I answered, but I am certain that my answer conveyed the conviction that such a question was philosophically naïve. Yet I should have known better. By the time I was an assistant professor, I was already living with a person diagnosed with severe to profound intellectual disabilities. With my inadequate and inauthentic answers, I was playing the philosophy game: conveying the presumed wisdom of the great canonical figures – rather than actually doing philosophy – questioning dogmas, taking seriously what I saw and understood, and interpreting these with the toolkits of critical and analytic inquiry. I knew my daughter, then labeled "severely to profoundly retarded," was just as human, just as morally valuable as anyone else, and yet I echoed a proposition that has stood since at least Aristotle. Beaudry is not playing at philosophy, but doing it here. And the philosophy he is doing is due in large measure to the fact that he has experienced a world constructed by and for neurotypical people, as seen through the eyes of his brother. As philosophers who have lived with a beloved person whose being gets occluded in the sorts of definition above, we know how much is at stake in getting the philosophy right. For in this definition of what it is to be human, we have the brick holding up the entire edifice of moral and political philosophy; ideas of robust moral status, dignity, and justice rest on it. No more so than in the conception of justice based on a social contract between rational contractors.

Since John Rawls resurrected social contract theory in the early 1970s, the idea that has dominated political philosophy is that the principles of justice are self-chosen by able-bodied and able-minded independent rational actors who are contracting with one another for social cooperation, based on mutual self-interest. Contract theory also prevails in moral theory, either as contractarianism (based on a Hobbesian understanding of mutual self-interest) or as contractualism (based on Kantian respect for contractors as ends-in-themselves). But what happens to those who are not "rational animals" – the fully functioning rational agents of contract theory?

When I eventually confronted this question, there were few philosophical answers – indeed, the question seemed not to be on the philosophical horizon at all. As I pondered where in the philosophical understanding of justice do people such as my daughter fit, it became increasingly obvious that the naïve student's objections pointed to a potential flaw in almost all traditional philosophical systems, for the claim to universality was belied by those people to whom the definition did not necessarily fit. Feminist philosophers and race theorists had already begun to dismantle the myth of philosophical universality. They revealed that the scope of the universal quantifier was never *all* human beings – no more than Jefferson's "all men are created equal" was to apply to slaves or free women. It now seemed that questioning the long-standing definition of "man" as a "rational animal" might be out of bounds no longer.

By the 1990s, the cracks in the hegemonic approach to the nonstandard body and mind were evident. In the spirit of feminist philosophers, race theorists, and anti-colonial scholars, some philosophers followed the lead of scholars in other disciplines and began their critical philosophical study of disability. In the late 1990s, I finally undertook the task of addressing the question posed by the philosophical naïf: what about those humans who may not be rational, or who may lack certain rational capacities – how do they partake in the human moral universe? Taking my experience with my daughter as a fixed point, and Rawlsian theory as an exemplary formulation of contract theory, I asked whether a theory of justice that neglected the existence of people such as her could be an adequate theory of justice.

Beaudry tells us that "[i]ntellectual disability affects two to three percent of the general population" and, of these, about 5 percent are considered severely to profoundly intellectually disabled. It is this group that is least able to be accommodated by contract theories of justice. It is a relatively small group – it is the "hard case" for theory. Many philosophers will say that we should no more do philosophy than formulate laws based on hard cases. Still today, more and more philosophers concede that the question of whether a theory can include people with severe intellectual disabilities needs answering. At the very least, one needs to consider if the exclusion is, or is not, a significant fault.

Beaudry unequivocally takes the stance that excluding the severely disabled individual from the scope of justice and morality is a fault or error of some kind. He presumes the equal moral worth of all disabled people, including those with severe and profound intellectual disabilities. Happily today there are enough philosophical views on how to repair this fault to justify an entire volume; we've come a long way from the total neglect of disability in philosophy.

Beaudry lays out the various positions he explores with powerful clarity and thoroughness. We see a number of philosophers picking at the edges of social contract theory or even at its core elements, with the intent to make it fully inclusive. While some try to reconstrue contemporary contract theories, others insist on revising our understanding of people with severe and profound cognitive disabilities in order to retrofit them into the standard theories. Beaudry examines all these theories and finds each wanting. It seems that the following anecdote is pertinent here: A couple lost while hiking in New England come across an old native dweller and ask him for directions. The crotchety old New Englander replies, "[W]ell if I was trying to get to there, I wouldn't start from here." Beaudry's arguments give us a very convincing reason to suspect that proponents of justice as a contractual agreement looking for a way to include people with very significant cognitive disabilities are like our lost hikers: their starting point will not get them to their desired destination.

The book that Jonas-Sébastien Beaudry graces us with is a carefully argued, analytically formidable response to all those whose starting point is contract theory and whose endpoint is the inclusion of people with severe and profound disabilities into a theory of justice. With precision, rigor, and generosity, he explores the most promising attempts to make contract theory compatible with a conception of justice for those with significant intellectual disabilities. He demonstrates how some attempts allow *almost all* to be included, but still leave out those whose disabilities are most significant. As he interrogates various theories, he demonstrates that in each case the view either ends up using the intellectually disabled in an instrumental fashion, leaves them with something short of full robust moral status, or includes them but only by unwittingly smuggling in noncontractual values and concepts. The comprehensiveness and thoroughness of Beaudry's investigation has no equal in the literature. It is a definitive work.

Should we then forsake contract theory? Some philosophers such as Martha Nussbaum have abandoned contract theory altogether, in some measure because it fails to explain why we owe justice to those with cognitive disabilities. For several decades, feminists and race theorists have pointed out the limitations of contract theory, arguing, for example, that the social contract is one made by men to control women and women's sexuality and reproduction (the sexual contract) or that the social contract is made between white men to rule over and control black and brown men and women (the racial contract) (Carole Pateman, *The Sexual Contract* [Stanford: Stanford University Press, 1988]; Charles Mills, *The Racial Contract*

[Ithaca: Cornell University Press, 1997]). That is to say, the contractual conception of justice depends on the subordination of some groups – those who were never meant to be contractors. Yet contract theory, whether it is Hobbesian contractarianism or Kantian-based contractualism, is a hard theory to give up for it has much to commend it, and arguably it can even be especially useful for those who were originally excluded. It gives us an understanding of when power is legitimate and when it is not. It offers a good understanding of how strangers might come to agree to cooperate under conditions that are deemed fair by all. It extolls values we cherish, such as equality and freedom.

Beaudry urges that we do not have to give up contract theory. Instead, we need to acknowledge that it cannot tell us what is just or unjust in every sort of relation, between every sort of relata. We need other ways to extend the concept of justice to include those who don't fit the Procrustean bed of the independent, rational, full-functioning cooperator or to help with those areas of life where we mostly need to act with other-regarding motivations.

Beaudry demonstrates the importance of including the significantly intellectually disabled in our philosophical considerations, not only because we can better understand what we owe to them, but also because doing so throws light on concepts such as contract-based theories of justice. The "hard case" shows us that we should not drop the intuition that this group of people have robust moral status and should be treated justly, but instead drop the conceit that contract theory is all we need for moral and political theory. As Beaudry writes, the difficulty lies not with contract theory, but with thinking that the "idealized model of non-tuist interpersonal relations, associated with a model of relations between strangers, will exhaust the moral roles that people play." Acknowledging the robust moral status of the profoundly and severely intellectually disabled can best be done by recognizing the moral obligations in the roles we assume and the relations we have to this extremely vulnerable population, where other-regarding concerns predominate. This group is owed justice, but it is rarely justice as understood in contractual terms or for contractual reasons. Beaudry urges us to consider a role- or relation-based morality in which the nature of the relation figures in how we think of what is right and just in the different sorts of relations we enter and in the roles we assume.

In this book, we have a great resource for thinking about contract theory, its scope, value, and limitations – ones that emerge as we attempt to make contract theory more and more inclusive. What Beaudry has done has been to clear the ground for all who labor in these fields. By showing us what contract theory can and cannot do, it cuts through the thicket, opening better paths to take to arrive at the source and nature of the justice we owe to those who are noncontractors, but who cohabit the moral universe with us. As the book illustrates the philosophical value of beginning with the hard case, we find ourselves needing to concede that we need a morally pluralistic approach. Now we can stop wrestling with contract theories of justice – stretching, pulling, and twisting them to try to make them fit all sorts of individuals to whom justice is owed. With respect to the question of contract theory and people with significant cognitive disabilities, Beaudry's is likely to be the last word. While we can keep contract theory for a limited set of relations, we also need to roll up our sleeves and locate a better "here" so we can go to "there."

Eva Feder Kittay
New York
February 16, 2020

Acknowledgments

I have received a lot of help throughout the conception, writing, and revision of this book. Amongst the many professors, mentors, colleagues, and students to whom I owe a debt of gratitude, I am especially indebted to John Gardner and Anita Silvers, who both sadly passed away in the summer of 2019. I am also grateful to Carolyn Ells, Leslie Green, Eva Kittay, Kevin Toh, and John Vorhaus. Their generous insights and support were priceless. Many other scholars helped me along the way, including Paula Bodington and Derek Parfit, who gave me generous advice. Many friends have also discussed this project with me, especially Aruna Nair and Hakan Külcü. I thank my research assistants, Elizabeth Bateman, Zoë Christmas, Christopher Little, and Matthew Palynchuk, for their excellent editorial support. I am grateful to the University of British Columbia and McGill University for having provided me with an environment that allowed me to pursue research in the field of the philosophy of disability. I am also blessed with a family and friends who have always supported my academic goals.

1

Severe Intellectual Disability and the Social Contract

1.1 A CHALLENGE TO THE SOCIAL CONTRACT TRADITION

Social contract theories generally predicate the authority of rules that govern society on the idea that these rules are the products of a contractual agreement struck between members of the society. These theories assume the moral, political, and strategic importance of certain contractual features (for instance, equality and reciprocity between contractors) and they assume certain characteristics are held by the parties (for instance, mutual disinterest and rationality). These theories are appealing because of the value they place on these assumed features. Social contract theories employ a normative or descriptive narrative about the origins of society, presenting parties to the social contract as endorsing certain rules and principles when they set up basic social institutions. The two main variants of social contract theory have been called "contractarianism" and "contractualism." These variants can also be described as ethical theories that apply to discrete situations, rather than as political theories that legitimize the social structures that are agreed to through this contractual process. This moral and political tradition is most famously represented by Thomas Hobbes, John Locke, Jean-Jacques Rousseau, and Immanuel Kant and, in contemporary times, by David Gauthier, John Rawls, and Thomas Scanlon. I distinguish "contractarian" and "contractualist" theories later in the chapter (see Section 1.5). Where I refer to both theories, I use the general term "contractual."

John Rawls's *A Theory of Justice* is arguably one of the most important philosophical works of the twentieth century.[1] His text single-handedly revived political philosophy, resuscitated the social contract tradition, and connected this tradition to the values of contemporary liberalism. While this book focuses on a particularly

---

[1] The three monographs by Rawls that outline his theory of justice as fairness are: *A Theory of Justice*, rev. ed. (Cambridge: Harvard University Press, 1999); *Political Liberalism*, expand. ed. (New York: Columbia University Press, 2005); *Justice as Fairness: A Restatement*, ed. Erin Kelly (Cambridge: Harvard University Press, 2001).

recent *integrationist* branch of social contract theory – rather than on Rawls – it is fitting to consider how Rawls, as the most influential contemporary representative of the social contract tradition, justified the exclusion of people with severe disabilities from the scope of his social contract. Indeed, Rawls's position on this question frames the philosophical problem that I address in this book. He presents the "fundamental question of political justice" in the following terms:

> [W]hat is the most appropriate conception of justice for specifying the terms of social cooperation between citizens regarded as free and equal, and as normal and fully cooperating members of society over a complete life?[2]

Rawls's emphasis on social cooperation between citizens influences him (and traditional social contract theorists) to set aside a fundamental problem that severely disabled individuals face: namely, that they are unable to "cooperate" due to their disabilities. Rawls considers that this exclusion of severely disabled individuals could be remedied by the expansion of his theory, although he confesses to "lack[ing] the ingenuity to see how the extension may proceed."[3] Thus, Rawls writes that, should his theory of "justice as fairness" fail to encompass individuals with severe disabilities, it is possible that other accounts of justice or morality may deal with the "problem" of the severely disabled person's exclusion and thus effectively supplement his theory. For Rawls, measuring the damage that the exclusion of the severely disabled individual and of other groups does to his contractualist theory "must wait until the case itself can be examined."[4] This is the challenge that Rawls bestows upon the social contract tradition: can it ground a *robust moral status* for severely disabled people? If not, how deep a fault is this for the tradition, and can the tradition be effectively supplemented by alternative accounts?

I define with more precision what I mean by robust obligations or robust moral status in Section 1.3. At this point, it is only necessary to know that "robust" implies more than mere charity and connotes no less moral and political consideration than that which is owed to all nondisabled citizens.[5]

1.1.1 *Situating This Work*

This book explores whether and how one particular set of theories can provide moral and political grounds for owing robust duties to people with severe disabilities, or

---

[2] Rawls, *Political Liberalism*, at 20.
[3] Ibid. at 21.
[4] Ibid.
[5] "Citizenship" is being broadly understood as membership to a political community. The frontiers of a political community can, in turn, be defined in different ways. This book will be focusing on contractual justifications for counting someone as a subject of justice or as a moral agent/patient. However, the claim that people with disabilities deserve the same moral and political status as that of other members of a moral or political community could also be used (as a hypothesis or starting premise) to reflect on noncontractual justifications for moral and political status as well.

grounds for justifying their robust moral status, which is the corollary of such duties. These theories belong to the social contract tradition. While I am interested in assessing the merits of various theoretical grounds that justify the severely disabled individual's moral status, it is particularly important to see how social contract theory fares in this discussion because of its theoretical and practical omnipresence. Whether the key ideals and premises of social contract theory are meticulously defended by theorists or unreflectively adopted by practitioners as a matter of common sense, their influence in political, economic, and legal affairs is undeniable. This influence is felt through the importance that our political culture and our laws give to individual capacities for reasoning and autonomy. As I will explain in this chapter, people with severe disabilities, especially cognitive disabilities, suffer from "contractual expectations" which, in turn, serve to justify their exclusion from various spheres of social life. For instance, they may be excluded – partially or completely – from work, education, healthcare, voting, marriage, and other participatory roles within the legal system, such as that of witness, complainant, and respondent, though the politics and the law in these areas are being reformed in various jurisdictions to gradually better accommodate cognitive differences.[6] The United Nations *Convention on the Rights of Persons with Disabilities*[7] is a symptom as much as a catalyst of this ongoing evolution in capacity recognition.[8]

While I assume that people with severe disabilities do have a robust moral status, I leave the issue of justifying this status unresolved. Various scholars justify the robust moral status of severely disabled individuals in different ways and by applying different theories, ranging from Kantian to Wittgensteinian. However, this book does not deal with the revisionist challenge presented in the last section of this chapter, or at least not directly. Instead, the question that this book addresses is whether normative contractual philosophy can justify the position that we do owe robust obligations to the severely disabled individual, and, if so, to what extent it succeeds or fails in meeting these obligations. I am not concerned with distinguishing between obligations of morality and justice in answering this question, as my focus is whether severely disabled individuals have a robust moral status. As I explain later in this chapter, this position implies that the duties of justice are owed to severely disabled individuals because having a robust moral status should normally imply that one is a subject of justice.

---

[6] Consider, for instance, the recent federal law in Canada: *An Act to Ensure a Barrier-Free Canada*, RSC 2019, c 10.
[7] March 30, 2007, 2515 UNTS 3 (entered into force on May 3, 2008).
[8] See, e.g., Colin Barnes, "A Working Social Model? Disability, Work and Disability Politics in the Twenty-First Century" (2000) 20:4 Critical Soc Pol'y 441; Linda Barclay, "Cognitive Impairment and the Right to Vote: A Strategic Approach" (2013) 30:2 J Applied Phil 146; Richard D. Schneider and Hy Bloom, *Law and Mental Disorder: A Comprehensive and Practical Approach* (Toronto: Irwin Law, 2013).

To some readers, social contract theory may evoke an outdated artifact, a thought experiment used by seventeenth- and eighteenth-century philosophers. However, its contemporary versions have been enormously influential in philosophical scholarship, and its conceptual pillars have not only outlasted its early formulations, but they also animate the fundamental liberal commitments of Western societies, which still adhere to the individualist paradigm that Thomas Hobbes heralded centuries ago. In fact, one may fail to detect the ubiquitous and permanent presence of contractual thinking in our cultural background because it is so entrenched as to be invisible. The social contract tradition holds the promise, as old as philosophy itself, that reason can help human beings to organize a fair society thanks to the use of reason. The social contract operated a metaphysical restructuring of the foundations of our political order, by understanding human beings' desires and their capacity for reason and placing individual wills at the heart of the social edifice. For early modern thinker Hobbes, "the central political question becomes that of knowing how a multiplicity of individual wills can become a unique political will ... [and] one of the central juridical questions becomes that of knowing how to found a penal law that does not conflict with ethical individualism."[9] While theories of the social contract do not make the news, their basic assumptions about sovereignty, power, individualism, reason, and personhood pervade our culture, notwithstanding critiques of modernity exposing the historically contingent construction of the modern subject (along with its reasonable nature, desires, needs, quality of life, and aspiration to autonomy). Modern subjecthood is conditional upon possessing reasoning capacities. As Foucauldian scholar Achille Mbembe wrote:

> [I]t is on the basis of a distinction between reason and unreason (passion, fantasy) that late-modern criticism has been able to articulate a certain idea of the political, the community, the subject – or, more fundamentally, of what the good life is all about, how to achieve it, and, in the process, to become a fully moral agent. Within this paradigm, reason is the truth of the subject and politics is the exercise of reason in the public sphere. The exercise of reason is tantamount to the exercise of freedom, a key element for individual autonomy. The romance of sovereignty, in this case, rests on the belief that the subject is the master and the controlling author of his or her own meaning.[10]

Far from an innocuous thought experiment, the social contract is therefore a quintessentially modern theorizing of society and, incidentally, of the conditions of exclusion of those understood as lacking certain cognitive capacities that enable reasoning and autonomy.

---

[9] Yves Charles Zarka, *Hobbes and Modern Political Thought*, trans. James Griffith (Edinburgh: Edinburgh University Press, 2016), at 9. See also Yves Charles Zarka, *La décision métaphysique de Hobbes: conditions de la politique* (Paris: J Vrin, 1987).

[10] J.-A. Mbembe, "Necropolitics" (2003) 15:1 Pub Culture 11 at 13.

The kind of exclusion I am considering here may seem quite abstract to readers who would claim not doubting that even the most profoundly disabled individuals have equal rights and find threats to their moral status farfetched. Yet, these same well-meaning readers may unwittingly entertain ableist prejudices making it difficult to realize that their social arrangements marginalize, disempower, and otherwise oppress people with disabilities in ways that go undetected, as whatever harm people with disabilities endure are thought to be the necessary result of fair social arrangements, which in fact rest on problematic understandings of disability. The rights of people with disabilities are often not so much violated as they are suspended: people with disabilities are often not just mistreated as subjects, but their very subjecthood is threatened. For instance, analyzing "whether human rights law effectively facilitates the meaningful inclusion of people with disabilities in society," Canadian legal scholar Judith Mosoff found that "[t]he most striking characteristic of the adjudicated complaints was that individuals with severe disabilities were rarely the subjects of decisions."[11] Perhaps, then, disability activists and scholars should pay attention not only to the violation of abstract rights, but also to the very status of persons with disabilities as rights bearers and how this status is constructed through relations of power preceding, or supposed by, discourses of rights and discrimination.[12] Examining the social contract tradition's role in disabling certain human beings is a contribution to this general endeavor.

1.1.2 *Main Contentions*

The hypothesis that I test in this book is that social contract theory does not satisfactorily explain why we owe a serious concern or respect for persons with severe intellectual disabilities in our community (or why they have a "robust moral status"). In turn, this book explores the extent to which "integrationist" contractual theories – that is, contractual theories that try to remedy the exclusion of the severely disabled individuals – fail or succeed. This examination suggests that the social contract tradition excludes morally important dimensions of human relations from the spheres of morality or justice.

My primary goal is to reveal various contractual expectations that pervade our moral, political, and legal culture and constitute an oppressive orthodoxy. To put this another way, I want to reveal the conceptual structure of a "disabled contract."

---

[11] Judith Mosoff, "Is the Human Rights Paradigm 'Able' to Include Disability: Who's In – Who Wins – What – Why" (2000) 26:1 Queen's LJ 225 at 225.

[12] This suggestion mirrors Hannah Arendt's criticism of the Rights of Man, worth only as much as the political will to protect them. "From the beginning," Arendt writes, "the paradox involved in the declaration of inalienable human rights was that it reckoned with an 'abstract' human being who seemed to exist nowhere" (*The Origins of Totalitarianism* [New York: Meridian Books, 1958], at 291). For Foucauldian critiques of medicolegal apparatuses constructing disability, see Shelley Tremain, "On the Government of Disability" (2001) 27:4 Soc Theory & Prac 617.

This work mirrors the critical ambition of Charles Mills and Carole Pateman, who revealed the structures of violence and domination that compose a racial contract[13] and a sexual contract,[14] respectively.[15] In similar terms, the title of this monograph, *The Disabled Contract*, refers to a conceptual apparatus that is used to justify, normalize, or naturalize unfair, immoral, or oppressive social structures. More specifically, this conceptual apparatus connotes the idea that the exclusion of PWD (persons with disabilities) and PSID (persons with severe intellectual disabilities) can be justified on contractual grounds or that harmful forms of integration can constitute "contractual compensation" for delaying integration, namely by forcing a "contract" on people with different needs and capacities. In a more literal way, this title suggests that our social contract is "disabled" in the sense that it fails to enable some people and, additionally, that the disabling/enabling power it generates is arbitrary.

A Rotten Social Contract
If we took the unbridled individualism that dominates our political culture seriously and imagined how it would translate in a social contract including PWD, the results may be bleaker than what any of the revisionist or integrationist contractual theories I examine in this book would formally propose. We could imagine a "social contract" involving the PWD and the PSID in the following way: an unspoken cultural agreement, that could have organically taken place through the industrial revolution, would segregate PWD from increasingly specialized means of production. Such social isolation, even accompanied with a duty of charity toward the PWD, would be seen as more economically advantageous than the social integration of PWD and less disruptive to the meaning of labor within a capitalistic framework. This evokes Mike Oliver's historical description of disability, as "ultimately produced by the functional needs of capital for a particular kind of work force."[16] If we accept (something that contractual thought cannot easily justify) that PWD are already a part of the community and *must* fit somewhere within it, we could imagine that a separate "contract" occurred between able-bodied people and disabled, especially severely disabled, individuals. This "contract" would have been unilaterally imposed by the powerful able-bodied contractors, who simultaneously act as trustees for PWD's interests, and who are moved only to give them scraps off

---

[13] Charles Mills, *The Racial Contract* (Ithaca: Cornell University Press, 1997).
[14] Carole Pateman, *The Sexual Contract* (Stanford: Stanford University Press, 1988).
[15] Those sexual and racial structures of oppression need to be revealed since they are made invisible within traditional understandings of the social contract. Mainstream contract doctrine both constitutes and perpetuates oppression, in part by rendering it invisible within the seemingly neutral language of rights and values it promotes and the prescriptive (but race- or sex-neutral) or descriptive accounts of society formation that it puts forward.
[16] Michael Oliver, *The Politics of Disablement* (London: Macmillan, 1990), esp. at xii, 27. See also Anita Silvers, "Formal Justice" in Anita Silvers, David Wasserman, and Mary Mahowald, *Disability, Difference, Discrimination* (Lanham, MD: Rowman & Littlefield, 1998), 13.

the political table because of PWD's already-established status as members of society. (Of course, under this model, PWD are not full citizens or full persons.)

The general terms of this hypothetical rotten social contract would have been the following: PWD would "contribute" by enduring social exclusion whenever this would be convenient for the social order. In return for letting the modes of production run as they do, and not seeking integration in the labor force (in a culture where one's status as a laborer is partly determinative of one's status as a person), PWD's basic needs would be provided for. This charitable kind of providence would be the first expense to be cut in times of economic hardship, and for many PWD – being literally voiceless, and most being powerless – the enforcement of this rotten contract would not be guaranteed. It would be left to the discretion of parties who may eventually gain from not enforcing it, namely by keeping more resources for themselves, or because cruelty toward "less than full persons" within one's community would distinguish and heighten one's own status as the "fullest" kind of person – self-serving pity and cruelty being the darker sides of the charity coin. Of course, alienation and segregation are not traded at a fair table of negotiation as a form of social contribution. Oppressed people are not considered entitled to *not* be alienated, segregated, or more easily sacrificed. However, by presenting this imposed indecent cost as traded, we can sense how poorly PWD, and especially PSID, fare under a contractual idiom. I will not attempt to flesh out the reality of this hypothetical rotten contract with historical and empirical data. Instead, I will examine whether even the most promising, integrationist versions of the social contract succeed at integrating PWD within their scope.

Although this work is primarily a critique of the social contract tradition, it also supports a more positive program of research that emerges from the examination of specific failures of this tradition. In the last part of this book, I elaborate on the moral dimensions missing from mainstream contractual thinking and point to the pitfalls that any alternative account must heed. I also suggest a theory that integrates seemingly clashing contractual and relational concerns and answers to the preliminary criticisms that are obstacles to this program of research. Thus, this book has a dual aim: to question or curtail the breadth of certain key assumptions of social contract theories and to contribute to research on the moral and political obligations that are owed to people with severe disabilities.

1.1.3 Terminology: PSID (Persons with Severe Intellectual Disabilities)

I will generally use the acronym "PSID" (persons with severe intellectual disabilities) to refer to the group of persons who pose the challenge to the social contract tradition that I am examining in this book.[17] I also occasionally use the term

---

[17] I hope that the very use of an acronym is at least no more dehumanizing than the commonly employed "PWD." Writing "persons with severe intellectual disabilities" throughout this book

"cognitive" or "mental" instead of "intellectual" to qualify their disability. I may also use the word "impairment" instead of "disability." I may also use person-first language, such as PWD, or disability-first language (as "the severely disabled" or "a disabled person"). Although I will generally adhere to a person-first language and to the terms "intellectual" and "disability," this book does not use a uniform terminology to better interact with a variety of scholarships and texts that use different terms to refer to identical or overlapping phenomena. (For instance, the section below uses a disability-first language, since it examines a medical text in which such language is predominant.) Readers should infer from the context whether I use those germane terms to make broader assertions (e.g., that apply not only to PSID but also to PWD or to severe physical disabilities) or to mirror a particular author's terminology. Generally speaking, disability referents in this book signify individuals who, as a result of their disabilities, lack "contractual" capacities – that is, the (generally intellectual) capacities required by different strands of the social contract tradition to be considered a full moral or political subject. Like other philosophers writing about intellectual disabilities, I do not take any of those terms to refer to "natural kinds" (i.e., "a grouping that reflects the structure of the natural world rather than the interests and actions of human beings"[18]), or to be self-evident or unproblematic.[19]

Consider a few common challenges to disability-related terminology. The terms "dysfunction," "impairment," "disability," and "handicap" are sometimes distinguished to refer to more or less socially constructed phenomena, or to draw attention to medical or social components of a situation. The same can be said of person-first language, which is sometimes preferred by those who wish to want to avoid the term "disabled person" because it seems to imply that someone's "personhood" itself is disabled or that someone is not a full person, whereas a "person with a disability" emphasizes her personhood first. The French expression *une personne en situation de handicap* (literally, a person in a *situation* of handicap/disability) not only detaches personhood from disability but also suggest that "handicap" is a "situation," thereby inviting to consider that this situation may be partially, if not totally, socially created. The traditional, reductionist, version of the social model of disability insisted that disability is *nothing but* a social phenomenon (e.g., physical barriers, such as a lack of a ramp to access the post office) added on top of some actual physiological differences in a PWD's body, referred to as "impairments."[20] However,

---

seemed too distracting. Stipulating that "disability" in this book refers to "severe intellectual disability" would have been the most elegant solution but it would have been a source of confusion, as most of my comments apply to PSID, and not to PWD generally.

[18] Alexander Bird and Emma Tobin, "Natural Kinds," *The Stanford Encyclopedia of Philosophy* (February 2017), plato.stanford.edu/archives/spr2018/entries/natural-kinds/.

[19] See, e.g., Licia Carlson, *The Faces of Intellectual Disability* (Bloomington: Indiana University Press, 2010), at xv.

[20] The "social model" of disability has gained currency from the seventies onward and has effectively become an orthodoxy of its own in many fields – from sociology to civil rights

those mainstream observations are themselves problematic. Some scholars may prefer to use the term "disabled person" to draw attention to disability. This is meant to emphasize society's responsibility in creating disability. "Disabled person" would always implicitly mean "person disabled *by* a particular social context." Challenges to personhood are not at the forefront of those scholars' concerns. Others may problematize the rigidity, artificiality, or oppressive features of identity politics, or the insidious reintroduction of natural kinds in disability discourses through the notion of "impairments." Some may point out that the very act of setting apart PSID as a distinct category of persons or of using words like "different" or "exceptional" may imply a problematic commitment to certain standards of "normalcy." While earlier waves of disability scholarship sought to identify, name, and redefine certain oppressed groups in more positive or empowering ways, later waves of disability scholarship problematized the "oppressed identity" used in these earlier emancipatory narratives. This theoretical progression is reminiscent of the "waves" of gender and race studies. It could be answered that theoretical investigations must start somewhere, and that using the category of PSID is a useful way to criticize theories that treat PSID as outliers, even if those theories themselves relied on the problematic assumption that PSID is a valid category to use to discuss who falls beyond the scope of morality. We must, in other words, take the assumptions of the people we criticize seriously – or seriously enough to get to the point of analyzing the arguments they make on the basis of those assumptions – unless we are to reject their views wholesale rather than engage with them.

I try to circumvent those debates, but I cannot avoid them entirely. If anything, my preferred person-first language (PSID) reflects this book's assumption that human beings with exceptional (and commonly assessed as "lesser") cognitive abilities are equally important members of our moral and political communities. The issue of how (and how much) phenomena and categories of "intellectual disability" are socially constructed and the biological and historical origins of these phenomena are left open. Although a social constructivist view tends to impute responsibility on the society that created the "problems" PWD suffer from (such as

activism. For a general introduction to disability models, see David Pfeiffer, "The Conceptualization of Disability" in Sharon N. Barnartt and Barbara M. Altman, eds., *Exploring Theories and Expanding Methodologies: Where We Are and Where We Need to Go (Research in Social Science and Disability, vol. 2)* (Bingley: Emerald Group Publishing, 2001), 29. For my own critical view on the debate between proponents of the "medical model" and proponents of the "social model" of disability, see Jonas-Sébastien Beaudry, "Beyond (Models of) Disability?" (2016) 41:2 J Med & Phil 210. On the debate about the construction of "impairment," as opposed to "disability," see my "The Vanishing Body of Disability Law: Power and the Making of the Impaired Subject" (2018) 31:1 Can J Fam L 7. In the history of disability waves, see the first part of my "Welcoming Monsters: Disability as a Liminal Legal Concept" (2018) 29:2 Yale JL & Human 291. For a more general survey of the complex enterprise of defining disability, see my "Theoretical Strategies to Define Disability" in David Wasserman and Adam Cureton, eds., *The Oxford Handbook of Philosophy and Disability* (New York: Oxford University Press, 2019).

exclusion, devaluation, and inequality), to fix said problems, this book assumes that, even if PWD *were* a natural kind, their communities would still owe them the recognition of their robust moral status.

Let me now refine certain descriptive and normative understandings of intellectual disability in order to delineate the category of PSID used in this book with more precision.

1.2 WHO ARE THE "PERSONS WITH SEVERE INTELLECTUAL DISABILITIES"?

1.2.1 A Medical Picture

My goal is not merely to set out a definition of PSID in order to proceed with my argument. Rather, I wish to begin my argument by examining the choices that theorists make when they define a category of people. A medical definition is helpful to begin understanding who PSID are, although I will problematize this definition in the following subsections. The fifth iteration of the *Diagnostic and Statistical Manual of Mental Disorders* (DSM-5), published by the American Psychiatric Association (APA), defines intellectual disability as a neurodevelopmental disorder:

> Intellectual disability (intellectual developmental disorder) is characterized by deficits in general mental abilities, such as reasoning, problem solving, planning, abstract thinking, judgment, academic learning, and learning from experience. The deficits result in impairments of adaptive functioning, such that the individual fails to meet standards of personal independence and social responsibility in one or more aspects of daily life, including communication, social participation, academic or occupational functioning, and personal independence at home or in community settings.[21]

Intellectual disability (the term that gradually replaced "mental retardation" in medical literatures) affects 2–3 percent of the general population.[22] Eighty-five percent of intellectually disabled people belong to the group known as "mildly" disabled people.[23] The APA classifies three other levels of severity for intellectual

---

[21] American Psychiatric Association, *Diagnostic and Statistical Manual of Mental Disorders: DSM-5*, 5th ed. (Arlington, VA: APA, 2013), at 31. The American Association on Intellectual and Developmental Disabilities (AAIDD), formerly the American Association on Mental Retardation, defines intellectual disability in a similar way: "Intellectual disability is a disability characterized by significant limitations both in intellectual functioning [such as reasoning, learning, problem-solving] and in adaptive behavior, which covers a range of everyday social and practical skills. This disability originates before the age of 18" (Robert L. Schalock et al., *Intellectual Disability: Definition, Classification, and Systems of Supports*, 11th ed. [Washington, DC: AAIDD, 2009], at ch. 1).

[22] See Donna K. Daily, Holly H. Ardinger, and Grace E. Holmes, "Identification and Evaluation of Mental Retardation" (2000) 61:4 American Family Physician 1059 at 1059.

[23] Paul Harrison et al., *Shorter Oxford Textbook of Psychiatry* (Oxford: Oxford University Press, 2017), at 487–88.

disability: moderate (constituting 10 percent of the intellectually impaired population), severe (constituting 3–4 percent), and profound (constituting 1–2 percent).[24] The category of people I am concerned with in this work corresponds to the two latter groups – the severely and profoundly intellectually disabled.[25]

The DSM-5 suggests that both mildly and moderately disabled persons can take part in roles and activities that are normally expected of adults within their community, sometimes in supervised settings, and sometimes independently (in the case of mild disability).[26] For instance, the mildly intellectually disabled person "may function age-appropriately" in matters of personal care and recreational skills but needs more support than her peers in terms of the organizational and decision-making skills pertaining to her well-being.[27] Likewise, she may obtain competitive employment, but only "in jobs that do not emphasize conceptual skills."[28] By comparison, people with moderate intellectual disabilities have lower practical skills and require more interventionist support than people with mild intellectual disabilities.

In contrast, severely and profoundly intellectually disabled persons require constant support and are more limited in their ability to participate in their communities. For example, both groups have limited verbal skills that are used primarily to communicate rather than to explain, and the profoundly intellectually disabled person "has a very limited understanding of symbolic communication in speech or gesture" and expresses her "desires and emotions largely through non-verbal, nonsymbolic communication."[29] Likewise, neither group can "make responsible decisions regarding the well-being of self or others" and ongoing support is necessary to allow them to participate in vocational or recreational activities, when such participation is possible.[30]

Rather than focusing on the limitations of the individual to define the gravity of her disability, the American Association on Intellectual and Developmental Disabilities (AAIDD) focuses on the degree of social support that the disabled individual requires to flourish or to be integrated into their community. Mildly

---

[24] Ibid.
[25] In this sense, I follow the AAIDD's recommendation to the WHO to group "profound" and "severe" within a single category, for the following reason: "Collapsing all individuals with IQ scores below 40 into one category is more scientifically and psychometrically supported than attempting to impose a classification cut-off that is five standard deviations below the population mean (i.e., IQ score = 25). Existing standardized tests of intelligence cannot reliably or validly distinguish among individuals with IQ scores below 40" (Marc J. Tassé, Ruth Luckasson, and Margaret Nygren, "AAIDD Proposed Recommendations for ICD–11 and the Condition Previously Known as Mental Retardation" (2013) 51:2 Intellectual and Developmental Disabilities 127 at 129).
[26] APA, *DSM-5*, at 35.
[27] Ibid. at 34.
[28] Ibid.
[29] Ibid. at 36.
[30] Ibid.

disabled individuals are likely to require "intermittent" or "limited" kind of support, such as training or support during transitional or hardship period. By comparison, most moderately disabled people and all severely mentally disabled individuals require "extensive" support, which is characterized as support that is given on a daily and perpetual basis. This support is "pervasive" in the sense that it is required in all areas of life.[31]

These definitions are not neutral descriptions, even if they appear to be. They are only starting points; they can be used not only to discuss a group of human beings with cognitive particularities but also as a springboard to problematize their social context and their uses by philosophers and scientists. I use them because they are part of the discussions with which I engage, but I will now qualify them.

1.2.2 *(The Problem with) Defining the Group of "People with Severe Intellectual Disabilities"*

Like race or gender, disability is not a value-neutral feature of our physical world. The medical definition of intellectual disability is certainly helpful, but it is only one part of the story. Therefore, I start by adopting a DSM-inspired working definition of the category of severely intellectually disabled people, and then go on to explain various, crucial provisos that tell us more about the category of severely disabled individuals than the plain medical definition.

For the purposes of my working definition, "severely intellectually disabled individuals" would typically be described as a group of people with *relatively* low cognitive *capacities* that correspond to substantial *difficulties* or *limitations* to perform as well as "nondisabled" people in various *functional* areas of human life, such as the conceptual, social, and relational. The more *dependent* a person is upon others to perform in these areas of human life, the less *capable* one is (in terms of performing) either with or without *special* aid, and the more "severe" the intellectual disability.

The Contextual and Value-Laden Nature of Disability
The hardest part of defining the severely disabled individual is not proposing a definition, but rather factoring into that definition the relative significance of the notions that are italicized above: *relatively, capacities, difficulties, limitations, functional, dependent, capable,* and *special*. This is because definitions (similar to the one above) of severe disability tend to describe what we understand as certain, clear cases of severely disabled individuals, such as a nonverbal person who is unable to walk or meet basic needs such as feeding or cleaning herself, who is constantly supervised and given a high level of care, and who has no prospect of taking on the various economic, political, social, legal, or intimate roles that most of us will

---

[31] See Schalock *et al.*, *Intellectual Disability*, at ch. 1.

experience during our lifetime. These general definitions assume various circumstances that make some daily activities difficult for some disabled people, while these same activities are not intrinsically difficult for other members of the general population. Limitations are therefore created by our social environments because they are constructed to facilitate certain kinds of actions that correspond to statistically average human capacities. Similarly, since we are all dependent to *relative* degrees on other people, the "medicalization" of a certain threshold of *dependency* may depend on social contexts and expectations of *capacity*. Therefore, internalizing the issue of disability and making it an individual rather than a social problem creates a reductionist – and potentially oppressive – definition of disability. Finally, these definitions presuppose the superior value of certain activities or modes of performance of activities because these activities are predominant in a certain context, or because most people are able to perform them.

Given these difficulties, the most constructive approach to designing a definition of PSID is not to offer plausible, structural parameters that define the group, but rather to identify how these parameters quickly become problematic and to then use them in a heuristically helpful way. This approach can be achieved by adopting a definition that has epistemological modesty sufficient to ground awareness that its components are contextually relative and may be used to oppress or marginalize people simply because they fall on the statistically abnormal end of human capacities. In the next two subsections, I describe the concerns that we must keep in mind when using such a contested concept as disability, which can be used to denote a medical condition, a physical impairment, a statistical difference, a form of social oppression, and all of these phenomena occurring simultaneously.

Just as we cannot avoid this complex meshing of descriptive and normative components by relying exclusively on a "neutral" description of disability, we cannot also escape the risk of oppression by applying a purely normative definition of disability. For example, by defining PSID by their lack of "contractual capacities," we risk creating disabilities based on potentially arbitrary values. Instead of scrutinizing these values, we risk calling people "disabled" when they cannot relate to these values, hence reinforcing their intrinsic relevance to the narrative of disability. Therefore, we must remain attuned to the dynamic and ideological elements of the empirical and normative components of any definition of the severely disabled individual.

Two Difficulties in Defining the Severely Disabled Individual: Heterogeneity and Stereotyping

Now, let me discuss in more detail the concerns that we must keep in mind when working with the term "disability." The idea that there are sound moral generalizations to be made about PSID should be questioned. As I have shown above, the task of defining the category of profoundly mentally disabled individuals is difficult. This task faces two main challenges. First, the characteristics of this group are hard to pin down because they vary over time and from individual to individual. Moreover, PSID sometimes possess capacities, talents, and modes of communication which are not typical for nondisabled persons. These traits may be central to a particular severely disabled individual's flourishing but they are barely noticed or are not allocated significance in the lives of nondisabled people.

Consider numerous capacities – that is, for apprehending right and wrong, enjoying music, communicating through humor, physical touch, facial expressions, sounds, or comments that cannot be readily translated into semantically logical phrases. While these capacities contribute to social interaction and to individual well-being,[32] they do so in ways that may not be recognized in a culture looking for expressions of a "cognitively normal" will or agency. Our culture is also inclined to dismiss senses, actions, modalities of interactions and enjoyment that are not connected to labor or productivity since, some disability legal scholars suggest, it assumes that productivity is required for both citizenship and personhood.[33] As a result, they are undervalued or under-explored by social engineers, moral philosophers, and political theorists. We might identify this as the heterogeneity problem: the PSID group is so diverse in terms of traits – including "contractual capacities" – that generalized assessments purporting to apply to the group as a whole run the risk of ignoring morally relevant differences within the group. Strategies to overcome this problem must involve acknowledging the heterogeneity of the group in a meaningful way, either by resisting generalized statements or recommendations about the group as a whole, or by making space for case-by-case adjustments. We may note that, in general, PSID lack certain capacities or possess them to a lower degree, as long as we also take into account cases where these capacities are present (though perhaps not exercised as independently) and remain aware of other cases where these same capacities are completely absent. This book reflects this flexible definitional strategy by highlighting many ways in which PSID have more capacities than they are presumed to have. While this approach corrects common "leveling down" generalizations, it equally avoids the risk of overestimating cognitive capacities, by pointing out that, in some cases, certain capacities are absent or are insufficient for contractual integrative strategies to work, suggesting that other strategies are required in such cases.

The second challenge to defining the category of PSID relates to defining "mental disability" within different social contexts. Mental disabilities are rife with moral evaluations and are more obviously socially constructed than, say, measles and chicken pox. Our lives are filled with activities – such as taking part in family life, social events and relationships, and earning a living – that are valued differently

---

[32] See, e.g., Eva Kittay, "At the Margins of Moral Personhood" (2008) 5:2–3 J Bioethical Inquiry 137 at 143.
[33] See, e.g., Dianne Pothier and Richard Devlin, eds., *Critical Disability Theory* (Vancouver: University of British Columbia Press, 2014), at 2, 17.

within and across different valuation systems. People who can do more of these activities have access to more value; people who can do fewer of them will have access to less. Below a certain "disability" threshold, it seems that the incapacity to access some valuable life activities calls for moral and political responses of a special order. Getting these responses right is extremely difficult, not only because it is hard to isolate the morally relevant factors in each case, but also because "nondisabled" people act in bad faith, and/or are epistemologically situated in a position that limits the ethical quality of their assessments of value. For example, it may be less threatening or costly to categorize some people as an "aberration" within a valuation scale, rather than to question one's beliefs about valuable activities, blameworthiness, and responsibility. The best strategy to deal with this problem is to remain aware of the social dimensions of, and implications for, any category of severely disabled individuals, and then to see whether it is possible to phrase objective statements about the severely disabled person in comparative or relational terms. This is to avoid concealing the fact that systemic advantages are given to another group — or that such advantages are not the result of natural or inevitable states of affairs, but rather are the results of social choices that are based on power or values. These choices, in turn, ought to be carefully scrutinized.

In sum, definitions of disability found in medical and philosophical literatures can be criticized on account of (1) overgeneralization, or a failure to holistically assess all relevant criteria and (2) failure to recognize the elements of social constructivism at work in a definition or failure to recognize the potential prejudices that these elements import into a definition. These two problems are evident in the DSM-5, which defines intellectual disability as involving "impairments of general mental abilities that impact adaptive functioning in three domains, or areas" of skills: conceptual (i.e., "language, reading, writing, math, reasoning, knowledge, and memory"), social ("empathy, social judgment, interpersonal communication [...], friendships," and similar relational capacities), and practical ("self-management [...] such as personal care, job responsibilities, money management, recreation, and organizing school and work tasks").[34]

The DSM's definition of mental disorder, including in its most recent version, has long faced criticism that it encourages overdiagnosis, false positives, and the "pathologizing"[35] or "medicalization of all problem behaviors and relationships"[36] and of using "intrinsically normative"[37] (rather than purely factual) biomedical

---

[34] APA, *DSM-5*, at 37.
[35] Joel Paris, "Preface" in Joel Paris and James Phillips, eds., *Making the DSM-5: Concepts and Controversies* (New York: Springer, 2013), v at vi.
[36] B. J. Rounsaville *et al.*, "Basic Nomenclature Issues for DSM-V" in David J. Kupfer, Michael B. First, and Darrel A. Regier, eds., *A Research Agenda for DSM-V* (Washington, DC: American Psychiatric Association, 2002), 1 at 3.
[37] Massimiliano Aragona, "The Concept of Mental Disorder and the DSM-V" (2009) 2:1 Dialogues in Philosophy Mental & Neuro Sci 1 at 4.

terms.[38] The British Psychological Society (the Society), among others, has been critical of the DSM definition. They note that overdiagnosis can cause stigmatization and isolation of individuals by casting their differences in a pathological or negative light. This problem is worsened by the fact that the evaluative criteria are "'symptoms' that all rely on subjective judgments" and rely on an assessment of values associated with "current normative social expectations."[39] Moreover, intellectual disabilities are not subjectively examined within a relational framework but rather are identified as "located within individuals."[40] This classification not only works to miss "the relational context of problems and the undeniable social causation of many such problems,"[41] but also, as the Society suggests, it assumes an unchallenged relational framework of "nondisability." That is, the relational framework is made up of relations taking place between people without disorders, which then assumes that "disorder" is only defined by a failure to partake of relations between people without disorders.[42]

Another aggravating factor in the use of a quasi-legislative categorizing instrument such as the DSM is that the body which created the manual could be unduly influenced by "powerful interests, both corporate and public, that could profit from a highly inclusive diagnostic system."[43] Commentators have argued that these interests may not only include influence from actors who ought not to be legitimate players in the debate – like pharmaceutical companies – but also from actors at the very center of the debate, like psychiatrists. Writing about the biopolitics of defining "mental disorders," Warren Kinghorn argues that "the project to define 'mental disorder' arose in the 1970s and early 1980s as a way to burnish the authority of psychiatry and specifically of *DSM-III*" and that the DSM-5 also attempts "to persuade [...] that there exists an appropriate, safe, and nonthreatening clinical 'space' within which diagnosis and treatment can be rightfully exercised."[44] Some, like Kinghorn, conclude that there is no such "safe space"[45] and that the DSM cannot aspire to categorize mental disorders as "natural kinds" nor should it use a language suggesting it can.[46]

---

[38] See also Jamie Walvisch, "Defining 'Mental Disorder' in Legal Contexts" (2017) 52 Int'l JL & Psychiatry 7.
[39] British Psychological Society, "Response to the American Psychiatric Association: DSM-5 Development," *The British Psychological Society* (2011), at 2, www1.bps.org.uk/system/files/consultationpapers/responses/DSM-5%202011%20-%20BPS%20response.pdf.
[40] Ibid.
[41] Ibid.
[42] Ibid.
[43] Paris, "Preface," at vi.
[44] Warren Kinghorn, "The Biopolitics of Defining 'Mental Disorder'" in Joel Paris and James Phillips, eds., *Making the DSM-5: Concepts and Controversies* (New York: Springer, 2013), 47 at 48.
[45] Ibid.
[46] Ibid.

To help us understand how fluid and adaptable a definition of the severely disabled individual should be, we must remember that in some imagined – and perhaps future – social contexts, the very notion of disability may lose not only its meaning but the medical or political purposes that drive it today. However, we must have a way to name a group of people we want to protect from exclusion or oppression while being aware that the very act of naming (and perhaps even some affective features of our desire to help by naming) might come at a cost for the named group. Any definition might misconstrue or misunderstand their needs and capacities, for example, by failing to conceive of more accommodating contexts in which their needs and capacities would be different.

From Medical to Philosophical Definitions

The criticisms of the DSM's definition of mental disorder also surface within philosophical literatures on mental disability. These criticisms relate to the risks of overgeneralization, implausible essentialism, stereotyping, the disregard of relational components, and the risks of being too individualistic in our approach to the condition of lacking certain cognitive capacities. Another criticism centers on the fact that key value judgments about certain capacities (and not of other capacities or relational features) are assumed to be the correct evaluative standard for determining disability.[47]

On one hand, philosophers talking about mental disability are often interested in particular individual traits that they want to isolate to assess their moral significance. On the other, these specific traits should correspond to a category of concrete people if their theoretical conclusions are to be applied in the real world. Yet disability categories are at least partly socially defined and are the object of various criticisms. Philosophers may therefore be tempted to discuss certain traits in the abstract and hold that their conclusions apply to whomever possess these traits, regardless of whether anyone possesses them or not, or regardless of their medical or social categories. In doing so, theorists face the charge that they are doing a poor job as applied ethicists when they cannot point to an actual group to whom their analyses refer. And when philosophers do claim that their conclusions apply to a particular social category, and claim that they can define that category with certainty, they risk facing the same criticisms that medical experts face.

Social contract thinkers are no exception. When they reflect on the issue of justifying the inclusion of the severely disabled individual in society, they focus on the moral and political consequences of lacking the intellectual capacities required to be a "contractor" (in the political sense – i.e., of participating in some version of a social contract) or to have "contractual relevance." This includes the ability to

---

[47] See, e.g., Carlson, *The Faces of Intellectual Disability*; Eva Kittay, "The Personal Is Philosophical Is Political: A Philosopher and a Mother of a Cognitively Disabled Person Send Notes from the Battlefield" (2009) 40:3–4 Metaphilosophy 606.

elaborate and to live by a conception of the good life (which implies autonomy), a sense of justice, rationality, and a capacity to threaten or benefit others through individual and/or collective arrangements. Determining which of these capacities matter will depend on the version of the contractual theory that is put forward.

Integrationist contractual thinkers cannot define PSID as a category of people lacking enough of these capacities to be a contractor or to have contractual relevance. They must keep the notions of "PSID" and "noncontractors" distinct if they want to argue that severely disabled people have, despite appearances, contracting capacities and/or contractual relevance. However, instead of expanding an empirically sophisticated definition of mental disability, they implicitly define the category of disabled people they are talking about as those who are *traditionally* seen as lacking "contractual" capacity or relevance but who, once we better qualify these capacities or their conditions of exercise, do in fact possess (enough of) them.

As a result, some of their conclusions may be transposed to people other than PSID in terms of failing to meet a threshold of contractual relevance, such as the very young or the elderly. However, I seek to focus on PSID: their impairments – namely, of conceptual, social, and practical skills that are of contractual relevance – are not only the most severe ones amongst living human beings in a conscious state, but these impairments are also thought to keep the severely disabled individual under the threshold of contractual relevance throughout their lifetime. Indeed, the group that best exemplifies these traits is that group defined as severely and profoundly intellectually disabled by the medical community. However, I only endorse the DSM's definition insofar as it refers to the capacities on which contractual thinkers focus. This definition is subject to the empirical challenge that many people classified as severely disabled under the DSM do, in fact, have some contractual capacities. In this work, I incidentally contribute to making such a case and therefore question whether the medically categorized "intellectually disabled" are as conceptually, socially, and practically impaired as the DSM suggests.

In sum, my use of a DSM-like definition is heavily qualified because the category of "severe intellectual disability" used in this work has an inherent normative dimension connected to moral status. The DSM's definition, however, aims at a criticized kind of objectivity and therefore does not venture into the territory of evaluating its moral and political consequences. Therefore, bodies like the APA or the AAIDD may evaluate the degree of support needed by severely disabled individuals to thrive without problematizing traditional normative standards of thriving. This reflects a scientific penchant for adopting an inductive approach and a philosophical penchant for applying a deductive one. For better or worse, medical researchers are more likely to be flexible in their consideration of normative meanings rather than in terms of the consequences of their empirical findings, whereas certain philosophical analyses are more likely to first determine proper axiological standards while leaving their empirical suppositions more liberally open to challenge. This is because medical researchers are primarily interested in achieving descriptive clarity, while philosophers are primarily interested in posing philosophical questions. I now turn to these philosophical questions.

1.2.3 Philosophical Implications of Belonging to the Category of PSID

What philosophical problems does the group of PSID raise? We consider this group as made up of beings who possess significantly less cognitive capacities than the species' norm, which implies that they have little, if any, practical rationality and self-consciousness and are unable to survive, let alone flourish, in a community, without intensive support. As far as social justice is concerned, the question of the extent to which the state should fund support for PSID in order for them to attain a certain level of well-being is a major area of philosophical investigation. This belongs to a line of inquiry that is concerned with determining PSID's specific needs and delineating what they are morally entitled to as robustly morally considerable beings. Yet there is a more fundamental inquiry which seeks to explain whether and why severely disabled individuals are indeed robustly morally considerable beings entitled to equal moral consideration. This is the question of their moral status.

Here are the two ethical pulls that are at the heart of the challenges that cognitive disabilities present to moral, political, and legal philosophy:

(1) It is a very widely and commonly held moral position that severely disabled individuals have a robust moral status.
(2) Liberal modern philosophy has traditionally emphasized the importance of autonomy and moral agency, both requiring sophisticated cognitive capacities. It has grounded the authority of the state, and the specialness of the value of our lives, on such bases.

Thus, how are we to account for the robust moral status of PSID if they are characterized by being significantly deprived of such capacities? While some philosophers see these two questions as incompatible – or at least requiring a choice of "camp" on either side of what seems like a conceptual divide – the integrationist contractual endeavor takes up the challenge of reconciling both questions. The theory argues either that cognitively able people contractually create a political world in which they make a special place for PSID, even though the latter have not contributed to its creation, or that severely disabled individuals are actually able to make such a contractual contribution. This book tests the validity of this contractual belief, according to which both ethical questions are reconcilable.

1.2.4 Why PSID?

The fact that the group of severely intellectually disabled individuals has particularly little power and few capacities – relatively to most people – makes it one of the most confrontational test cases for integrationist theorists and, indeed, mainstream liberal assumptions. It is hard to conceptualize the capacities and needs of the severely disabled individual in a way that resembles the needs of the traditional moral, political, and legal subject, just as it is hard to stretch traditional conceptions of the subject itself to include this person. Unlike other "marginal" subjects – like infants and elderly people who have not yet gained (or who have lost) many of their physical and mental capacities – integrationist philosophers cannot use traditional arguments to circumvent the hard question that I raise in relation to the severely disabled individual: why are these powerless or otherwise incapacitated human beings owed serious moral consideration? While many disabilities can be effectively accommodated (or are the results of socially engineered contexts), persons with severe disabilities tend to defy normalization, making it harder to argue that they meet the criteria necessary to demonstrate a robust moral status. Their existence and the ethical demands they make on a largely able-bodied society must lead us to question the validity of these traditional criteria.

In the case of other powerless or helpless human subjects, other than PSID, the criticisms that I present in this book may simply go unnoticed because the marginalized group is saved by a defining feature of its category. For instance, young human beings are generally protected by their connection to their future capable self, while older humans are generally saved by their association to their past capacities and social contributions. However, the permanent state of PSID prevents theorists who are otherwise sympathetic to the needs of vulnerable human beings from relying on theories of potentiality and identity to justify their moral status.

A preliminary objection against integrationist philosophers is that the group of PSID is, in reality, quite small. However, this is a poor objection for two reasons. First, it is morally wrong. If severely disabled individuals matter, then it is not valid to say that they can be neglected because there are so few of them. This position is key in supporting narratives of minority rights and discrimination claims within legal normative theory. Second, many of my reflections and conclusions presented here apply not only to people who live with severe intellectual disabilities but also to people with physical disabilities or less severe disabilities, as well as to ethical subjects who (for better or worse) are not necessarily considered to belong to the category of "disabled." This includes those such as elderly people who have lost many of their physical and mental capacities and children, infants, and fetuses who have not yet acquired these capacities. It also applies to victims of ageism or ableism who are assumed to have fewer capacities or lower quality of life than they really have. These reflections can also encompass people with mental or physical illnesses that are periodic or temporary.

Why, one might object, do these groups need the fundamental protections that preservationists (who claim that all human beings deserve a robust moral status) try to justify? After all, I just conceded that these other groups (such as infants or the elderly) are saved from radical exclusion by some feature of their group, such as their potential to become moral agents. Moreover, the idea that mere humanity confers exceptional worth is still culturally powerful, at least within popular discourses and political rhetoric. However, my point is that integrationist arguments for inclusion based on these features continue to come under scrutiny because, I suspect, they are not very convincing. This does not necessarily mean that human exceptionalism is wrong, but only that its proponents ought to think harder about how to justify their conclusions to avoid charges of arbitrariness or speciesism.

Let me illustrate my concern with grounding status on potentiality by considering the case of an infant who would "matter" only because she has the potential to become a moral agent later in her life. Most of us would agree that it would be unequivocally wrong to abuse this child physically, even if there was a way to carry out this abuse that would not impinge on her future agency or capacity to become a fully cooperating citizen. This – the question of intrinsic moral value – is the hard question that I do not want theorists to duck by showing empirical data indicating that the child's future agency *would* be affected by this abuse, or by positing a metaphysical theory about the child and the moral agent being indistinguishable. It is perhaps the hardest question that moral philosophers face, now that the doctrines of the sacredness of life or of human exceptionalism are difficult to maintain without their theological foundations.[48]

Medical technology gives us increasing control over life. Bioethics and general public opinion now have to consider how to regulate sensitive "right to life" issues such as prenatal screening, abortion, infanticide, euthanasia, and genetic enhancement. How cognitively disabled people should fare within this new technological and moral world is not only an urgent matter for the population of cognitively disabled people to resolve[49] but also for *us* – the "cognitively able" – as we may be mistaken in our belief about the degree of autonomy, dependency, and vulnerability that characterizes human nature, and that moral and political philosophy has traditionally idealized. Preservationist arguments may not only serve to protect and improve the lives of very vulnerable people within our society but could also help us come to term with our own vulnerability and the fluctuating nature of our physical and mental abilities. I put PSID at the center of this book, rather than bracketing them as exceptions, because this group most radically questions traditional assumptions about what is valuable in human life and relations. However, as mentioned earlier, many of my comments, arguments, and conclusions apply to other disabilities as well.

---

[48] See, e.g., Peter Singer, *Unsanctifying Human Life: Essays on Ethics*, ed. Helga Kuhse (Oxford: Blackwell, 2002).

[49] See Jean-Marie Le Méné, *La trisomie est une tragédie grecque* (Paris: Salvator, 2009) as an illustration of the grave consequences that framing disability discourses in a particular way can have on a specific group of disabled people.

1.3 ROBUST MORAL STATUS

The notion of moral status (or moral standing) is both very common and widely disputed, largely because it can be based upon entirely different axiological grounds, and can generate diverse normative implications, depending on the theoretical framework employed. For example, moral status is sometimes considered to be a scalar property, but other times it is not. In the latter case, "moral status" may be synonymous with another germane and contested concept, "dignity." In the former, where it is considered to be a scalar property, we first need to distinguish between higher and lower statuses. Even within a scalar account, above a certain threshold of requirements, theorists will often focus on one "special" status which they will call "full" or "strong" moral status.[50]

Although some hold that moral status is essentially a disputed concept, the following definition seems broad enough to encompass all its variants: moral status is a property which confers upon the individual who possesses it a special moral considerability. The special moral considerability that is owed to beings with a full moral status is generally taken to be special kinds of attitudes or treatment, such as respect and concern, and it corresponds to functional privileges, such as being entitled to hold certain moral rights.[51]

However, we need to give a more comprehensive definition of moral status, as the above description of the nature and scope of moral considerability and its implications does not reveal exactly what is desirable about such a status from a contractual perspective. From a contractual point of view, I use the term "robust moral status" to connote a property which confers on its possessor a moral entitlement to take part in the process of constructing social institutions and deciding their governing rules, and/or the entitlement to having one's interests considered during this process on an equal footing. These are the "robust obligations" that are owed to entities with robust moral statuses.

---

[50] A majority of theories, including contractual ones, simply assume that people either possess or do not possess a moral status and the properties said to underlie it. Even when these properties obviously come by degree, theories will make use of a threshold to reach the same "all-or-nothing" result: one is either below or above the threshold, one is either within the "range" of possessing a property or not (see Rawls, A Theory of Justice, at 444–45). The prima facie incompatibility between the fact that robust moral status-granting properties come by degree and the fact that moral status is often used as an all-or-nothing notion raises the suspicion that moral reasons extraneous to the former scalar properties explain their nonscalar implications. Whether or not this way of conceptualizing moral status as correlating all-or-nothing entitlements is the best use of the notion is not a matter that I will discuss here. Insofar as social contract theories are concerned, "a being either has or does not have the crucial property that confers rights. It is like the mark of Cain, conferring moral untouchability on whoever displays it" (Loren E. Lomasky, Persons, Rights, and the Moral Community [New York: Oxford University Press, 1997], at 189).

[51] More generally, a moral status correlates certain characteristics of the value of an entity (for instance, nonderivativeness) as well as certain constraints on the way in which it may be fittingly related (for instance, it may not be used only instrumentally).

Robust obligations can be further characterized by the stability of their foundations and their nonoptionality. Thus, these obligations differ notably from those based on stipulations that, for example, are agreed to by able contractors on the basis of mere desire or preference. Robust obligations need not be absolute, but they must be based on some stable properties that are internal to an entity or on stable relations that the entity has with other contractors or with society (i.e., the collectivity of contractors). If the contractual obligations that society or individuals have in relation to entities with a robust moral status are optional and unstable, then they would not correspond to any concept of full moral status that presently exists in bioethical or political literatures. Perhaps there are grounds for examining the possibility of a plural, scalar, optional, unstable, and relative (in other ways) strong moral status, in spite of the historical and political implausibility of this status. However, such an examination falls outside the scope of this book. Contractual grounds for a robust moral status are almost always considered to have the characteristics of stability and nonoptionality.[52] That is, parties to contractual negotiations express their will within certain constraints. The nature of these constraints – and the parties' characteristics *qua* negotiators, self-interested beings, reasonable beings, and/or valuers and self-valuers (depending on the account) – limits the expression of parties' wills. This is done in such a way that makes granting a robust moral status to an entity a much less optional and more stable affair than, say, choosing how they want to spend their Saturday night, and broaches the broader question of determining how society should be organized so that, *inter alia*, they spend most of their Saturday nights doing activities that they prefer.

The contractual grounds for a robust moral status are, from the most direct to the most indirect: (1) having what it takes to be a contractor; or (2) having what it takes to contribute to a contractual society; or (3) possessing contractual relevance. To have "contractual relevance" is to have other properties that are unrelated to participating to contractual endeavors but that give contractors strong contract-related reasons to grant beings who possess them an equally important status.[53] By "contract-related reasons," I mean reasons that are related to the moral agent's exercise of her contracting capacities or to the success of a contractual society. As I explain in Chapters 3 and 5 of this book, if these reasons are not sufficiently contract-related, then their grounds and stringency need to be justified in a noncontractual account. Also, "contractually relevant" beings must not only have relevant properties that

---

[52] We will deal with an exception in Chapter 5.
[53] I do not mean to give equality a distinctive definitional importance here. It is simply the case that the implicit or explicit concept of "full moral status" within contractual thought entails *one* kind of strong status. Even though nothing precludes, in theory, the consideration of a political theory granting a variety of scalar statuses to different beings possessing status-giving properties (such as the capacities to benefit others contractually, or to have more or less sophisticated contracting capacities) to different degrees, it is simply not an option considered in contractual thought (or that would be seriously considered in mainstream liberal moral and political literature). Membership in a contractual society is assumed to be an all-or-nothing quality.

provide contract-related reasons for granting them a robust moral status but they must also be the kind of entities upon whom we *can* confer a robust moral status. As we see in Chapter 5, theories that justify granting a robust moral status to entities that do not have subjective interests or that do not partake of any goods (such as life, play, and social life) are odd and unconvincing.

A definition of the grounds and implications of robust moral status will become relatively exhaustive depending on whether we apply a contractualist or contractarian framework for interpretation. It would not be controversial to assume that, according to a contractualist definition, robust moral status connotes a property that confers on its possessor a moral entitlement to special concern and respect. The terms "concern and respect" here are given their ordinary meanings, and they are "special" because: (1) they are ways of nonderivatively valuing certain entities and considering these entities to be their own source of value;[54] (2) they are nonoptional or noneasily defeasible obligations; and (3) they correspond to "robust" duties, which are both moral duties and duties of justice. According to this framework, it would be inaccurate and unfair to refuse to grant equal consideration to the interests of beings with a robust moral status when deliberating on considerations of justice (such as the design of fair social institutions or the redistribution of limited resources). However, this specific definition does not match some contractarian accounts, which associate robust moral status with a self-interested stance from which a moral agent will choose to respect an entity for prudential reasons rather than because she recognizes the entity's nonderivative value.

For the purposes of this book, I need not make the case that the doctrine of moral status is a good idea, or investigate its best and most exhaustive definition.[55] Rather, I use the term robust moral status comparatively, to see whether contractual arguments justifying the position that nondisabled people have it also hold for PSID, who would therefore be equally entitled to it. This comparative method – comparing the status of "central cases" of beings with full moral status within contractual thought to the status of "marginal cases" – befits Rawls's method of incremental extension, which the inclusivist branch of contractual thought has adopted. It may be that the doctrine of moral status, as scoped in contractual thought, is flawed in terms of not being sufficiently pluralist or relational and lacking the ability to translate into all the proper moral attitudes. My conclusion suggests

---

[54] This applies regardless of whether these two characteristics are different from one another and, if it is controversial, whether they are already implicit to the ordinary meaning of concern and respect.
[55] In favor of this view, see Mary A. Warren, *Moral Status: Obligations to Persons and Other Living Things* (Oxford: Oxford University Press, 2000). For opposing views, see Anita Silvers, "Moral Status: What a Bad Idea!" (2012) 56:11 J Intellectual Disability Research 1014 and Joseph Raz, *Value, Respect, and Attachment* (Cambridge: Cambridge University Press, 2001), at 127–29.

that this is the case. However, we cannot assume this final position from the start, and thus we must first ask whether one of the available contractual accounts for the bases of robust moral status can convincingly apply to PSID.

I conclude this discussion of the concept of robust moral status by briefly explaining its relation to other, related concepts – namely dignity, personhood, equality, intrinsic value, and moral rights – in order to explain why I focus on robust moral status instead of these concepts. One might suggest that I focus on the notions of dignity or personhood rather than on robust moral status, as these are the conditions that we ought to secure for severely disabled individuals. However, even though the terms "dignity" and "personhood" may be more common than robust moral status, focusing on them exclusively in this context is not ideal. First, this is the case because these concepts are just as ambiguous as "robust moral status." Therefore, to address this ambiguity, we would need to agree on a comprehensive definition of these terms that fits the contractual theories that I explore in this book, much as I have to do for robust moral status. Second, it might do greater violence to the philosophical traditions that underpin these concepts to state that a being endowed with "dignity" must either be (in direct or indirect terms) a contractor or have contractual relevance, and that this status primarily implies representation within the contractual society-building process. In many influential accounts of the notions of personhood and dignity, these contract-related conditions are either absent or merely incidental to the core definition.[56] According to these accounts, "personhood" and "dignity" are kinds of robust moral statuses that are suffused with noncontractual elements. Of course, contractual thinkers might propose a new account of "personhood" and "dignity" but these notions are so enmeshed with noncontractual ideas that it is less confusing to choose a more neutral terrain of challenge for this investigation. Third, different accounts of the notions of "personhood" and "dignity" imply very different grounds and normative consequences: for instance, Kantian[57] and Hobbesian[58] understandings of dignity are antithetical. Likewise, while a contractualist and contractarian understanding of robust moral status would also be different, these accounts would at least overlap according to the definitional elements of "robust moral status" that I set out above. Lastly, it is not certain that contractual theories need to challenge noncontractual accounts of personhood and dignity in order to propose contract-related grounds for robust moral status. For example, contractual theories may hold that some "persons" are not subjects of justice.

---

[56] For historical and conceptual surveys of noncontractual accounts of dignity, see Remy Debes, ed., *Dignity: A History* (New York: Oxford University Press, 2017); Jeff Malpas and Norelle Lickiss, eds., *Perspectives on Human Dignity: A Conversation* (Dordrecht: Springer, 2007).
[57] Immanuel Kant, *Groundwork of the Metaphysics of Morals*, trans. and ed. Mary Gregor (Cambridge: Cambridge University Press, 2012), at 42.
[58] William Molesworth, ed., *The English Works of Thomas Hobbes of Malmesbury*, vol. III: *Leviathan* (London: John Bohn, 1839–45), at 76.

One could argue that my main focus ought to be equality *per se* since I am concerned with showing that severely disabled people are *equally* entitled to robust moral status as other people. Although I will deal with issues related to equality when they arise, I do not think that securing "equality" for PSID ought to be the primary goal. Apart from familiar objections to the position that equality has intrinsic value, the contractual thinkers that I engage with do not deal with equality as a foundational concept. For them, equality of status is incidental to the fact that severely disabled individuals have direct or indirect contractual relevance. Equality is also a side effect of their nonscalar view of robust moral status, which makes this robust moral status equal for all. In other words, these theorists argue that severely disabled individuals are entitled to special consideration as morally considerable beings and as subjects of justice because their properties demand it. Further, they argue that the fact that this consideration is equal reflects both their equal contractual relevance and the nonscalar feature of their conception of robust moral status, rather than the intrinsic importance of equality. Besides, I am of the view that a primary focus on equality (in contrast to a focus on specific rights, for example) would undermine a contractual position, if I am correct in claiming that contractual thinkers require equality of a single, nonscalar robust moral status for pragmatic rather than empirical reasons or for philosophical reasons that have little to do with contractual premises. I will return to this discussion in Chapter 5. Lastly, equality of *treatment* is not a goal for severely disabled individuals, given the particularities of their needs. Although I am not investigating the difficult question of what it would mean, in terms of concrete distribution of resources, to give a severely disabled person equal representation and consideration, in Chapter 4 I explore whether – and in what sense – it would be unfair to *a priori* limit the support given to them in terms of considerations of equality.

Two other concepts are closely connected to the notion of robust moral status: intrinsic value and moral rights. "Intrinsic value" is another disputed concept, which I take to mean "final" or "nonderivative" value, or to be an antonym of "instrumental" value.[59] An entity with intrinsic value has a *telos* that goes beyond serving somebody's ends. In other words, it is more than an instrument. The valuing attitudes that are directed to an intrinsically valuable entity are not directed at or derivative upon something else beyond this entity. This (plausible but not undisputed) account of intrinsic value can have the same meaning as robust moral status in some contexts, such as contractualist accounts of robust moral status, but not in others, as with some contractarian accounts which grant only derivative value to other contractors. However, it should be noted that a robust contractarian account will seek to secure as stable and as comprehensive the conceptual grounds for citizens' rights as this theory can offer. The generality of robust moral status thus

---

[59] See, e.g., Christine Korsgaard, "Two Distinctions in Goodness" (1983) 92:2 Philosophical Review 169.

tends to be favorable for contractarian accounts, but as far as contractualist accounts are concerned, the two concepts (robust moral status and intrinsic value) can be taken to be synonymous if one assumes that both warrant the same kind of moral considerability. However, this assumption is problematic for contractual theory, as having intrinsic value might be justified on noncontractual grounds and, if this were enough to secure a robust moral status, then it would provide a noncontractual account of robust moral status, which goes beyond the scope of this book. However, there might be an account of intrinsic value which retains its contractual dimension and which attributes robust moral status to PSID. I explore this possible account in Chapter 5.

Finally, the notion of moral rights is not significantly different from the notion of robust moral status. A robust moral status will, of necessity, translate into a being having some moral rights. Indeed, without moral rights associated with it, robust moral status would not mean much at all. The difference between the two concepts is that "moral rights" refers to a list of moral entitlements that are possessed by an entity, whereas the "moral status" of this entity refers to the condition of an entity in the eyes of moral agents. Therefore, whether this condition can be reduced to a list of moral entitlements that renders the concept of moral status, a (redundant) shorthand for that of moral rights, is a question that merits a comprehensive review of how philosophers apply the concept of "moral status." However, there is no need to undertake such a review here, as I assume that we can meaningfully use the notion of moral status, if only because most other authors do. Certainly, the case can be made that, even if used as a mere shorthand, the term "moral status" has utility. Consider if I were to describe to you someone who possesses a number of rights – for example, a right to ask you questions in some circumstances, which you have an obligation to answer, or the right to exercise physical force upon you or constrain your freedom of movement in some circumstances. Now, alternatively, I could simply refer to the status of a policeman (or your parent, if you are a minor). Similarly, contractual authors assume that the status of a "contractor" comes with a list of rights, for example, the right to have one's interests represented in a society-building process.

I should also point out that the notion of robust moral status is, in both its contractualist and contractarian formulations, the strongest moral and political status that individuals have within society. Therefore, its implications go beyond the notion of a more basic or rudimentary status (that correlates to fundamental rights), which would require less demanding conditions to be met and would imply only the most basic rights. In Chapter 5, I explore the connections between these two accounts of basic entitlements (reflected, e.g., in some human rights conventions and discourse) and contract-based robust moral status. My concerns are that these accounts may not be based on contractual premises and that, even if they were, they would secure a lesser status for PSID that would translate into diminished political representation and lesser entitlement to a redistribution of social resources.

1.4 WHY SOCIAL CONTRACT THEORY?

Many theorists have tried to ground the special status of cognitively disabled people in contractual theories. Some, like Martha Nussbaum[60] and Eva Kittay,[61] have concluded that Rawls's model – which they considered to be the most promising contractual model for doing so – failed to ground this status. They therefore argue that we must now look in noncontractual frameworks to explain the robust status of people with severe disabilities. In *Frontiers of Justice*, Nussbaum writes:

> Now of course we immediately want to say that people with impairments and related disabilities are not unproductive. They contribute to society in many ways, when society creates conditions in which they may do so. So social contract theorists are just wrong about the facts; if they correct their false factual assumptions, they can fully include people with impairments and their unusual needs, mitigating the disabilities associated with these impairments. A defense of social contract theory along these lines is, however, doomed to failure.[62]

The anti-contractual criticism is twofold. Empirically, no feat of social arrangements can turn individuals with severe disabilities into productive contractors. Conceptually, no matter how we broaden or modify the contractual notions of reciprocity, cooperation, production, participation, or society as a collective venture

---

[60] See Martha Nussbaum, *Frontiers of Justice: Disability, Nationality, Species Membership* (Cambridge: Harvard University Press, 2006).

[61] Eva Kittay, *Love's Labor: Essays on Women, Equality and Dependency* (New York: Routledge, 1999). Whether or to what extent Kittay rejects, rather than amends, Rawlsian contractualism is not entirely clear, because Kittay makes substantial additions to Rawls's theory of justice as fairness, such as suggesting a third moral power, "a capacity to respond to vulnerability with care," an additional primary good (care), and a third principle of justice, the "principle of social responsibility for care" (at 102, 113). Kittay herself insists on the important lacunae within Rawls's theory – mostly due to its failure to take dependency sufficiently into account – and sees "no natural way" (at 113) of inserting her dependency concerns into a Rawlsian framework. Some, like Noëlle Claire McAfee, may still suggest that Rawls would be receptive to Kittay's modifications (see Noëlle Claire McAfee, "Book Review of *Love's Labor: Essays on Women, Equality and Dependency* by Eva Feder Kittay" (2001) 32:3 Metaphilosophy 344). Others may find that those modifications assume values or emotional propensities that would not be universal, neutral, or mutually disinterested enough to easily fit a Rawlsian approach to justice. Thus, Anita Silvers and Michael Ashley Stein associate *Love's Labor* to an ethics of care (see Anita Silvers and Michael Ashley Stein, "Disability and the Social Contract," Book Review of *Frontiers of Justice: Disability, Nationality, Species Membership* (2007) 74:4 U Chicago L Rev 1615 at 1620). Given this ambiguity, Kittay's *Love Labor* could reasonably be interpreted as taking either a feminist Rawlsian or a care ethics orientation. Given my own inclination to reconcile the insights of those sometimes diverging approaches to justice, I intuit that elements of both can serve to flesh out the theory of equality that Kittay ultimately wishes to endorse: "a connection-based equality, an equality that *recognizes* needs based on our functioning through periods of dependency and caring for dependents. A connection-based equality is one concerned less with resources as such and more with capabilities and functionings" (Kittay, *Love's Labor*, at 187).

[62] Nussbaum, *Frontiers of Justice*, at 105.

for mutual benefit, when we rely on these requirements for identifying members of society, people with severe disabilities cannot meet them, unless we also integrate many nonhuman beings (animals and plants) into our society. Not only would this solution face the problem of the scarcity of resources to be distributed among such a wide "society" but it stretches the notion of society beyond anything recognizably contractual.

In contrast, the theorists whom I consider in this work, such as Lawrence Becker and Anita Silvers, have chosen to adapt integrationist contractarian and contractualist models so as to include people with severe disabilities within their framework, and they provide a contractual justification for their robust moral status. These thinkers have taken up Rawls's challenge of conceptual incrementation. One of the strongest objections to this integrationist contractual endeavor could be framed as such: why should we look in the social contract tradition for a justification for the robust moral status of PSID if these individuals (as well as other social "marginal cases" of people apparently not in possession of contracting capacities or strong "contractual relevance") are typically taken to be the social contract tradition's Achilles' heel? Another objection could be put this way: since I conclude that social contract theories are not the most promising way of grounding the robust moral status of people with severe disabilities, why should I spend time elaborating on critiques of these theories, instead of looking for alternative theories?

1.4.1 Criticizing the Social Contract and Contractual Integrationists

First, it is helpful to theorize the foundational forms of exclusion that go unnoticed by policymakers and jurists who create or endorse unhelpful moral, political, and/or legal statuses in response to severely disabled people's needs, and who thus fail to question the validity of mainstream liberal assumptions. This work contributes to future research on the moral and political groundings of the rights of profoundly mentally disabled people and it curtails the breadth of certain key assumptions of social contract theories. I am interested in questioning the universality of the moral and political subject that is put forward by the social contract tradition and to show the exclusionist impact of mischaracterizing the moral, political, or legal subject. As such, as I mentioned earlier, my approach has some similarities with Carole Pateman's *The Sexual Contract* (1988) and Charles Mills' *The Racial Contract* (1997), which, respectively, show how and why women and nonwhites are left out of, and are oppressed by, contractual theories and practices of social justice. Pateman shows how the social contract upholds the patriarchy and supports the domination of men over women instead of engendering freedom and equality for all. She shows that our social contract conceals another, more fundamental, "sexual contract." Similarly, Mills reveals that a "racial contract" dictates the identity of the subject of contract theory, essentially designed to enforce white supremacy. In both cases, an oppressive contract takes place between members of a dominant class in order to exclude and subjugate other populations (i.e., nonwhites and women).

Unlike other authors who promptly discard social contract theory in order to direct their efforts toward presenting an alternative theory, I follow Pateman and Mills in acknowledging the tremendous influence that the social contract tradition has had on liberalism and social justice. My main task, then, is to reveal the weakness of these foundational pillars of contemporary legal and political thought, and to critically examine whether "integrationist" contractual thinkers can overcome the exclusivist impact of social contract theory. Whereas the "intermales contract" justifies various forms of domination over women and the "interwhites contract" justifies various forms of racial imperialism and colonialism, the "ableist" or "disabled" contract taking place between nondisabled agents justifies various forms of exclusion (isolation, under-appraisal, and disrespect) of people with disabilities. The challenge I make to the social contract tradition seems, in a sense, to be even harder to overcome than to the sexual and racial contracts identified by Pateman and Mills; PSID seem to lack the qualities required of the contractual agent and – unlike being a white person or being a man – certain cognitive capacities seem to be inherently essential to the identity of a contractor, however one conceives of this entity.

Even though alternative discourses might ground the robust moral status of severely disabled individuals elsewhere, the severely disabled person would still not be a subject of justice according to contractual accounts. This exclusivist conclusion deserves scrutiny, given the influence of social contract theory on our political tradition. Contractual concepts of reciprocity, cooperation, productivity, and fairness are the omnipresent background of the contemporary political and legal horizon. This dominant ideology requires significant undermining before alternatives to it can be realistically heard. As Mills put it, contract talk is "the political lingua franca of our times."[63] Pateman similarly speaks of the contract doctrine's "extraordinarily widespread influence."[64] The mainstream and ubiquitous nature of the contractual justification of robust moral status is created not only by the historic influence of the social contract tradition and the contemporary literature it underpins but also by its central, foundational position within modern moral and political philosophy. It also underpins everyday political parlance and enforceable legal language prioritizing values of equality and freedom, and the capacity to act autonomously and consent. Therefore, showing how the social contract tradition excludes a certain group of agents that lacks the cognitive capacities of the "normal subject" is not only of interest to social contract scholars but also reveals how mainstream political philosophy has until recently methodically left the phenomena of disabilities, dependence, and vulnerability out of its analysis of justice.

---

[63] Mills, *The Racial Contract*, at 3.
[64] Pateman, *The Sexual Contract*, at ix.

1.4.2 *The Value of Contractual Relation*

Second, it is likely that moral and political traditions that have become mainstream have some wisdom to offer, even though mainstream theories may convey oppressive or wrongheaded ideologies. Taking contractual theory seriously allows us to examine some of its core values and to consider whether we can preserve them while simultaneously critiquing other aspects of the tradition. I believe that a contractual framework is useful in our thinking about morality and justice, as it properly reflects key liberal values – the importance of autonomy, the merit of elaborating a conception of the good, aspiring to live by it and by doing so, to flourish, the concept of making plans and being held to our word, the benefit of being rewarded for our social contributions, and held accountable for our social failings and the social virtues of reciprocity and impartiality. These values are so central to human life and social arrangements that it is easy to understand why many scholars would be reluctant to put contractual theory aside when dealing with the robust moral status of PSID and to argue instead that the social contract tradition can successfully integrate these people into its framework and explain their moral and political status in contractual terms.

There is currently a divide between thinkers who go beyond contractual theory to explain the duties we hold toward people with severe disabilities and thinkers who try to expand social contract theory to include them. Examining strategies of expanding the social contract doctrine is hardly a futile endeavor. John Rawls explicitly left the issue of whether severely disabled individuals could be included within the scope of justice as fairness to be dealt with later, if possible, by the extension of the theory.[65] In fact, severely disabled people might prove to be not an *exception* that can be brought within the bounds of social contract theory, but rather the "outlier" that forces us to reexamine the assumptions and criteria we use to turn people into outliers. However, even that line of reasoning need not be fatal to contractual theory.

Moreover, it would be salutary for contractual theory if it could expand so as to include people with severe disabilities. The exclusion of this group of people is detrimental to social contract theories, as the adequacy of theories of justice – as Lawrence Becker notes – "is now measured partly by [their] success in dealing with justice for the disabled."[66] Contractual authors may react differently to the failure of their theory to encompass severe disabilities. They may either simply recognize their limitations (something that Rawls explicitly conceded),[67] or they may claim to still occupy the whole terrain of available justifications for robust moral status. In the former case, they must develop ways to balance claims made by beings with

---

[65] See Rawls, *Political Liberalism*, at 20–21.
[66] Lawrence Becker, "Reciprocity, Justice, and Disability" (2005) 116:1 Ethics 9 at 9.
[67] See Rawls, *Political Liberalism*, at 20–21.

contractually based and noncontractually based robust moral status. However, adopting the latter position risks contributing to a refutation of contractual theory.

It may be less confrontational or more constructive to say that I am testing the compatibility between the strong moral pull that dictates that we have a robust concern for people with severe disabilities on the one hand and, on the other, that we have continued adherence to the social contract tradition. Indeed, I ultimately conclude that the social contract framework cannot completely and accurately explain all of the robust duties we owe to severely disabled individuals. I also conclude that this finding does not imply that the social contract tradition must be jettisoned but rather that we should narrow its claim to the whole of the territories of morality and justice.

Nonetheless, my primary interest lies with the moral status of severely disabled individuals rather than with social contract theory. I use this theory because many scholars writing about PWD hope to explain their robust moral status in a broadly contractarian or contractualist way. Although I initially shared their optimism, I am now unconvinced that this approach can provide all PWD, notably PSID, with a suitable place in the moral world. This conclusion allows me to shift my attention to other (relational) solutions that complement and/or nest contractual frameworks.

1.4.3 *Learning from the "Opposing Camp" and Overcoming the Opposition between Camps*

Let me point out two further benefits of seriously considering unlikely but paradigmatic solutions to this issue. One could insist that a more natural way to start such an investigation on the status of PSID would be to first look at theories that are traditionally understood to be more likely to justify their moral status. This could include forms of human exceptionalism or humanism, care ethics, moral conceptions of partiality, empathy or sentimentalism, or duties toward occurrences of vulnerability that characterize people with severe disabilities and disability-related needs and dependencies.

Insofar as we may have to challenge conceptions of the person and of her worth that have been cornerstones of liberal politics since Hobbes, it is relevant to ask first whether present-day liberalism really cannot make room for our strongly held moral concern for PSID. After all, it would be fairly momentous to state – particularly at the opening of a work politicizing concepts including care ethics – that the social contract tradition (and Rawls's theory of justice) is a "dead end" for the severely disabled person, or a dead end *tout court* and that, short of finding a pluralist compromise, the latter may be an inevitable implication of the former. Dismissing a mainstream tradition tends to isolate its critics, making it easier for the dominant ideology to present them as radicals that ought not to be taken seriously.

By engaging with the case of PSID from a contractual perspective, I invite anti-contractual thinkers to consider the merits of the social contract tradition, and

I dissuade contractual thinkers from discarding the test case of severe disabilities as an exception to a general rule that should be properly dealt with "later." Postponing treatment of this glaring flaw in social contract theory tends to deflate the impact of one's failure to deal with this "dead end" and to condone the lesser political status of people with severe disabilities. Giving a fair chance to arguments that defend the importance of contractual relations for disabled and nondisabled people alike enables us to strike a more accurate balance between interests in social contract theory, as opposed to switching completely to a one-sided, noncontractual alternative. Many authors speaking from within these apparently conflictual traditions tend to reject social contract theory or to reject alternative accounts of the robust moral status of severely disabled individuals. Little consideration is given to whether their separate insights could each be acknowledged within a more flexible, pluralist framework. As a result, the strong dichotomies that are set up in debates around the robust moral status of PSID (e.g., care *versus* justice, partiality *versus* impartiality, charity *versus* justice) are unhelpfully rigid.

To put this another way: starting from an approach that we suspect to be problematic can help us to identify more precisely those narrow points of disagreement that are perhaps fixable. Delineating morally important dimensions of human relations by analyzing what social contract theories mistakenly exclude has the dual advantage of (a) making the determination of these elements less arbitrary and (b) further justifying why we ought to modify or abandon certain contractualist or contractarian aspirations. This is because an emphasis on the moral weight of noncontractual relations would then be the result of an elimination process that would test our intuitions by confronting them with mainstream, well-established assumptions, rather than strawman arguments.

1.4.4 *Choosing to Deal with the Most Unlikely of Contractors*

PSID, within the broader group of PWD, are less able to act autonomously, to develop a conception of the good life or second-order desires, to demonstrate self-awareness and awareness of others, to help or threaten others, to work and to participate in cooperative endeavors. We could say that they are the most unlikely of contractors. However, when we take seriously the idea that PSID have a robust moral status, this requires us to recognize that they also have a claim to question the criteria used to grant moral status, contractual or otherwise. Thus, by choosing "the most unlikely of contractors," I encourage my reader to reject the possibility of "normalizing" people with disabilities by forcing them into a philosophical framework that almost fits them, rather than facing the truth that it may not, and then having to build a theoretical home that either fits them, or leaves them out in the cold and denies their robust moral status. To choose a less outlying class of contractors would dodge the contractual bullet. To choose a more other-regarding, sentimentalist, or humanistic philosophical framework for this work would deprive

PSID from an opportunity to knock at the contractual door and, if necessary, to blow our political and social house down.

Lastly, even without assuming that PSID have the right to question the criteria of robust moral status, one can still learn valuable lessons from engaging with vivid conceptual contrasts in philosophy.

1.5 THE CONTRACTUALISM–CONTRACTARIANISM DISTINCTION

This book will explore integrationist contractarian and contractualist strategies. Contractualism and contractarianism are ethical normative theories which can be used either as moral theories to explain the grounds of moral norms or as political theories used to justify the legitimacy of political power.[68] As political theories, they are known as "social contract" theories. They all – contractarian, contractualist, moral, and political – have in common the belief that "agreement (either hypothetical or actual) has moral significance"[69] and that "whether an action is right or wrong must depend on whether the act accords with or violates principles that are, or would be, the object of a suitable agreement."[70]

The notion of a contract or an agreement existing between rational people is compelling because of its seeming simplicity. However, the notion is also complex and ambiguous, because a contract is not a basic notion or value, but rather refers to a bundle of intuitions, conventions, and values which must all be argued for rather than assumed. Contractual theories are not merely conventionalist. That is, the norms at the outcome of the contractual procedures are not valid just because they have been contracted for, but because the act of contracting took place within a particular situation and allowed for the expression of particular agent capacities. Indeed, both the contractual situation and the contractors are generally idealized.[71] The normative content underlying contractual discourse must also be explained. As we begin to investigate this explanation, we see two clusters of ideas appear, and even though both are located within the conceptual history of the social contract, they center around incompatible theoretical commitments, values, and assumptions. I follow Stephen Darwall in calling these two clusters of traditions

---

[68] See, e.g., Simon Blackburn, *Oxford Dictionary of Philosophy*, 2nd ed. (Oxford: Oxford University Press, 2008) *sub verbo* social contract; Ann Cudd, "Contractarians," *The Stanford Encyclopedia of Philosophy* (August 2012), plato.stanford.edu/archives/fall2012/entries/contractarianism/.

[69] See Christie Hartley, "Justice for the Disabled: A Contractualist Approach" (2009) 40:1 J Soc Phil 17 at 17.

[70] Stephen Darwall, *Contractarianism / Contractualism* (Malden, MA: Blackwell, 2003), at 1. Darwall adds "between equals" at the end of his definition. Although it is accurate of all theories we will be concerned with, I prefer not to put it in this most basic definition, because "equality" can be understood in very different ways and "inequality" only affects the moral significance of an agreement when it affects the expression of uncoerced will which is what centrally matters.

[71] *Ibid.*

"contractarianism" and "contractualism," as some philosophers have recently noted that this has become a common distinction.[72]

Contractualism can be said to center around the value of autonomy – the capacity to govern oneself. Autonomy is closely associated with Kant, whose conception of dignity (or moral worth) was based on a person's capacity to know and endorse the moral law. The act of contracting with others to lay out principles of justice and laws is a way to become the authors of the laws or to endorse the political structure that enacts them. *The social contract allows people to be legislators*. It expresses people's rational and autonomous nature, and grounds the legitimacy of political power and the content of legal and moral norms upon these traits.[73] (It does so, it is worth noting, to the exclusion of those who are not seen as relevant to justice, and sometimes to morality.) The procedure of contractualist rule-making is therefore grounded on the value of a "common perspective" in which individuals engage or partake.[74] By engaging "contractually" with other people – that is, by making sure that the norms we impose upon them are reasonable or justifiable to them – we recognize this special value that they have, describing it as being priceless[75] or having "inviolability."[76] The contract is not a way around this special value, as it would be if contractual agency or freedom was itself something that agents could put on the negotiating table. Rather, the contract is a means to *express* this value. Thus, people's capacities to be reasonable and rational are honored, esteemed, or respected rather than used (or rather than *merely* used, as they can be respected in spite of, or through, their use). The object of the contractualist conception of equality is this value and the capacities or potential for it. Though people's intellectual capacities vary and even though we can say that people are more or less autonomous for other reasons (e.g., one may be more submissive or less authentic in their relationships), they are still to be treated as moral equals, because this treatment is required by their nature and their needs, and because only in this way they can lead a moral and (some would add) a flourishing or happy life.

Contractarianism is easier to explain because it takes as its starting point the ordinary, transactional understanding of contract. That is, when contracting, we

---

[72] See, e.g., Hartley, "Justice for the Disabled," at 17; Cudd, "Contractarians." Note, however, Cynthia Stark's resistance, in her "How to Include the Severely Disabled in a Contractarian Theory of Justice" (2007) 15:2 J Political Phil 127 at 128 (fn. 4). She prefers to keep the contractualist–contractarian distinction to distinguish moral from political theories (i.e., Scanlon from Rawls). I note that terms like "moral theories" and "theories of justice" may also operate this distinction.

[73] See Kant, *Groundwork*, at 36–43; Immanuel Kant, *The Metaphysics of Morals*, trans. and ed. Mary Gregor (Cambridge: Cambridge University Press, 1996), at 92.

[74] For instance, through the Rousseauian "general will," as part of the Kantian "kingdom of end" or behind the Rawlsian "veil of ignorance." See Darwall, *Contractarianism / Contractualism*, at 5–6; Hartley, "Justice for the Disabled," at 17–18.

[75] See Kant, *Metaphysics of Morals*, at 186, 209.

[76] See Rawls, *A Theory of Justice*, at 24–25.

rarely consider what our action implies in terms of respect for ourselves and for others as free agents, though this is what contractualism asks us to do. However, contracts generally occur against a transactional background where it is permissible for contracting parties to concern themselves only with maximizing the satisfaction of particular desires, regardless of whether these desires are noble or moral and regardless of the impact that this transaction has on counterparties.

This understanding of contract may be commonplace, but it is obviously not neutral, as it relies on a conception of people as primarily guided by self-interest, and the position that this self-interest is not constrained by moral norms, but simply guided by higher degrees of self-interest. Here, reason is instrumental in achieving one's ends and is not symptomatic of any special value other than power. As such, contractarianism is usually associated with Hobbes, who (prior and) antithetically to Kant, based the value or worth of people on their "price; that is to say, so much as would be given for the use of [their] power" and defined their dignity as their "public worth" (the former being relative to the "buyer" and the latter set by the State).[77] In the Hobbesian ethical framework, what is "good" is simply that which is desired. "Power" is central to this framework, as it is one's "present means [...] to obtain some future apparent good."[78] Unlike contractualism, which starts by prizing autonomy, contractarianism has a descriptive starting point that focuses on people's shared traits of rationality and self-interest as well as their currencies of power. The conception of equality at work in political contractarianism is not ideal, but factual: it assumes an equality of power. This equality is more questionable, but social contract theories assume that the weak can team up against the strong and that every Goliath has his David, making it prudent to grant an equal political status to everybody (above a certain threshold of capacities). Contractarian theories of justice can therefore be presented as prudential rather than moral.

To consider the contrasting points of both traditions, a fair contractualist society is one in which principles of justice allow for mutual respect, while a fair contractarian society is one in which principles of justice are mutually advantageous. The social contract allows contractualists to be moral legislators, whereas it helps contractarians to get what they want. Both traditions explain robust moral status – in particular, the status of a subject of justice – in terms of contracting capacities. For example, contractualism may require certain levels of autonomy, rationality, reasonableness, a sense of justice, moral agency, and other traits that contractors should pay attention to for moral reasons. Contractarianism, on the other hand, requires power, namely the power to help or hurt others and the power to make them contractors strategically worth bargaining with. It is generally assumed that the severely disabled individual lacks both sets of capacities.

---

[77] See Molesworth, *Leviathan*, at 76.
[78] Ibid. at 74.

These traditions have been described in various ways: as Hobbesian and Kantian,[79] as "subject-centered justice" and "justice as reciprocity,"[80] as theories of justice "founded on the notions of impartiality and individual well-being" and as theories of justice "founded on the notions of self-interest and mutual advantage."[81] However, none of these pairings or dichotomies are perfect. For instance, a terminological focus on mutuality or reciprocity in the contractarian tradition alone may overlook the idea that – as is the case in Rawls's theory, itself sometimes characterized as mixed, sometimes as contractualist – reciprocity can be a form of respect, although this will depend on what is being reciprocated and what reciprocity is taken to mean. Conversely, Jean Hampton uses the Kantian-Hobbesian dichotomy but presents a form of Kantian contractarianism. Lastly, Buchanan writes that "the term 'subject-centered' seems apt since it serves to emphasize that moral status depends upon features of the individual herself other than her power to affect others for good or for ill."[82] However, both contractualism and contractarianism are "subject-centered" to the extent that, though they disagree on the conception of the subject, they both effectuate a shift away from a natural political structure, or from an objective list of goods and toward centering our political, metaphysical, and ethical world around human beings.[83] Since Buchanan refers to the "contingency objection" to contractarianism (which I address in this book), perhaps terms like "derivative" or "contingent" may have been sufficient. However, this labeling of objections would have loaded the dice by focusing on an aspect of contractarianism that contractarians themselves do not find salient. Given the problems of these pairs, Darwall's terms "contractualism" and "contractarianism" – though stipulative (and perhaps partly *because* they are not self-explanatory in a way that would also cause confusion or ambiguity) – are useful technical terms to adopt for the purposes of this book.

Indeed, both traditions seem to exclude individuals with very serious (especially intellectual) impairments from the scope of justice, if not from morality altogether. Some within these traditions consider that the treatment of PSID (and others with different kinds of disabilities) belongs to an ethical sphere other than that of the morality of justice, such as charity or love. It is obvious why, from a contractarian

---

[79] Jean Hampton, *The Intrinsic Worth of Persons: Contractarianism in Moral and Political Philosophy*, ed. Daniel Farnham (New York: Cambridge University Press, 2007).
[80] Allen Buchanan, "Justice as Reciprocity versus Subject-Centered Justice" (1990) 19:3 Phil & Pub Aff 227. Buchanan characterizes *justice as reciprocity* by "the claim that only those who do (or at least can) make a contribution to the cooperative surplus have rights to social resources" (at 230) and *subject-centered justice* by the idea that "basic rights to resources are grounded not in the individual's strategic capacities but rather in other features of the individual herself – her needs or nonstrategic capacities" (at 231).
[81] See Becker, "Reciprocity, Justice, and Disability," at 12.
[82] See Buchanan, "Justice as Reciprocity," at 231.
[83] Far from being dissociated from contractarianism, such a shift is characteristic of Hobbes's early modern contractarian theory. See generally Zarka, *Décision métaphysique*.

point of view, persons with severe disabilities would be excluded from the political community: they do not pose a threat and cannot engage in reciprocal, mutually beneficial, tit-for-tat transactions. Even if persons with severe disabilities could engage in some sort of transaction, they may still fail to be granted the full status of subject of justice and be exploited. Note that, from a contractualist point of view, people who are only *physically* impaired would still possess the capacities required to be granted a robust moral status, since they are able to act autonomously – that is, to develop and pursue a conception of the good life. (Rawls's exclusion of the severely physically disabled from his contractual deliberative process on account of their inability to be "normal and fully cooperating members of society over a complete life" reflects the *contractarian* elements of this theory.[84]) On the other hand, it could be argued that severely *cognitively* disabled people are not moral agents and cannot be said to belong to the moral community, if Kant was right that moral agency is indeed a *sine qua non* requirement for belonging to the moral community. If PSID cannot reciprocate respect, the attitude of respect may not even apply to them. This is why philosophers debating the moral status of human beings have focused on cognitive (rather than physical) impairments[85] and why I choose to focus on this harder case – even if some of my reflections apply, *mutatis mutandis*, to severely physically disabled individuals as well – especially within a contractarian paradigm.

To understand how difficult it is to grant a "free entry ticket" to moral and political communities to PSID within a contractual framework, and how logical this exclusion is from within the contractual tradition, it may be helpful to think of a youth soccer team or a math club. We can understand that the soccer team will not allow an obese student on their team because the child runs too slowly. Although we do not find this rejection charitable (or helpful to the obese student, whose health may improve by playing sports), we can see why it is rational with regard to the goal pursued by self-interested soccer players. Some may even find it moral, given their understanding of the need for excellence in sport. As for the math club, let us imagine that it is driven by a love of science and discovery, and that the members are less motivated by a chance of winning contests than they are by learning. The students understand that they stand a better chance of finding the solution to a mathematical problem presented in a national contest if they put their heads together and work constructively as an intellectual team. We may find them

---

[84] Rawls, *Justice as Fairness*, at 167. Though, again, it depends on how cooperation, reciprocity, and respect are understood. One may hold an account of respect that would require reciprocity or the capacity to reciprocate, and that would not excuse anyone from those requirements, even on the grounds that one is not responsible for being unable to reciprocate. Such an account would seem to bring its author under the contractarian umbrella.

[85] See David Wasserman *et al.*, "Cognitive Disability and Moral Status," *The Stanford Encyclopedia of Philosophy* (August 2017), plato.stanford.edu/entries/cognitive-disability/; Eva Feder Kittay and Licia Carlson, *Cognitive Disability and Its Challenge to Moral Philosophy* (Malden, MA: Wiley-Blackwell, 2010).

ungenerous to refuse membership to someone who is failing math (although being part of a math club may help the failing student to improve), but we can also see why they would consider it absurd to grant membership to someone who cannot help them achieve their goal. These examples show that when we size these concepts down to specific contexts, the contractualist and contractarian exclusionary frameworks seem more justified because they fit the self-appointed, stipulated ambitions of smaller groups. The problem with contractualism and contractarianism is that, when they are taken to be a theory of justice, they purport to apply to society as a whole rather than to particular communities or to a subset of social relations, such as clubs or private associations. In this book, I ask whether contractual theories of justice applied to society *as a whole* can integrate PSID. If they cannot, I ask *why* they fail to do so and *how* they could be acceptably downsized.

1.6 STARTING POINTS: PRESERVATIONISTS AND REVISIONISTS

Let me conclude this chapter by examining a primary assumption I make in this book: that excluding the severely disabled individual from the scope of justice and morality would be a fault or error of some kind. How can this assumption be justified? Most of us assume that excluding the severely disabled individual from our community of other, equally important members, is wrong. Although we might not be clear on what "equal importance" precisely involves, most of us believe that a theory of justice has failed where it is unable to competently explain why it provides less than full moral status to certain groups.

However, this assumption is not shared by all moral and political philosophers. Some theorists challenge the assumption that people with severe disabilities – especially mental disabilities – deserve the same moral and political status as their nondisabled fellow citizens. These theorists have been referred to as "revisionists" because they propose to revise our moral intuitions rather than preserve them.[86] Some revisionists suggest that a person with disabilities lacks important capacities, and that this makes her life less desirable than the life of a nondisabled person. For instance, Jeff McMahan[87] and Peter Singer[88] conclude that human beings with significantly lower than species average cognitive capacities have a lower moral status, based on the lesser value of their lives. They reject a kind of human exceptionalism, according to which being a member of the human species would suffice to justify granting a robust moral status upon an individual. They are committed to interspecies impartiality and propose that moral status should supervene on traits, capacities, or interests that should matter regardless of the entity

---

[86] This revisionist/preservationist distinction is found in Agnieszka Jaworska, "Caring and Full Moral Standing" (2007) 117:3 Ethics 460 at 463–64.
[87] Jeff McMahan, "Challenges to Human Equality" (2008) 12:1 J Ethics (2008) 81.
[88] Peter Singer, *Practical Ethics*, 3rd ed. (New York: Cambridge University Press, 2011).

(human or nonhuman) in which they occur.[89] Taking this position to its practical conclusions means it is less bad to sacrifice the interests of severely disabled individuals or, indeed, to end their lives, compared to the sacrifice of nonhuman animals who possess the relevant capacities or interests to a higher degree.

I mentioned some points on which both Singer and McMahan agreed; let me say a little more about some of their respective views. McMahan's "tiered" morality implies that different human beings fall under different moral regimes, and it is not equally wrong to kill this or that individual.[90] In lower tiers, the weaker the capacities, the weaker the constraints that would prevent killing or sacrifice.[91] An individual's level of mental capacity may determine how important she is by determining whether she possesses any kind of special inviolability or whether it is permissible to neglect her, or less wrong to sacrifice her interests than the interests of others. The low status that an intellectually disabled human could have means she "may be treated in a consequentialist manner."[92] Even her most basic interests (e.g., in life, or in physical integrity) may be sacrificed for the sake of someone else's interests or, arguably, traded for other goods or desirable states of affairs in the world: money, health, resources, art, or games.

Singer wrote that "when the death of a disabled infant will lead to the birth of another infant with better prospects of a happy life, the total amount of happiness will be greater if the disabled infant is killed."[93] In cases where infants lack the traits that would underlie a right to life (such as the capability "of seeing themselves as distinct entities over time"), infanticide may be justified because of the displeasure or burden a parent would experience.[94] Utilitarian premises of this kind may potentially justify recommending harvesting the organs of severely disabled orphan children, who would be kept socially isolated so that they would be mourned by a minimum of people.[95] Utilitarians may well factor public disgust at these policy

---

[89] We find this commitment in Singer's "principle of equal consideration of interests" (*ibid.* at 20) and in James Rachels' commitment to "moral individualism" in *Created from Animals: The Moral Implications of Darwinism* (Oxford: Oxford University Press, 1990), at 173, endorsed by Jeff McMahan, "Our Fellow Creatures" (2005) 9:3–4 J Ethics 353 at 354.

[90] See McMahan, "Our Fellow Creatures," at 355.

[91] For similar comments on James Rachels, see Peter Byrne, *Philosophical and Ethical Problems in Mental Handicap* (New York: St Martin's Press, 2000), at 9–10.

[92] See McMahan, "Challenges to Human Equality," at 98.

[93] Singer, *Practical Ethics*, at 163.

[94] *Ibid.* at 161.

[95] Contrast with Singer's comment on experimenters' "bias in favour of their own species whenever they carry out experiments on nonhuman animals for purposes that they would not think justified them in using human beings at an equal or lower level of sentience, awareness, sensitivity, and so on" (*ibid.* at 58). One should add that animal rights activists can, in theory, use Singer's comparisons between animals and severely mentally disabled people to argue for leveling up the treatment of animals rather than leveling down the treatment of humans. However, if philosophers or policymakers accept some version of Singer's "principle of equality" or Rachels' "moral individualism" and are committed to comparing states of affairs occurring within entities (humans, nonhuman animals, plants,

strategies into their calculation of the practicability or morality of these approaches. This calculation may lead them to oppose such disquieting proposals, at least until the public has overcome its squeamishness. The problem with this utilitarian countermove against their own policy positions is that they do not consider our strong aversion to organ harvesting as a distinct source of normative obligation. Rather, they consider that this aversion is a mere psychological phenomenon that creates a sense of displeasure or repugnance.

In sum, accepting that a person's claim to life, concern, love, or respect is made hostage to possessing particular kinds of capacities, may lead to nonintuitive conclusions. Some revisionist conclusions are illiberal in nature, as they logically imply the presence of "moral castes" within a society of people, where humans are ranked across a spectrum of the permissibility of sacrificing them, with severely disabled individuals at the one extreme of this spectrum. Indeed, some of these conclusions could form a *reductio ad absurdum* argument against these revisionist views.

Surely, the "preservationists" respond, something has gone wrong within revisionist theory if it leads to such unpalatable and cruel conclusions.[96] Preservationists insist that all human beings deserve a robust moral status in spite of being differently cognitively and physically endowed. In order to justify this conclusion, preservationists have traditionally claimed that belonging to the human species is enough to justify receiving the highest kind of moral status. More recently, moral philosophers who take a preservationist stance have understood moral status in relational terms. For instance, some have argued that relations of dependency and care, parental relations, or kinds of solidarity arising from membership in the same species can all provide morally relevant grounds to justify giving the highest kind of moral regard to human beings with severe intellectual disabilities.[97]

---

robots, angels, etc.) as though the situatedness of those entities did not matter, their ethical analyses may well lead them to a leveling down of the status of certain human beings. Some philosophers thinking about the rights and welfare of human and nonhuman animals are concerned with the limits of interspecies comparisons because, *inter alia*, they can potentially harm humans and other animals alike. The status of humans lacking species-typical capacities is no longer secured on relational grounds (social, familial, biological, cultural connections, for instance) and the status of animals is forced into an anthropocentric framework. See, e.g., Cora Diamond, "Eating Meat and Eating People" (1978) 53:206 Philosophy 465. This is not to say that comparisons are undesirable. In a trivial sense, everyone must agree with Singer that they are "unavoidable" (Peter Singer, "Speciesism and Moral Status" [2009] 40:3–4 Metaphilosophy 567 at 568). The work of other philosophers drawing comparisons between animals and people with disabilities suggest that it is not comparisons *per se* that are damaging, but a comparativist stance that atomizes and decontextualizes situated beings and abstracts them away from the moral complexity of different forms of life. See, e.g., Sunaura Taylor, *Beasts of Burden: Animal and Disability Liberation* (New York: The New Press, 2017); Sue Donaldson and Will Kymlicka, *Zoopolis: A Political Theory of Animal Rights* (Oxford: Oxford University Press, 2011).

[96] For a critical review of the implications of McMahan's view for people with disabilities, see Kittay, "Margins of Personhood."

[97] See, e.g., Kittay, "Personal Philosophical Political"; Bernard Williams, "The Human Prejudice" in *Philosophy as a Humanistic Discipline* (Princeton: Princeton University Press,

Unfortunately, the philosophical commitments of each side of this debate often make "preservationists" and "revisionists" unresponsive to the other's claims. Disability activists point out that they were once the babies whom utilitarian bioethicists suggested euthanizing.[98] Equally, disability philosophers lose patience with the debate when their mentally disabled siblings and children are substantively compared to animals and identified as second-class citizens or "less than" persons.[99] On the other side of the debate, revisionist philosophers insist that the relational standpoints of preservationists are clouded by emotions and prejudices. These exchanges border on name-calling, and death threats have been issued outside of academia (and almost supported from inside).[100] Revisionists are compared to Nazis and preservationists to racists.[101]

Rather than entering into an extensive review of this argument, I start from the position that revisionist conclusions are indeed wrong, and that the severely disabled individual has a "robust moral status." Though such a position makes it unnecessary to give a detailed account of the context and chronology of this primary philosophical disagreement, it remains helpful to provide a brief overview of the two main revisionist positions so as to properly situate my own argument. Unlike Rawls, the first group of revisionist theorists (in the vein of Singer and McMahan) need not be concerned by the failure of the social contract to fully account for the role of persons with severe intellectual disabilities in our society or, at least, not on the grounds that people with severe disabilities enjoy a moral status that would make this shortcoming wrong.

A second group of revisionist philosophers applies a more collectivist or relational focus to their research. Rather than being concerned with the individual value of lives or private states of affairs, they seek to ground membership to our political or moral community in individual capacities to take part in specific social relations. For instance, David Gauthier concludes that "the congenitally handicapped and

---

2009); Cora Diamond, "The Importance of Being Human" (1991) 29 Royal Institute Phil Supplements 35. For an enlightening survey of the literature in the area, see John Vorhaus, *Valuing Profoundly Disabled People: Fellowship, Community and Ties of Birth* (New York: Routledge, 2018).

[98] For an insightful and well-known comment on Peter Singer written by a disability activist, see Harriet McBryde Johnson, "Unspeakable Conversations," *The New York Times* (February 16, 2003), www.nytimes.com/2003/02/16/magazine/unspeakable-conversations.html.

[99] Consider Kittay, "Personal Philosophical Political."

[100] See, e.g., Jenny Teichman, "The False Philosophy of Peter Singer," *The New Criterion* 2:8 (April 1993), www.newcriterion.com/issues/1993/4/the-false-philosophy-of-peter-singer.

[101] To be fair to preservationists, most of them would agree that animals are treated terribly, and that the widespread neglect of animal welfare and animal rights is a sign of speciesism (an arbitrary disregard for the value of nonhuman lives). They have much more trouble with the contention that widespread repugnance at the thought of casting severely disabled people at the margins of our moral community is also a kind of speciesism, nonmoral feelings, or misfiring moral ones, morally similar to the affective response racist people have toward mixed-race marriage.

defective [...] fall beyond the pale of a morality tied to mutuality."[102] Similarly, Jean Hampton claims that "[t]here is something absurd about inquiring into the morality of the relationship between, say, a mother and her newborn infant" or between people who are "radically unequal in capacities."[103] A deep commitment to reciprocity leads some revisionists to hold that relationships between able-bodied people and members of society with less capacities to reciprocate (such as human beings with severe intellectual disability) fall not only "outside the province of distributive justice"[104] but also beyond the province of justice and morality altogether. Hampton, for instance, is sympathetic to feminist views that see *moral value* in relations involving powerless people, but concludes that to consider such relations to be *moral* is "evaluatively inept."[105] Susan Dimock follows Gauthier's and Hampton's commitment to a mutuality requirement and explicitly holds that human relationships that cannot meet this requirement (such as those between "the completely infirm and their caregivers") fall "beyond the realm of morality, because we are beyond the realm of interaction and so beyond the realm of normativity."[106] This book examines challenges to this exclusionist position and to related views that stop short of asserting that the severely disabled individual falls *beyond* the scopes of morality and justice, but then also cannot explain why they would fall *within* them.

It is worth noting that most people – both in and outside of academia – are either "soft" or "folk" preservationists or, at least, not hardliner revisionists. By this, I mean that most people would not align themselves with either kind of revisionism, but instead hold that commonsense morality dictates that even people with very low cognitive capacities are not more "sacrificable" than others, and that relationships that nondisabled people have with these people can be governed by morality and justice. They are, however, "soft" or "folk" preservationists because they may be unable to justify their beliefs and because they sometimes endorse policies and behaviors that assume a less than robust moral status for people with disabilities. This positioning might suggest a weakness of will, or that their preservationist commitment is partly rhetorical in nature. However, it is generally true that most revisionist philosophers express some discomfort with their conclusions about disability or attempt to mitigate the impact of their policy solutions on severely disabled people in marginal ways. Most of us who think deeply about the lives of people with disabilities – whether we are philosophers, lawyers, doctors, or nurses, and whether we have a disability ourselves or a disabled family member or not – believe that we owe something of considerable moral significance to people with profound

---

[102] David Gauthier, *Morals by Agreement* (Oxford: Oxford University Press, 1987), at 268.
[103] Hampton, *The Intrinsic Worth of Persons*, 32–33.
[104] *Ibid.* at 33.
[105] *Ibid.* at 38.
[106] Susan Dimock, "Why All Feminists Should Be Contractarians" (2008) 47:2 Dialogue: Can Phil Rev 273 at 285.

intellectual disabilities. For example, most of us are appalled when we read about the mistreatment of severely disabled individuals in institutions that are ostensibly dedicated to providing them with care. And our assumptions that society has failed to protect or properly care for severely disabled individuals implies their prior entitlement to that care and protection.

This consensus view is worth describing because it illustrates how most people, including philosophers, rely upon their own intuitions and experiences in formulating their ethical positions. Preservationists may, for instance, start from their real or imagined experience of relating to people with lower cognitive capacities than the average person. Likewise, revisionists may start from their commitment to impartiality, to the importance of specific goods, such as moral agency, or to the importance of reciprocity for healthy moral relations. In drawing from their experiences and from abstracted theoretical frameworks to select their hypotheses, premises, and approaches, both groups inevitably rely on their intuitions about which of their beliefs are weightier building blocks upon which more movable pieces can be rearranged, whether they consider the weightier building blocks as immovable "ethical bedrocks"[107] or as shiftable, revisable, temporary scaffolding.

This may sound obvious, but it addresses the potential objection that I am asserting, rather than proving, that people with severe disabilities are persons and should be treated in a way that reflects that they are not lesser beings than humans with different intellectual capacities. Consider Peter Byrne, a philosopher of disability who shares this assumption and who wrote that he cannot make sense of his experience of love and care toward his autistic son, "unless [he] accept[s] that love and its associated attitudes are revelatory of value and unless the fact of common membership of a human community [suffices to ground equal respect and personhood]."[108] Similarly, I grew up with my brother, Richard-Alexandre, who has an intellectual disability and a mental illness. I saw my brother's lifelong struggles to "fit in" in a society that is simply not set up in a way that will maximize his social integration, self-esteem, and well-being. I also had other significant experiences with persons with cognitive disabilities and illnesses of different kinds. This inevitably affects the set of intuitions I begin from, the weightiness of some of my beliefs, and my inclination to find certain philosophical methodologies more insightful than others. This does not necessarily mean that all "preservationists" are determined not to question beliefs they are experiencing as foundational and/or providing meaning or coherence to their identity and/or their moral agency. But it does mean, as Byrne puts it, that we cannot "abandon a human point of view"; that is, "we cannot reason about [how we are to treat each other and the rest of the planet] other than by using insights and forms of argument immanent in human

---

[107] I borrow this term from Jenny Teichman, *Social Ethics: A Student's Guide* (Oxford: Blackwell, 1996).
[108] Byrne, *Philosophical and Ethical Problems*, at xi.

reasoning about value."[109] Examining the parameters and normative implications of the assumed entitlement of severely disabled individuals to a robust moral status in the context of the social contract tradition may not only help us to assess this tradition's capacity to account for, and recognize, this status. It may also help us to better justify, understand, or adjust this status. It may help to reach alternative frameworks that would better justify this status, but such new frameworks may also invite us to amend or specify the meaning and content of this status.

Incidentally, I think that acknowledging the breadth of this consensus on the entitlement of the severely disabled individual to a robust moral status lends the preservationist approach the sort of "democratic virtue" that philosophers – wishing to engender a fruitful exchange between theorists and the *demos* (the populace as a political unit) – encourage.[110] The fact that we can point to historical and contemporary abuses or mistreatment of people with disabilities does not destabilize this position, as few people joining this conversation would side with Nazi euthanasia programs, for example. If anything, the public reaction to past and current events that deny the robust moral status of severely disabled individuals further justifies the assumption that severely disabled people do have a robust moral status.

Finally, revisionists could point to the danger of beginning this debate from the *status quo*, which often conceals systemic oppression. They may, for instance, anticipate that any theoretical work starting with the premise that persons with severe mental disabilities have a robust moral status would imply sanctification or elevation of the membership to our species as a sufficient and necessary condition to have moral relevance. However, this need not be the case. I find it hard to see how protecting vulnerable people who have severe disabilities would oppress anyone, human or not. Besides, the inchoate set of intuitions that all human beings matter – regardless of how physically or cognitively impaired they are – while undeniably widespread, is not really part of a political or theoretical *status quo*, except at a high level of abstraction and in rights rhetoric. Traditional strands of human exceptionalism are not particularly good news for people with severe disabilities, seen as broken specimens rather than exemplars of a superior kind. While some have worried that certain animal ethicists have exploited disabled people in order to advance the status of animals,[111] the reverse concern seems bizarre. First, because animals are regrettably so widely neglected in moral and political thought that they can hardly be used as a stepping stone for marginalized human minorities. Second, because the considerations that underlie much of care and disability ethicists' work (which resist the "intelligist," "ableist," or "sanist" tendencies that find their way into

---

[109] *Ibid.* at 65.
[110] See James Tully, *Public Philosophy in a New Key: Volume 1, Democracy and Civic Freedom* (Cambridge: Cambridge University Press, 2009), at 3–11.
[111] See Carlson, *The Faces of Intellectual Disability*.

mainstream moral, political, and legal theories[112]) are more likely to open, rather than close, avenues of research paying attention to the unique texture of animal vulnerability as well.

To sum up, anti-speciesist critiques best reach their target when they attack radical strands of human exceptionalism[113] that few, if any, philosophers of disability endorse. Animal ethicists and philosophers of disabilities may just as well agree on the importance of paying attention to the distinctive textures and content of inter- and intraspecies relations and/or species-related norms.[114] And both may resist strands of human exceptionalism that tend to exalt not humanity at large, including in its frail and interdependent features, but a "central case" of humanity – a particular specimen of humans used as an ideal benchmark for all others. (Revisionists are no less liable to use such benchmarks.[115]) I am therefore sympathetic to anti-speciesist arguments but have trouble seeing how they can credibly be levied against my assumption that vulnerable, disabled, human beings historically cast at the margins of our moral communities should enjoy a robust moral status. Thus, far from being reactionary, views that assume as a starting point that the status of people with severe disabilities should be *preserved* may in fact *revise* some foundational tenets of liberal ideology and sustain a greater sensibility to inter- and intraspecies vulnerability and dependency.

1.6.1 *The Dis-Citizenship and Lesser Personhood of PSID Are Real Problems*

Soft preservationists may find this defense of a preservationist starting point frivolous. They think, of course, that no one outside of specialized philosophical circles doubts that people with disabilities are "persons" and "citizens." This assumption is mistaken. Disability advocates and theorists face generalized resistance to the recognition that second-rate citizenship and truncated personhood *are* granted to many human beings, for no other reason than they have different physical and cognitive capacities. No one would suggest that North American societies are no longer sexist or racist simply because it no longer has laws on the books that declare slaves to

---

[112] *Ibid.* See also Michael L. Perlin, *The Hidden Prejudice: Mental Disability on Trial* (Washington, DC: American Psychological Association, 2000); Simo Vehmas, "Discriminative Assumptions of Utilitarian Bioethics Regarding Individuals with Intellectual Disabilities" (1999) 14:1 Disability & Society 37.

[113] Consider, e.g., Tibor Machan, *Putting Humans First: Why We Are Nature's Favorite* (Lanham, MD: Rowman & Littlefield, 2004).

[114] Consider, e.g., Taylor, *Beasts of Burden*; Kittay, "Margins of Personhood." For my own thoughts on the matter, see my "Of Apes and Men" in John Huss, ed., *Planet of the Apes and Philosophy: Great Apes Think Alike* (Chicago: Open Court, 2013); "From Autonomy to Habeas Corpus: Animal Rights Activists Take the Parameters of Legal Personhood to Court" (2016) 1 Global J Animal L 3; "Are Animals Persons? Why Ask?" (2019) 9:1 J Animal Ethics 6.

[115] Consider Jeff McMahan, "Cognitive Disability, Misfortune, and Justice" (1996) 25:1 Philosophy & Pub Affairs 3 at 16–17.

count as three-fifths of a person for legislative representation purposes,[116] or that women are not "persons" for the purposes of eligibility for Senate office.[117] In recent years, more attention has been paid to discrimination of oppressed minorities that takes indirect, systemic, or otherwise deceptive forms. The denial of ableism is as pronounced as the denial of concealed racism and sexism. As Judy Rohrer writes, the rise of disability rights awareness in the United States in the 1990s – thanks to the introduction of the *Americans with Disabilities Act* – was then followed by a "period of conservative backlash" and derision:

> One reason these attacks gained ground is that many Americans have difficulty believing ableism exists, which, ironically, allows this form of discrimination to persist. The general disbelief regarding the oppression of those with disabilities is one of several components of ableism.[118]

In other words, the belief that PWD are treated like full persons and full citizens relies on a (ableist) misunderstanding of disability advocacy, which is dedicated not only to helping differently embodied human beings access mainstream society but also to raising awareness of the reality that society has been built by and for nondisabled people. These nondisabled people then assume that nondisabled bodies can legitimately be used as a benchmark for policymakers to quantify and select the goods they distribute and the modes of access to those goods.

While the harvesting of organs of mentally disabled orphans belongs to dystopias, the increasing access to preconception screening and routinization of prenatal screening does not. In spite of the positive effects for prospective parents (in terms of enabling greater freedom of choice), these screening techniques can be understood as part of a state-endorsed eugenic endeavor and can be interpreted as conveying a negative message about the value of PWD's lives. At the other end of a person's lifespan, one may consider euthanasia and assisted suicide, which are legalized in a growing number of states. Some, including scholars and activists within disability communities, are concerned that people who access medical aid in dying may have internalized ableist prejudices and not have proper access to alternative solutions to deal with their isolation, condition, or pain. The medicolegal frameworks put in place to regulate these new technologies and treatments cannot afford to ignore the underlying ableist cultural vectors at work, especially since they are given voice in routine value judgments (e.g., about health, aesthetics,

---

[116] US Const art I, § 2, cl 3 (1788), known as the "three-fifths clause," calculated the number of seats a State would have in Congress by stipulating that slaves would count as three-fifths of a person.

[117] The Supreme Court of Canada held that women were not "persons" under the section of the Canadian Constitution stipulating conditions of eligibility to be appointed to Senate (*Reference re: Meaning of the Word "Persons" in s 24 of the BNA Act*, [1928] SCR 276).

[118] Judy Rohrer, "Ableism" in Susan Burch, ed., *Encyclopedia of American Disability History*, vol. 1 (New York: Facts On File, 2009), at 2.

deservingness, the wrongness of killing) that all citizens – including parents, health practitioners, and patients who have become severely ill or disabled – are liable to make.

Ethical issues that arise at the beginning and end of life (such as prenatal screening, postnatal discontinuation of treatment, and euthanasia) may offer dramatic illustrations of the value of life, the right to life, and the wrongness of killing or suicide. Similarly, the suspension of legal capacity when people are placed in protective care regimes also creates a striking illustration of the denial of rights or standing. However, PWD suffer from more commonplace categories of social neglect and exclusion. PWD and their families must constantly struggle to access healthcare, education, work, and other goods that nondisabled people take for granted, and they must also struggle – often in vain – to access special kinds of support that nondisabled people do not require. PWD often lose these battles of attrition, simply because they do not possess the economic resiliency that is required to win them. They also experience the limitations that legislators and judges place on how far society will go to enable them, in spite of having a body that does not fit the norm, to live a flourishing life. These more habitual forms of discrimination (e.g., denying access to social services and failing to design social institutions and facilities that can accommodate PWD) often go unnoticed, including by many well-meaning "soft" preservationists, who are willing to endorse the lofty statement that all human beings matter equally, but are more ambivalent about working out the normative implications of this position. Do PWD matter enough to transform our society to accommodate them? Do they matter enough for nondisabled policymakers to rethink the organization of social institutions and design of facilities from the ground up, as though PWD had been represented at the table of negotiation from the beginning? Those are the hard questions that soft preservationists often do not ask because they are under the spell of a medicalized conception of disability that makes it a biological and private problem, instead of a social and political one.

Vindicating a preservationist stance is far from frivolous, given that American and European societies endorse a "regime of dis-citizenship," that is, "a system of deep structural economic, social, political, legal, and cultural inequality" for PWD.[119] The assumptions made by the social contract tradition are only a fraction – though a representative fraction – of potentially ableist assumptions at work in our culture, such as "the ideology of productivity and efficiency"[120] and the fetishization of the "normal" body.[121] There is an important difference between the pseudo-humanist hunches that PSID deserve to be welcome in our communities, or that PSID possess certain attributes of personhood and citizenship, and the actual preservationist

---

[119] Pothier and Devlin, *Critical Disability Theory*, at 1.
[120] *Ibid.* at 18.
[121] See, e.g., Lennard J. Davis, *Enforcing Normalcy: Disability, Deafness and the Body* (London: Verso, 1995).

position that PSID deserve full moral and political consideration within our communities, rather than charity, pity, or minimal welfare.

1.7 STRUCTURE AND SUMMARY OF THE BOOK

This book assesses the two kinds of integrative strategies that social contract theory can adopt to include PSID within the scope of contractual justice and, more generally, that contractual theory can use to include PSID within the scope of morality. These strategies are as follows:

(1) Challenging the idea that the PSID do not have contracting capacities (i) empirically (claiming that they do, contrary to what we assumed) or (ii) conceptually (claiming that they do, once we loosen our understanding of required capacities). This would confer the status of direct contractors to PSID.
(2) Finding or assuming that PSID do not have the required "direct" contracting capacities but holding that there are other reasons which justify their representation in contractual procedures, and that these reasons are compatible with the contractual assumptions inherent in these procedures. That (i) PSID may be able to take part indirectly or passively in society, as is required; and/or (ii) they may have capacities or properties that make it necessary or robustly obligatory for contractors to provide the means for their social integration. We may call these two aspects (i) their "passive" or "indirect" contractual capacities and (ii) their "contractual relevance."

This book is divided into two parts, the first of which focuses on contractarianism.

In this first chapter, "Severe Intellectual Disability and the Social Contract," I have introduced the notions of PSID, of robust moral status and explained social contract theory and its two main branches (contractarianism and contractualism). I have presented my hypothesis that contractual moral and political thought cannot provide a compelling justification for the robust moral status of PSID and I have justified the choice of this hypothesis.

In Chapter 2, "Inclusive Contractarianism," I focus on contractarian arguments to bring PSID into our political community. The most obvious argument to do so is by showing that it is advantageous for other members of the community to include them in their "cooperative venture." This inclusion can be done either directly – by showing that PSID can bring more to the table than we usually expect, especially if we think of their input differently – or indirectly – by showing that their integration into our community indirectly benefits us, even though their input seems insignificant and even though they are mostly passive beneficiaries. I argue that this first kind of justification seems empirically dubious and the latter (rule-contractarianism) offers a problematically derivative or contingent status to PSID. I then turn to

Lawrence Becker's recent contractarian argument to grant PSID a robust political status. While he succeeds in making the case that integrating the disabled could be mutually advantageous, his conclusion remains contingent upon a crowd of exclusively self-interested beings agreeing with his empirical wager, which becomes less convincing when applied to PSID. I conclude that taking a collectivist, multipartite stance on reciprocal relations to elaborate a kind of rule-contractarianism remains a promising avenue, if the contingency objection could be met by rendering the inclusion of PSID as less of an opportunistic happenstance and more of a necessity based on their traits and on the nature of the contribution they can provide.

Chapter 3, "The Capacity to Trust as a Contractual Basis for Robust Moral Status," focuses on the essay "Justice through Trust," by Leslie Francis and Anita Silvers, which in my view makes the best contractarian argument to include PSID among the rank of contributing contractors. Silvers and Francis insist on abandoning the misleading metaphor of the social contract as a tit-for-tat exchange. Instead, they argue that society is more accurately conceived of as a multipartite, complex net of transactions which fundamentally requires a climate of trust in which any being able to trust or be trustworthy can participate. Their theory answers the contingency objection by rendering the robustness of PSID's status necessary in an essential way. PSID's contribution to fostering a climate of trust can be said to occur not in spite of their disability and its corollary vulnerability and exploitability but partly because of it.

The chapter is structured as follows. I first present the account of justice through trust and defend it from a few potential objections. I then consider the nature of trust and discuss how we can understand it in a self-regarding or an other-regarding way to reveal a tension that I explore further in the following sections. On one hand, trust as self-regarding seems more compatible with contractarian assumptions. Yet this principle also faces the problems of being too instrumental to contractors and is likely to provide a status for PSID that is too contingent or derivative. Indeed, not all people with profound disabilities will have the capacity to trust. On the other hand, trust as other-regarding – as important as this may be to morality and justice – may not be as essentially connected to social contract theory as Silvers and Francis argue. Although a trust-based conception of contractual justice goes a long way in integrating PWD, these tensions tend to confirm that contractarian theories have difficulty in genuinely accommodating people with particularly severe disabilities.

The second part of the monograph explores contractualist alternatives.

In Chapter 4, "People with Severe Intellectual Disabilities as Active Citizens," I assess five strategies that contractualist thinkers have put forward to conceptualize PSID as active participants to the social contract. These consist of focusing on (1) PSID's talents; (2) their capacity to have a conception of the good; (3) their ability to "engage" with others or play a "part" in society; (4) their potential to develop (further) contractual capacities; and (5) their need for assistance by "collaborators" or "cognitive prostheses" in the nurturing and exercising of these capacities.

1.7 Structure and Summary of the Book 51

Instead of conceptualizing PSID as different from the able-bodied population and elaborating a theory which nonetheless justifies granting them a robust moral status – as theorists of passive citizenship do – I explore how we could "normalize" PSID, that is, conceptualize them as contractors, just as we do with other members of society. I explain and criticize the two ways in which this could be done: (1) by modifying the benchmark requirements for counting as a contractor or (2) by arguing that PSID do meet these requirements, despite appearances to the contrary. According to a contractualist account, this integrative strategy takes the form of arguing that PSID can elaborate a conception of the good life as well as partake in society's cooperative endeavor, provided they have proper support. I explore how prejudices contribute to concealing the socially constructed dimension of disability, as well as the harm caused to PSID by being conceptualized as burden-like passive beneficiaries instead of talented contributors in need of appropriate support. However, while this approach is promising in terms of its application to less seriously disabled individuals, I find that social support, including "mental prostheses," is not a plausible solution for many profoundly disabled individuals, unless this support is conceptualized in a way that alters it beyond recognition, or that takes it beyond the autonomy-based contractualist paradigm to which it purports to be attached. I consider the other strategies mentioned above but I conclude that they cannot escape one of two pitfalls: either they modify contractualist requirements to the point of overstepping its boundaries and gesturing at alternative theories, or they are not empirically warranted.

Chapter 5, "People with Severe Intellectual Disabilities as Passive Citizens," gives a critical exploration of the various ways that PSID might be included within the reach of contractual justice as passive citizens – that is, as citizens who nevertheless lack the requisite abilities to enter into contractualist processes. First, I consider contractualist attempts, such as that of Christine Korsgaard, that try to reconcile this "passive citizenship" with robust moral status. This is done by moral agents conferring moral status on nonrational beings that are worthy of moral consideration. I show that this reconciliation either relies on (or imports) noncontractualist values and grounds to justify robust moral status, or otherwise leave us hopelessly indeterminate when it comes to prioritizing the moral status of PSID over other nonrational beings like plants and nonhuman animals. I then consider Rawlsian attempts at defending passive citizenship, such as Adam Cureton's proposal. I argue that such attempts are problematic for two reasons: They either clash with other notions within the Rawlsian framework or render PSID's moral status too contingent, thus making PSID vulnerable to the whims of contractors in the original position. I also consider Cynthia Stark's view that the shared basic needs of PSID supply us with strong reasons to include PSID within the Rawlsian framework of justice. I argue that this strategy falls short of its aim – it relies, like Korsgaard, on values that are not internal to the Rawlsian or, more generally, contractualist framework.

Chapter 6, "Other-Regarding Concern and Exploitation," explores feminist contractarianism, which suggests that the morality of private relationships should be assessed from a self-interested point of view, in part because other-regarding concern may play a role in exploiting parties in intimate relationships. Variants of feminist contractarianism draw from both Kantian and Hobbesian strands of contractarianism (which I respectively call contractualism and contractarianism).

I suggest that the feminist contractarian criticism of other-regarding concern overreaches. While other-regarding concern can indeed be connected with exploitation, systematically replacing it with a self-regarding stance goes too far. Other-regarding concern is an important moral attitude, not only in private relationships but also within social ethics and theories of justice, which cannot, in my view, satisfactorily account for the robust moral status of PSID without incorporating it.

Showing how contractual theory underestimates other-regarding concern even in a context where it is most plausibly relevant informs us of why it could similarly fail in the wider context of justice between strangers. Debunking contractual assumptions against other-regarding concern confirms that there is no reason not to develop noncontractual ethical frameworks that better account for human dependency and vulnerability.

In the concluding chapter, "Beyond Contractual Relations," I explore the implications of contractual theories' failures to satisfactorily justify the robust moral status of PSID. Social contract theory can justify a robust moral status and meaningful social integration for many people with cognitive impairments. However, (1) not all PSID can fit within a contractual framework; and (2) in many cases, there are salient facts about PSID that ought to guide their treatment and (the mode of their) social integration.

I gesture toward a pluralist, relational approach to morality, in which agents must balance moral attitudes that connect to different relations, such as respect toward a fellow contractor and looking after a vulnerable being entrusted to our care. I suggest that such a relational account of morality offers a promising way to reconcile our seemingly conflicting intuitions about the grounds for the robust moral status of all human beings. I argue that we should not discard social contract theories, but rather give them their due place, which involves limiting them to the relations or circumstances to which they apply. I am not yet making the case for integrating theories of care ethics, concern, empathy, or fiduciary relations in a theory of justice, or in a parallel theory complementing it, but I deal with a few objections that social contract theorists may raise against such an endeavor.

2

Inclusive Contractarianism

Persons with Severe Intellectual Disabilities within a Society of Self-Interested Contractors

2.1 GENERIC INCLUSIVIST CONTRACTARIANISM

In this chapter, I will first consider the traditional contractarian arguments to include PSID within the social contract before considering more progressive ones. While seeking to expand our understanding of (1) contractarian goals and (2) how to best attain these goals, I will adhere as faithfully as possible to traditional contractarian commitments and approach the subject of disabilities from that standpoint. If this approach fails to justify integrating PSID, I will then revisit the contractarian theoretical notions that justify the attribution of moral status. However, the more we expand or reconstruct these notions, the more likely we are to inadvertently move beyond contractarianism's boundaries altogether.

Let me begin with a question: Within a contractarian framework that assumes the self-interest of parties to social conventions, could Abby, a contractor, make self-interested choices to protect herself against the eventuality of becoming a profoundly disabled person? This would seem logical within a contractarian logic, because it would be rational for Abby to make provisions for periods of her life during which she will be vulnerable and dependent on others to survive, as in her old age, or after an incapacitating injury or illness. In order to assess the plausibility of this suggestion, I must first say more about what I mean by "depending on others," and I must consider the standpoint from which Abby would make this self-interested choice.

2.1.1 *Depending on Oneself*

If Abby accumulated enough money to pay for a wheelchair (in the event that she loses the ability to walk) or for someone to cook her meals and/or feed her (if she became unable to do these tasks), she would then be depending on others, but only in a weak sense. From another perspective, we can see that Abby still ultimately depends on herself for survival, in that her ability to look after herself depends upon her financial resources.

Pushed to its limits, the dichotomy between depending on oneself or on others is reducible to the paradigms of self-regarding and other-regarding interpersonal social frameworks or interactions. An intuition that underpins my criticism of social contract theory in this book is that the theory has difficulty cohering with ordinary intuitions if it tries to operate without other-regarding concerns. Especially when it responds to vulnerability, it seems that contractual thinking must import a source of moral obligation toward others that precedes the contractual act of will. This intuition conflicts with contractual thinkers' willingness to establish a system that is motivated by self-interest. In this system, Abby does not have to fear that she will be left to die when her bank account is depleted, but only because others realize that they are similar to Abby, inasmuch as they also face the prospect of suddenly becoming so disabled that their lives would impose greater costs than benefits on the contractually collectivized pool of talents and resources.

The picture of the world set out here (or, more precisely, the conception of human nature, justice, and the legitimacy of caring for oneself first) is one in which everyone is expected to carry their own weight. Through reason and self-interest, individuals in this world realize that they may be better able to amass more wealth in a certain type of social structure than in another, and so they opt for the more profitable structure. They also realize that they may not be able to carry their own weight due to the possibility of a debilitating event that would render them dependent on others, and this situation could occur in a context in which they have not made sufficient provisions for their future disabled self. In this scenario, a disabled person may be dependent on not only their past selves but also on other people. These other people, fearing that the same outcome might happen to them, may agree to a collective insurance scheme. However, people in this world would ultimately be relying on their past selves (individually and collectively), who were clever enough to make arrangements for the possibility that they may become disabled and thus unable to care for themselves. Should the needs of this group become too extraordinary or somehow rendered ineligible under the terms of the agreed "insurance scheme," then this group would have no recourse to the assistance of others as a matter of justice.

Such a description would *permanently* exclude PSID who at no point in their lives have been in a position to negotiate with others. That is, they have never been in a position either to promise to contribute to the common pool of resources or to threaten to disrupt the peace (in a Hobbes-like scenario of the state of nature) should their demands not be met. In this traditional contractarian view, permanently disabled people like the PSID are understood to be unprofitable contractors (hereinafter "UC") because their needs throughout their lifespan exceed what they can ever potentially contribute.

There can be no "veil of ignorance"[1] at work within this simple version of contractarianism because the veil of ignorance expresses a substantive idea about justice: it imposes impartiality upon the process. Briefly, the veil of ignorance is a theoretical assumption maintaining that parties to imagined negotiations of the principles of justice upon which social arrangements are premised are unaware of their own social conditions or personal traits and preferences. Such a veil is designed to ensure that, since parties are unable to make decisions in their own self-interest, they will opt for social arrangements that would be reasonably acceptable to the various social groups to which they may turn out to belong. Contractors like Abby would only endorse an impartiality-maximizing negotiating posture if it best fulfilled their interests. However, Abby already knows that she is not profoundly and permanently disabled, even though she may still become a UC if she becomes disabled at some point in her life. Fairness, from this unsophisticated contractarian perspective, reflects, rather than corrects, the existing power dynamics. This brings us to a discussion of the standpoint that individuals are meant to take in order to calculate with whom it is in their best interest to negotiate, and to what social structure it would be most beneficial to adhere.

2.1.2 *From Which Temporal or Epistemological Standpoint?*

I have considered above the most relatable (in the sense of being closest to everyday contractual acts) case of individuals who negotiate with one another, taking into account their present state, which includes an assessment of the power accumulated by their past selves and their likely prospect of future power. This is an ordinary standpoint from which to calculate whether someone may become severely disabled to the point of becoming a UC – that is, their potential needs exceeding their profitability. Indeed, we never know whether we could become a UC. Therefore, this ordinary standpoint allows prospective UCs to get a free ride at the expense of other contractors. Considered from this contractarian point of view, this "free rider" outcome is less than ideal. (I note that this standpoint would, nonetheless, at least justify excluding PSID, assuming that science can reliably inform us that a permanently and profoundly mentally disabled individual who is a UC will remain so.)

Another standpoint from which to test contractarian ideals involves employing a "crystal ball" conceit to test the cost–benefit balance of people's lives. This crystal ball analogy has almost the reverse effect of a veil of ignorance that facilitates impartiality. By having access to this cost–benefit crystal ball, a future UC could strategically opt in to a social structure that enables them to maximize their actual productivity in order to compensate for their future inability to cover the costs of their extraordinary needs. For example, they could opt to work two jobs instead of

---

[1] John Rawls, A *Theory of Justice*, rev. ed. (Cambridge: Harvard University Press, 1999), at 118. See Chapter 5 for a discussion of Rawls's device of the "veil of ignorance."

one or to buy into an insurance scheme for classes of UCs rather than distributing the cost of their needs on others by increasing everybody's insurance premium. Of course, for many UCs, no productivity adjustments would be possible and they would be altogether excluded from the scope of justice. Other UCs would not be able to get the agreement of profitable contractees to set up a social structure that enables them to contribute to the common good, as setting up this accommodating social structure will not be profitable overall. The cost of setting up the accommodation may be greater than the benefits obtained by the accommodated individuals' productive output, particularly if the required accommodation is too specific, varied, or extensive, or if the target group of disabled individuals is too small for the adapted production structure to be made profitable or feasible, thanks, for instance, to an economy of scale.

While this standpoint fits more comfortably within the contractarian ideals of putting oneself first and the principle of justice expressed as "to each their own," it does not make for a very appealing social justice structure. One may respond that this contractarian ideal is not realizable in any event, as there exists no cost–benefit crystal ball. Yet this practical objection does not address the issue that, even as an ideal state of being, this structure is unsatisfactory. Furthermore, it is far from a fictionalized worldview. We already invest in research that enables increasingly sophisticated assessments of the chances that our children will suffer from a variety of genetic conditions such as Down's syndrome. In this context, it is not far-fetched to imagine that we could develop health policies that differentially benefit certain "castes" of people with disabilities, naturally moving to the outcome that some castes will simply stop receiving help from the state, depending upon the severity of their disability and other factors, such as their age. While many such developments are matters of speculative ethics, genetic discrimination is not. Intuitively, we resist such a bleak model of justice. Therefore, in order to understand the appeal of this contractarian model, one must imagine something contrary to what the veil of ignorance suggests. That is, instead of thinking that one could be a UC, one must already know that one is not. One may then be inclined to think that we have imperfect obligations of charity toward the UC, rather than more robust obligations of justice. In this model, the outlier– the UC – must recognize that her misfortune, no matter how debilitating, is not remedied as a matter of justice, but is properly dealt with individually as a subject of charity.

I do not have faith in this contractarian perspective. The wrongness of these positions can be most clearly stated by examples that test their effects across different groups. However, testing the practical effects of this perspective goes beyond the scope of this book, as I assume that a theory of justice that does not account for profoundly disabled people is problematic. In such a theory, not only would PSID be excluded, but so would many other UCs. The resulting picture idealizes a world where people each carry their own weight instead of leaning on one another (in terms of relying on other-regarding virtues or ideals that imply more than a charitable obligation). Many scholars suspect that these self-interested positions fail to capture what is of value in human life and to reflect the noncontractual and normative content of human relations. For example, Jean Hampton rejects this view as too instrumental in nature and because it makes too little of human intrinsic worth;[2] Silvers and Francis argue that it makes for a society without genuine trust within which we would not want to live.[3]

Regardless of whether these ordinary or idealized contractarian standpoints are ethically appealing or plausible, they exclude PSID. In the next section, I consider other contractarian alternatives based on the idea that PSID could be profitable contractors, contrary to what has been assumed so far.

2.1.3 Must PSID Be UC?

If the basic contractarian test to determine status as a subject of justice (and corollary entitlements) is whether an individual is a profitable contractor – that is, someone with whom it is worth contracting because doing so will improve our common lot – must PSID be deprived of this status? Could PSID contribute, directly or indirectly, to a contractarian society in a way that would validate their claim to social membership? Here, I assume that such validation warrants as robust a moral status as contractarian theory can justify.

The standpoint from which one answers this question is not neutral, moral, or otherwise. I am not referring to the temporal standpoint (as I do in the section above) but rather to the social, institutional, or structural state of affairs that frames this question. Indeed, whether or not we have a crystal ball (or similarly effective genetic tools) that tells us whether an individual would, on the whole, be a profitable contractor to bargain with, we cannot assume that profound intellectual disability would necessarily correspond to unprofitability unless we also make empirical assumptions about this disability or social assumptions about the ways in which mutually beneficial endeavors should be set up and benefit us.

Philosophers in the social contract tradition are well-known for invoking a pre-social state – a "state of nature" – which implies some substantial assumptions about human nature and the things that humans value. The (in)correctness of these assumptions then confers (or not, if implausible) normative and descriptive appeal upon the contractual theory that, in turn, builds on them. It also presents a pragmatic prospect of durability or enforceability for the social arrangements that flow from this theory.

---

[2] Jean Hampton, *The Intrinsic Worth of Persons: Contractarianism in Moral and Political Philosophy*, ed. Daniel Farnham (New York: Cambridge University Press, 2007), at 11–12.

[3] Leslie Francis and Anita Silvers, "Justice through Trust: Disability and the 'Outlier Problem' in Social Contract Theory" (2005) 116:1 Ethics 40. We will come back to their arguments and the issue of whether they are truly contractarian in the next chapter.

In contrast, disability theorists have long problematized the claim that disabilities are natural, or that they should be categorized as strictly biological issues to be treated medically, like other illnesses. Mainstream disability theory favors another model – the social model of disability – that is meant to assist us in seeing how disabilities are socially constructed. Although I do not think that this model of disability should entirely supplant other models (for reasons that I discuss briefly in Chapter 1), I reference this debate to note one of its widely accepted conclusions: that there is a social dimension to the construction of disabilities. This is evidenced by the way in which the failure to meet the species-norm standards or to possess statistically standard physiological or psychological functions, can constitute a disabling handicap in one social context, but not in another.

For example, a departure from the species-norm standards such as stuttering would not prevent a person from being a lawyer or a politician, barring the prejudice and discrimination which can occur when people hear a stuttering lawyer plead a case. Likewise, anti-Semitic people might prevent a Jewish person from performing a job for which they are qualified, and sexist people might be antagonistic toward women who run for political office. Giving weight to these prejudices may seem unwise or imprudent since these individuals are just as able as others to competently perform their work.[4] The inclusivist contractarian idea would be to extend this position to PSID who, with some accommodation, could perform work from which they are currently excluded based on their disability. The question thus becomes, are we making prejudiced and unprofitable choices?

Committing, for the moment, to this generic, nonrule-based version of contractarianism, I will illustrate how these intuitions about external preferences hold up when we try to apply them to PSID who seemingly have too few capabilities or talents to be "profitable" human beings. Speaking of others as instrumental to our ends has turned many people away from the Hobbesian brand of contractarianism. I believe that the case of PSID is one of the numerous instances where the exception properly leads us to question the norm, rather than bringing the exception in line with the norm (what we may call the "normalizing problem"). However, if we allow our token contractarian to hold the position that instrumentalizing one another is a sound way to develop a moral theory or a theory of justice, then here are three ways in which people with severe disabilities can avoid being a UC and be useful to a society set up to capitalize on the abilities of most in order to achieve its goals, such as prosperity, security, and justice.

---

[4] I note that the contractarian who would share this intuition would not reject stutterers, Jewish people, and so on, from a social joint venture as long as they can carry their own weight and contribute to their own welfare. She may be prejudiced, but not to the point of expecting social arrangements to grant her more importance than anyone able to contribute meaningfully to society. Therefore, she would accept that her preference not to integrate certain stigmatized groups in her community would not be given weight, even if their sheer presence would be displeasing to her and thus indirectly affect her well-being. I will come back to the issue of "external preferences" in the next section since contractarian theory can make room for them.

First, we could say that PSID help to create jobs. Caring professions, though poorly paid and underdeveloped, constitute a context in which they can realize their talents and their ideal selves in a way that is consistent with their conception of the good, in addition to enabling them to make a remunerable social contribution. Second, we could say that weak and vulnerable people help us develop more comprehensive healthcare institutions and new technologies that will benefit all of us, as we all fall prey to dependency upon such institutions at some point in our lives. Third, we could say that the vulnerability of PSID and other people with profound disabilities teaches us about our own vulnerability. This is an important benefit for our own peace of mind, as the vulnerable and dependent beings that we are – all suffering from shame and anxiety to some degree – may learn to acknowledge, rather than deny, our limitations. Being put in caring relations with particularly dependent and vulnerable people trains us to accept and endorse a caring role toward ourselves and others as a socially acceptable way of living. Further, the adoption of a caring role can lead us to expect others to do the same, which weakens the view of society as a busy, ruthless "dog-eat-dog" world, and invalidates the idea that the dominant social role of a contractor is the only legally and socially sanctioned role.

It is not worth making a stronger case for each of these hypotheses right now. I will return to the worthwhile aspects of each of these three arguments in the chapters that follow, as they are understood within more complex frameworks than the generic contractarianism I present here. For now, I only want to point out that, apart from being problematic on their own terms, these three suggestions all invite a challenge to contractarianism.

To problematize these suggestions in broad terms, my main contention is that they only recognize that PSID have a contingent and relative value. One might say that I cannot hold this against them, since this generic contractarianism does not treat more able people with any greater deference. Other flaws include recognizing that the caring industry has historically played a large part in the social isolation of people with profound disabilities, as I explore in a later chapter the position that PSID should in fact be given is an active, rather than passive, contributory role in society. Further, the second and third solutions are not only instrumental in the sense that they are applicable to all persons in a contractarian framework but they also state explicitly that PSID are not themselves the primary beneficiaries of this policy. In other words, it is as though the disabled person's identity as a contractor has already been diminished; her interests have become an object of negotiation, but she has a lesser claim to a seat at the negotiating table as a full contractor herself. Contractarians thus integrate the disabled person's interests and the caring relations toward them into their agenda, just as they might vote in favor of the large-scale production of chessboards, given that chess has been found to have a calming effect on general social relations. (We see the PSID playing the part of the chessboard in this analogy.) These arguments are also empirically controversial, the second particularly so.

However, in terms of determining the prominent conceptual flaws of these suggestions, we see that they all assume, in some way or another, what needs to be proven. The first argument assumes that we ought to subsidize care work for people with severe disabilities rather than considering the bleak alternative of not doing so, or of letting the costs of such caring employment be assumed by those who are personally attached to PSID. It may also subtly assume that there is some value in developing a caring self that is more objective, higher or less optional than any general taste or preference.[5] At worst, it treats PSID just like any other source of work, implying that PSID could be replaced in social accounting, for example, by the production of chessboards. Their status is too contingent to count as having even a kind of "contingent importance" like that of more able contractors if, by "importance," one merely means a Hobbesian understanding of dignity as the "public worth of a [human being]... set on him by the commonwealth" and marked out by titles and offices.[6] The same goes for the second argument. If contractarian society found a way to develop scientific knowledge and caring institutions without PSID, then this society could do without these disabled people. Thus, their inclusion relies on a (dubious) empirical gamble. At best, the view that would make people with disabilities (and not chessboards) the necessary[7] object of job-creating policies is that there is something meaningful about engaging in caring roles, and that policies supporting these jobs thus reflect some meaningful value (in contrast to the chessboard policies). This view assumes the existence of a moral pull prior to, or coexistent with, the self-interests of contracting parties.

The same objection can be made in relation to the third hypothesis, which does not assume a concern for PSID, but only for ourselves (nonseverely intellectually disabled). However, the way in which it voices this concern – acknowledging our vulnerable and dependent nature and the importance of this fact on our happiness – seems to imply a social theory of justice or a moral theory that goes beyond the core assumptions of contractarianism. More precisely, the realization that vulnerability and dependence matter so much in our lives would, because of the implications of these rich concepts, imply a normative relational stance. According to such a stance, the goods needed to deal with our vulnerability- and dependency-related needs cannot be properly socially pursued within a contractarian framework that is founded on self-interest. I unpack these ideas further in the chapters on other-regarding concern, and I revisit them in the conclusion.

---

[5] For an exploration of the idea that care occupies a central place in human existence and moral life, consider Nel Noddings, *Caring: A Feminine Approach to Ethics & Moral Education* (Berkeley: University of California Press, 1984).

[6] William Molesworth, ed., *The English Works of Thomas Hobbes of Malmesbury*, vol. III: *Leviathan* (London: John Bohn, 1839–45), at 76.

[7] Or *more* necessary than chessboards, since we are trying to give PSID a status that is robust but still conditional in contrast to other accounts of robust status that would be conceptually incompatible with conditionality or derivativeness altogether.

I raise these points here, only to show that a traditional or generic form of contractarianism needs considerable conceptual tinkering before it allows PSID to be integrated as actively or passively profitable members of society. In some cases, people with profound disabilities may not be empirically profitable after all, or they may be less profitable than alternative options. Normatively, contractarianism risks assimilating PSID to the status of objects contracted for, as opposed to considering them to be competent contractors in themselves.

2.2 MORALIZED CONTRACTARIANISM

I will now address a problem that runs through the background of my analysis: the prompt assumption that the question of integrating PSID is worth exploring, and the empirical optimism about the results of doing so. These features may have the effect of importing noncontractual and moral constraints into contractarianism. In the previous section, I took the examples of refusing to hire stutterers, women, or Jewish people as examples of prejudiced and unprofitable decisions. However, the inclusivist contractarian question (are we making prejudiced and unprofitable choices?) may not always be justified from a contractarian point of view more interested in finding a profitable outcome than an unprejudiced one. Not only are profitability and prejudice distinct notions, but it can be profitable to be prejudiced.

First, in some cases, PSID may not be capable of doing the work of a given position. The examples of stutterers, women, or Jewish people stand at the other end of the justified–unjustified spectrum of professional exclusion – that is, where inclusion is justified because the person is able to perform the work regardless of the impact of prejudiced external preferences. However, let us imagine that we have a case of someone who is paralyzed and who therefore needs a machine or an assistant to type for her. Exclusion in these circumstances seems justified if the job is that of a typist. Alternatively, we might have a case where there is prejudice against hiring someone as a typist who is able to type, but who has bipolar personality disorder. In this case, the refusal to hire her is not rationally justified when compared to the decision not to hire someone on the grounds that they cannot carry out the job's central activity or inherent requirements. In between these two extremes, we have a wide range of prejudices that are presented as natural obstacles that are either to be lamented or fixed, rather than being seen as the result of opportunistic social choices.

The second problem is that, unlike what I have described above, according to a contractarian account, external preferences[8] may serve as rational justifications. As

---

[8] See Ronald Dworkin's distinction between a "personal preference for [one's] own enjoyment of some goods or opportunities" and "external preferences for the assignment of goods and opportunities to others, or both" (*Taking Rights Seriously* [London: Bloomsbury Academic, 2013], at 234).

we have seen, contractarianism (or a bold and traditional version of it) is willingness to make opportunistic choices. However, it will only aim at purity from prejudice if this is the most profitable outcome, which renders antiprejudiced attitudes and policies contingent on their profitability, measured in terms of self-interested preferences between bargainers. For people with contractarian dispositions, what to do about the prejudices of others is always an open question. In some cases, it would be too expensive to change those preferences and we have to simply tolerate them. For example, an employer might decide that it is too costly to hire PSID because customers will not like them and will not buy products that are prepared by them. Similarly, a self-interested bargainer may admit people of color into her establishment, not out of respect or because of principles of equality, but because she realizes that her business ultimately yields greater profit when she accepts a larger clientele. Whether prejudices are desirable or not depends upon the contingent benefits or loss of profit they bring.

Inclusivist contractarian accounts (those that include PSID) are somewhat optimistic (or naïve) when they assume that contractarians will come around to the idea that they are "missing out" when they exclude certain marginalized people. As we saw, this is simply not always the case. Second, even when an inclusivist contractarian proposes a plausible picture of social arrangements that integrates specific outliers in a way that would yield an overall beneficial outcome, one may ask why she is going out of her way to integrate these outliers. Generally, inclusivist contractarian arguments only aim to show that able-bodied contractors will be better off if they integrate PSID into society. Among the multitude of possible social arrangements that would be beneficial for most people, there is often a nagging arbitrariness in preferring one that happens to integrate PSID. Inclusivist contractarianism seems constrained by moral notions of prequalification requirements for being a member of society. It builds on these constraints to create a specific theory of contractarian roles that befit PSID who are to play a contractarian part in this philosophical framework. It also does not look elsewhere to try justifying PSID's robust moral status.

This moralized contractarianism would, for instance, problematize or strictly scrutinize any "prejudiced" starting point from which we begin to assess someone's potential input. Though a requirement of profitability would still be the decisive factor, it would tend to be applied more liberally toward those who have traditionally been discriminated against (thus, assuming such discrimination is wrong) and more stringently toward policies that would heighten exclusion instead of mitigating it. For example, if one begins thinking about the productivity of PSID with a barter economy in mind – populated by individuals who must each produce a good to be traded with others – this structural view of production from which we contemplate acquiring and relinquishing some rights under a social contract would exclude PSID out of hand. The fast-paced, normalized, industrial means of production in the modern economy would be even more exclusive.

2.2 Moralized Contractarianism

Problematizing these starting points, while still aiming to reach the optimal outcome, would involve imagining beneficial social arrangements that allow PSID to actualize their talents in order to properly assess the contribution they could potentially make, and to weigh this against the cost of accommodation or revamping of current social structures. Some philosophers – notably Anita Silvers – have made arguments in support of the idea that this inclusivist standpoint would successfully justify the inclusion of PSID. I will explore two versions of this argument in this book: one in terms of disabled people who can be active contributors (in Chapter 4) and one in terms of disabled people who occupy a more passive role, but who still participate in relations that are profitable (trust-enhancing) to society (in Chapter 3). Briefly, my conclusion is that these arguments do not succeed in supporting the integration of the most severe cases of intellectual disability. Further, they even fail to satisfactorily explain the integration of a larger group of less severe cases of disability. In other words, even when we have moralized the standpoint from which we assess the potential input of contractors – that is, even when we do not exclude PSID's input because of prejudice, external preferences, or a failure to be open to imagine new forms of social production and mutually benefitting structures – we find that some PWD are just unable to be integrated on the basis of this inclusivist account.

The unsophisticated, generic form of contractarianism that I analyze here – which I use to explain why contractarianism is prima facie ill-suited to justify a robust moral status for PSID – is similarly unable to incorporate PSID. This position is shared by many prominent scholars, including John Rawls, Martha Nussbaum, Eva Kittay, and David Gauthier.[9] Gauthier, for instance, wrote that "[t]he primary problem is care for the handicapped. Speaking euphemistically of enabling them to live productive lives, when the services required exceed any possible products, conceals an issue which, understandably, no one wants to face."[10] Similarly, John Rawls, whose theory contains mixed contractarian and contractualist elements,[11] considered this a potential and indelible taint to his theory. Lastly, Martha

---

[9] See, e.g., Eva Feder Kittay, "When Caring Is Just and Justice Is Caring: Justice and Mental Retardation" in Eva Feder Kittay and Ellen K. Feder, eds., *The Subject of Care: Feminist Perspectives on Dependency* (Lanham, MD: Rowman & Littlefield, 2012), at 257, 267.

[10] David Gauthier, *Morals by Agreement* (Oxford: Oxford University Press, 1987), at 18.

[11] I focus on a contractualist reading of Rawls. Whether the idea that his theory contains contractarian elements is plausible is an exegetic matter that I will not explore in this book. Nonetheless, I note that the idea that his theory is a hybrid makes sense a priori. Rawls's emphasis on a community of people mutually respecting one another is closer to contractualism, whereas Rawls's emphasis on finding a political solution for relatively self-interested persons to overcome their irreducible disagreements in the most beneficial way has a contractarian flavor. For an argument to the effect that Rawls's theory is a hybrid blend of contractualism and contractarianism because it contains both the prudential aim of mutual advantage and the Kantian ideal of mutual acceptability, see Martha Nussbaum, *Frontiers of Justice: Disability, Nationality, Species Membership* (Cambridge: Harvard University Press, 2006), at 54–67.

Nussbaum has used the exclusion of persons with severe disabilities as an argument in favor of (at least partially) rejecting social contract theory.[12]

These renowned philosophers, though working within a contractualist framework, do not rely on anything more foundational than the simple set of ordinary contractarian intuitions that I have presented here. This is why I explore more nuanced arguments made by those who think that PSID can (almost always) make a contribution in order to verify whether these verdicts hold up under scrutiny or whether, as I suspect, the optimistic assumptions of these inclusivist contractarian arguments conceal prior noncontractual commitments. In the next chapter on social contract as trust-enhancing, I challenge this summary rejection of contractarianism's capacity to meaningfully integrate PSID. I consider whether PSID can be granted the robust status of contractors under a more progressive description of the capacities that enable (virtually all) PWD to be profitable contractors, namely, the capacity to take part in relations of trust and therefore to participate in the formation of a climate of trust. However, in the present chapter, I want to examine another important essay in the field, which presents the contractarian arguments that I have been considering in their most sophisticated form. I now turn to this argument to show that I have not simply been attacking a contractarian straw man. Rather, I will demonstrate that the fundamental criticisms of generic contractarianism are hard to evade without one first making substantial modifications or expansions of contractarian goals and strategies.

2.3 WHEN THE "TOUGH CROWD" RETHINKS RECIPROCITY

Political philosopher Lawrence Becker has produced scholarship of considerable importance for philosophers of disability, notably on the notions of habilitation and reciprocity. His work on the latter notion is what interests me here. He has shown how reciprocity is generally oversimplified and how, when properly understood, it could allow impartialist and mutual advantage theories of the social contract (categories that correspond roughly to contractualism and contractarianism) to "[go] a long way toward answering the challenge that disability poses to theories of justice."[13] While Becker does go a "long way," he still does not offer a way out of the contingency and derivativeness objections presented above which affect generic contractarianism. However, he offers us an opportunity to distinguish between two kinds of challenges that disabled people must face in order to not be outliers within a contractarian theory of justice: (1) not having a recognized robust moral status (i.e., not being represented as equally important and entitled parties in contract-like proceedings); and (2) being excluded from the scope of justice altogether (i.e., not

---

[12] *Ibid.* at 98–99.
[13] Lawrence Becker, "Reciprocity, Justice, and Disability" (2005) 116:1 Ethics 9, at 12.

being owed anything as a matter of justice).[14] Unsurprisingly, Becker successfully addresses the second challenge. Yet the status of PSID remains too derivative in Becker's account. It does not constitute a robust moral status (in the contractarian sense of robustness), though Becker resists this conclusion.[15]

Becker focuses on "mutual advantage theories," which I take to be contractarian in nature. (Despite the possibility that "mutual advantage theory" and contractarianism overlap imperfectly, this would not be significant for our analysis.) His justification for integrating disabled people within our political community parallels my analysis of the generic contractarian account above. That is, in order to be given serious prudential consideration by the idealized self-interested rational agent – who hesitates to choose between a state of unregulated exercise of power and warfare or abiding by principles of justice; one needs to either pose a threat to the contractarian agent or have something to give her that would make it rational for the agent to negotiate peacefully. According to such a view, PWD able to perform attacks or valuable reciprocal exchanges would be integrated into the political community. Other people with disabilities would be indirectly (and not directly) integrated – in the sense that society would take their interests into consideration – for two reasons: (1) able people could become disabled themselves and (2) caregivers and careworkers are strong enough to act as allies and will issue threats to others and demand benefits for the disabled people that they love.[16] We have seen that (1) does not apply in the case of permanently and severely intellectually disabled people

---

[14] There is a third kind of challenge. Contractualism and contractarianism can provide principles to structure a moral theory as well as a theory of justice. Although Becker does not deal with moral theories more generally, later on, I consider a more radical challenge to the moral status of PSID, which is to exclude them not only from the reach of justice but from morality as well.

[15] Becker, "Reciprocity, Justice, and Disability," at 17, 37.

[16] A variant of (2) is that able contractors, "while fortunate in their own abilities, might have long-lived but seriously disabled children, friends, and neighbors – people whom they love deeply and whose welfare is inextricably connected, psychologically, to their own" (*ibid.* at 17). Let me now answer two potential questions that could be raised in relation to this variant as I develop the argument in this chapter. First, I will try to distinguish the "tough crowd" from the "caring crowd" on a different basis than Becker, namely, that the caring crowd's commitment extends to more than strict self-interest. One could flag, like in the previous quote reproducing a Hobbesian idea, that caring for our close ones is another form of self-interest. The first answer is a disagreement on the basis of assumptions about human psychology. The second answer is that, even though this would sometimes be the case, it could still be said that the caring crowd values more than strict self-interest. The third answer is that the caring crowd would not accept these political terms; they could not accept that the ethical and political weight to be given to their disabled loved one would be a mere appendix to their own status, or a factor determining their own happiness, like a taste or a preference (see, e.g., Peter Byrne, *Philosophical and Ethical Problems in Mental Handicap* [New York: St Martin's Press, 2000]). Fourth, the caring crowd would not, therefore, accept terms of negotiation that would ab initio prevent PSID from having as robust a political status as anyone else.

Second, as we deal with the contentious notion of a "tough crowd" and a "caring crowd," one may wonder if we could belong to both crowds. I do not exclude this possibility – in fact, it would reflect my position that we take part in different relations over our lives. However, even if this were the case, I will artificially separate both crowds for the sake of this discussion.

since they are not a category to which people belong by disease or accident. However, Becker shows why, with a modified conception of reciprocity, strictly self-interested agents would try to "restore mutually advantageous reciprocal relationships between the wrongdoer [i.e., the burdensome disabled] and the wronged [i.e., the nondisabled],"[17] namely, by "rehabilitating" the disabled. He also applies argument (2) to this end – hinging on the advocacy of the people who love and care for PSID – which I will now address.

2.3.1 Addressing the "Tough Crowd" First

Becker begins with the idea that we cannot let go of mutual advantage theories (contractarianism) for Hobbesian-like reasons. Mutual advantage theorists, however, must address what he describes as the "tough crowd problem;" otherwise, social stability cannot be achieved. Becker defines the tough crowd problem as "the problem of persistent, life-and-death conflicts between people who are politically engaged and willing to deal with each other – rather than fight as a first resort – but who have irreconcilable views about human good and the good life."[18] While this sounds very much like Rawls's description of the ineliminable reality of disagreement about comprehensive conceptions of the good life, in my reading of Becker's essay, Rawls's account is not what he takes the tough crowd to be, and, therefore, not what the tough crowd problem really is.

Becker associates the tough crowd with Thrasymachus's crowd, who asked Socrates why we should choose justice over "a way of life … based on the unfettered exercise of power."[19] The tough crowd, Becker claims, includes a diverse range of political actors such as "hard-boiled political realists, opportunistic free-riders, enthusiastic anarchists, resourceful skeptics, cultural relativists, ideologues of all stripes, members of militant religions, [and] relentless advocates for special interests."[20] This group is composed of "those whom we regard as powerful but evil, powerful but amoral, powerful but unreasonable, or powerful but badly wrong in their conception of the good life."[21] Put otherwise, they are people united in their belief that rational self-interest is the only shared trait that helps overcome disagreement in a mutually profitable way. Likewise, the tough crowd believes that nothing other than an understanding of power and self-interest can lead to social stability. Thus, as they deploy their instrumental reason and become engaged in a contractual procedure, the tough crowd becomes made up of (generic) contractarians.

Becker only describes crowds that favor self-interest to the point of giving it lexical priority over all else in society-building and constitutional arrangements. We are left

---

[17] Becker, "Reciprocity, Justice, and Disability," at 31.
[18] Ibid. at 13.
[19] Ibid.
[20] Ibid. at 14.
[21] Ibid.

to conclude that those who believe that vulnerability and dependency have important moral dimensions (and thus that we ought to care for PSID and PWD) are the "relentless advocates" or "caregivers" to whom Becker refers.[22] The "tough crowd" may be opposed to the "caring crowd" – a group that thinks that other propensities are just as fundamental to human forms of life and that social stability can be arrived at without self-interest. While not an opposition made by Becker, there is no way around this dichotomy: the caring crowd is the most important alternative to the tough crowd. This is due to the fact that no one is challenging Rawls's finding of ineliminable disagreement among people regarding comprehensive conceptions of the good life, and no one doubts that "in a pliant, like-minded company we have the luxury to consider political arrangements that are fully satisfying even, perhaps, to pursue some form of ethical perfectionism."[23] Everybody also agrees that, in spite of deep and enduring disagreements, we can hope for some common ground. Otherwise, we have an enduring and hopeless problem. What should be problematized is that the tough crowd assumes that the caring crowd will agree that there is no hope for social stability outside of accepting that the only language of negotiation must (within a social contract theory account of social justice) be fundamentally based on self-interest.

There is ambiguity in Becker's essay about whether the tough crowd is characterized by (1) a shared commitment to giving fundamental, exclusive priority to self-interest (the contractarian crowd or the tough crowd as I defined it) or (2) by rational people facing ineliminable disagreement about comprehensive conceptions of the good life (*all* the crowds, according to Rawls). This ambiguity allows Becker to say not only that political philosophy's primary problem is dealing with the fact that disagreement about the good between members of a society is unavoidable, but also that its primary audience is Thrasymachus's crowd – that is, the tough crowd or the generic contractarians.[24] It also allows him to include the caring crowd within the tough crowd.[25] In doing so, Becker silences the fact that the caring crowd does not share the Hobbesian assumptions of the tough crowd, such as the inevitability of "permanent warfare" or the impossibility of a sustainable commitment to social structures that fail to capitalize on individual self-regarding drives.

While objections could be raised by my interpretation of the terms above, this move is intellectually important for four reasons. First, while it could be said that I am hijacking Becker's terms to a degree, I am only giving back to Rawls what belongs to Rawls by pointing out what looks like a contractarian attempt to capture a Rawlsian-like category of rational people living under the conditions of justice. Second, I am not purposefully misinterpreting Becker's terms, but only insisting

---

[22] *Ibid.* at 14, 16.
[23] *Ibid.* at 14.
[24] *Ibid.* at 13.
[25] *Ibid.* at 15.

that we do not conflate the tough/contractarian crowd with "everybody." This is in order to give conceptual space to challenge the generic set of contractarian assumptions about people (and what they have in common) and disagreement (and how to overcome it). Of course, Becker can embrace a contractarian point of view – a move that I appreciate – for it offers us the opportunity to see the limits of an unapologetically contractarian attempt at including PSID within our political community. Third, I think that this redefinition is important because, regardless of whether Becker would concede to my point, we must deal with the tough crowd's *real* problem. Leaving the problem posed by Rawls's crowd (everybody disagreeing about the good) to subsequent chapters in which I analyze contractualist solutions, I now turn to the problems posed by Thrasymachus's crowd. Recall, this is a subset of those disagreeing about the good and who insist that only a traditional contractarian solution prioritizing self-interest will lead us to social stability, which is powerful enough to hold the rest of us hostage to their view, regardless of whether they are morally right. I deal with a moralized version of putting self-interest first in a different chapter, as Becker's argument does not try to moralize contractarianism but rather presents it as a self-interested story about the proper understanding of power and reciprocity and its ability to retain the tough crowd's attention.[26] Fourth, to illustrate the contractarian assumption that the tough crowd is viewed as the only group from which justice should be constructed, consider a passage in which Becker seems to recognize the conceptual distinction between the "tough crowd," the "rest" (the ones whose negotiating terms are silenced), and a third "bargaining group" that social contract theory uses to elaborate a system of social justice:

> [I]n any philosophically plausible mutual advantage theory, the *bargaining group* must include at least everyone that the *tough crowd* must include for strategic reasons – everyone, for example, whose exclusion from the process is likely to undermine the effectiveness or stability of the conventions, contracts, and institutions that are advantageous to the *tough crowd*.[27]

As this suggests, the tough crowd is granted a close connection to the bargaining group because of their power, their recalcitrance, and their self-interested minds. They are already part of this bargaining group, which is completed incrementally by adding other individuals to it, notably from the caring crowd whose exclusion could turn out to be unprofitable.

Given these problems, I reformulate the tough crowd problem as I did at the start of this section: they hold us hostage to their negotiating terms which are fundamentally grounded on self-interest, the constitutional, legal, and social consequences of which must reflect and maintain the priority of self-interest. They will accept nothing less than the satisfaction of their terms under the threat to social stability.

---

[26] *Ibid.* at 17–18.
[27] *Ibid.* at 16 (emphasis added).

2.3 When the "Tough Crowd" Rethinks Reciprocity?

This threat holds as long as it is not profitable to question or challenge their negotiating terms or to reject them entirely – that is, as long as the risk of a certain degree of social instability is not preferable. However, one notes that this is a risk that is incomparably lower than a state of perpetual warfare, which may be taken by theorists less timorous or pessimistic than Hobbes, who was known for surrendering important rights and freedoms for the sake of social stability.

Ultimately, Becker's stance has a Hobbesian flavor because of its emphasis on social stability. He fears that not dealing with the tough crowd will preclude social stability in that they "will repeatedly scuttle other political arrangements at the constitutional level."[28] Likewise, he notes that, in failing to construct commitments of justice on the basis of this rational self-interest alone, "we have little chance, short of perpetual warfare, of protecting the disabled."[29] This Hobbesian fear of perpetual warfare reflects a bleak view of human nature – or at least of the tough crowd, whose conception of "human nature" becomes the only political philosophy that should be of interest,[30] for questionable pragmatic reasons.

Here are a few criticisms that can be directed to an approach that grants such importance to the tough crowd:

1. We probably do not want to use an overtly and unapologetically amoral starting point for a theory of justice.[31]
2. If the tough crowd holds the rest of us hostage to its negotiating terms (which also reflect its views about what matters in human life and human interactions), then it is exercising some sort of tyranny over the rest of the society. Liberal justice requires that no group imposes its will upon all others. So, if the tough crowd forces the caring (or any other) crowd to adopt its primarily self-interested negotiating terms and societal structures, it is not clear whether the resulting arrangements qualify as "just."
3. We cannot be sure that no other scenario of escaping perpetual warfare is factually implausible.[32] For instance, the caring crowd may hold that self-interest is important, while not considering it to be the only common denominator in terms of a profound and stable basis for negotiation between people who have deep disagreements about the good.
4. The caring crowd could, itself, challenge the established constitutional order if their fundamental views about what is owed to them and to vulnerable human beings are silenced. There is no reason to assume

---

[28] *Ibid.* at 14.
[29] *Ibid.*
[30] *Ibid.* at 15.
[31] *Ibid.* at 17–18, 23.
[32] *Ibid.* at 14.

that the tough crowd alone is powerful enough to threaten to destabilize the social order and "repeatedly scuttle the established constitutional order" out of love for themselves, while the caring crowd would not do the same for other motivations – like, for instance, out of love for their disabled children or partiality toward other vulnerable and dependent groups. We should not expect the caring crowd to be more or less "pliant" than the tough crowd lest we confuse meekness with kindness, submissiveness with tolerance, self-effacement with other-regarding concern, weakness with care, and the inability to put up a fight with empathy.[33] Countless civil rights movements, resistance movements, and groups that protest the harm suffered by their fellow human beings illustrate that self-interest may be accompanied with other kinds of motivations, such as people acting out of love or in solidarity with others. Such acts of protest do not lead us into a state of permanent warfare. On the contrary, it can in fact have the effect of further stabilizing the social order.[34]

---

[33] This is not an admission that the tough crowd is right in claiming that the only way out of an "unprofitable" disagreement is to focus on rational self-interest alone. Rather, it is a claim that focusing on rational self-interest alone may not be sufficiently profitable for the caring crowd. It does not mean that the caring crowd is unresponsive to reason or at least no more or no less responsive than the tough crowd is: both of them value some things deeply, and both of them are rational and reasonable enough to see that they must distinguish between what they value and the strategies (and underlying shared values) that make a conversation and a stable social order possible. It is not prima facie implausible that making some room for other-regarding concern and empathy in our description of justice could lead to stable social arrangements, even without moralizing too soon a theory of justice that would rather track shared traits about human beings. These shared traits could include empathy, dependence, and a tendency to cooperate and socialize, among others. Michael Slote's application of his theory on caring and empathy to justice is such an argument: *The Ethics of Care and Empathy* (London: Routledge, 2007) and *Moral Sentimentalism* (Oxford: Oxford University Press, 2010). We will also turn to Silvers and Francis' theory of "justice through trust," which tracks the natural cooperative tendencies of human beings, who work *both* solitarily and collectively.

[34] It is possible that my claim may sound naïve, perhaps even more so within a book that focuses on theories that are wholly immersed in the liberal paradigm of autonomy. While I cannot fully defend my position here, I note that people have historically rallied to claim the rights of others, especially vulnerable groups like children and mentally disabled people. Further, if empathy, solidarity, and other-regarding concern do *not* have countless and all-pervading social functions within the institution of the family through the practices of socialization as well as being motivating factors to pursue meaningful projects, it is hardly the well-oiled Hobbesian punishment system – necessary though it might be – that would ensure social stability. I am only raising these perennial issues to ward off a quick dismissal of the idea that human beings may universally agree on more than being selfish and rational, even when it comes to seeking the terms of a society-building procedure. The claims that humans are cooperative social beings and that they are dependent on one another may be as compelling and the normative consequences of those claims may not be so easy to dismiss. See Alasdair MacIntyre, *Dependent Rational Animals: Why Human Beings Need the Virtues* (Chicago: Open Court, 1999).

2.3.2 *Derivativeness of PSID's Status Secured through Their Caregivers*

As a result of his contractarian and instrumentalizing approach, when Becker argues that social institutions will be adapted to cater to the needs of both the disabled and their defenders (by which he means their caregivers, unless the disabled are themselves able enough to be threatening), it will not be for the sake of the disabled. Rather, it will be "for the sake of efficiency and for the sake of stability."[35]

PSID are not able to directly threaten social stability and, as a result, they have no direct moral status. Granted, the people who love them or have caring relations with them may have such solid bonds with them that this indirectness or derivativeness is less threatening to PSID's well-being than it might otherwise be under this contractarian view. However, I am not focusing on these derivative statuses (though we can easily think of grounds for such statuses as a last philosophical resort, should we be unable to provide PSID with a robust moral status).

As for my critique of generic contractarianism, my criticism of the particular derivativeness or contingency of PSID's moral status in Becker's account is not a criticism of the instrumental aspect of this status, as everybody is instrumentalized in a contractarian account. The instrumental status of nondisabled citizens is, nonetheless, the robust moral status provided by a traditional Hobbesian or contractarian framework, even though it would not be recognized as a robust moral status within, say, a contractualist or Kantian framework. There is a plausible notion of a robust moral status within Hobbesian contractarianism, which is used by Becker. In fact, while using an instrumental, strategic, self-serving rationality instead of notions such as dignity qua priceless value, contractarian theories of the moral status of subjects of justice reach a similar end point in terms of robustness and equality of status. This shows that, although the concept of what counts as a robust status may change radically from one philosophical standpoint to the other, there are surprising commonalities between philosophers in terms of trying to explain and justify a nearly[36] universal robust moral status, even though they start from very different foundations. Becker echoes Hobbes in his explanation of this:

> [T]he only sort of strategic situation in which every member of this crowd would make an agreement with the others is one in which no other individual can dominate anyone else or can dominate a few into forming a coalition against the rest. The result is one of the major features of the bargaining situation imagined by

---

[35] Becker, "Reciprocity, Justice, and Disability," at 17.
[36] Critical theorists would hasten to add that this idea of "near universality" is not only insidious because there is a world of difference between "universality" and "near universality" (namely, a gap within which marginalized and oppressed groups have traditionally fallen) but also because the very appeal to the notion of "universality," albeit qualified, helps dynamics of power and exclusion to masquerade as bona fide attempts to reach universal inclusion within seemingly objective theories.

social contract theorists: namely, one in which all parties to the bargaining are roughly equal, free, and independent.[37]

However, the status of PSID is contingent not only upon their being instrumental to others, but also upon being instrumental (or, rather, the object of partial preferences) to people who care for them who are, themselves, instrumental to others. Thus, they are valued not only derivatively but, as it were, "doubly derivatively."

Does it matter if one is removed from a direct status once, twice, or thrice, or even instrumentalized at all? My answer is simply that, if a contractarian theory grounds robust moral status on power, then there is a substantial difference between holding that someone is directly powerful and holding that someone happens to be powerful through her contingent role within social matrices or her contingent relations with powerful agents. Since the foundations here are more fragile, the moral status of PSID cannot be said to be robust. The fact that most of us would not trust such an indirect robust moral status within an ideal contractarian society and would prefer to be granted an ordinary robust moral status is an indication that PSID's moral status is a mitigated kind of robust moral status.

Becker would resist my characterization of the contractarian status as too derivative.[38] He, too, seeks to find grounds for a *robust* status for PSID (or at least as robust a status as contractarians can grant). He claims:

> [T]he basic structure that idealized bargainers design not only will be designed *from the beginning* with the disabled in mind but will be designed *for* the disabled and *for* their caregivers as well as for the bargainers themselves. These considerations will not be derivative matters but central ones.[39]

The word "matters" here is ambiguous. In one sense, the interests of the disabled will be considered by the idealized bargainers in the very design of social institutions. But the disabled person's status remains derivative because the idealized bargainers must consider them in the first place. This consideration is derivative or contingent on the consideration that we have toward the agents who love and care for PSID and for ourselves, should we need these caring institutions.[40] A possible argument is that caregivers can require the tough crowd to grant a more robust (less derivative) status to the cared-for: they will accept nothing less for those they love. However, this honorific membership to our contractarian political community is still contingent upon the caregivers' attitudes toward PSID. To truly make it non-derivative, the tough crowd should borrow the point of view of the agents caring for disabled people. However, in a contractarian view (whether the generic one or the one of Becker), the bond that unites the caregivers with PSID is not required by

---

[37] Becker, "Reciprocity, Justice, and Disability," at 14–15.
[38] *Ibid.* at 37, fn 30.
[39] *Ibid.* at 17.
[40] *Ibid.*

justice. If justice is a matter of rationally maximizing self-interest and of granting a robust status to people in order to contract with them, given that contractual rational dealings are more mutually advantageous relationships than, say, war, the tough crowd has direct reasons to deal with the caregivers of people with disabilities, but not with PSID themselves. PSID only come into the picture as one of the personal preferences that able-bodied contractors want to secure for themselves. However, if the tough crowd *did* borrow caregivers' perspectives on PSID, they would then become concerned for PWD in an attitudinal way that could not be reduced to, or dependent on, the concern the tough crowd has for the caregivers. Only then could the tough crowd be disposed to grant PSID a nonderivative robust status and, whether this would be a matter of justice or not, it would be neither tough (in the sense of strictly self-interested) nor contractarian.

One may be alarmed by the contingency affecting the status of PSID within a contractarian framework that assumes a strictly self-interested picture of individuals when these individuals reflect upon what they owe to one another as a matter of justice, and perhaps also of morality. Entrusting the treatment of PSID to the tough crowd is like putting sheep and wolves in the same enclosure and hoping that they can coexist harmoniously.

Becker argues that, "for strategic reasons alone,"[41] contractarian theories can justify a robust status for PSID. But his best argument is not to be found in his advocacy of the indirect view, for the reasons set out above; rather, it is by offering an understanding of PSID as directly worthwhile fellow contractors. He does so by showing that many PSID can actually reciprocate once the notion of reciprocity is understood in a richer and more complex way.

2.3.3 Rethinking Reciprocity

Becker explains that the concept of reciprocity is oversimplified in Western philosophy in four ways: it is understood to require (1) "[d]irect, one-to-one exchanges"; (2) "[i]n-kind returns"; (3) voluntariness, that is, be the subject of a voluntary transaction; and (4) "that the things exchanged must be of equal value in some agent-independent sense."[42] Becker suggests a more comprehensive account of reciprocity, which is constituted by proper accounts of "fittingness and proportionality" for the good and bad received.[43] A "fittingness standard" defines "the range of things that count as goods for the recipients, and in the case of reciprocating for bad things, the standard is to return corrective good for bad received."[44] Standards of proportionality state that "for the good we receive, we respond with an equal

---

[41] *Ibid.*
[42] *Ibid.* at 20–23 (emphasis removed).
[43] *Ibid.* at 20.
[44] *Ibid.* at 23.

marginal sacrifice and... for the bad, our corrective responses be directed to restoring and sustaining productive reciprocal relationships."[45]

I have little to contribute to his view of reciprocity, which I find plausible[46] and helpful in understanding what constitutes proper returns in good and bad within "transactional relations" that should be understood – for the sake of transactions based on the well-being of the parties taking part in them – in such contractarian terms.[47] Nevertheless, my criticisms of this inclusivist strategy will consist of taking notice of the two apparently unredeemable flaws of generic contractarianism that surface here. First, the dubious empirical wager that PSID are indirectly profitable or threatening enough to have their interests socially accounted for and, second, the oddity of framing our obligations regarding justice and morality in terms of power when it comes to our dealing with PSID.

On Becker's account of fittingness, the "issues central to justice for the disabled"[48] are framed under the rubric of "bad received"[49] (rather than goods received) in need of corrective steps (the fitting corrective response to maintaining productive reciprocal relationships). This initial viewpoint of seeing disabled people as a burden is problematic, as we will see in Chapter 4, on active citizenship. These corrective measures aim to "restore and sustain productive reciprocal relationships" that are "mutually advantageous."[50] However, one can wonder what sort of reciprocal relationship could be made possible (rather than "restored") through social accommodation. Not all PWD can become productive members of society through rehabilitation programs. Furthermore, not all PWD can be encompassed by a contractarian effort to normalize them, and it is far from obvious that those who can, either partially or completely, will be able to offset the costs of required accommodation.

Becker's account of proportionality trades on the familiar idea that "we cannot reasonably assume that the notion of [a balanced, fair and proportional transaction] involves equal, dollar-for-dollar values for the parties."[51] He also emphasizes that reciprocal proportionality must be understood by being placed "into its larger

---

[45] *Ibid.*
[46] Although I note that this ultimately relies on some empirical assumptions that could be challenged and are difficult to prove. I suspect that I am favorable to his views because I already think that we should broaden our understanding of reciprocity, whether or not it serves the tough crowd's interests, among other things. For instance, reciprocity may later serve to measure what members should contribute to the benefit of whom and when, and what sort of responses – accolade, higher salary, jail time – are merited when they succeed or fail, rather than to be an exclusive criterion for membership to society.
[47] However, I believe that such relations are far from sufficient in terms of discussions about fundamental issues of justice such as membership to the political community, robust moral status, or representation of interests at the early stage of society building.
[48] Becker, "Reciprocity, Justice, and Disability," at 26.
[49] *Ibid.* at 23.
[50] *Ibid.* at 25.
[51] *Ibid.* at 26.

context–specifically, into its role in the project of creating and sustaining mutually advantageous social relationships generally."[52] We will return to both of these ideas, which are most successfully employed by Silvers and Francis. At this point, let me just state why they are not as successful within a more individualist (in contrast to Silvers and Francis's) contractarian account. Of course, an advantageous exchange does not need to be dollar for dollar. The value can be subjective to each of the traders and one of the traders may receive less value (even if once it is adjusted to subjective valuing). Yet this trade can still be a good deal if the trader chooses it freely. The problem, however, is that PWD may not be able to trade, even if we admit this inequality of currency (in kind and amount). Becker's answer, similar to that of Silvers and Francis, is that the very fact of sustaining trading relations with PWD constitutes a social advantage. This is an empirical claim that can be questioned. (Becker is not referring to Silvers and Francis's claim that relations of trust between disabled and able people are themselves valuable in and of themselves. That view has issues of its own, which I will deal with in the next chapter.) Instead of relations of trust or any other sort of nurturing relations, Becker is focusing on the type of relations sought by the tough crowd: "mutually advantageous social relationships."[53] Becker's two suggestions are that (1) we should adopt the proportionality requirement so as to not completely exclude "the young, old, poor, powerless, unlucky, and disabled"[54] and thus completely extinguish the hope of a mutually advantageous project and (2) excluding them would produce "resentments [,] ... social instability and economic efficiency."[55] However, it is unlikely that many PSID have the capacities to contribute proportionally (even on Becker's adjusted notion of proportionality) in a way that would prompt the tough crowd to bargain with them. It is also dubious to assert that the tough crowd would fear PSID's resentment, even supposing they *are* able to resent their exclusion or abandonment. Of course, the caregivers, on the other hand, are able to contribute to and threaten social stability but the idea considered here is whether PSID can themselves be seen as parties to the contract (as Silvers and Francis will suggest). If they cannot and, in fact, can only benefit from their caregivers' partiality toward them or from some other social arrangements designed for able contractors, then this solution raises the issue of derivativeness and contingency that I have explored in this chapter.

Becker's version of contractarianism – which is more sophisticated than (but retains some damning features of) generic contractarianism – cannot provide a satisfactory basis for the integration of PSID. The key reason for this is that, although Becker expands our notion of reciprocity in a way that enables contractarians not to miss out on profitable deals with PSID, it is simply too empirically dubious to assert

[52] *Ibid.*
[53] *Ibid.*
[54] *Ibid.*
[55] *Ibid.* at 27.

that PSID constitute an untapped resource. Further, if we consult our ordinary intuitions about why we ought to grant people with disabilities a robust status within our political community, this appears to be a somewhat outlandish account of justice that purports to not be amoral. To overcome this flaw of contractarianism, we would need, if it is even possible, a contractarian account that not *only* challenges too restrictive a view of reciprocity but also reconceptualizes the kind(s) of profits that PSID can procure, so that they can more plausibly and less contingently be said to have something to trade.

Becker recognizes that contractarianism is stuck with a "residue of injustice," that is to say:

> [T]o impose unfair arrangements on individuals (especially the powerless) for reasons unrelated to those individuals' particular interests, needs, ... claims [or capabilities]. A theory does this when it locates the crucial determinants of individual entitlements and just distributive arrangements "outside" some individuals – for example, by defining a bargaining procedure that effectively excludes some people, or an aggregation of expected consequences that discounts their interests, or a conception of excellence or flourishing that is inappropriate for them.[56]

His answer to this is that we cannot expect more from a contractarian theory.[57] He is skeptical that doctrines of inherent human dignity (notably nonconsequentialist right-based theories) – though they would avoid the contingency objection – can successfully and defensibly "construct interpersonal rankings of inherent individual rights that will yield a unique solution to every priority problem between the disabled and others."[58]

I should emphasize that Becker's criticism of nonconsequentialist right-based theories is not a wholesale rejection of any noncontractarian theory of justice (or theoretical elements that contribute to such a theory). Although it is not my goal to develop a full-fledged alternative, I am favorable to the idea that fiduciary relations have a normative content that cannot be reduced to mutual advantage, although I suspect this argument would need to take into account the nature of the relations at stake, as well as the circumstances and consequences of the choices that present themselves. I acknowledge Becker's point that dealing with conflicts between the claims of disabled and nondisabled people represents a greater challenge within a theory of justice that is not unified around a single set of principles (such as the goal of mutual advantage between strictly self-interested contractors) and that such an approach would admit competing fundamental moral pulls. Here, I can only refer to J. Baird Callicott's simple but compelling answer that doing the right thing for the right reason is important, as well as Mary A. Warren's response (to criticisms of her claim that there is a plurality of grounds for moral status) that simplicity is not the

---

[56] *Ibid.* at 37.
[57] *Ibid.*
[58] *Ibid.* at 38.

only philosophical virtue to a theory. I would also highlight, as Silvers and Francis do, that normalization of the harm caused to PSID – that is, by receiving benefits on the basis of a theoretical framework developed to cater to the needs, claims, interests, and capabilities of nondisabled people – is far from insignificant.[59] This harm is even greater when we deal with PSID whose needs and capacities differ even more widely from the norm than in the case of other disabled people. I agree with Becker that "[i]t is hard to see how one could ask more of a mutual advantage theory of justice on [the issue of the disabled]."[60] But I hope, for PSID's sake, that Becker's pessimism regarding alternative theories is unjustified, as I do not share his optimism regarding the welfare of PSID within an idealized contractarian society.

Before turning to Silvers and Francis's theory of justice through trust in the following chapter, I wish to conclude this chapter by emphasizing that contractarian accounts awkwardly steer a course between Charybdis and Scylla when they deliberate on PSID's status. Either they implicitly introduce a noncontractual, qualificatory criterion to be granted (or specially considered for) robust moral status that is incompatible with contractarian fundamental premises or they must exclude PSID along with other UC. Ultimately, I think that contractarians cannot give up on the features of contractarianism that taint it with an unsatisfactory derivativeness without giving up on the key commitments of contractarianism.

2.4 TWO OBJECTIONS: BITING THE CONTRACTARIAN BULLET OR ADMITTING AN UNSPOKEN QUALIFICATORY CRITERION

Contractarians do not have an independent criterion for membership to the contracting community. That is, Abby only gets to join the community if it is profitable to have her on board. There is no further eligibility criterion such as, for example, questions about who counts as humans or persons. We could bring horses in if it is profitable to do so.

A first contractarian position may be that there are very few "presocial" cases in which one can plausibly argue that PSID can be regarded as profitable members of the emerging contracting community. In other words, and as I have shown above, the tough crowd would have no interest in dealing with them at all. In the "naked"

---

[59] J. Baird Callicott, "Intrinsic Value in Nature: A Metaethical Analysis" (1995) 3 Electronic J Analytic Phil; Mary Anne Warren, *Moral Status: Obligations to Persons and Other Living Things* (Oxford: Oxford University Press, 2000); Leslie Francis and Anita Silvers, "Thinking about the Good: Reconfiguring Liberal Metaphysics (or Not) for People with Cognitive Disabilities" in Eva Feder Kittay and Licia Carlson, *Cognitive Disability and Its Challenge to Moral Philosophy* (Malden, MA: Wiley-Blackwell, 2010), at 237. (See their criticisms of Nussbaum in particular.)

[60] Becker, "Reciprocity, Justice, and Disability," at 37.

position of a presocial order[61] in which the contract is being formed, why would anybody include PSID? They have nothing to bring to the bargaining table.[62]

The progressive inclusivist contractarian would answer that contractarians can be long-term planners and, even from a presocial state perspective, they may see that the integration of disabled people through institutions that allow them to be productive would be profitable overall.

The objector would insist that contractarians cannot soften their propositions in order to let the weaker participants have more of a role and must therefore consider the cases where, barring implausible optimism, a group of self-interested bargainers would think it better if a noncontributing PSID had been excluded from the outset, even though she is now, regrettably, "one of us." Now that PSID are here, it is more difficult to remove them because of cost (including people's negative reactions to mistreating vulnerable humans). But the question of whether it would be better if this group of people was not around is, on principle, open to contractarians to answer. Further, considering this question can translate into government-sponsored, economically sanctioned, and/or socially encouraged eugenic policies, such as those in place regarding prenatal detection of cognitive deficiencies.

[61] This first remark could be problematized. Nondisabled people could not develop their abilities either if left to themselves as newborns. The contractors in the presocial state must have developed their contracting capacities, thanks to some form of community support. Therefore, the state of nature scenario is not neutral in terms of the support it assumes has been dispensed – it assumes that the central case of "negotiator" received support to develop her abilities (e.g., a capacity to communicate) but that PSID were deprived of any needed additional support. The fact that such a "state of nature" thought experiment would assume that only people able to achieve a high degree of autonomy should count as negotiators would not necessarily be arbitrary, insofar as only these people become "profitable contractors" and such a requirement is central to contractarianism. However, this view should integrate those disabled people who are able to become profitable contractors but require more support than the statistical average. However, it would still exclude most PWD who would remain UC in spite of any (presocial or social) support.

[62] By contrast, on the contractualist side, it may seem that the contract is superfluous if one imagines an independent criterion that renders one eligible for being a contracting party. Thus, if we can use the independent criterion as the direct route that enables eligibility, why bother with the contract? If, as the objection goes, the contractualist identifies PSID as "persons" who are eligible to be in the contract for the purpose of contractualism, then why not just treat the fact that they are persons as evidence to decide how they should be treated and not as a threshold condition for the contract? The answer to that objection is that that there is no such independent contractualist criterion, at least not one that is explicitly acknowledged. Persons are contractors, and that implies that they possess specific contracting capacities amounting to "moral powers." The moral capacities that justify granting a robust moral status on a contractualist account are to be deployed during the *contractual* process of building social institutions and their moral salience cannot be detached from their contractual dimension. Indeed, as we will see in the chapters on contractualism, if we simply accept that PSID are worthy of a robust moral consideration without offering them adequate contractual representation, they will suffer from institutional exclusion because some of the social settings will be ill-fitted for them. The contractual process is not only about securing membership to the political community; the contract is also a modal device telling us how to treat social members and the sort of constitutional arrangements and policies that they can expect.

2.4 Two Objections

Two answers to this problem that can be provided by an inclusivist contractarianism (or perhaps an unwittingly moralized version of contractarianism) are that even self-interested people will be strongly averse to such solutions. They may desire, for their own sake, a social climate that is not so ruthlessly calculating, if only because it may penalize them. We return to this argument in the next chapter. The second answer goes back to the fact that the tough crowd may not be statically associated with a particular group of individuals. We can all suddenly find ourselves belonging to the caring crowd – or likely to be in it – if we have a disabled child, no matter how socially unprofitable that child is. Therefore, the contractual presocial story is odd here, since we cannot eliminate the fact of vulnerability from the human condition. Lamenting the fact that we are now regrettably "stuck" with people with severe disabilities supposes that we could have it any other way.

However, both answers presuppose that we are bad at detecting the truly profitable in human life. This is an increasingly dubious position, as are our social motivations, which historical harmful treatments of PSID demonstrate. In other words, contractarians must face the tough crowd. The tough crowd may indeed put the brakes on policies designed to marginalize or remove profoundly disabled people from society because of the psychological cost to others, the demoralization of our productive population, or the fear that they or their children could be next. But because contractarianism provides an idealized explanation of who ought to count as a member of society, these contingent considerations would not justify granting PSID as robust a moral status as a contractarian account can provide.[63] This is part of the nature of this idealized account.

Let me summarize the problem of introducing a noncontractarian criterion for granting robust moral status. Hobbesian contractarians imagine a state of nature in which we are faced with the question of whether to establish a civil society. They argue that the marginal advantage for "us" to do so is enough, so long as the problem of free-riders (people who enjoy the benefit of security without contributing) is dealt with through coercion.[64] In this story, there is an amorphous "us" and the fundamental question asks: what are the prequalifications for being part of this "us"? Are there prequalifications that would justify granting a robust moral status before considering the usual contractarian reasons for doing so?

There are two scenarios in which this could occur. According to the first, there is no prequalification. That is, there is nothing that counts as granting eligibility in advance of the contract being made. The relevant "us" is defined as everyone from

---

[63] I set aside the idea that contractarian criteria may create various sorts of moral statuses or even exclude or downgrade members who fall beyond a certain productivity level since, although one could criticize contractarianism precisely for not closing this conceptual window (or even opening it), it is not something that is remotely politically plausible in the current state of the liberal philosophical tradition that I deal with here.

[64] See generally Anthony de Jasay, *Social Contract, Free Ride: A Study of the Public Goods Problem* (Indianapolis: Liberty Fund, 2008).

whom the others could obtain a marginal advantage. Each person is considered eligible only inasmuch as it would be advantageous for each of the others to bring that person in. If this is the case – and we see that it is – then we have a problem to resolve in the state of nature in deciding which people are not "us" when they do not have a marginal contribution to make. The second scenario is that there are prequalificatory requirements, which would moralize a contractarian theory. This scenario brings contractarianism closer to a contractualist theory by not grounding it in self-interest alone. There would be features that "we" share that make us eligible for a robust moral status independently from the advantage that we would bring to the group.

Contractarians may talk as though they believe the first theory, but in practice, they embrace the second theory, because they have always modeled the birth of society on the hypothesis that it will include some weaker participants.[65] This is not just a society of the strongest. If they are indeed making inroads into the contractarian commitment to seeking out the most profitable deal for themselves, then what is the extent and breadth of these inroads? How does this alternate view compete with their traditional contractarian commitments, and how do they justify the fact that it does not completely supersede these commitments? More importantly, what are these unspoken prequalificatory requirements? Why are babies included? Are they only included because they have the potential to grow up to be warriors or CEOs?

The contractarian ideal response is that, yes, babies can eventually benefit us or be a threat to us, and they are therefore part of "us." But, as Gauthier suggests, the same claim does not apply to the permanently disabled, especially those who will not contribute to the pool of common resources.[66] For PSID, there must be an additional and unspoken background of social bonds (and, if there are, we should wonder whether this same background does not apply to babies and competent adults as well). We already have an undertheorized but strong idea of what the "us" refers to. This moral pull is at work in both contractarian and contractualist accounts, even though they do not acknowledge it and explain social membership exclusively in contractual terms. These moral prequalificatory requirements are not to be integrated into contractarian accounts because they are not coherent with them.[67]

---

[65] One could also ask, without further moral constraints, what would prevent contractarians from dealing with threats in a very different way than by integration? Unlike in the contractualist account of requirements that include sophisticated cognitive and moral powers, the brute powers that contractarians refer to are not closely or conceptually linked to respect. The proverb advising one to keep one's friends close but enemies closer may not always hold, and neither may Hobbes's empirical conviction that a civil contract with groups threatening us is the best way to protect ourselves. The fact that some potentially threatening individuals must be contracted with rather than disposed of does not mean that the same holds for all potentially threatening or costly individuals.

[66] See Gauthier, *Morals by Agreement*.

[67] This is evident on prudential contractarian accounts, but I still have to show that this is also more likely than not for Silvers and Francis's seemingly moralized contractarian account and for the contractualist accounts we will explore next.

2.4 Two Objections

We know that contractarians want self-interest to be the only negotiating modality in precontractual negotiations, but do they want self-interest to be the only condition for entry into these negotiations? If so, it is not clear how this could be thought of as the basis for founding a society. Given these parameters, why would they include anyone in the group who was not the fittest and most competent? Weaker people might pose a threat, but only if they can unite, and not if we fight them one at a time. The strongest cannot prevent the weakest from uniting and forming their own social contract, but then, within that other social contract, the same problem would arise. Why would middle-ranking "weaker ones" include the weakest ones in their society? Following this line of thought, we can marginalize a small group that is no threat to anyone. This group – to which PSID would surely belong – can safely be left to die without fear of retribution. Short of adding some moral constraints to this scenario, it is hard to see how contractarianism can provide a working, realistic account of liberal society as we envision it. It may well be a better justification for a stratified society with castes or communities coexisting hierarchically.

If David Gauthier and Eva Kittay are right to say that it is a kind of wistful contractarian metaphor to speak of the productivity of certain PSID (Gauthier would take this to justify the exclusion of PSID from the scope of justice and Kittay, the rejection of contractarianism), then inclusivist contractarians like Becker are too optimistic about the success of rehabilitation[68] and about the likelihood that the tough crowd will find it beneficial to negotiate with the caring crowd. They also read either too much or too little into the importance of the relations with PSID that even self-interested contractors will have as family members or prospective family members (as their self-interest may include, in a Hobbesian account, the interests of their close family members, whose well-being is linked to theirs). Inclusivist contractarians assume too much if they think that these relationships alone will preclude contractarians from considering whether a purge may not be, on the whole, more effective, given that, by definition, they are open-minded to the possibility. They also do not go far enough when they fail to acknowledge and explicitly endorse what seems to be their unspoken moral pre-qualifications that ultimately explain why PSID cannot simply be left out, gradually marginalized, or even eliminated in a way that would result in the social benefits outweighing the psychological costs of such an action.

---

[68] Becker, "Reciprocity, Justice, and Disability," at 26.

3

The Capacity to Trust as a Contractual Basis for Robust Moral Status

3.1 A TRUST-BASED CONCEPTUALIZATION OF THE SOCIAL CONTRACT

In their 2005 article, Leslie Francis and Anita Silvers problematize traditional contractual accounts for excluding persons with disabilities (PWD). The exclusion of PWD in traditional contractual accounts results, they explain, from the requirement that only people with roughly equal capacities are able to partake in the social contract, which is understood principally as a process of bargaining for mutual advantage. This "homogeneity requirement," as they call it, provides that groups of individuals who do not possess the required physical or intellectual capacities to contract stand outside the boundaries within which parties can contract.[1] The properties required to partake in the bargaining process that determines the rules governing social arrangements are, in turn, influenced by the socially dominant group.[2] Thus, as they explain, this "requirement invites doubts about [the outliers'] legitimacy as participants, deflecting attention from their ideas and attenuating the value of reaching mutual agreement with them."[3] In other words, the interests of those outliers are bound to be neglected or at least remain hostage to choices made by participants of the social contract.

Silvers and Francis's illuminating essay challenges the exclusion of disabled people by questioning the necessity and the historical predominance of an aspect of the contractarian tradition that has been taken for granted: that "social contract theory [must be] understood as a process of bargaining for mutual advantage."[4] They note that this bargaining paradigm does not enjoy the weight of tradition that it

---

[1] Leslie Francis and Anita Silvers, "Justice through Trust: Disability and the 'Outlier Problem' in Social Contract Theory" (2005) 116:1 Ethics 40, at 46.
[2] *Ibid.* at 45–47.
[3] *Ibid.* at 46.
[4] *Ibid.* at 41.

purports to have. Instead, Silvers and Francis claim that the interpretation of the social contract as a bargain "bears the mark of a comparatively recent, nineteenth-century legal theory of contracting, one that has continued to be influential but has also been the subject of ongoing criticism."[5] Importantly, while the contractual process was often conceived as a way to deal with human vulnerability and dependency,[6] the bargaining model obscures this by assuming that the negotiating process takes place between roughly equal and independent parties. However, from a legal point of view, the vulnerability of one party to another is fertile grounds for coercion, which may vitiate a contract.

Rather than understanding the social contract as being based on a bargain, Silvers and Francis essentially propose a different requirement: the capacity to trust. This requirement appears to only be a qualified challenge to the homogeneity requirement; parties who are able to trust are not homogeneously endowed with the intellectual and physical capacities that enable them to bring an equal contribution to the joint venture (or a contribution sufficient to interest other parties to bargain with them) in terms of the products traditionally expected from this cooperation, such as mutual enrichment and protection. However, they suggest that (1) all parties are endowed, albeit to varying degrees, with a capacity to trust and be trusted; and (2) all parties contribute to this joint venture, but they do so indirectly by making their community more trust-facilitating. Thus, it is not the homogeneity of relevant individual capacities that is being challenged per se, but the nature of these capacities – that is, trust, in opposition to sophisticated cognitive capacities. Their argument also raises the idea that morally relevant capacities – ones warranting access to the ethical community and justifying the status of an equal political participant in it – must be directly linked to an input, or should enable the individual to produce this input by herself, outside of a community. Hence, Silvers and Francis make conceptual room for another sort of input on the part of apparently extremely limited contractors.

This is not to say that other-regarding motivations and a culture of trust have always been central to the contractual tradition, which is the alternative position that Silvers and Francis promote. Social contract theorists may not have made use of other-regarding motivations and trust to the extent that Silvers and Francis do, even if those theorists' arguments were not mere projections of dyadic bargaining and were instead aimed at creating a certain political climate or culture. For instance, Hobbes's social contract did take human vulnerability (notably, to one another) into account, but aimed at achieving a climate of peace that did not require more than self-regarding reasoning on the part of the subjects. Therefore, Silvers and Francis must make the case for their "other-regarding"[7] and trust-engendering social

---

[5] *Ibid.* at 43.
[6] *Ibid.* at 74.
[7] *Ibid.* at 60.

contract. Other-regarding concern means concern for others, whereas self-regarding concern means concern for oneself.

Their strategy is to retain a contractual understanding of justice and a justification for inclusion into the ethical community that designs the principles of justice. While remaining within this contractual framework, they replace the understanding of the social contract as *bargaining* with an understanding of the social contract as a tool for *building trust*: trust underlaid by other-regarding concern and trust underlaid by self-regarding concern.[8] As they write, justice has often been seen as the minimal individual commitment to which equally strong, smart, and strategically minded, self-interested agents can accede. Justice may also be seen, however, as a principled practice that will be agreed to by other-regarding agents of very different abilities, depending on one another and seeking relationships that can be sustained.[9]

They add that "[t]he principles of justice formulated through and for trust will not be concerned with equally enriching the individual interests of the parties but with effectively strengthening the bonds between them."[10] In turn, they must explain (1) why building trust and bonds would be a central goal of justice and (2) how this conceptualization of justice would justify including mentally disabled people who are capable of trust. The second element of their justification is easier to satisfy than the first. Once it is established that the social contract requires a social framework that is responsive to people's abilities or needs to "achieve successful personal trust relationships"[11] (i.e., once (1) is established), to prove (2), one need only add the premise that including outliers in the ethical community that designs the principles of justice will help to achieve this end.

The claim that including outliers in the ethical community will aid in building trust is plausible. I would be more skeptical if Silvers and Francis referred only to the trust that exists in a particular dyadic relationship and held that this relationship had to be mutually beneficial, therefore inferring that justice reigned when social institutions facilitated anyone able to trust to directly benefit from particular trusting relationships. If that were the case, then (2) would not follow as easily. It seems likely that PSID can take part in relations of trust but it is less likely that their trustees will always directly benefit from these relationships. Further, one may be willing to

---

[8] This is my interpretation of Silvers and Francis's argument – and it may be one that they would disagree with – but I think it is the best way to make sense of it, since they seem to evoke two different notions of trust. While they can certainly say that a culture of trust would have both elements, they cannot equate them as they are clearly different. Nor can they say that trust based on self-regarding elements alone does not classify as trust, which is what they seem to imply at several points, such as when they refer to Francis Fukuyama's comment that people who do not trust one another can only cooperate through a costly negotiated contract (*ibid.* at 61). It is plausible that parties may enter such a contract precisely to secure trust, albeit a trust that is based on distrustful negotiations.

[9] *Ibid.* at 68.
[10] *Ibid.* at 74.
[11] *Ibid.* at 45.

accept that it is plausible that person A's capacity to trust would ground some duties toward A, but equally one might fail to see – barring further arguments – why these would be duties of justice.[12]

Silvers and Francis' understanding of trust as a key element of justice is collectivist, in that it has more to do with a climate or a culture of trust reigning in a community than with particular and individual relations of trust occurring within that community or an individual need for trust. However, this position does not fail to take stock of the capacity to trust. On the contrary, the contemplated just, trust-engendering social framework is responsive to the capacity to trust, as well as to the "human conditions of vulnerability and dependence."[13] This collectivist approach is reflected in the suggestion that the entity benefitting is the cooperative culture itself, rather than particular parties to an exchange.

On this more complex picture, the discretionary commitment to trusting each other by parties whose capabilities differ sustains cooperation not because the parties necessarily reciprocate directly with each other but because their interactions enrich another kind of entity, the cooperative scheme (or the social climate, the community culture, or society itself).[14]

This conception of the social contract as primarily aimed at improving trust within a community does not disregard mutual benefits. Individual interests will be satisfied *through* this trust rather than being the primary goal of the social contract. The purpose of contracting is to "[develop] bonds of confidence."[15] The underlying empirical assumption is that this will better "[help] map understandings (typically but not necessarily articulated as a set of principles) that facilitate parties' awareness of each other's expectations about how each will behave" rather than "jockeying for position against one another."[16]

Inspired by Annette Baier, Silvers and Francis make a case for the fundamental importance of trust and that we should therefore not jump to conclude that social contracts grounded on self-regarding motivations alone can do away with trust. In some basic sense, trust is a necessary condition of any human enterprise. Without trust in the laws of physics, in the worth of our actions, in other people, we would

---

[12] Rawls adopted such a position toward animals, for instance, suggesting that their capacity for pleasure and pain would justify duties of compassion and humanity, but not duties of strict justice. See, e.g., Martha Nussbaum, *Frontiers of Justice: Disability, Nationality, Species Membership* (Cambridge: Harvard University Press, 2006), at 331–32.

[13] Francis and Silvers, "Justice through Trust," at 59. At least, I will treat their argument as such, as I think that their text favors this interpretation, as the following quotes will show. If they meant something more individualistic, they would run into the problem that is mentioned in the previous paragraph and I would think it is still worth exploring this collectivist option, as it is very promising.

[14] *Ibid.* at 45. Although it may sound like it, this is different from saying that it is the community itself (as an entity having an existence distinct from that of its members) that is benefited as the final recipient of justice or as an intrinsically valuable end.

[15] *Ibid.* at 59.

[16] *Ibid.*

not achieve much. For example, I would not start moving rocks to build a monument without some trust that the rocks I position will not be removed by other people, or, indeed, the trust that it is worthwhile to build this monument. Of course, this basic sense of trust as an ability to predict how certain entities will behave (e.g., a rock is likely to stay where I place it) does not capture the more specific dimensions of trust that exist between beings able to subjectively expect – and respond – to trust. Here, we are only dealing with trust toward other beings who are able to be trusted in that richer sense. But since human activities often (if not always, to some degree) take place within a community, the far-reaching importance of this trust should not be neglected, especially when conceptualizing social arrangements and the impersonal institutions that citizens must be able to trust to a minimal degree to ensure their endurance. As Niklas Luhmann notes,

> A system – economic, legal, or political – requires trust as an input condition. Without trust it cannot stimulate supportive activities in situations of uncertainty or risk. [...] *The lack of trust* [...] reduces the range of possibilities for rational action. It prevents, for example, early medication. It prevents, above all, capital investment under conditions of uncertainty and risk. It may lead to a bad life in moral terms, because one no longer expects to be rewarded after death. It may reduce public interest in innovative art which is not yet recognized and confirmed by the establishment of experts. Through lack of trust a system may lose size; it may even shrink below a critical threshold for its own reproduction at a certain level of development.[17]

Are these sufficient justifications for position building a climate and culture propitious to trust as the central goal of justice? Are they strong enough justifications for putting trust before mutual benefit? Why should we not, for instance, conceive of trust as being less central, or a mere means to gain personal benefits? Can trust-centered social arrangements be desirable for more compelling reasons? For one thing, the above justifications do not treat trust as intrinsically valuable. Indeed, it would be problematic to make such a claim. Annette Baier reminds us of the obvious fact that "not all the things that thrive when there is trust between people, and which matter, are things that should be encouraged to thrive"[18] and that "[w]e cannot simply label trustingness a virtue."[19] In support of this position, she evokes the case of exploitation and the trust between criminals. Silvers and Francis are aware of this problem and do not make such a claim.[20]

Ultimately, we should not expect Silvers and Francis to provide us with a more substantial answer (in opposition to a procedural one) to the question of why trust

---

[17] Niklas Luhmann, "Familiarity, Confidence, Trust: Problems and Alternatives" in Diego Gambetta, ed., *Trust: Making and Breaking Cooperative Relations* (New York: Basic Blackwell, 1988), at 103–4.
[18] Annette Baier, "Trust and Antitrust" (1986) 96:2 Ethics 231, at 231.
[19] Annette Baier, "Trusting People" (1992) 6 Ethics 137, at 137.
[20] See Francis and Silvers, "Justice through Trust," at 64.

should be a key social good. Their strategy is to retain the proceduralist justificatory methodology of social contract theory instead of opting for the realization of more substantial goods or capabilities, virtues, or practices, like caring. They suggest a progressive understanding of such a contractualist procedure taking place within a culture of trust. Their suggestion that the participants to such a procedure have other-regarding motivations and a desire to cultivate a culture of trust is not unrealistic. In fact, it plausibly modifies Rawls's often criticized assumptions regarding the moderate selfishness of participants within his proceduralist justificatory argument. On this point, Silvers and Francis agree with Nussbaum that it is not "clear whether the rabbit of justice can really be pulled out of the hat of rational self-interest."[21]

The result of basing justice on building trust is that anyone who has the capacity to trust can be a subject of justice – that is, they can be active parties to the sort of society-building agreement that theories of social contract contemplate. Unlike the bargaining paradigm of the social contract, the integration of PSID as full members of society under this trust-based paradigm does not face obstacles from their inability to significantly reciprocate the benefits they receive or their lack of cognitive abilities to contract or represent themselves. It also evades the difficulties arising from assigning a trustee to represent them. In sum, Silvers and Francis argue in favor of the capacity for trust being sufficient grounds for both disabled and nondisabled people.

I interpret their argument as contractarian, even though they do not draw a line between the contractualist and the contractarian branches of the social contract tradition and make references to authors of both traditions. Perhaps a contractualist reading of their argument would be possible – notably by emphasizing that a climate of trust would facilitate a climate of mutual respect – but I choose to leave this kind of argument for later discussion (taking special note of Christie Hartley's arguments on this point), and thus I do not interpret justice through trust in a contractualist way in this book. While I could argue that this reading of Silvers and Francis makes the best available contractarian case to include PSID (and/or to reveal that contractarianism cannot escape the dilemma of excluding these people or importing foundational noncontractarian premises), I also think that it is the most plausible reading of their argument. Even when they forcefully criticize the centrality of self-regarding concerns, reasons, and motivations, as well as self-interest and selfishness in the social contract tradition, and appear to want to side with Nussbaum on the difficulty of grounding justice on rational self-interest, it seems that the other-regarding attitudes they introduce do not run as deep as would be the case in a foundationally other-regarding framework. Indeed, they contrast an influential

---

[21] Quoted in *ibid.* at 60. Silvers and Francis refer to Martha Nussbaum, "Beyond the Social Contract: Toward Global Justice," Tanner Lectures on Human Values (Canberra, November 2002 and Cambridge, March 2003), tannerlectures.utah.edu/lectures/documents/volume24/nussbaum_2003.pdf. However, it appears that this quote has been edited from the lecture.

"adversarial" contractual relationship of strategic give-and-take with an alternative bonding contractual relationship "promoting stable compliance with mutual expectations."[22] However, even though other-regarding attitudes are deployed in this alternative contractual model, they ultimately serve (or are nested in) what seems like a relatively traditional contractarian, self-regarding goal of "stabilizing cooperation" in the most "effective" way.[23] Silvers and Francis take kinds of trust (self- or other-regarding) to be crucial *instrumental* dispositions that are required for collaborative activity (hence the title "Justice through Trust"). Practicing justice involves collaborative activity, which requires not merely agents who are trustworthy, as well as able to trust but also requires cultivating a community climate of trust. Inclusiveness facilitates building this climate of trust.[24] These instrumentalizing and self-regarding features of justice through trust lead me to categorize it as a contractarian theory, despite Silvers and Francis's resistance to a reading of this self-regarding element. It will be part of my argument to suggest either that justice through trust embraces this self-regarding dimension and excludes PSID or that it incorporates a more fully other-regarding approach and thus ceases to be contractual.

In the following two sections, I develop a critical assessment of two problematic issues that I see with Silvers and Francis's argument. The first set of problems has to do with the nature of trust and the second set of problems has to do with questioning whether Silvers and Francis's understanding of trust is really as closely linked to social contract theory as they suggest.

My main claim relating to their conception of trust is that it does not need to be fundamentally other-regarding if it is an instrument to attain contractarian ends. However, if it is self-regarding, it seems to exclude PSID. Yet, we can still insist on integrating an other-regarding kind of trust within the social contract in an instrumental way. While Silvers and Francis propose that this kind of other-regarding trust is crucial to the social contract, I contend that it is only crucial if we value it for noncontractual reasons that have been imported into their contractual framework. However, if these reasons have substantial normative implications, then they do not need to be framed in contractual terms and, indeed, doing so would conflict with a procedural, contractual framework that endeavors to avoid making such substantial assumptions.

I have no problem accepting that other-regarding attitudes are key in justifying disabled people's robust moral status. I also agree that trust, in particular, is an attitude or a disposition that may partly justify granting this robust moral status by, for example, being one of the affective, cognitive, or conative bases for granting robust moral status to a being on a variety of noncontractual accounts. As well, it forms an

---

[22] See Francis and Silvers, "Justice through Trust," at 60.
[23] *Ibid.* at 58–61.
[24] Personal communication with Anita Silvers (Winter 2012).

important part of a moral agent's proper response to the robust moral status of PSID by, for example, honoring their trust, if the person can trust.

3.2 THE NATURE OF TRUST

3.2.1 *The Problem: Justice through Trust – But Which Kind of Trust?*

Is the version of trust that Silvers and Francis advocate the only, or even the most plausible, candidate to complement the social contract doctrine? If other understandings of trust better fit the social contract doctrine (but exclude PSID or other outliers), what would justify choosing Silvers and Francis's understanding of trust over such alternative understandings? One potential concern is that they may be tinkering with contractarianism in order to achieve inclusivist results in an arbitrary way.

For instance, can we think of trust as being entirely compatible with the bargaining paradigm and with a culture of promoting self-interestedness and individualism? And, if so, is this interpretation of trust a better match with the notion of a social contract? May it be interpreted as a bargain or a cooperative scheme? If so, are there other reasons why we should still prefer interpreting the social contract through the lens of an other-regarding understanding of trust? And are these reasons necessarily (or even best) expressed through contractual thought?

It seems that we can indeed conceive of trust in a self-interested, self-regarding way that would be compatible with the bargaining model of the social contract. But, first, I should clarify what I mean by trust, as there are many parties to a trusting relationship. The terms "self-regarding" and "other-regarding" can also be misleading since I am in fact referring to the attitudes or motivations of the trusted individual rather than to the attitudes of the trusting one. Also, I have delayed defining the notion of trust in order to first deal with its ambiguity and the problem it causes for Silvers and Francis's argument.

Baier defines trust as an "accepted vulnerability to another person's power over something one cares about, in the confidence that such power will not be used to harm what is entrusted."[25] Trust is therefore a mental phenomenon with cognitive, affective, and conative dimensions.[26] Even though self-regarding trust and other-regarding trust may encompass different cognitive, affective, and conative elements, as well as different kinds of "confidences" or expectations and different entrusted objects, they both fall under this general definition, which we can use for this chapter.

---

[25] See Baier, "Trusting People," at 152.
[26] Annette Baier, "Trust," Tanner Lectures on Human Values (Princeton University, March 1991), tannerlectures.utah.edu/_documents/a-to-z/b/baier92.pdf, at 111.

Whatever beliefs, feelings, or intentions trust involves, they are experienced by the trusting party, not the trusted one. However, trust obviously implies a relationship between trusting and trusted parties. Understanding how trust comes to be and how it is maintained therefore requires an understanding of the mental state that the trusted party has toward her trusting activities. These may be directed toward the individual trusting her, toward the object with which she is entrusted, toward the community or culture of trust within which this discrete trusting event takes place, or toward herself, that is, toward her personal, moral ideal as a trustworthy person or her reputation.

The "culture of trust" within which trust takes place calls for a conceptual analysis. Silvers and Francis, for instance, seek to make the case for a trust-based understanding of contractarian justice and they are interested in such a "climate" or "culture" of trust as it underlies (i.e., allows for and is allowed by) the social contract. A culture of trust is characterized by the fact that it creates favorable conditions for the dependency of trusting individuals and the reliability of trusted ones.[27] Focusing on the mental state of the trusted party is helpful to understand what helps or hinders a culture of trust, insofar as it is revealing that party's reliability, reliability being central to a culture of trust.

Reliability is indeed a key ingredient of any contractarian account of justice. It is uncontroversial to state that a social contract will engender some degree of reliability and predictability and therefore of trust. The disputed points are (1) whether this trust is not only facilitated or made possible by a social contract but is also a preexisting condition for it and (2) whether the trusted and trusting parties' attitudes are opportunistic and self-regarding or other-regarding. Whereas many traditional contractual theories of justice assume that parties to the social contract are self-interested, some progressive understandings of social contract or of justice more generally suggest that (a) social agreements to achieve justice should be at least seen partly as a strategy deployed by individuals who are already parties to relations of trust and who are trying to fortify, extend, and multiply such relations and (b) people designing principles of justice may be animated by more other-regarding motivations than mainstream social contract theory assumes.

The notion of trust can have different meanings, which is a hurdle for Silvers and Francis's argument.[28] In particular, they use it within two different contexts where

---

[27] See "Justice through Trust," where Silvers and Francis explain that "[a] culture of trust supports people's depending on each other and therefore supports individual reliability" (at 44, fn 12) and that "[a] climate of trust supports people's depending on the economical, political, or legal system and therefore contributes to social stability" (at 43, fn 11).

[28] Allow me to make two more definitional clarifications regarding the objects that trust could have and the kind of attitude or thought that trust could be. First, one could distinguish "trusting that individual A will do X" from "trusting that B (other people, entities, or circumstances) will get A to do X." It is debatable whether, in the latter case, one is trusting A, B, or both. It depends on whether one sees trust as an attitude, the "focal point" of which is the fact that X was performed by A (and is thus directed at A), the realization of X, or the ultimate or

trust could reasonably be expected to imply some different features: the trust that members of a society want to foster for cooperative endeavors to take place and the trust that people with intellectual disabilities can give or receive. It is essential that these two notions overlap – or are connected in a causal way – if Silvers and Francis's argument that fostering the latter kind of trust is desirable because fostering the former kind of trust is desirable is to succeed. However, they do not sufficiently argue that both understandings of trust overlap and it is not obvious that such overlap can be assumed. For instance, if trust is taken to mean an expectation that people will behave a certain way, all that should be needed to secure stable cooperation would be inductive confidence in the ability to predict someone's behavior. This would be a different understanding of trust from the kind that a PSID has toward her caregiver – namely, that the caregiver has her best interests at heart. I "trust" that a purse of gold would be taken if I left it on a pavement at a busy metro station because I "trust" in the predictability of people's untrustworthiness.[29]

The kind of trust necessary to stabilize social cooperation may have attitudinal and behavioral elements that are different from the ones taking place in relations with PSID. Perhaps not enough attention has been paid to the particular nature of relations between nondisabled citizens and caring relations with mentally disabled individuals. For example, insofar as there would be specific normative codes regulating these different relations, it is not obvious how fostering "trust" within a close, personal relationship would equally foster "trust" as an instrument of wide social cooperation between strangers. Perhaps in the former case, some specific mental

---

salient conditions for X to occur. These comments are related to the second distinction: trust could be a personal attitude in the sense that it would be directed at the trusted one, or reside in impersonal thoughts of probability and predictability, or an amalgamation of both. (Imagine A saying, "don't you trust me?" and the interlocutor answering, "Of course I trust you, but I just don't think you can do X," which probably means "I trust your disposition and willingness to do X, but not your capacities to do X.") Some may be tempted to reduce trust to a matter of predictability and interpret the great differences between, say, evaluating the predictability of Abby (a prospective shoplifter), of the police, and the circumstances of Abby paying for goods before leaving the store. This, along with the sunrise and astrological physics, or the daily behavior of the dog, its breed's protective instincts, or its barking, may be differences in types of predictability. This assumes that the fact that we focus on someone's virtue when evaluating the predictability of a person's behavior is only incidental: people are the kind of entities whose behaviors can be predicted by looking at their virtues, among other things. Others may lean toward interpreting trust as a more personal attitude that attaches only to beings who can meaningfully respond to trust, and to conceive predictability as a condition of its rationality. Again, some may want to insist that trust is a composite that cannot be reduced to a single attitude, object (or "focal point" within this object), or calculation of predictability.

Silvers and Francis only minimally typologize the notion of trust and do not dwell on these two distinctions. The trust they are spotlighting attaches to individuals, such as bargainers and caregivers, but it can also take the form of confidence that deals carried out within a climate of trust are likely to be realized. However, moving from one understanding of trust to another is problematic, as I argue in this section.

[29] I owe this example as well as the Humean reference of inductive confidence to Paula Bodington.

states are required for "trust" to take place which are not required in the latter. Indeed, perhaps only certain, consistent behaviors will be enough to secure "trust" in the latter case. It is also possible that in the case of the kind of trust needed to secure a trust-fostering contractarian society, it is not necessary that the trusted parties know that they are being trusted, or at least that they are trusted by anyone in particular. In the case of a PSID trusting her caregiver, on the other hand, this trust may require the caregiver to be aware of it. Alternatively, perhaps trust in caring relations may be imposed upon a PSID who "trusts" her caregiver because she has no other choice but does not "trust" the caregiver in another sense, and thus resists the relationship of trust imposed on her. In such a case, the difference between the imposed trust and the heartfelt trust may be the nature of the entrusted object. In the above case of imposed trust, the object may be the welfare of the disabled person, and in case of the heartfelt trust, it may be the disabled person herself.[30] Such a personal dimension to the relation of trust may not be required for an understanding of trust as qualifying a social climate.

In sum, it is problematic to assume that fostering or hindering one kind of trust would foster or hinder another. I think that the kind of pluralist, relational view of morality that I present in the conclusion of this book helps us to detect the problem, which is to assume that the notion of trust does not fundamentally change, nor is it transferable from one kind of social relation to another. This is evidently problematic when we think that some relations have different normative frameworks. However, even without defending or endorsing such a view, it is easy to be skeptical of the claim that improving trust within caring relations toward PSID is causally connected to improving trust within contractual relations between strangers. We might just as naturally expect that certain spheres of our social lives (such as relations within the family or toward the particularly weak and vulnerable) do not raise the same sort of expectations regarding what object one can entrust to whom.

The fact that trust could be defined in terms of varying dispositions, behaviors, attitudes, motivations, affects, or epistemological components points to a deep notional ambiguity. I cannot explore which account or accounts of trust we ought to adapt in different relational contexts, as it is not necessary to assess whether Silvers and Francis claim that a trust-based and trust-fostering contractarian theory of justice can provide a robust moral status for PSID. I rely on Baier's broad definition of trust as a touchstone concept and make only one important subdivision of kinds of trust: self-regarding and other-regarding. I think this distinction best reveals what I aim to show: justice through trust must either exclude PSID or weaken its claim to be a contractarian theory. Self-regarding trust is the trust that is used instrumentally and

---

[30] The caregiver's responsive attitude to the trust of a person with a profound disability would be different if it is directed at the states of affairs undergone by the person rather than the person herself. For an elaboration on this idea, see Elizabeth Anderson, *Value in Ethics and Economics* (Cambridge: Harvard University Press, 1995).

3.2 The Nature of Trust

valued derivatively to serve the interests of self-interested contractors. Other-regarding trust expresses contractors' other-regarding concern for the well-being of fellow parties in relations of trust, though what is at issue here is whether these relations of trust can correspond to contractual relations.[31]

Let me close this section by clarifying the notions pertaining to the topic of trust and the reasons why the ambiguity of the notion is problematic for Silvers and Francis. I return to the claim that we do not need to understand trust in an other-regarding way. In the next two subsections, I argue that, on a contractarian account, self-regarding trust or instrumental other-regarding trust may constitute all the trust contractarians need to attain social stability and a climate that is favorable to cooperative endeavors. If this is the case, then the robust moral status of PSID is grounded on quite fragile – that is, empirically questionable or overly contingent – bases. In the following section, we will turn to a sturdier, other-regarding notion of trust that Silvers and Francis propose. This trust would provide a better basis for the robust moral status of people with severe disabilities; however, it does not seem to be required in a contractarian account. Further, even if it were, I note in the fourth section of this chapter that many PSID would still not possess the robust moral status-granting capacity to trust, and it seems odd to grant a robust moral status to many of the PSID who would have this capacity because such a capacity does not lie at the heart of *why* we ought to grant them a robust moral status.[32] In the fifth and final section of this chapter, I emphasize that other-regarding trust still matters, but that it matters because of reasons that are unrelated to the contractarian master premises. Within contractarianism, at worst, trust must simply be self-regarding and must be used as a tool of predictability and coercion to make sure trusted people comply with expectations. At best, other-regarding trust may be used as a means to foster a general climate of contractual trust (i.e., trust facilitating cooperative endeavors of all kinds). Even if we assume that fostering self-regarding trust will improve the general contractual trust – which is far from obvious given the particularity of the relations within which self-regarding trust takes place – it would still make other-regarding trust too derivative or contingent to ground the robust moral status of PSID. As stated above, this will be the case unless contractarianism takes the importance of other-regarding concern to justice more seriously, thus abandoning its contractual aspirations.

---

[31] Silvers and Francis do not make this distinction themselves, and they seem to suggest that these two kinds of trust are fungible, which may be correct at the level of how both self- and other-regarding sorts of trust are reflected into similar behaviors and attitudes. Yet it is problematic in terms of explaining whether and how closely these sorts of trust are linked to the social contract tradition. Since this is the main point of tension that I see in their argument, I will take a stand on what exactly I take them to mean by their use of "trust" in the third section of this chapter.

[32] This last argument is not meant to do more than point to an intuitively odd aspect of a trust-based contractarian account of the robust moral status of a PSID, as I am not yet offering an alternative account, the merits and "oddity" of which could be compared with the contractarian one.

3.2.2 *Trust as Self-Regarding*

The trusted person's motivations need not be other-regarding. It is possible to trust someone even though we know that she is purely selfish. Someone may simultaneously have the reputation of being opportunistic and selfish and of being reliable. This sort of individual may in fact be the model bargainer. To deny the name of trust to the attitude directed at her seems unwarranted and fits the idea of "trust as expectation" that is present in Silvers and Francis's argument. If to trust is to accept[33] being placed in a situation of vulnerability vis-à-vis someone who has "power over something one cares about, in the confidence that such power will not be used to harm what is entrusted,"[34] nothing in this definition implies that this confidence must be matched with a belief that the person with power over our well-being cares for us. Consider that A entrusts B to do X, and B stands to lose a significant amount if she does not properly do X (e.g., she will not be paid by A, she will face expensive legal prosecution, etc.). If the consequence of not complying with her obligation is costlier to B than to betray A's trust, then it is neither naive nor foolish of A to trust B, all things being equal.

In this case, A's trust is made rational by the fact that B is self-interestedly motivated to avoid the bad consequences that would ensue from betraying A's trust. Silvers and Francis are right to point out that legal apparatuses guaranteeing cooperation through "rules that must be negotiated, agreed to, and enforced" come with transaction costs,[35] but such an enforcement scheme does not mean that the typical relation of two business partners, indifferent to each other's happiness (other than if this happiness serves them in turn) does not involve trust. B may also acquire the reputation of being trustworthy in order to facilitate future exchanges with other parties who are aware of her reputation of reliability in an equally self-interested way. Other parties may be aware of this motivation, and this is why A should worry if this is B's last promise, or A was only counting on B's self-interested motivation to maintain her reputation for future promise-based exchanges.[36] In sum, trust can be understood prudentially and instrumentally as a means to achieve predictability.

---

[33] While there may be situations where trust is not "accepted" or imposed, Silvers and Francis are not considering such options. One may think of Oliver Wendell Holmes's "bad man" only wishing "to avoid an encounter with the public force" rather than wishing to behave ethically ("The Path of the Law" [1897] 10 Harv L Rev 457, at 458) and coping with, rather than endorsing, legally entrenched trust-fostering norms, as a counterexample. However, the "bad man" has still accepted the relations of trust that are imposed upon him in the sense that he would not infringe them out of a fear of being caught. That much we can trust him with.
[34] Francis and Silvers, "Justice through Trust," at 62. The authors cite Baier's definition.
[35] *Ibid.* at 61, where the authors rely on Francis Fukuyama's work on trust.
[36] However, one could remark that it is common that people who get into the habit of respecting various rules out of fear of sanction or other self-interested and amoral reasons are more likely than not to "stay in character" even when they have a chance to "get away with it." This may be out of habit or because they have developed a virtuous character through the imposition of particular behaviors or, most probably, for both reasons. I am not relying on such a possibility,

One might argue that this trust in "bad men" is of a significantly different nature to other sorts of trust. If the "bad man" did not honor the trust placed in him because he was held to not be responsible for his actions, the trust we would have toward him would be very different from other varieties of trust. For example, if a woman puts a tracking device and camera on her partner and threatens him with great harm if he so much as looks at another woman, then she might "trust" him not to commit adultery, as the cost for him would be too great. "Some trust!" the husband might retort. Perhaps this kind of trust might only be readily recognized as "trust" in the context of less personal relationships.[37]

I think the objection is really that "trust as rational expectation" does not imply that one is expecting particular other-regarding attitudes (as in the example above, love or faithfulness) from someone else. In the above example, the object of the expectation is a behavior: not cheating on one's partner. I grant that this may not be the kind of trust that the wife wants to have in her husband, but I do not believe that this disqualifies it from being classified as trust, although, perhaps this type of trust is of such low value that even calling it "trust" may seem derisory to the wife, who might have intended to mean what faithful lovers generally mean by trust. In that sense, I would also not dispute that "trust as rational expectation" is not a trust befitting certain personal relationships, even though it is still trust according to our definition and, more importantly, it fits plausibly within the theoretical background privileged by contractarianism.

This objection does point to the idea, however, that trust concerning the husband's sincerely faithful attitude to his marriage is more desirable and would generally imply that he can be trusted in terms of behaviors as well. In other words, this suggests that we can use other-regarding trust instrumentally and profitably as it is susceptible to do more for us than self-regarding trust. This line of thought – though empirically challengeable – would also support the claim that to foster other-regarding trust is desirable even within a contractual framework that privileges a self-interested standpoint. However, this would only make other-regarding trust an instrumental tool in the contractarian arsenal and the idea that contractarians would necessarily prefer it over self-regarding trust is questionable. Let me explore why in the next section.

3.2.3 The Benefits of Self-Regarding Trust

I agree with Silvers and Francis that a community of self-interested agents seems less likely to foster trust than a community of agents that are concerned for each other's

---

as it is too approximate and uncertain, and because (more importantly) I am considering the fictional possibility of purely self-interested and systematically opportunistic individuals. But the participants of a real-life bargaining framework based on self-interest alone would measure what are, in practice, the odds that someone would act cooperatively, for whatever reason.

[37] I owe the example of the "trusting" wife to Paula Bodington.

well-being. However, there are good grounds to question this hypothesis or at least the evidence that supports it.

My starting point is the idea that it could be beneficial to agree to play a game – that is, to adhere to certain posited rules that constrain its participants in specific ways – in which we momentarily and restrictively limit our concern toward others. This starting point is probably diametrically opposed to that of Hobbesian or rational-choice contractarianism, which assumes egoism or non-tuism between people who, as Susan Dimock explains, do not have "sufficiently robust preferences for the well-being of others" to motivate them to "act morally just because doing so realizes the good of others."[38] In real-life ordinary bargaining, we may not be asking ourselves "is the person I am contracting with getting a good deal as well?" not because, I suggest, we are fundamentally disinterested in the fate of others and concerned only with our own, but because we are trying to be good bargainers. To play the bargaining game correctly, we may have to silence, to some extent, some other-regarding propensities (e.g., our natural sense of empathy). My second, related claim is that this position may not only be advantageous for ourselves but may also further (self-regarding) trust.

I do not deny that we show concern toward others that is robust enough to motivate actions on our part; I am only considering the plausibility of the view that we should sometimes suspend concern if the relation calls for it. That is, I am not merely saying that we should suspend a parent-like concern in favor of a different sort of concern in certain cases, but rather we should suspend concern altogether, up to a point. It is possible, and it may be moral or fair, to suspend one's concern for another because the bargaining game requires it. The moral demand that bargaining makes on us probably draws its normative force from the respect we owe to ourselves and to others for having chosen to engage in bargaining. In this view, therefore, bargaining may well have an other-regarding component, but it would demand a suspension of this other-regarding component. This other-regarding component may remain latent in the sense that we remain disposed to engage in other-regarding attitudes anew, should our contracting partner fall below a certain threshold of well-being. However, the suspension renders this disposition inactive.

I do not necessarily endorse this view, but it reconciles the idea that self-regarding trust is a good thing with the idea that we are not essentially nor exclusively self-concerned beings. This implies that we could value self-regarding trust without endorsing a restrictive conception of contracting parties as selfish[39] and being in denial of "the human conditions of vulnerability and dependence."[40] Therefore, these flaws cannot be levied against making a central contractarian political and

---

[38] Susan Dimock, "Why All Feminists Should Be Contractarians" (2008) 47:2 Dialogue: Can Phil Rev 273, at 279.
[39] See Francis and Silvers, "Justice through Trust," at 60.
[40] Ibid. at 59.

social use of self-regarding trust, as Silvers and Francis implicitly suggest.[41] The envisaged position is that, in ordinary bargaining situations, we ought not only to suspend excessively paternalistic concern but suspend other-regarding concern altogether. Whatever other-regarding motivation there is, it is at work on another level of the agent's consciousness. This claim implies not only that this is a descriptively more accurate portrait of an agent's psychology in bargaining situations, but also that agents have other-regarding reasons to suspend their other-regarding concern. Said reasons derive from the nature of the bargaining relation.

The idea is that concern is not only (1) inappropriately paternalistic at times but (2) it is always unwelcome in contractual relations, even if it underlies a less paternalistic attitude of respect. Respectful behaviors within such relations can be secured by a conceptual framework only making use of the contractors' self-interest.[42]

Consider how the claim that "real concern is undesirable" resonates with real-life situations of bargaining. Often, once parties have agreed to play a bargaining game, they consider it inappropriate to show or be shown concern, as suspending mutual concern – up to a point – is one of the bargaining rules to which they have agreed. Some business relationships require a mask of indifference to our fellow contractors' personal affairs or welfare, as embodied in the expression "nothing personal – it's just business," or in the Alexandre Dumas quote: "In business, sir, one has no friends, only correspondents."[43] This is why a business partner may be resentful when one references personal problems as an excuse not to perform professional obligations.

However, people invoking their personal circumstances with respect to their welfare expect other-regarding concerns from the other people partaking in their common venture. The expectation of other-regarding concern can be seen as a trump card, in the sense that it suspends the ordinary rules of the game – but it can also be seen as an attempt to cheat if the card was not initially dealt (scenario 1). It is not so if the excuses fall within specific categories that the parties agreed to at the outset (scenario 2), because then one is invoking the normative strength of everyone's initial commitments, rather than expecting everyone's compassion. To illustrate scenario 2, consider an employment contract that makes generous provisions

---

[41] See, *mutatis mutandis*, Jean Hampton, *The Intrinsic Worth of Persons: Contractarianism in Moral and Political Philosophy*, ed., Daniel Farnham (New York: Cambridge University Press, 2007) arguing that "putting oneself first" is compatible with the recognition of the intrinsic worth of oneself and others. See also her "The Wisdom of the Egoist: The Moral and Political Implications of Valuing the Self" (1997) 14:1 Social Phil and Pol'y 21. I elaborate on these ideas in Chapter 6.

[42] I do not think that this would be real respect. Given my attitudinal view of respect, I would identify respect by examining the attitude that underpins the behavior rather than the behavior itself. Here, the attitude is ultimately motivated by self-concern rather than concern or respect toward others. It is not really respect, but rather a prudential and self-interested attitude. The position I am presenting here in favor of self-regarding trust holds that this is all that is needed.

[43] *The Count of Monte Cristo* (Open Road Media, 2014, originally published in 1844), at 583.

for parental leave. For scenario 1, in contrast, consider a small company that must fire 20 of 50 employees and the manager chooses which employees to let go on the basis of seniority. However, employee A argues that she has two young children in school, is a single parent, and so should not be let go because she will not be able to provide for her family. This is different from the parental leave case, as no provision was previously agreed to about giving preference to people with children in case of downsizing. Co-workers may feel cheated if they judge that A is trying to circumvent or ignore the rules of the game that were previously agreed upon. If "special circumstances" trump cards are allowed, employees B, C, and D may also start comparing their well-being, challenges, vulnerabilities, and responsibilities. B is 55 years old and knows that her age will virtually make it impossible for her to find a new job in her field of work. C is young and single but has massive student debt. D has a number of friends depending on her financially, or may be personally invested in her work in a way that being fired would subjectively devastate her in a way that would affect her identity more than it would for A, B, and C. Evaluating whose claim is most worthy of concern is, at the very least, problematic, if not impossible. Different parties – even if we assume they are acting in good faith and consider this conundrum from a detached, impartial point of view – may still disagree.

Further, the last thing bargainers want is their fellow bargainers telling them what the goods they are trading are really worth to them. A key advantage of the traditional understanding of bargaining is that it allows traders to make subjective assessments of the worth of what is being traded. Arguably, it seems to be part of the concept of bargaining that a third party – an outsider to the bargain – could not objectively decide the most desirable outcome of the bargain for all parties involved. Thus understood, bargaining has the advantage of recognizing agents' capacities to choose for themselves – or, rather, the superiority of reaching an agreement over the possibility of settling the agreement on the basis of a substantial theory of goods.

Refraining from calling upon other-regarding concern circumvents the difficulty of prioritizing needs and vulnerabilities. Hence, it seems that it is sometimes best to leave aside evaluations based on other-regarding concern, just as it is sometimes best to allow individuals to plan for their own needs through contracting and choose the level of risks she is willing to take.

The claim that it may be best to leave evaluations based on other-regarding concerns aside is appealing. An obvious objection is to point to the risk of suspending one's concern or empathy for others. Even within bargaining games, suspension of concern may lead to horrific exploitation and dehumanization. We, humans, are skillful at categorizing people in ways that free us from the burden of meeting their needs and addressing their suffering, and theoretical justifications for suspending concern or empathy should be approached with caution. However, I am only presenting a position that supports suspension of concern *within certain limits*. One may still point to the risk of suspending concern, even within those limits. The danger of hardening oneself within these limits or making oneself indifferent to the fate of others is that, even within this space where it is supposedly safe to be ruthless and self-regarding, other people may in fact be owed our concern. There might also be particular and circumstantial limits that we have failed to stipulate. While I find that this criticism is plausible, it is not obvious that the dangers it considers outweigh the benefits provided by suspending concern.[44]

Another criticism of the position that bargaining-facilitating trust can be advantageously based on self-interest is that the bargaining model reflects an adversarial, war-like relationship rather than one that achieves efficiency and respect (which are difficult to measure). As such, this bargaining style may, echoing the familiar feminist criticism of masculine "ideals," reflect a gendered preference. Such a gendered preference may lead to a quick dismissal of the claim that maintaining an underlying and effective other-regarding concern while doing business may be no less efficient and respectful. For example, the movie *Potiche*, directed by François Ozon, centers on Suzanne Pujol, a woman who takes the place of her husband as the head of his company when he becomes sick.[45] Her "maternal" way of doing business – which does not imply naivety and softness, but is characterized by a concern for her employees, rather than the more traditional and adversarial model of management – leads to better results for all parties. The movie ends with Mrs. Pujol moving into the political arena and suggests that her "maternal approach" to management could be equally successful there.

The opposing position insists that mutual concern – of the employees toward management, and of management toward the workforce – would be a disaster: inefficient at best, worsening disagreements at worst, and preventing parties from settling on a narrower terrain of agreement that is constrained by clear bargaining rules. This position holds that it is better for everyone at the outset to behave in an adversarial way that promotes one's own interests. However, it could also be said that indifference may, on the contrary, prevent fruitful negotiations. Putting oneself in another's shoes in a concerned, rather than purely prudential way, may give negotiators insights into the other party's needs (even unexpressed ones) and allow them to propose terms that are more agreeable to all and are more likely to lead to a

---

[44] Notably, because if proper constraints have been established, it seems unlikely that a lack of other-regarding concern would yield terrible results. It is much more likely that, if exploitation occurs, it would not be out of a failure to see that the bargaining framework has flaws, but because of a weakness of will to do something about it. One could answer that this weakness of will may in fact be perpetuated by a bargaining framework that facilitates self-deception about individual or collective other-regarding duties. By contrast, if one is concerned with the well-being of others, then one would more readily become aware of the lacunae of a bargaining framework. However, it could also be said that one can find enough resources in self-interest and autonomy to correct a defective or immoral bargaining framework. Consider Iris Marion Young's "social connection model" to explain why we have the responsibility to help people beyond our nation. She maintains that exploitative structures ought to be corrected, not because of an other-regarding or charitable concern for the exploited, but because of a responsibility generated by the unfairness of a self-interested bargain ("Responsibility and Global Justice: A Social Connection Model" [2006] 23:1 Social Phil and Pol'y 102).
[45] *Potiche* (France: Mandarin Cinéma, 2010).

successful agreement. Indifference can also cause considerable transaction costs, as Silvers and Francis note. It can also foster egocentric or ruthless attitudes that slow or stiffen negotiations and incite parties to be suspicious and to "stick to their guns."[46]

Another argument against grounding bargaining on other-regarding trust or concern is that other-regarding attitudes can be invoked in bad faith. Whatever concern strangers have for each other, it may fail to motivate their actions, especially when their own interests are at stake. Here, it is unnecessary to set out examples of strategic use of other-regarding concern in bad faith; the political and business worlds are replete with them.

In sum, the position that favors building trust on self-interested attitudes would rather base itself on developing bargaining ethics and on correcting and improving the limits beyond which parties should drop the mask of indifference (according to my account). This position may also be based on the motivation to act prudentially in a contractee's welfare because it is in a party's own interest to benefit from this concern (the Hobbesian or rational-choice account) and to develop mechanisms to swiftly modify limits to indifference and to better respond to particular needs – especially basic and urgent ones – should they arise.

An alternative position would rather bet on developing frameworks that filter varieties of other-regarding concern, channeling the right concern at the right time. Both positions reflect assumptions about how self-regarding or other-regarding human beings are, and the sort of bargaining and social contract that would best correspond to, or correct, human nature, as well as determining whether autonomy or concern should be centrally valued.

The position that self-regarding trust is more beneficial than other-regarding trust, and the opposing position, are both reasonably plausible. My point is to show that Silvers and Francis have not discarded the idea that self-regarding trust and the game of mutual disinterest can result in sustainable cooperation, stable compliance, and a productive process. While I agree with them, my reasons differ from their own, as their reasons are in line with their aspiration to remain within the contractarian tradition. They claim that other-regarding trust will ultimately sustain cooperation better than self-interested bargaining. Moreover, this ensures that their argument (and its moral appeal resting, it seems to me, on something more fundamental) is at least partially hostage to an empirical one.

3.2.4 *Trust as Indirectly or Derivatively Other-Regarding*

The attitude of the trusted party could have an indirect, other-regarding dimension that would consist of respecting the trusting party as a chooser. However, such a

---

[46] We will come back to the potential desirability of instrumental "other-regarding" trust in the next section. Here, I wish to make the case that other-regarding trust, instrumental or genuine, is not obviously better than self-regarding trust.

dimension would seem to be compatible with the bargaining model of contract. On this account, there would be no need to appeal to a trust-based model of respect to explain that kind of other-regarding concern on the contractor's part. I will now explain what I mean by respecting other people *qua* choosers and why this attitude would be indirectly other-regarding.

Self-interested, rational individuals can detect that other individuals are like them in many ways. In particular, they can detect that they have similar needs, worries, powers, and bargaining capacities. If these parties are self-interested and rational – all things being equal – it becomes possible to cooperate with them to strike a mutually beneficial deal. Presented like this, the agent who recognizes that other people are, like herself, autonomous choosers, valuers, or project-pursuers[47] can still be entirely selfish and use this knowledge to pursue immoral ends such as exploitation. For example, the mutually beneficial deal could be "if you become my slave, at least you will not starve to death." However, in the argument I am contemplating here, there is more than an opportunistic recognition of other people's capacities. Closely associated with the detection of those capacities is respect, reverence, concern, or some other-regarding attitude toward the being that possesses them. This represents a jump from a prudential reasoning of instrumentalizing others to a moral attitude toward others that requires justification.

For example, one might argue that it is a condition or implication of an agent's autonomy that she would give particular normative weight to the autonomy of others. More generally, one may think that moral agents ought to be concerned with beings who share their plight and their need for certain goods. My point here is not to address issues about the stringency or effectiveness of such concerns, but simply to point out that these attitudes would be other-regarding.

However, I would like to point to a middle ground that implies a less than fully other-regarding attitude, but that still implies an other-regarding attitudinal dimension. Essentially, A indirectly respects B by the very fact of bargaining with B. Even if A is indifferent to B's general well-being, and even if it cannot be said that A "cares" or is "concerned" for B, A's recognition of B's status *qua* bargainer/chooser implies that A has some other-regarding attitudes toward B, even though these attitudes are initially and ultimately rooted in self-interested bargaining.

For instance, A (as an individual or a country) could abide by a certain agreement (or treaty) in a way that benefits B (as an individual or country) and thwarts A's own short-term interests. A seems to be benefitting B in a way that is not self-serving. Although A may be able to explain her reasons in an entirely prudential and self-interested way, she is still engaging in an other-regarding frame of mind in fulfilling her obligations toward B and, indeed, this frame of mind may be necessary to perform some of those obligations. If A is not really concerned about B and is only

---

[47] See, e.g., Loren E. Lomasky, *Persons, Rights, and the Moral Community* (New York: Oxford University Press, 1997).

acting in a way that serves her own interests, and these actions incidentally create outcomes that seem to reflect a concern for B, then she may not be able to properly fulfill her part of the deal. This scenario applies particularly well in the case of someone hired to perform care work. Consider the case of a babysitter who throws herself in front of a car to save a child from being run over. She risks her life doing this, and we can question whether she would have acted this way if she had time to reflect on the risks involved. However, she was "in the moment" of the performance of her contractual obligation to another, and so her own interest receded to make room for the interest of the child she was obligated to care for. A similar example – not involving caring work – would be the case of a soldier risking her life in the course of her duty.

An objection to this position is that, in these cases, the agent is simply being irrational or is deluded. Unless she is concerned for the fate of other entities (such as the child or the child's parents, her fellow soldiers or her country) or unless she is trying to be virtuous, the agent is just doing a poor job at acting in her self-interest, rather than doing a good job at acting in an other-regarding way. One may respond by claiming that the agent could not properly fulfill her part of the bargain without engaging in less than strictly self-regarding thought. One could also point out that such a temporary – if not ultimately – other-regarding attitude is quite common within a bargaining culture, even one that seems to embrace agents' primarily self-regarding attitudes. Once someone has agreed to build your house, or cut your hair, or babysit your child, or oversee a business or humanitarian project, there is a sense that the good worker – one who takes her job seriously – is not merely counting down the hours until she can leave, or telling herself that she is only doing this job because of the money. Of course, this may not hold true for all activities. Certainly, the more alienating the work, the more likely one may have exclusively self-regarding thoughts about it. Yet alienating work may be indicative of a failure to secure a self-interested deal or may suggest exploitation, rather than indicating the incompatibility of bargaining with indirectly other-regarding concern.

Another similar argument is that to have concern for oneself implies having some other-regarding attitudes. Someone could abide by the rules of a community of choosers who recognize each other as such out of self-interest. In this context, taking oneself seriously out of self-concern implies that one also takes their community seriously and, it follows, some concern for the members of that community.

Lastly, a major reason for encouraging a culture in which mutual other-regarding concern underlies trusting relations is that it appears to be beneficial for everyone. It encourages trusting in other people's reliability without requiring assurance of their compliance, diminishing transaction costs. In addition to a quantifiable advantage, it provides an emotional benefit – to do business with opportunistic strangers, like negotiating with enemies, is more emotionally intensive than dealing with people who are concerned with us, even limitedly. And in many cases, this other-regarding concern can go so far as to encourage parties to seek a nonexplotative agreement (i.e., a result that is not merely strictly mutually beneficial but that takes into account how well each party is doing and how much each is benefitting from the bargain). Silvers and Francis also underline the stability that such an other-regarding trust provides. All of these advantages make other-regarding trust instrumentally desirable.

The other-regarding component of A's attitude would not be the result of mere accident, inadvertence, or irrationality. Instead, it would be an important, perhaps necessary, part of bargaining. The day-to-day basics of many jobs require at least a partial reduction of self-interest and an increase of other-regarding interest, such as taking customers' or patients' needs seriously. This requires endorsing certain other-regarding attitudes and taking one's vocation seriously, which demands losing sight of the potential benefit and relating to one's art or profession as per the standards of that trade or profession. This may reflect an empirical fact about the way humans conceive of their roles in a psychological sense, but the operation of a contract sometimes does indeed require us to endorse an other-regarding view – or at least we should adopt such a view if we wish to fulfill our contract in the best possible way. This account would also explain why A's concern for others would be limited to the kind of other-regarding concern that is required by A's role, and would fit more naturally with the notion of contracting than with the idea that A is just more fundamentally concerned with the fate of others. A's other-regardingness would be limited to (1) the other-regardingness that is implied in considering the other party as a bargainer and (2) the other-regardingness specifically contracted for. Point (2) is the idea that, while executing her part of the deal that serves B's interest, A will adopt a less than strictly self-regarding attitude. This leads us to a picture of self-interested parties who are willing to adopt some limited, other-regarding attitudes that are nevertheless ultimately grounded on self-interest. Such a picture fits comfortably with the notion of contract, which requires both a certain degree of self-interest from the parties as well as some cooperative dimensions.

So whether trusting parties are indirectly respecting each other and paying tribute to their respective autonomies by implicitly recognizing each other's capacity to bargain, or whether they are endorsing other-regarding attitudes, they are not ultimately concerned for others. That is, their attitudes are ultimately self-regarding or anchored in self-interest. Therefore, this sort of other-regarding attitude is not a real concern, as it is contingent upon serving the agent's own interests. This indirect other-regarding trust is compatible with the bargaining paradigm and a culture of self-interest.

What is the implication of a possibility of "self-regarding other-regarding trust" (and its potential desirability within a contractarian framework) for Silvers and Francis's conclusions? They try to pit contracts against trust[48] in a way that seeks to oppose bargain-like contract with trust-based and trust-engendering contract. However, I have been highlighting the position that trust need not be an

---

[48] See Francis and Silvers, "Justice through Trust," at 61.

other-regarding attitude.[49] As a result, while Silvers and Francis are right about the benefits of trust, it is not obvious why the same benefits could not be obtained from a self-regarding understanding of trust compatible with the bargaining paradigm of contractualism.

It is possible that Silvers and Francis may prefer their trust-engendering contractual theory of justice over a bargaining-like contractual theory because of its potential benefits. It is plausible that a trust-engendering social contract, based on other-regarding trust, would yield some benefits that a bargain-like social contract based on self-regarding trust alone would not. Notably, there is the general, underlying knowledge that the members of this bargaining community do not care for each other in a way that is not ultimately self-serving. This is not the sort of community that encourages social connectedness and feelings – like solidarity and a sense of belonging – that are bound to enrich the individual's life. We simply crave more genuinely other-regarding relations within our personal and communal lives, not just seemingly concerned, affable and polite interactions with fellow contractors eager to create a friendly atmosphere among otherwise self-interested bargainers. A community fundamentally rooted in individual self-interest would not prevent isolation from other human beings, a lack of belonging or loneliness. It may even be a somewhat threatening community to be part of, and it would seem alien to any known society.

However, the conceptual possibility of a society made of strictly self-interested bargainers does limit the claims that Silvers and Francis can make against the bargain-like model of contract, since relations of trust between self-interested parties are possible and probably more beneficial than they imply. Thus, it becomes less obvious that the bargain-like model of social contract – even though it does not provide the benefits of belonging and community as well as the trust-based model does – provides these benefits indirectly, as well as providing other benefits directly, and in a better way than the trust-based model. Notably, one may challenge Silvers and Francis's empirical assumption about the stability and security offered by both sorts of social contract theories.

In this section, I have shown that "self-interested" or "indirectly other-regarding" trust is already quite beneficial to contractors and to the making of a social contract. In particular, this trust seems to provide the means to "promot[e] stable compliance with mutual expectations" and "stabiliz[e] cooperation"[50] in a satisfactory way. It seems plausible that the inclusion of PSID to this contract would promote trust even further, but this is an empirical hypothesis, and may not prove correct.[51] Even if the inclusion of PSID did significantly further trust between able-minded people, the

---

[49] Ibid.
[50] Ibid. at 60.
[51] For instance, while able-bodied people may be relieved to see that social arrangements take care of PSID's well-being, and may even note that PSID "trust" they will be treated well, they may still not see how those arrangements secure trust in their own lives, affairs, and

inclusion of PSID as parties to the social contract would come at a great cost. The fact that they stand almost exclusively at the receiving end of the mutually beneficial relationship that is central to the idea of a fair contract makes them very costly. To call human beings "costly" or "expensive" may (rightly) seem repugnant and distressing, but these reasons have probably little to do with the fact that we are missing facts about their "profitability," such as the fact that not abusing the trust of PSID warrants a reputation or climate of constancy and trustworthiness, both at the individual and collective level.[52]

In sum, this section has provided grounds to question (1) the idea that the bargaining model does not rely on trust (which is what Silvers and Francis imply when they pit those "concerned to facilitate a culture of trust" against those "seeking their mutual self-interest"[53]) although this trust is not based on other-regarding feelings; and (2) the hypothesis that a trust based on other-regarding feelings will do a better job at securing agreements, comforting expectations regarding other people's behaviors,[54] and facilitating the trade of one's liberties for social cooperation.[55]

Despite my arguments above, I do not deny that a strong case can be made in favor of other-regarding concern or trust being crucial components of our moral and political lives. It is evident that such a trust – paradigmatically exemplified by the trust that exists between a child and a parent – has its virtues, which self-regarding trust does not seem to have. Instead, my question is whether these virtues are best expressed in a contractual theory? Silvers and Francis are probably right to assert that justice is a matter of encouraging not only self-regarding, but also other-regarding trusting relations, mutual dependence, and sustainable relationships.[56] But is this a contractual matter? This is the topic of the next section.

3.3 OTHER-REGARDING TRUST AND THE SOCIAL CONTRACT

Silvers and Francis propose an understanding of social contract that takes place within and reinforces a culture (or climate) of trust.[57] This section considers whether the notion of trust – and, more particularly, trust based on other-regarding concern that Silvers and Francis propose – is indeed linked to the notion of a social

---

negotiations. In other words, they imagine that the trust cementing many of their social interactions takes place within a different moral/political sphere than the one where certain vulnerable people are placed to benefit from certain special protections. This hypothesis, too, relies on an empirical wager that may be misguided.

[52] See Francis and Silvers, "Justice through Trust," at 68.
[53] Ibid. at 68.
[54] Ibid. at 60.
[55] Ibid. at 75.
[56] Ibid. at 68.
[57] As mentioned, Silvers and Francis take trust to be not only the result of a social contract but also a condition for it – that is, "a foundational element in bargaining itself" (*ibid.* at 67).

contract, or whether the desirability of trust may be better explained in other ways. While I have no doubt that trust is indeed important, I explain this importance by reference to other traits of the human condition. Although Silvers and Francis do consider human traits (such as vulnerability and dependency),[58] they go further than claiming that other-regarding trust is particularly important. Indeed, they interpret the social contract as being essentially trust-based and trust-engendering.

A potential criticism of their position is that the notions of trust and contract are not conceptually linked or are not as closely intertwined as Silvers and Francis present them to be. That being the case, a certain kind of trust may well lead to the social inclusion of PSID and to granting these persons a robust moral status, but not on a contractarian basis. This criticism can be interpreted in a strong and a weak way. But before I present these two versions, let me state what I understand Silvers and Francis to be saying about (1) how trust and the social contract are connected and (2) the nature of trust, as their understanding of trust differs from the concepts I presented as plausible contractarian options in Sections 3.2.2–3.2.4.

3.3.1 Preliminary Clarifications: Trust as "Other-Regarding" and as "Inherent" and Not as Merely Instrumental to the Social Contract

While no one questions that the social contract engenders *some* sort of trust, Silvers and Francis suggest that trust is central to (rather than part of) the social contract. As such, they object to a specific, widespread, contractarian understanding of trust as instrumental. Rather than seeing trust as merely one of the goals of the social contract, or as a contractual means to achieve its other goals, they see trust as inherently interlaced with the social contract. For Silvers and Francis, the social contract is not an event that uses or incidentally builds or capitalizes on trust: it consists *of* building trust.[59] The trust fostered by this social contract is also the motivating force that drives social cooperation and cohesion, by contrast (say) to sustained self-interest and a legitimate authority backed up by a potential use of force, which we could call a "Hobbesian trust."[60]

Another dimension of trust contemplated by Silvers and Francis is that it appears to be other-regarding. While it seems that they want to talk of "trust" more generally, as they seek to contrast their conception of trust with that of the "Hobbesian trust," they are forced to exclude strictly self-regarding and instrumental trust. Their account arguably echoes a virtue-based one: the climate of trust they have in mind

---

[58] Ibid. at 59.
[59] Ibid. at 74.
[60] In a way, the Hobbesian does not trust the person with whom she is dealing as much as she relies on state authority to intervene should her fellow bargainer defect from her engagements. I write "in a way" because it can still be said that she "trusts" her fellow bargainer, but this trust is ultimately grounded on something "outside" of that bargainer, which would not be the case, for instance, if she was relying on the bargainer's virtue.

is one where people are trustworthy, and where this "virtue" should be fostered, and not just as an instrument to serve individual opportunism. However, their account remains contractual since this "virtue" is desirable only because it serves social cooperation and, for that reason, it is desired by the parties to the social contract.[61] The virtue of trustworthiness implies that someone will not try to opportunistically escape her obligations – by, for instance, finding some sort of legal loophole – as a systematically and strictly rational, self-interested agent would. A defender of a "Hobbesian trust" would say that satisfying the other party's expectation by not tricking her is something that can also be explained in egoistic terms (e.g., the desire to establish a reputation so that one may facilitate future deals). However, when we think of someone as virtuously trustworthy (i.e., when we think of trustworthiness as a virtue), we do not consider one's motivation to live up to the expectations placed on her to be purely self-interested. Rather, we see it as an attempt to perform in a way that an ideally trustworthy agent would. However, does this ideal of trustworthiness imply other-regarding concern? Is the virtuously trustworthy individual "other-regardingly" trustworthy?

On a definition of trustworthiness that is focused on predictability or expectations, this does not seem to be the case. For instance, while one may be a "person of her word" because this is an ideal reputation to achieve (rather than because the Sovereign has the power to constrain her), this does not indicate that this trustworthy individual will necessarily have concern for others. No aspect of being "a person of one's word" implies that one would feel the compulsion to "give one's word" in an other-regarding way. That would involve other motivations – and perhaps other virtues – but not necessarily trustworthiness. As we saw, there can be an other-regarding dimension to trust. But one could suggest that, when we speak of "other-regarding trust," we conflate different notions that are not necessarily analytically connected. Instead, "other-regarding trust" is a shorthand for trust regarding an entrusted object which must be treated – in order for trust to be honored – in an other-regarding way, or with an other-regarding attitude. This is reflected in Baier's definition of trust as the "accepted vulnerability to another person's power over something one cares about in the confidence that such power will not be used to harm what is entrusted."[62] It so happens that certain entrusted objects (say, oneself *qua* lover) will be harmed if they are not related to in an other-regarding way. Some may insist on keeping the notion of trust distinct from other-regarding concern, simply because it may lead us astray to suggest that a trustworthy individual must engage in other-regarding attitudes toward entrusted objects.

A counter-argument holds that when we think of a trustworthy person, we naturally expect that this person will care for the trusting party's well-being. The

---

[61] I am not strictly saying that their account is a virtue-based one, since the value of this virtue is contingent upon contractual thinking. However, the fact that it is easily – if not best – understood by reference to a virtue (rather than to a merely opportunistically developed trait) gives us a further insight into their conception of trust and helps us to establish whether it is self- or other-regarding. This is a distinction, I repeat, that they themselves do not make.

[62] See Baier, "Trusting People," at 152.

trusted party may not care for the entrusted object in an other-regarding way but may care about the one-trusting in an other-regarding way. To put this another way, the trusted party will be concerned for the trusting party and interested in improving her well-being within the boundaries defined by the terms of their trust. We can see this understanding of trust at work when we tell a friend that "I trust that you will repay the loan that I gave you," or "you can trust me: I will repay this loan." We can distinguish these from the general statement that "we trust banks." The former is a richer understanding of trust, as it analytically incorporates some other-regarding elements. It would mean that if the trusted party does not have an other-regarding attitude underlying the discharge of her obligations as the trusted party, she will not be trustworthy. Thus, the relation to which she is a party is not really one of trust, but rather one of sheer predictability. However, it seems to me that this is only the case within certain relations of trust – paradigmatically, the one taking place alongside or within a relation of care between a parent and a child. Elements of other-regarding concern, valuing or motivation toward the trusting party or the entrusted object (which may be the party herself, or some aspects of her life, or expectations of future actions involving her) are not necessary for all kinds of trusting relations. However, in many relations where we trust someone, we will be more trusting if we are convinced that the trusted party has our well-being at heart rather than just her own, that she cares about us, or that she respects us in a strong, other-regarding sense, for instance, if she believes it is imperative that she does not treat us as a mere means.

The problem that this causes for Silvers and Francis is that there is a need for a substantial bridge between the trust taking place with PSID and the trust required by a social contract, otherwise fostering the former may not improve the latter. If we limit Silvers and Francis's argument to self-regarding trust, it would not succeed at including PSID, even though they can enter relations of trust. This is because, while PSID can enter relations of trust, Silvers and Francis's argument only works to explain why – once they are *already* parties to such relations – entrusted agents should live up to their expectations. But why would contractors enter into relations of trust with PSID in the first place? (Or why would they respond to the unilaterally "imposed" trust of people with disabilities, or endorse the role of one-trusted when they are accidentally confronted with this obligation?) We need to add some noncontractual ingredient to this picture or to tell a more complex contractual story, as Silvers and Francis do, when they state:

> Trust carries not only an element of risk but also an element of anticipatory confidence. What better way to gain faith in others' willingness to be fair, and thus to be induced to cooperate with them, than by observing their willingness to commit and honor commitments to people unable to proffer material incentives or impose penalties, or by learning of their reputation for doing so?[63]

---

[63] See Francis and Silvers, "Justice through Trust," at 69.

This quote shows how Silvers and Francis use trust simultaneously as a tool of predictability and as a vehicle for other-regarding attitudes. Instead of justifying the position that we would engage in relations of trust with PSID on the basis of their robust moral status (which would then need to be justified on some other grounds), people with these disabilities are held to have a robust moral status because engaging in relations of trust with them – the group most defenseless against a breach of trust and the easiest to exploit – shows how trustworthy we fundamentally are. They use trusting relations with people with severe disabilities as a way to promote certain virtues which, in turn, promote social cooperation. However, it is not clear that this conclusion has more to do with trustworthiness than some sort of other-regarding concern. If I say: "I treat a vulnerable person well; doesn't that show that I would be trustworthy toward you?" I am probably referring to two different virtues. What I really mean is that "I am good/caring/generous toward a vulnerable person; doesn't that show that I am generally virtuous and therefore, you may expect me to be trustworthy to you as well?" I could also mean that the trusting relations that I have with disabled people are infused with *other-regarding* trust, which makes me the sort of agent whose trustworthiness is special: it is underlaid by an other-regarding concern from which you, potential fellow contractor, would also benefit.

One argument against such a bridge would be to insist on the particularity of role-based relations. For example, one could answer the question asked in the previous paragraph as follows: "No, it shows that you are a good caregiver, but I still expect you to be a ruthless negotiator." Indeed, demonstrating a virtuous character through one kind of relation or life activity does not necessarily correlate to a globally virtuous character. I do not conclude that Silvers and Francis are mistaken to connect one's propensity to other-regarding concern, trustworthiness, or a composite notion of other-regarding trust toward PSID with a propensity to exhibit similar virtues within other relations, notably socially cooperative endeavors that are central to the social contract tradition. Rather, I am suggesting that this connection must still be argued for and I have reservations about it that are based on the plurality of relations (and of the attitudes, virtues, or dispositions – including trustworthiness – that apply to different relations). As a result, though I agree with Silvers and Francis that valuing other-regarding attitudes (including responses to trust) toward PSID is essential for explaining their robust moral status, I find it risky to ground this robust moral status on the fact that the "other-regarding trust" we would show them is, in turn, connected to the kind of trust that contractarians are after.

In conclusion, the sort of trust whose compatibility with the social contract I explore here has two properties: it is (1) other-regarding (i.e., it is underlain by other-regarding concern),[64] and (2) seen as an inherent, rather than an incidental, part of contracting.[65]

3.3.2 *Other-Regarding Trust Is Not So Closely Intertwined with the Social Contract*

A weak version of this claim (or criticism) would be that other-regarding trust and the social contract are not conceptually necessary to one another. A stronger version of this criticism would be that the notion of other-regarding trust and the notion of contract are incompatible. The former would adulterate Silvers and Francis's version of contractarianism, as it can then be compared (and potentially, unfavorably compared) to the alternative bargaining model, as I did in the previous section. The latter criticism poses a more serious obstacle to their claim that the social contract can be linked to other-regarding trust. Something fundamental about the notion of contract – whether one between self-interested parties or one between other-regarding parties – prevents it from being a manifestation of other-regarding concern or trust.

If agents are already other-motivated, why would they need to make a contract? Silvers and Francis would probably respond by saying that this question supposes a view of contract as an enforcement mechanism (to secure trust between initially distrustful parties) rather than as "outcomes of processes of developing trust."[66] The problem could then be posed as: why would these processes assume a contractual form? Or, in the stronger form of the criticism: can these processes assume a contractual form? In other words, can we meaningfully use the concept of contract to connote such processes?

There are two main reasons to formulate processes of other-regarding trust in a contract-like way, though before I address these reasons, I note that it is not

---

[64] At any rate, I will take Silvers and Francis's argument as an occasion to discuss whether the endeavor of marrying the social contract and other-regarding trust is promising. If they mean to do something else than that, I am either not sure that (1) there is not a confusion of virtues at work or (2) they are not falling back on purely self-interested trust, which is insufficient to include all PWD, at least as per the logic of their argument. Another reason why it is worth discussing other-regarding trust is that I believe that other-regarding attitudes are key in understanding the robust moral status of people with severe disabilities, and I am therefore interested to make my argument progress in the direction that I find the most promising, to see what would – and what would not – be the best framework to give expression to an other-regarding trust and the other-regarding concern underlying it. It also seems structurally sensical to go through the varieties of trust (self-regarding, derivatively, and ultimately other-regarding) that can sustain the social contract and the contractual role of PSID. In any case, I think that my attribution of views to Silvers and Francis is fair but, were I misguided, I would claim to utilize a reasonable reading of them as a heuristic foil (at times) and ally (at others).

[65] In other words, while the Hobbesian also thinks that the social contract aims at social cooperation, she does not suppose that trust is necessarily the way to secure it. She sees the social contract as rational bargaining, and only contingently as trust-building.

[66] See Francis and Silvers, "Justice through Trust," at 61.

immediately clear how either reason makes meaningful use of the notion of contract. By meaningful, I mean that the notion of contract must add a conceptual element to a discussion of trust that is not already implicit, and that this element must plausibly be called "contractual." This term implies that a stipulative definition of "contract" would not do, as the idea of contract within social contract theory includes specific definitional elements. Silvers and Francis do dispute these elements, and I take them to be saying that the object of a social contract is to create institutions (or more generally, a social context) which facilitate particular instances of (self- and other-regarding) trust, constancy, or "stable compliance with mutual expectations" that stand outside of an adversarial negotiating framework between self-interested parties, as well as (to stem from and reinforce) a culture of trust that includes an affective dimension of bonding and other-regarding concern, and a disposition to depend upon (and be depended upon by) others.[67] Do these elements imply some expression of binding uncoerced will, which seems to be the common denominator of any plausible definition of contract?[68]

First, let us consider the idea that an agreement or a contract would further reinforce other-regarding trust. It is evident why an enforceable contract will put self-interested parties' minds at ease and allow for (self-regarding) trust, but it is unclear how the contractual form would itself buttress other-regarding trust. If contracts are merely expressions of preexisting relations of trust, or of renewed statements of trust, or of the parties' intentions to abide by, preserve, or augment these other-regarding attitudes, then what exactly do they do (and how do they do it) if they add nothing to these relations of trust? Alternatively, if they multiply or (re)assert them more boldly, can these assertions or statements be considered – in any way – contracts?[69] The notions of assertion and of other-regarding trust, rather than that of contract, seem to explain why a "contract" would further reinforce trust.

---

[67] *Ibid.*
[68] Sustaining social cooperation fairly may be the goal of social contract theory – as Silvers and Francis point out – but it is not necessarily the goal of all contracting: one may contract with a killer. Also, I see no reason to question their comments on the history of social contract theory concluding that contract theory has long been concerned with creating a "protective social order" since we are all vulnerable (see my discussion of a more traditional, rational-choice form of contractualism in the previous chapter) rather than to be a bargain between mutually disinterested parties (*ibid.* at 60, 74–75). However, these *goals* are not the contract itself, but its object. It is through the expression of binding, uncoerced will that they are attained.
[69] One possible answer is that they are promises, and in that sense, a binding expression of will. However, this would give the social contract a unilateral feel that is not in line with the characteristics of mutuality and collectiveness that are not only attached to the tradition of social contract, but that Silvers and Francis do not wish to let go of either. In any case, this promise would be binding because of the autonomy of the party who made it. Yet that leaves it up to the party to promise something other than trust. If we are to base the social contract on the spontaneous promise of other-regarding "trustability," then we need to say more about trust and, it seems to me, to discuss why trust matters, within or outside of a contractualist framework.

The second potential justification for "contractualizing" other-regarding trust is a rather practical one. Contract is a useful instrument to clarify the content of our obligations and avoid the costs that result from confusion, redundancy of work, etc. It does seem that contracting as a form of making clear plans, channeling our efforts, and so on, quite usefully provides predictability and increases efficiency. However, I think that this justification can be understood in two different ways, and neither one seems to ultimately require the binding expression of will.

In the first case, the contract is between parties who already trust each other, and so the agreement looks more like planning than contracting; the binding character of the planning would not be contract-like.[70] Consider a case of planning that is underlaid by mutual concern – such as fraternal love – such as plans that a brother and his sister make to go fishing together on the weekend. Since the interests of the parties converge – ensuring each other's happiness – there is no reason why the plan would not be easily altered to accommodate each sibling's schedule. For example, the sister understands that her brother has too much work and cannot get away from the city at a certain time, etc. Here, this agreement seems to do away with the binding dimension of contract, or at best, to make it contingent on serving the best interests of the parties. However, a contract that is not binding is not much of a contract.

In the second case, the contract takes place between parties who do not trust each other, but who contract for the well-being of someone who trusts each of them. For instance, a mother contracts with a baker for the well-being of her son, who will eat the bread she buys from the bakery. Here, we should not confuse the categories of people with whom we would not need such a binding agreement (the mother and her son) and with whom we need a binding agreement because of their devotion to each other's welfare is far from secure (the contractual relation between the baker and the mother). Once we distinguish these two categories, it seems that the former does rely on other-regarding trust but does not really need the notion of contract to secure an already existing trust, while the latter does need the notion of contract precisely because there is no (or not enough) trust and because this contract is based on self-regarding concern alone. This distinction is fairly obvious: feelings toward my children are evidently different from feelings toward the people with whom I contract for the well-being of my children. However, it is important to distinguish between these two categories because, if we talk of both relationships in the same breath, it can be tempting to conclude from the fact that contractual agreements indirectly serve trusting relations that we include other-regardingness in our understanding of this contract. One can easily understand that the former relation is other-regarding, but not contractual, and that the latter is contractual, but not other-regarding.

---

[70] It can be contingent upon the fact that, as things unfold, it still best serves the interests of all parties involved. Without enforcement, why would it be otherwise? Not because parties will naturally abide, for abiding's sake or for the sake of the other parties. Other-regarding concern toward other parties may indeed justify the position *not* to abide.

This discussion leads me to conclude that, while it is easy to see how an enforceable contract can improve trust between mutually disinterested parties, it is not as easy to see how a contractual agreement would, in itself, play a role in improving other-regarding trust. I am not claiming that this may never be the case. Instead, I am suggesting that, in many cases of pseudo-contractual processes that foster other-regarding trust, the notions of asserting or clarifying relations (rather than contracting) actually foster trust, and contracts serving these trusting relationships do not necessarily take place between the parties to those relationships.

One final reason to be suspicious of a marriage between contract and the mutual concern that underlies certain trusting relationships is that it could corrupt such relations. The notion of contract – that is, the binding expression of wills founded upon the respect for the parties' autonomy – provides contracting agents with motivations that may distort rather than reinforce other-regarding and concerned motivations. For example, consider how awkward and uncomfortable discussions about prenuptial agreements can be. It is not unimaginable that such discussions eventually threaten some marriages. This might be because the contractual aspect of marriage has nothing to do with the other-regarding, loving relationship which is (typically) the prime aspect of marriage. When a romantic partnership is broken down into its practical financial elements, the parties might be divided between their contractual, self-interested selves, and their united partnership. This marital relationship is particularly complex because the welfare of each separate party is fused with the success of the common venture, yet a romantic commitment often implies that each party shall/should put the welfare and happiness of the other before their own. Notice how, in this scenario, the other-regarding aspect of marriage does not need a contract, while the financial contract contemplates separation (i.e., the failure of the other-regarding aspect of marriage) and incites the parties to assume the self-regarding stance of their future divorced-self. In my view, the fact that marriage has both other-regarding attitudinal aspects and self-interested contractual ones does not suggest that we are dealing here with an other-regarding contract (no more than we can conflate the relationship between a mother and her son with the relationship between the mother and the baker). On the contrary, these different dimensions point to two different – potentially incompatible – relations.

Not all relations based on other-regarding trust may be corrupted in similar ways, but certainly many would be. Consider contracts between friends and family. Silvers and Francis could answer that this corruption only arises because I assume that the contract asks the parties to take a self-regarding stance that is incompatible with their other-regarding one (such as the engaged couple who are asked to put themselves in the shoes of their future divorced selves to reach to a prenuptial agreement). Of course, some other contracts – especially the social contract – can be other-regarding and can ask the parties to take an other-regarding stance.[71]

---

[71] Here is an illustration of the sort of response that Silvers and Francis might provide to this criticism. Some, like Onora O'Neill, have criticized the intense multiplication of forms and

However, a contract – even one that takes into account the fact that human beings live vulnerable lives of mutual dependence and recognizes that fact in its provisions – would still require parties to determine what is most beneficial to their own (other-regarding) selves and to set the terms they would like themselves and others to be bound by, thereby presuming that all of the parties distrust each other. This is in spite of the general understanding that everyone (i.e., each party) is capable of other-regarding concern and craves other-regarding trust. Appealing to a contractual process seems to be an admission of distrust compatible with the idea that we want to create the opportunity for trusting relationships through this contract between distrustful parties. Again, the other-regarding aspects of the mother–son relationship are not somehow passed on to the mother–baker relationship simply because the latter serves the former.

As I noted in the previous section, this position does not deny the picture of contractors (and human beings, generally) as more other-regarding than the rational-choice or Hobbesian models of social contract theory would suggest. On the contrary, human beings live in relationships of trust all their lives – as family, friends, and community members – which suggests that such relations are central to human life. Instead, the question is whether the social contract can, should, or does constitute such a relationship.

3.4 CAN ALL PSID TAKE PART IN TRUSTING RELATIONSHIPS?

Silvers and Francis understand trusting and being trustworthy in a way that does not imply "sophisticated ratiocination." Most vulnerable humans know when it is safe to put their welfare in the hands of another or, if they stand at the trusted end of the

procedures to ensure that parties have consented in medical contexts (*Autonomy and Trust in Bioethics* [Cambridge: Cambridge University Press, 2002]). However, instead of being an expression of trust, these numerous, formalized expressions of autonomy cultivate *distrust*. If you must sign a form before you do anything, it puts you in a position where you could be blamed for trusting, rather than rewarded for not putting yourself in a vulnerable position. Silvers and Francis would say that *this* sort of contract is primarily aimed at protecting the parties' "atomistic" autonomy in a way that already presumes that contracts do not reflect trust but rather distrust, which is what Silvers and Francis challenge. If we think that contracts reflect trust, we instead suggest that the contract can stipulate that the patient can trust the doctor and that the institutional framework should ensure that the doctor is reliable, so that the parties can afford dependency. This would be the sort of contract that encourages dependency, vulnerability, and trust.

I have been questioning how much of a "contract" (properly speaking) that assertion of trust would be. I am also suggesting that the aspects that would be binding expressions of will (i.e., contractual) may be indicative of distrust. For instance, a patient may fear that the doctor would fail to suggest an experimental, very expensive treatment, and a doctor may fear being sued. Lastly, I will suggest that the fact that contracts emphasize the value of the contractors' autonomy undermines the value of trust by making it incident to or contingent upon the contract, and undermines the needs of people in trusting relationships or other caring-type relationships (like doctor–patient relationships).

trusting relationship, how to earn that trustworthiness. As Silvers and Francis state, "[s]mall children can sense the consequences of being inconstant, unreliable, or dishonest – that is, of being untrustworthy – well enough to be deterred by them."[72] Even animals, they continue, can "learn what behaviors they must exhibit to gain and hold the other's trust."[73]

One problem is that this ground for being a subject of justice excludes those people who are unable to be actively part of a trusting relationship, even at the receiving (or trusting) end. While this is likely an extremely small group, individuals who are incapable of (giving or receiving) trust certainly exist.[74] For instance, disabilities or mental illnesses can leave people in a vegetative state, or in a state that otherwise impedes their capacity to express trust, such as advanced stages of Alzheimer's. Some other conditions, such as psychopathology, deprive an otherwise intelligent person of the ability to relate to other human beings in an other-regarding way. For instance, a psychopath may opportunistically trust others, but only in a self-regarding way – that is, she may only be able to superficially "grasp" the motivations or the behaviors of the person she trusts.[75] Do we want to exclude all such individuals from the ambit of justice? I should note here that, if the capacity to trust was a sufficient rather than a necessary condition for inclusion, this group (people unable to trust) would not necessarily be excluded, but their inclusion would depend on whether there are other plausible grounds for including them.

The fact that Silvers and Francis's argument may not cover all PSID (and other people unable to take part in trusting relationships) is not a criticism of their argument. On the contrary, I want to highlight that their argument covers a significant portion of PSID. So significant is the segment of PSID included in Silvers and Francis's argument, in fact, that their contractarian approach to

---

[72] Francis and Silvers, "Justice through Trust," at 68–69.
[73] *Ibid.* at 71.
[74] Of course, I do not have statistics on the number of people who are not able to meet the psychological criteria required to take part in a trusting relationship. Even if statistics were available, they would prove controversial given how difficult it is to draw definitive conclusions about the mental capacity of many nonverbal people with disabilities.
[75] It may be said in such a case that she is still in a relationship of trust, if only at the receiving end of this relationship. But one could think that (1) individuals with such capacities would be expected to reciprocate to be properly said to be parties to relations of trust (given the collective, mutual aspect of trust) or (2) her self-interested, opportunistic understanding of the trust from which she benefits prevents her from really being in a relation of trust. In the case of (2), despite the appearance of this trusting relationship, it is in fact another sort of relationship that is possibly exploitative or manipulative. This could be motivated by her constant mental state of wanting to exploit the other through trust, rather than being a fair (albeit self-interested) bargainer in a relation of trust. Finally, (3) pathologically anti-social individuals may lack sufficient capacities to empathize with other contractors standing in a similar situation, in terms of having desires and contracting capacities of their own. Objectifying fellow contractors might still fit the most self-interested versions of contractarianism (though it could count as contractualist), but lacking empathy may, if anything, hinder one's capacity to communicate and negotiate efficiently.

integrating physically and mentally disabled people into a theory of justice would already make tremendous progress in social contract theory. Further, we should not ignore the value of pragmatism: their effort to remain within a contractual justification political scheme seems less radical and perhaps more achievable than alternative explanations which can be harder to translate into palatable and communicable public policies. Their view counters an important "miscategorizing problem" – most people who are classified as having "profound mental disabilities" are often associated with the most severe cases of disability among the group.[76] Silvers and Francis force us to recognize that the sort of trust that exists between able-minded people is not essentially different from the trust that exists between humans who have dramatically lower capacities. This invites us to more carefully examine those cases where we have previously assumed that trust is impossible to establish. For example, even PSID who seem unable to distinguish between individuals might still be engaged in a "nonpersonalized" trust: in a competently caring environment, they may grow to be receptive of care in a more trusting way than they would be if they had spent years in an abusive institution.

In addition to the trust-based contractarian model reaching (what I believe to be) the morally correct conclusion that most disabled people should be within the ambit of justice, the relative nonradicalism of the trust-based contractarian model may be more attractive to public policymakers than competing justifications. However, this approach holds the inclusion of PSID hostage to the assumption that the designers of a fair society do indeed value and prioritize securing a culture of trust and trustworthiness between members of the community.[77] It is not obvious that parties to the social contract would prioritize establishing a trust-facilitating environment, that is, an environment that allows for (mutually reinforcing) trustworthiness where all relations of trust – either between strangers who contract together and between caregivers and the cared for – are somehow conflated. To put the query another way, must the development of this broad-ranging "trustworthiness" be such a central social goal of a fair society? Since Silvers and Francis have taken the contractarian route – which has faith in parties' wisdom, rationality, moral insights, and (they would add) other-regarding moral motivations – they can only hope that the contractual procedure yields such a result. However, is it obvious that parties to the social contract would agree to this? Maybe Silvers and Francis *have* got something right about the human condition, and this broad, polymorphous trust is indeed what we individually and collectively need. Perhaps if we establish this sort

---

[76] See, e.g., Licia Carlson, *The Faces of Intellectual Disability* (Bloomington: Indiana University Press, 2010).

[77] By this "trust" they must mean more than the trivial idea that the parties must use some sort of trust. Of course, any kind of contract would imply some sort of trust, but it could be a trust secured by authority and self-interest, as I have said. They must assume that the participants in the design of the social contract will want to establish a setting that is propitious for trusting relations that go far beyond trust insured by authority and self-interest alone.

of social model, we will realize that it works better for us as a community and as individuals. Yet, if they have miscalculated or misunderstood the moral motivations for respecting people with severe disabilities, then the social contract would not yield that result. Moreover, given Silvers and Francis's proceduralist commitment, there would be no higher ground and no substantial goods to use as a trump card against the results of their procedure for telling contracting parties that they have gotten it wrong and have misunderstood their best interests. We are left, in other words, with Martha Nussbaum's worry that at least some disabled people would not be "productive" enough to fit in a society founded upon contractarian premises, even if their productivity has been argued for in a new way.[78]

3.5 HOW IMPORTANT IS TRUST?

So far, I have criticized both the idea that the social contract is compatible with "trust-building" and the stronger claim that its participants are best served by a "trust-building" understanding of the social contract. I have suggested that such an understanding may not be the best (or even intuitively correct) way of securing the position of all people with disabilities within our ethical community. However, trusting relations with PSID are intuitively of great moral importance, and if I do not think that the importance of this trust is best understood in contractual terms, I need to illustrate how we might otherwise explain it. There are two questions to explore related to the importance of trust: *how important is trust?* and *how is trust important?* Or, if we put these questions another way (1) is trust as important or central as Silvers and Francis take it to be? and (2) on what is this importance grounded and how is it to be "cashed out"?

3.5.1 *The Problem of the Derivative Importance of a Contractarian Trust-Based Status*

A noncontractarian focus on other-regarding trust might be able to avoid a problem with the contractarian account. This problem is that the emphasis on the value of a trusting culture or trust-fostering political arrangement – as opposed to the value for PSID of being integrated as full members of our ethical community – seems to suggest that the latter value derives from, or is contingent upon, the former.

X's capacity to trust seems like a good grounding for moral obligations toward X. But does that imply that we have robust duties toward X, including duties that relate to a robust moral status such as duties of justice? A conception of justice based on trust is far from unimaginable but would need to be argued for. It does not seem that Silvers and Francis have provided, or tried to provide, such a conception of justice. Indeed, their intention to remain within a contractual framework is central

---

[78] See Nussbaum, *Frontiers of Justice*, at 105.

to their argument, and so they must retain the position that justice is a matter of fair contracting. Contracting is not replaced by trust as a foundational justification for authority, rather it becomes closely connected to it, notably by being the goal of contracting. They still have "contractarian faith" that proceduralism is able to generate good outcomes, rather than in the pre- or nonprocedural identification of such substantial goods.[79]

If one argued the simpler claim that one can be a member of the ethical community if one has the capacity to trust, then we could establish the claim that those with mental disabilities who able to trust are owed a robust moral status. But it is not certain that such a claim would succeed and, at any rate, Silvers and Francis's argument is more subtle and complex than that. They do claim that there should be no outliers and that disabled individuals should be included in an ethical community – even if they cannot significantly reciprocate in terms of their social contribution – *because* this fosters a climate of trust. It seems that two statements follow from their argument:

1. Disabled people are only "derivative subjects"[80] of justice. Their inclusion seems warranted by the impact of their inclusion on society, which "enrich[es] another kind of entity, the cooperative scheme (or the social climate, the community culture, or society itself)."[81] This stands in opposition to the goal of enriching the lives of PWD in a direct way.
2. If we accept the view put forward in (1), then a PSID's capacity to trust has, in itself, nothing to do with their inclusion in our ethical community, except to the extent that including beings who trust us within our community makes for a desirable or good environment.

As we have seen, Silvers and Francis's underlying position is that an agent who does not exploit the most exploitable person must be reliable. I have challenged this idea: someone could abide by ethical principles that require her not to exploit vulnerable people but that still allow agents to be ruthless or even callous toward others. One could also say that a person might have less to gain from exploiting a person with a profound mental disability than from exploiting more physically capable people, such as recently arrived migrants who are susceptible to working long hours in a sweatshop. That said, the claim remains true when it refers to the community rather than to specific individuals. If a state makes provision for the most easily exploited groups in society, able contractors will know that they live in a state that pays attention to the human conditions of vulnerability and dependency, including their own. However, this consequentialist way of approaching the issue

---

[79] Francis and Silvers, "Justice through Trust," at 53–54.
[80] Nussbaum's terminology. See *Frontiers of Justice*, at 327.
[81] Francis and Silvers, "Justice through Trust," at 45.

instrumentalizes people with disabilities, since the primary goal pursued is to build trust within the community, not to have concern for people with disabilities.

We may also detect a denigrating undertone in our attitude toward people with disabilities if we imply that "if we have integrated *these people*, we must indeed be living in some bleeding-heart community!" Of course, this is not the goal that Silvers and Francis pursue in either substantive or formal terms. Instead, their underlying ethos seems to be the idea that "my community recognizes and grants the proper moral weight to human dependency and vulnerability, from which I myself am not immune." But this sort of justification takes us either toward a self-interested version of the social contract or toward a justification of Silvers and Francis's argument that is based on the importance of human dependency and vulnerability, both of which can do without this trust-based version of contractarianism. It seems hard to escape the position that we instrumentalize PSID and PWD more generally if we adopt their account.

To address the criticism that we would only be giving importance to PSID derivative if we included them insofar as they serve the cooperative social scheme, trust-based contractarians could claim that relations of trust require us to avoid endorsing such a calculating, instrumentalizing outlook or attitudes. The apparently paradoxical suggestion is that it would be in our self-interest to temporarily suspend our self-interested or community-oriented "moral focal point," which should be directed toward the trusting individual in a noninstrumentalizing way. I have already mentioned this possibility but, whether or not it is plausible, other problems remain. I comment on two of these problems in the next sections.

3.5.2 Does Their Capacity to Take Part in Trusting Relations Explain Why PSID Should Be Subjects of Justice?

Do Silvers and Francis assume that human beings with disabilities are particularly important outliers? I find that their treatment of the issue of trusting animals reveals tension in this regard. On the face of their argument, they are not arbitrarily focusing on the disabled. Rather, disabled people are an important group of individuals who are deprived of capacities that are traditionally assumed to be necessary to participate in the cooperative design of a fair society. Disabled people possess the capacity to trust and, often, to be trusted. And any outlier able to trust or be trusted should fall within the scope of justice and be equal political participants.[82] Some entities, like plants or rocks, do not have the cognitive capacities required to trust, but some animals do trust humans, and Silvers and Francis consider that they are therefore owed trustworthiness in humans.[83] However, it is not clear how far down this path they intend to travel. For instance, they go on to say that "[c]hildren who torture

---

[82] *Ibid.* at 49.
[83] *Ibid.* at 72.

animals often grow into adults who treat other people cruelly. The man who whips his malnourished fallen cart horse strikes us as someone to avoid in doing business."[84]

This statement appears to suggest that they mean to curtail our duties toward beings who are able to trust only to the extent that it creates a trusting community of humans. The derivative aspect of the duties owed to animals – "derivative" because it serves the community of people who "really matter" – is analogous to Kant's position[85] and is subject to the same criticism. Surely, we want to give more than a right not to be tortured (or other derivative and limited privileges) to PSID. But if Silvers and Francis are really promising full political integration to outliers, then why curtail it in the case of animals? They state that animals could be "active participants in shaping principles that nurture a climate of trust."[86] However, they seem to retreat from this position about the status of animals when they proceed to ask what this status should imply. We cannot only trust the *status quo* to inform us on this matter if we recognize in animals the power to provide a real input into the creation of a fair community. Surely, many of us agree that torturing our pets is wrong, but it is instead these subordinating relationships (such as domestication) that need to be questioned. We should consider the prejudices that are embedded in ideas like breeding animals for enjoyment or for food or hunting animals for sport. The status that animals would benefit from within a theory of justice based on contracting with trust therefore highlights how dangerously minimalistic a derivative status can be.

Silvers and Francis's treatment in the case of animals also highlights that it is unclear whether *all* vulnerable human beings would really count as inliers within a trust-based contractarian theory of justice. Some domesticated animals, such as dogs, may become actively attached to people and act as though they belong to a human–dog "pack." But others like chickens and cows may not recognize a bond with humans in the same way, and the implications of this for their status is unclear. And what about wild animals? They may only have intraspecies relations of trust (or no propensity to trust altogether), but they are still vulnerable to human actions. Silvers and Francis do not reduce the notion of trust to that of vulnerability (and

---

[84] Ibid.
[85] *Lectures on Ethics*, ed. J. B. Schneewind, trans. Peter Heath (New York: Cambridge University Press, 1997), at 212–13. In his lecture "On Duties to Animals and Spirits," Kant argues that "duties towards [animals] are indirect duties to humanity." Animals have no intrinsic worth or dignity, but they are still not to be treated merely as means, insofar as they are, at least in some respect and in some circumstances, sufficiently analogous with human beings. Therefore treating them well will cultivate virtues (Kant mentions the propensity to properly respond to human merit) or emotions (Kant mentions "tenderness") that will then be directed at human beings. This view will be criticized by those who believe that animals have some kind of nonderivative value.
[86] Francis and Silvers, "Justice through Trust," at 71–72.

I think they are correct not to), but this results in their theory excluding many animals and, it seems, some people with severe mental disabilities as well.

Finally, it is not clear that treating animals well would indeed foster a climate of trust. Recall that Silvers and Francis's criterion for distinguishing the morally relevant trust is whether it will foster a culture of trust. As I mentioned, they say that a man who whips his malnourished cart horse and therefore does not grant the animal a pleasant existence is not a man we want to do business with. Not all businesspeople would agree. After all, hunting and exploiting the environment have been traditional settings and objects of contractual arrangements, including theories of the social contract.

The claim that a person who treats animals well is more trustworthy nonetheless remains plausible, but perhaps not because we intuit that she honored the trust the animal gave her – and would therefore also honor the trust we would give her. We may come to trust this person because we intuit that she properly responded to the vulnerability she detected in an animal and we would judge her to be virtuous enough to similarly fittingly respond to the vulnerability she would detect in us. We may also distrust her, knowing how some people act kindly toward certain animals, like their pets, and callously toward fellow human beings. In sum, behaviors toward people with severe intellectual disabilities or toward animals are not necessarily based on attitudes that can be reliably projected onto (expectations of) behaviors toward people with average cognitive skills. The interspecies transfer of trusting attitudes that Silvers and Francis are considering further highlights how a trust-based contractarian theory of justice may not pay enough attention to the relational texture of the community – that is, the multitude of relations and roles people occupy within it, and how said roles and relations modulate (arguably for valid moral reasons) trustworthiness.

It could be that contractual parties more readily trust someone who treats certain vulnerable beings well but not others, because the parties happen to already care for one group more than another. If this concern for others is warranted by some moral (nonprejudiced) reason, it needs to be explained in reference to quality or value other than trust. I do think there are ways to distinguish the relationships that we have with animals from the ones we have with humans, but it may be difficult to do so if we rely only on the notion of trust. Using the capacity to trust as the cornerstone to bring outliers into the ethical community – unless it is paired with some other (and potentially competing) moral grounds – makes it hard to explain why disabled people should be owed something different from what is owed to animals that are also able to trust. This distinction is worth making because, among other reasons, animals and humans with disabilities are different sorts of beings and are part of different relationships with other humans. This is a particular example of the more general problem that the specialness or particularity of the moral status of PSID is not fully and solely explained by a reference to their impact on a trusting culture. The fact that Silvers and Francis's contractual trust-based account of justice allows for an assessment of interspecies contribution tends to suggest a justificatory broadness that misses what is particular about PSID and their relations with other humans, especially given the tensions that this assessment creates.

Another problem with the broadness of the criterion of an unsophisticated capacity to trust is that the more basic the definition of trust we adopt, the less appealing trust is as sufficient (and Silvers and Francis seem to say, necessary[87]) grounds for being a potential participant to the social contract and thus a subject of justice. For instance, reduced to strictly dependent behavior, the idea of trust would apply to many beings, but it would be unclear why this sort of trust would matter so much. In fact, even a more cognitively sophisticated understanding of trust does not provide us with grounds to pay serious moral attention to a being, to find this being intrinsically important, and to divert our resources toward improving their welfare (should the right relationship between ourselves and this being be established). An enemy trusting me to betray my friends is a fool and her trust does not obligate me morally. There seems to be nothing normative[88] about trust in and of itself. What makes worse to harm my little brother who has grown to trust me, than to harm a child I do not know, can be explained by the relationship between my brother and me (one of care and/or of brotherly love), rather than trust (although trust may well have evolved from that relationship and might indeed infuse it). Whether, why, and how much trust would be valuable, is the topic I deal with in the next section.[89]

3.5.3 Why Other-Regarding Trust May Still Matter within a Noncontractual Theory of Justice

Why is a climate of trust – or trusting relations more generally – desirable or good? Silvers and Francis's answer is that it best achieves the fundamental aim of social contract theory: to sustain social cooperation. It does so, they claim, by disposing participants to constancy and "promoting stable compliance with mutual expectations,"[90] notably by establishing the trustworthiness of agents (individually or collectively) by identifying that they are in other-regarding trust relations (i.e., trust underlaid by other-regarding concern). I agree that a climate of trust is desirable, but

---

[87] Ibid. at 69.
[88] This does not mean that trust is not valuable; it certainly enriches people's lives.
[89] In the case of Silvers and Francis's argument, what makes a capacity to trust normative is the fact that it is chosen by parties to the social contract (and they suggest that these parties would choose it because of the positive impact that relations of trust and a culture of trust will have on society). We would not value mentally disabled people *qua* trusters, but *qua* potential maximizers of social global happiness (assuming that to show trustworthiness toward vulnerable people with disabilities is a particularly good way of developing a culture of trust). The capacity to trust, thus interpreted, grounds the status of subject of justice because trusting individuals allows for greater social cohesion rather than because "trusters" are the sort of beings we should treat particularly well.
[90] Francis and Silvers, "Justice through Trust," at 60.

not (or not principally) because it facilitates expectations, reliability, and foreseeability between contractors. My way of explaining the value of trust makes it less foundational and central a good than if one sees it as the most basic and important condition to be met through the social contract.

A climate of trust is indeed desirable, *inter alia*, for the self-interested reasons set out in the previous chapter (i.e., on forms of contractarianism that assume self-interest and rationality). I would know, as an able or disabled citizen, that I (or my children, or my loved ones) would be taken care of, should I (or they) need this care someday. This would also allow me to live a less anguished, overcautious life in which I can take more risks to achieve happiness. It would also invite, if not obligate, me to be more reliable and disposed to help (either directly or via my government) dependent individuals, as I will have recognized the importance of making provisions for human dependency and vulnerability.

Contrary to Silvers and Francis, such a justification for including the disabled in our ethical community would not appeal to a capacity to trust. Rather, it would be based on concern for one's own vulnerability (and possibly that of others). The capacity to trust would be fostered because it benefits the "direct" contractor: the central member of the ethical community on a contractarian account, who is the uncontested possessor of a robust moral status on traditional contractarian grounds (a capacity to benefit or threaten others) and who decides to extend a robust moral status to beings on other grounds. PSID may then be granted an "indirect" robust moral status because this ultimately serves "real" contractors who directly merit a robust moral status.

The difference between direct and indirect inclusion into the ethical community may not initially seem significant, but it is practically and conceptually relevant if one wants to use trust as grounds to establish robust moral status. Is there something about the capacity to trust that would make someone a full member of our ethical community, regardless of the impact that her membership has on the community? That is, would an individual capacity to trust ground the other-regarding concern that underlies the non-Hobbesian contractarianism that Silvers and Francis defend?

It seems to me that the answer is in the negative. The capacity to trust is precious, on a trust-based contractarian account, because of its impact on the community. However, the capacity to trust is important not only because it serves the community; it also serves the individual and is important because the individual is important. (This importance is not based on the capacity to trust, otherwise, this would be circular reasoning.) It is not the capacity to trust *per se* that matters, but the fact that a trusting relation is often an indicator of concern. The fact that X trusts me will not, in itself, make X important to me. It may instead indicate that she *is* important to me, and that I am already engaged in some concerned behaviors toward X that have caused X to have certain expectations toward me. Trust may crystallize or spell out these expectations, rather than having initially created them. It is also plausible that I will have no moral concern for and obligations to beings who (misleadingly) trust me, at least not in terms of that trust. By the same token, it seems that I may have strong obligations toward beings who do not have trusting expectations from me. In sum, it is not evident that a capacity to trust, in and of itself, would grant a robust moral status to PSID. It may serve the community's culture of trust, as Silvers and Francis argue, but then it is not clear how it would necessarily be the other-regarding sort of trust on which they capitalize.

3.6 CONCLUSION

While Silvers and Francis's trust-based and trust-engendering contractarian account of why PSID should be included in our ethical community represents an ingenious contribution to social contract theory, it has two significant weaknesses. First, their account still excludes some members of the group whom we identify as severely intellectually disabled. On its face, this does not reveal a lacuna in their argument, unless I assume that no group of people should be excluded from the design of a fair society. However, it seems that Silvers and Francis would themselves be dissatisfied with the outcome that some mentally disabled people remain outliers as they appear to assume that their theory encompasses *all* outliers.[91] They only mention in passing that "almost everyone" can trust, and immediately after this statement assert that "[e]ven the most vulnerable individuals may be parties to trust."[92] As we have discussed, not everyone is able to be "parties to trust" unless we define this ability in ways that end up being problematic within a contractarian account. Secondly, it seems plausible that a culture of trust would more readily flourish in a society that creates a special, protective place for those disabled individuals who are deprived of cognitive capacities that enable them to trust. However, Silvers and Francis's argument lacks the internal resources to make this case, as they have chosen to focus on an internally, individually possessed capacity.[93] Their argument could still

---

[91] Silvers and Francis maintain that "no one should have to be an 'outlier'" (*ibid*. at 44). However, as I have noted previously, this statement is implicitly qualified. They must imply that *some* sort of properties qualifies a being to be an "inlier," otherwise stones, ferns, and rabbits would also be outliers. Without these qualifying properties, a being could not even be an "outlier," as to stand outside of a community one needs to be the sort of being who can *stand* in some position vis-à-vis a community, either as an insider or an outsider. This way of presenting the issue of exclusion or integration reveals that the ethical investigation of this matter must not focus exclusively on the understanding that some individual properties matter in and of themselves (i.e., inside or outside of a community) but should also investigate how a community is defined in a morally relevant way.

[92] *Ibid*. at 69.

[93] If the criterion for being integrated into the social contract is simply that this inclusion would foster the climate of trust, one could argue that X could be included in this society even if X cannot take part in relations of trust themselves. However, in this case, the problem of the lack of correlation between the contractors' relation with X and the climate of trust would be even more pronounced, and so would the derivativeness of X's robust moral status, even supposing that this can be a robust moral status. What would this inclusion mean if it cannot be understood in terms of taking part in a social matrix of trusting relations? How would it

provide a justification for integrating the vast majority of people with disabilities, and be read along other grounds for social inclusion. Different (and potentially non-contractual) grounds may explain why people with the most severe of impairments ought to be granted equivalent status to able-bodied people.[94]

However, the justifications that Silvers and Francis offer for including PSID still face another problem: they do not fully capture the important reasons why PSID "matter" in a way that requires their inclusion in our ethical community. One could say that their argument already provides sufficient reasons for considering PSID as parties to the social contract and that it does not need to aim at being a full account of what is owed to this group of people. However, these reasons might include incorrect or questionable assumptions or claims. Notably, as I have suggested, this contractarian argument instrumentalizes people with these profound disabilities: we would care for them and recognize their role as members of society because doing so encourages a culture of trust where nonmutually beneficial relations could take place and be fostered.[95] Since the way in which PSID benefit or threaten us is very indirect (by fostering or hindering a collectively beneficial culture of trust-facilitating institutions), it leaves the issue open for someone to claim that we do not need to

---

benefit X? Such an inclusion would likely be ultimately justified by a preference or belief shared by community members rather than because X is a contractor like them. (Consider, for example, integrating ancient sculpted rocks into the social contract on the basis that they are considered by some people to be benevolent spirits securing trust.)

[94] That is, by having their interests considered by the designers of a fair society to be as important and worthy of consideration as the interests of the other "moral legislators," leaving aside for now the complex issue of whether they themselves – like Silvers suggests here and elsewhere – should be considered to be active legislators or participants.

[95] As we have seen in the previous chapter, this criticism is not addressed to Silvers and Francis's argument specifically, but rather to a broad variety of contractarianism that assumes that parties to the social contract must be able to contribute to this collective endeavor or to threaten the social order should they be left outside of it. Silvers and Francis's argument has the advantage that it could be used to make the case that we should include PSID without modifying these contractarian assumptions. However, this is not their intention. They challenge these assumptions by noting that parties can also have other-regarding, not only prudential and self-interested, motivations. Although I interpreted their argument as a trust-based contractarianism, their argument draws from different varieties of social contract theories, which we could associate with both contractarianism and contractualism. Sometimes Silvers and Francis appeal to the logic of the former tradition by considering how disabled people could contribute to social cooperation, namely if they were involved in the adoption of its terms and could therefore request a structure that would allow them to be "productive" (*ibid.* at 49, 69). At other times, they appeal to the Kantian idea that "[c]entral to the point of contracting is that each party is respected as in some broad sense being a chooser" (*ibid.* at 44). There is no (at least not immediately evident) contradiction in working on these two fronts, but given that the thrust of their argument centers on trust and its benefits, I take them to be dealing with the idea that including people with disabilities in our ethical community benefits us all, in a sense that fits better within the first, rather than the second, variety of social contract theory. They have more to say about the status of the disabled *qua* active choosers, but that is a topic that I will deal with in Chapter 4, so as not to confuse the arguments favoring the inclusion of PSID and in order to better analyze their respective merits.

include some severely disabled people at an early stage of the social contract. This argument does not seem to necessarily require that we give these people an initial important moral status. As I have suggested, people with these disabilities may be included at a later stage of the social design, when social architects think it beneficial to the community to integrate them, along with bridges, public libraries, and laws protecting heritage houses. From a contractual point of view, it seems that this is where this group of people most plausibly fit. This may seem wrong because we are aware of other key reasons why people with severe intellectual disabilities should be given a more important status than bridges. However, these reasons find a better expression in places other than in contractual thinking.

Even if Silvers and Francis's key insight is formulated in a way that emphasizes other-regarding trust rather than self-interest – by turning away from a bargaining paradigm to a trust-generating-based one – the criticism of instrumentalization is hard to avoid. Caring about very vulnerable beings may foster trust, reliability, and a feeling of community connection. This can also remind us that we are all potential recipients of community care and foster genuine other-regarding concerns, rather than mere other-regarding attitudes that are ultimately based in self-interest. However, these outcomes remain valuable only because they effectively promote the ends desired by contractors (and if there are no other better ways of promoting those ends).

Nonetheless, Silvers and Francis have provided what I consider to be the best approach of conceptualizing the notion of "mutual advantage" that lies at the heart of the social contract in a way that integrates this sort of benefit into the contractual balance. They have provided a compelling way of harnessing – within a contractual theory – the "multifaceted and diffuse benefit to society of interacting with [cognitively impaired individuals] and supporting them,"[96] as Nussbaum puts it. Many philosophers agree on this "diffuse benefit." The hard point of disagreement is whether it works within a contractual theory to justify granting a robust moral status to those like PSID.

Ultimately, I do not think that the social contract is the best conceptual framework to compellingly and entirely express the importance of such a special benefit. To respond to Silvers and Francis specifically, I am not convinced that relations of trust with PSID could even constitute such a benefit. On the contrary, it is more plausible to me that to ground the robust moral status of PSID on their capacity to trust puts the cart before the horse. In other words, we ought to engage in trusting relations with members of this group because they *already have* a robust moral status – one that is grounded on a different basis that needs further articulation. I reject the argument that trusting relations arise because PSID have a capacity to trust which indirectly and questionably contributes to a trust-based and trust-engendering social contract.

---

[96] See Nussbaum, *Frontiers of Justice*, at 129.

If we assume, as I do, that PSID have a robust moral status and should be owed stringent duties of justice, it is far from obvious that the capacity to trust is the most salient aspect of their robust moral status. The value of a climate of (other-regarding) trust – although one that plausibly fits their version of the social contract – does not best fit our ordinary intuitions about why we should honor the trust of PSID and why we should expect them to trust us. Discovering the real reasons for these positions would probably explain why we still owe these individuals a very important concern (and one that warrants integration into our ethical community) even when they lack the capacity to take part in relations of trust.

Let me conclude this chapter by referring to John Steinbeck's novel *Of Mice and Men*. For readers who are unfamiliar with the narrative, Lennie is a mentally disabled man and George is his best friend who cares for him. While they are working on a farm, Lennie strangles a woman – although he acts without intending to hurt her – and then runs away, pursued by a mob. George ultimately shoots and kills Lennie to spare him a harsher death at the hands of the mob. This story shows us that even though Lennie trusts George, the value and normativity of this trust cannot be grounded on the hypothesis that it fosters a social climate of trust. Lennie's existence and actions do not engender a culture of trust; inded, his actions hinder the communal climate of trust. George has no doubts about the stringency of his duties toward Lennie. Steinbeck suggests that George would not have his life (as Lennie's caregiver) any other way. At some point, George ruminates about his life and says how much easier it would be without Lennie, but he takes it back a moment later because he remembers the importance of this relationship in his life, the demands it makes, the meaning it gives. Lennie is not a burden: he just happens to be there, like George himself. To think of Lennie as a burden is to think of human beings as unburdened from one another or to think that this "unburdening" is a proper moral aspiration. This is precisely what, for better or worse, contractarianism generally assumes. Silvers and Francis challenge this assumption while paradoxically defending the questionable hypothesis that Lennie's capacity to engage in relations of trust entitles him to a robust moral status. However, in the novel, trust-fostering contractarians are the angry mob chasing him with rifles.[97]

---

[97] One may note that Lennie has betrayed the community's trust and the social climate of trust needs to be reestablished through his punishment. However, my point is that Lennie has no separate claim to a right to life if it turns out that his capacity to properly respond to trust is defective, due to his mental limitations. This story, *mutatis mutandis*, illustrates how one is entitled to a robust moral status on a trust-based contractarian account. It is not about Lennie being a subject of justice who must be duly punished. On the contrary, he has no special moral status left; he is chased by a mob to be summarily killed like an animal that has disturbed the community's tranquility.

4

People with Severe Intellectual Disabilities as Active Citizens

As illustrated in the previous chapter, the philosophers Anita Silvers and Leslie Francis have developed the elements of a theory of justice that can retain the social contract framework and fully integrate outliers such as people with disabilities. Both in their individual and joint writings, Silvers and Francis are probably the best representatives of the view that PSID possess the necessary capacities to be conceptualized as active participants within a liberal theory of justice and, more particularly, that they can be so conceptualized within social contract theory. Their theory of justice is characterized by an effort to maintain the paradigmatic features of liberal social contract theories, such as the requirement of autonomy, the capacity to have a conception of the good, and the possession of talents that contribute to the common social pool.

A notable feature of Silvers and Francis's arguments is that they redefine and broaden the notion of passive citizenship in comparison to other relevant theorists whose work I examine in Chapters 2 and 5. However, unlike other theorists of active citizenship, whom we will explore later in this chapter,[1] as well as to other theorists who confer a robust moral status on PSID on bases other than capacities that are pertinent to a social contract argument (whose work we will not explore),[2] Silvers and Francis do not render these notions less demanding by lowering the threshold for robust moral status or to be considered a full subject of justice. Instead, they

---

[1] Such as Christie Hartley, who conceptualizes the notion of mutuality and reciprocity as demanding only a sort of "engagement" in "Justice for the Disabled: A Contractualist Approach" (2009) 40:1 J Soc Phil 17.
[2] "Among the more inclusive criteria proposed are the capacity to communicate, or for minimal communication with other humans; to value or care; and to give and receive love; to form relationships characterized by reciprocity of care" (David Wasserman et al., "Cognitive Disability and Moral Status," *The Stanford Encyclopedia of Philosophy* [August 2017], plato.stanford.edu/entries/cognitive-disability/ [citations omitted]).

"elevate" PSID to more traditional standards for status or subjecthood.[3] While all three of the groups of theories[4] that I contrast reconceptualize these standards, Silvers and Francis do so in a less radical way by anchoring them in the liberal tradition and offering plausible reasons for doing so. By comparison, the "passive citizenship" theorists that I consider in Chapter 5 reconceptualize the standards to render the indirect integration of PSID as either innocuous or as compatible with a social contract (if not strongly or compellingly justified by it) that takes place between capable, active citizens. The "active citizenship" theorists, on the other hand, "lower" the standards for political community membership in order to capture a greater number of less capacitated beings.

We can see that Silvers and Francis situate the requirements for a robust moral status within liberalism, particularly in the ways that they anchor their theory of "justice through trust" and their views of conceptions of the good (as socially rather than independently scripted) within established liberal traditions. This approach counts in their favor – at least in pragmatic terms, as I mentioned in the previous chapter – insofar as they outline incremental changes to a valued tradition that is deeply embedded in our liberal political culture (and revived by Rawls), which they suggest we should better understand rather than overthrow. However, while simultaneously reconceptualizing liberal notions of the social contract in a relatively traditional way, they also do something that neither of the other two aforementioned groups do (or, at least, nowhere near as forcefully): they reconceptualize PSID themselves, or rather they devote a considerable amount of attention to illustrating how disabled people can individually be enabled to meet a (liberal) threshold, in contrast to only (or mostly) focusing on rethinking this threshold.

In seven of their essays analyzed in this chapter, Silvers and Francis develop a complex conceptual apparatus to make the case for the integration of PSID as described above. This includes sketching a theory of justice (justice through trust) and introducing some core elements of a potentially competing theory of justice

---

[3] Surely, the theorists who "lower" or "lessen" the threshold for robust moral status – contractual or not – would not consider that their reconceptualization implies any pejorative "lessening." They are simply getting to the truth of what should suffice to establish moral status or subjecthood within a theory of justice. Yet, it is part of Silvers and Francis's conceptual framework to be aware of the social and historical context within which disabled people have been conceptualized as objects of obligations (instead of subjects) and to suggest that pejorative tags (of being a noncontributing beneficiary and a "burden") may insidiously accompany such less demanding benchmarks, as we will see.

[4] That is, (1) contractarians, in Chapters 2 and 3, (2) contractualist accounts of active citizenship, in Chapter 4, and (3) contractualist accounts of passive citizenship, in Chapter 5. Note that I am analyzing different dimensions of the writings of Silvers and Francis in Chapters 3 and 4. It would be misleading to categorize them as "contractarian" or "contractualist" (either passive or active) thinkers, since their arguments, like those of Rawls, contain elements of both strands. The same can be said of most authors I use in this monograph. It would not be helpful to reduce these theorists themselves to a label; instead, I am using some of their arguments under specific labels for pedagogical purposes.

(justice for talents). They also engage in metaphysical, ethical, and sociological arguments that deal with autonomy, conceptions of the good, "cognitive prostheses," and prejudices toward the disabled, whereby we see people with disabilities primarily as objects of redistribution instead of as participants to be integrated into our ethical community. These elements fit neatly together like interlocking puzzle pieces. Their key components can be summed up in five premises or claims, which I list below. While I think that Silvers and Francis's conceptual apparatus constitutes the most compelling integrationist version of social contract theory to date, my analysis illustrates that it still does not fully reflect the reasons why we care for mentally disabled people. Therefore, I conclude that such a social contract theory does not satisfactorily explain *why* we owe the sort of duties that we owe to (severely) disabled people, even though it does correctly explain many of these reasons for these duties.

The five premises that make up Silvers and Francis's conceptual apparatus are as follows:

(1) PSID should be socially integrated rather than being the beneficiaries of compensatory distribution.
(2) The justifications for this integration are their talents and capacities to cooperate;
(3) as well as the fact that their integration to the social structure will enhance social trust;
(4) and their capacity for formulating a conception of the good.
(5) These capacities may require proper support, which is a support that must not become a kind of compensatory distribution (or else, it would contradict premise #1) but rather enhances individual capacities in a way that enables social contribution and integration.

Not all of the essays in which these premises are found focus exclusively on cognitively disabled people, but I apply this lens to their work and interpret some of Silvers's arguments as applying to PSID when I believe she would agree, and where her arguments allow for this interpretation. Note, I have already assessed the merits of premise (3) in my discussion of their theory of justice as trust, which was complex and promising enough to warrant a separate chapter in this book.[5]

---

[5] PSID's capacity to trust or foster trust is more convincingly read as a kind of passive participation, though it could also be understood as a nontraditional active kind of trust. It is also most simply and boldly stated as a contractarian integrationist argument instead of a contractualist one. This is why I chose "justice as trust" as representing the best contemporary contractarian case for (active or passive) citizenship. However, it may be associated with contractualism instead, though I suspect that taking the capacity to "trust" too seriously may imply the position of not taking other psychological capacities – that are central to contractualist doctrines – seriously enough.

Before I explore and problematize Silvers and Francis's arguments, I should explicitly link them to social contract theory. Their arguments are to the effect that PSID possess capacities that enable them to take part in a collective endeavor that is regulated by a social contract. These capacities are their talents and capabilities to cooperate and to elaborate a conception of the good, the proposition being that, with appropriate support, PSID are "contractually" useful. Silvers's attention to their social and philosophical representations (i.e., their social role as well as their roles within justice theories) enables us to see how both representations reinforce a common and harmful stereotype connected to a variety of social contract theories, which have trouble justifying the integration of PSID if they are only seen as objects of compensatory redistribution and/or as "burdens" rather than as valuable participants to contract-like moral, political, and social arrangements. In Silvers's words, "[d]istributive schemes that cast people with disabilities as supported by others rather than as supporting others thereby diminish their opportunities by denying them the identities they need to initiate mutual or reciprocal relationships,"[6] that is, relationships that constitute the sort of social cooperation that reasonable subjects of justice endeavor to pursue fairly.[7]

4.1 JUSTICE FOR TALENTS

4.1.1 *The Distributive Discourse of Compensation versus the Rewarding Discourse of Talents*

Silvers begins her essay "Formal Justice" with a dichotomy between PWD as vulnerable, dependent, and burdensome and PWD as potential social participants. The operational goals of justice associated with the former conception are distribution, separation, special treatments, and accommodation, whereas the operational goals associated with the latter conception are integration, similar treatment, and neutrality.[8]

The conceptual shift that Silvers makes is part of her contractualist integrationist strategy of conceptualizing PWD as active contractors and citizens as opposed to passive beneficiaries. On her account, focusing on redistribution at a later stage of the social contract procedures (as well as at a later stage of social cooperation and production) has inherently exclusivist consequences. Comparatively, by

---

[6] Anita Silvers, "Formal Justice" in Anita Silvers, David Wasserman, and Mary Mahowald, *Disability, Difference, Discrimination* (Lanham, MD: Rowman & Littlefield, 1998), 13 at 142.

[7] See John Rawls, *Political Liberalism*, expand. ed. (New York: Columbia University Press, 2005), at 16, 20, 50.

[8] Silvers, "Formal Justice"; see also Martha Minow, *Making All the Difference: Inclusion, Exclusion, and American Law* (Ithaca: Cornell University Press, 2006), at 20–21; Anita Silvers, "No Talent? Beyond the Worst Off! A Diverse Theory of Justice for Disability" in Kimberley Brownlee and Adam Cureton, eds., *Disability and Disadvantage* (Oxford: Oxford University Press, 2009), at 163, 167–69.

emphasizing social integration instead of accommodation or compensation, she characterizes disabled people as active participants or contributors, bringing them closer to the model of active contractors that I analyze in this chapter.

Silvers's dichotomy between integration and compensation is similar to Martha Minow's dichotomy between denying and recognizing difference and to Ronald Dworkin's dichotomy between the right to equal treatment and the right to be treated as equal.[9] Minow refers to this as the dilemma of difference: "when does treating people differently emphasize their differences and stigmatize or hinder them on that basis? And when does treating people the same become insensitive to their difference and likely to stigmatize or hinder them on *that* basis?"[10] Silvers is opposed to the idea that the "problem" of disability is one of (re)distribution, involving seeing the disabled as burdensome, deficient, and needy. The justificatory focus is put on "special needs" that require extraordinary allocations of resources; this philosophical framework is influenced by – and exacerbates – a pejorative or prejudiced way of thinking about people with disabilities. The resulting practices necessitated by such a view also have the harmful effect of furthering the social isolation of disabled people.

This isolation (or insulation) of the disabled both within concrete social institutions and within philosophy is the key problem against which Silvers fights. Her proposal is to shift the focus of justice considerations from distribution to integration.[11] In other words, the metric of justice should be social access, integration, opportunity to cooperate or participate in society and to express one's talents, rather than focusing on enabling PSID to partake of basic goods or capabilities that nondisabled people enjoy. Of course, one such good could, in fact, be social integration, but Silvers's point is to distinguish a focus on social integration with the focus on compensation for disadvantage. The models she criticizes too quickly abandon the possibility of integrating PSID, and instead redistribute resources by creating special – often protective and apparently well-meaning – regimes to assist people with disabilities. Such insular regimes, which correlate, I believe, to an insular kind of moral status, serve to isolate PSID, alienate them from society, hinder their self-accomplishments, and "cast them as exceptionally needy and thereby in deficit compared with other people."[12]

It is in this sense that Silvers contrasts distribution and integration. Let me justify this dichotomy and Silvers's focus on the integration side of it, since it could be challenged. One could, like David Wasserman, insist that a "just social response to

---

[9] Silvers, "No Talent," at 167–69; Silvers, "Formal Justice," at 126; Ronald Dworkin, *Taking Rights Seriously* (London: Bloomsbury Academic, 2013), at 227.
[10] Minow, *Making All the Difference*, at 20.
[11] Anita Silvers, David Wasserman, and Mary Mahowald, "Introduction" in Silvers *et al.*, *Disability, Difference, Discrimination*, at 4–5.
[12] *Ibid.* at 34.

disabilities must encompass distributive concerns"[13] and that the good(s) of integration, social participation, and contribution are simply goods to be *distributed*, among others. Instead of proposing a shift from distribution to integration, Silvers could have proposed a shift from distribution of resources and compensation for a lack of (normal) abilities to distribution of the conditions for being socially integrated. After all, it is not distribution *per se* that she is against, but rather the distribution of the wrong kinds of resources to people who are in dire need of inclusion and recognition as active citizens and talented contributors. In this sense, distribution may have the effect of further marginalizing, isolating, and labeling disabled people as burdensome and needy beings who should be merely brought to an average (or minimal) level of well-being by some standard of normalcy.

However, while Silvers's point *could* be made using the idiom of distribution, there are good reasons not to adopt distribution as her primary argumentative focus. Those reasons are found in the work of Iris Marion Young, one of the first "relational egalitarianists" to reproach the traditional redistributive focus of theories of justice. Young argues that (1) focusing on the distribution of material goods "tends to ignore the social structure and institutional context that often help determine distributive patterns."[14] In other words, people concerned with justice should challenge unfair elements within "decision-making power and procedures, division of labor, and culture," not just redistribute the outcome of a structurally unfair process.[15] In response to the objection that those very goods ("power, opportunity, or self-respect") could themselves be redistributed just like material goods, Young argues that (2) "[w]hen metaphorically extended to nonmaterial social goods, the concept of distribution represents them as though they were static things, instead of a function of social relations and processes."[16] In other words, distributive processes fail to question the origin and nature of the goods being distributed. While no one is denying that (re)distribution has an important role to play within social arrangements, the general point that Young and others[17] make is that traditional distributive foci lack the critical teeth that theories of social justice should have to challenge structural injustice. Young and others seek to place citizens in a position of equality vis-à-vis one another at a fundamental level – such as the level of being granted an equally robust moral status explored in this book – rather than to sweeten the (poor) deal of those citizens who unluckily inherited the short end of the stick. This

---

[13] *Ibid.* at 6.
[14] Iris Young, *Justice and the Politics of Difference* (Princeton, NJ: Princeton University Press, 1990), at 15–16.
[15] *Ibid.*
[16] *Ibid.*
[17] See, e.g., Elizabeth Anderson's "democratic equality," which "integrates principles of distribution with the expressive demands of equal respect [in seeking the construction of a community of equals]" ("What Is the Point of Equality?" [1999] 109:2 Ethics 287 at 289); or Nancy Fraser's approach to recognition as "the status of individual group members as full partners in social interaction" ("Rethinking Recognition" [2000] 3 New Left Review 107 at 113).

approach is particularly fitting for disability theorists approaching questions of justice, since people with disabilities are paradigmatic "outliers" whose demands for fair treatment characteristically take the form of a challenge of the very institutions that contributed to creating a social context in which they must beg for compensation for "their" inability to fit in. In other words, society's inaptitude to create accessible structures that would not have turned PWD into outliers in the first place is presented as the shortcoming of PWD, rather than a shortcoming of society.

That said, in the specific context of elements of Silvers's arguments that I am examining, I still think that many of the goods she discusses can be fruitfully thought of in distributive terms (in spite of Young's warnings) and should not be generalized to all issues of justice since no one is denying that redistribution can be a useful political concept. My view is that Silvers's concerns do not require us to categorically jettison a distributive approach *per se*. Instead, her crucial insight is that we ought to avoid the common move of casting PWD as worst off, have-nots, tragically "lesser" persons to whom the riches of able-bodied citizens are *redistributed* on the basis of their misfortune. While arguably not ideal (for the reasons that Young outlines), a distributive discourse is not problematic for the purpose of this chapter as long as it conceives of distribution in ways that focus on PWD's talents and avoids casting them as a somehow biologically determined category of "deserving poor." I suggest that Silvers's elements of a talent-oriented theory of justice could be operationalized both in distributive terms and in terms of structural and relational reforms. I will argue that we should remain open to the possibility that, in some cases, nurturing PSID's talents may be better formulated primarily in redistributive or remedial terms, rather than primarily in integrationist terms. This is because, (1) while we can and should work on creating a more universally inclusive society, we must also explain why we ought to care for PWD, whose gifts and talents may be idiosyncratic to the point of resisting normalizing measures, given the reality of exclusionist facilities and institutions. If it does not broaden its reach, "justice for talents" risks excluding a category of severely disabled individuals for whom available accommodation measures will not suffice. I also suggest (2) that in some cases, disabilities can indeed put people in an unfortunate and undesirable situation that should be compensated. I maintain a clear distinction between (a) the claim that certain aspects of disability sometimes denote undesirable states of affair and (b) the claim that PWD are always and necessarily worse off because of their impairments. Claim (b) does not follow from claim (a), and we can endorse claim (a), as I think we sometimes should, without endorsing claim (b). This position can be called an "axiologically open-ended" conception of disability, which means that people with disabilities can articulate some of their issues as undeserved problems while *also* insisting that their "disabled" minds and bodies are not to be systematically lamented. On the contrary, having a disability can be experienced as a neutral, or even a positive experience, in some contexts.

While not uncontroversial, this axiologically open-ended approach has the advantage of fitting the complexity of disability, namely of how disability is experienced subjectively and contextually. It has notably (and recently) been defended by Elizabeth Barnes.[18] Silvers herself has also argued for a "neutral" approach that would, on the one hand, require disability activists to accept that, sometimes, disability pride discourses should give way to attempts to "cure" "problems," and that, on the other hand, would require mainstream bioethics to stop assuming, as it has traditionally done,[19] that being disabled is necessarily a bad thing.[20] As long as it makes no such assumption, a compensatory lens will not necessarily convey the ableist message that Silvers wishes to uproot from theories of justice. Such an outlook that does not predetermine the negative or positive value of disability invites us to ask whether, and to what extent, measures that nurture the talents of PWD should (not) be justified in terms of other-regarding concern or care, rather than being formulated within the contractual idiom of reciprocity, productivity, and respect for autonomy.

4.1.2 *Social and Philosophical Prejudices That Isolate PSID from Active Participation*

While Silvers does not deny that PSID can and should sometimes be the object of care and recognizes that justice can also be a matter of compensation, she holds that it is a mistake to emphasize compensatory concerns in a theory of justice that deals with the disabled. She writes:

> There is all the difference in the world between conceiving of people with disabilities as equal and thereby as deserving only such differentiated treatment as is needed to reform social practice that excludes them and thinking of them as deficient and thereby as deserving of special benefits, entitlements, and exemptions to sustain them in their exclusion from the mainstream of commercial and civic life.[21]

Silvers suggests that people who are viewed as needing support, protection, or care are not "social persons in a full and meaningful sense."[22] This is due to the ways that society characterizes their state of vulnerability and dependence, using a certain

---

[18] Elizabeth Barnes, *The Minority Body* (Oxford: Oxford University Press, 2016); see also my "Theoretical Strategies to Define Disability" in David Wasserman and Adam Cureton, eds., *The Oxford Handbook of Philosophy and Disability* (New York: Oxford University Press, 2019) and my "Beyond (Models of) Disability?" (2016) 41:2 J Med & Phil 210.
[19] See, e.g., Simo Vehmas, "Discriminative Assumptions of Utilitarian Bioethics Regarding Individuals with Intellectual Disabilities" (1999) 14:1 Disability & Society 37.
[20] Anita Silvers, "On the Possibility and Desirability of Constructing a Neutral Conception of Disability" (2003) 24:6 Theoretical Medicine & Bioethics 471.
[21] Silvers, "Formal Justice," at 138.
[22] *Ibid.* at 141.

hyperbolic or pejorative tone (i.e., PSID's "extraordinary needs," "spectacular neediness" triggering a "visceral protective [psychological] response"[23]). If this is so, the claim that beneficiaries of support are not "social persons" in a full sense is easier to accept. However, the idea that caring and dependent relationships necessarily carry this negative connotation is still a claim that theorists who justify the duties of justice toward PSID on this basis would be uncomfortable with. Such theorists may insist that one can be the recipient of care, protection, and support without being characterized as spectacularly needy. Of course, such characterizations do exist in an ableist culture, but care ethicists, for instance, are likely to criticize a culture that belittles people in need of care. In other words, one can argue that there is nothing intrinsically wrong with dependence rather than (or in addition to) arguing that PWD are not dependent. Thus, Silvers's argument appears to limit the possibility of a disabled person being a subject of justice (or a "social person in a full and meaningful sense") to their capacity to be integrated. Her requirement that PWD be able to "initiate mutual or reciprocal relationships"[24] and support others is problematic, if we consider the limitations of some PSID.

My concern is that, no matter how progressive, helpful, and inclusive Silvers's proposal is, her attempt to make PWD fit within a mainstream model of the person and her construct of their robust political entitlements constitutes yet another normalizing strategy.[25] Although Silvers criticizes cases of wrongful normalization, such as capping PSID's social support relative to the level of "average talents" or to the lower threshold of a basic minimum, her own characterization of PSID has normalizing features. In some respects, forcing PSID into the traditional liberal model of person (or the contractualist model of social member) risks denying the fact that central aspects of PSID's lives – and of the relationships they have with nondisabled people – sometimes have as much, if not more, to do with caring for them as dependents as with enabling their participation and expression of talents to contribute to the common good. Important aspects of their relations, such as care and tailor-made dependency management, can also be regulated by principles of justice.

I believe that Silvers's proposal is sound in one respect: our philosophical and political focus on compensation is often prejudiced and can result in PSID only having an insular (and generally lesser) moral status than other persons. It is nonetheless unnecessarily reductionist. Even if PSID did have the contracting capacities and talents that Silvers assumes they would have if given the appropriate social support, their robust moral status should still be grounded on aspects of their identity and relations. Otherwise, PSID who, we may find, do not have the

---

[23] Ibid.
[24] Ibid.
[25] By "normalizing," I mean the attempt to conceptualize PWD as entitled to a robust moral status by considering the standards of a "normal," statistically average person, namely by examining the standards of capacities and needs that "normal" people have.

contracting capacities and talents that a contractualist framework requires in order to grant them a robust moral status, would not count as subjects of justice. In other words, while pleading for social reforms that would ensure integration is a promising strategy – and one long employed by proponents of the social model of disability – it is not sufficient to justify integrating PSID who defy normalization.

4.1.3 *Justice for Talents: Which Is Good and for Whose Benefit?*

It is not controversial to say that we take the notion of talent seriously: we recognize the value of cultivating and expressing individual talents and, by respecting people's talent, we show respect for individuals themselves, all while increasing the pool of common resources. In contrast, we generally speak of PSID's "talents," if at all, in a compassionate and metaphorical way, as though they do not really belong to the categories of "talented" or "exceptionally talented" people. Thus, to say that PSID should be conceptualized as a group of talented individuals (rather than talentless or burdensome individuals) or as persons who are entitled to have their talents supported beyond the realization of "average talents" is a more novel and controversial claim, but one worth defending.

Let me begin this discussion by pointing out a problem that affects Silvers's general argument regarding talent, namely the conflation of different (dis)advantages for disabled people. She pulls many conceptual strands into a single bundle of justice-related ideas, models, and strategies that she favors (the "integration" bundle) and, likewise, pulls many strands into a bundle that she criticizes (the "distribution" bundle). This bundling can be problematic when we realize that these different strands do not have to be pulled together and that distinguishing them would, in fact, allow us to see when contractual paradigms may not be the most appropriate lens to use when considering PWD's talents and needs. I have pulled apart a few strands of ideas in order to situate my agreements and disagreements with her position. The following are the conditions that a talent-concerned approach to justice should seek to secure:[26]

(1) Conditions to realize one's talents (the subjective standard);
(2) conditions to realize average or minimum talents (the socially "normal" standard or the objective basic threshold required for human flourishing);
(3) conditions to realize one's exceptional talents; and
(4) conditions to be socially integrated.

---

[26] Here, I understand "justice for talents" as a preference for social arrangements that take the opportunity to develop and express individual talents seriously, paying attention to the untapped potential of groups traditionally considered the "worst off."

One must also be clear about who should benefit from the fostering of talents – society or the individual – or, if both, whether one beneficiary has priority over the other. Lastly, talents could be used either as properties that justify granting a robust status to a being or as a notion guiding redistribution[27] to beings whose status is already secured. Silvers mostly deals with this second notion, as she generally assumes (where she writes on "justice as talents") that people with disabilities are already members of society. But portions of her argument may suggest that being talented is a robust moral status-granting capacity, insofar as the truly talentless fall outside the scope of "justice for talents."

These notions – redistribution and robust moral status – are distinct and should not be assumed to fall within the same category. Perhaps Silvers's claim is that they do (and they may), although I suspect that she only seeks to highlight that, in many cases, these notions are related in the sense that it is both good for the individual and for society to promote talents and exceptional talents, and that social integration allows for the realization of these talents for the individual's and society's sakes. These notions may certainly coincide, but sometimes they will not, and this becomes a problem when we must decide how to distribute limited resources and how to prioritize the realization of certain goods or needs over others.

For example, certain ordinary talents may coincide with social integration, while others may be exercised solitarily. The good of social integration and of talents should not be analytically connected as necessary for one another (unless we take "social integration" to mean having benefitted from an upbringing and from social resources that allow one to possess the capacities that one has, even as a hermit). The same may be even more true of extraordinary talents, if precepts about geniuses being misunderstood hold any truth. While the realization of one's ordinary and extraordinary talents will further one's well-being or flourishing, talents will not always serve society by, for instance, increasing the common pool of resources. Incidentally, we may define "serving the social good" loosely, but there is still a limit to the definition. While some talents, such as those possessed by an iconoclastic poet, may enrich humanity's heritage for generations, the exercise of other talents, such as meditating, will be for the individual's benefit alone. It is also unclear whether society owes a stringent duty to help a person develop their exceptional talents if other people have not had the chance to develop their ordinary talents. This "duty" to the individual with exceptional talents will be even more questionable if the ordinary talents of those others serve society more than they serve the individual.

Silvers does not abandon the compensatory distributive discourse altogether. Rather, she sets it aside to argue that people with disabilities should be granted

---

[27] Instead of using the idiom of "distribution," we could say that talent is a notion that can be used to guide the reform of social structures. In this sense, traditional outliers would take part in social processes delineating conditions of redistribution, as well as delineating the very nature of those talents, the role they play in society, and the thresholds or benchmarks used to develop and exercise those talents and conditions.

the conditions for their social integration and for the realization of their talents on a different basis. However, once the above distinctions are made, this conclusion is not so obvious, and a contractual account may not sufficiently explain PSID's entitlement to a robust claim to support their needs.

For instance, we could cap social support for the realization of people's "ordinary talents" at 60 percent (evaluated subjectively) given our limited resources, but then cap social support for the realization of people's exceptional talents at 10 percent.[28] If we decided to give more than the allotted 60 percent or 10 percent to disabled people, this would likely be a form of compensation for the losses that they incur in many areas of their lives, as opposed to the simple result of an assessment of the value of their talents. However, in more general terms, although I believe that justice for PSID can be framed as "justice for talents" in many respects, I do not think that approaching their special needs in redistributive terms is always nefarious. I would be inclined to say that promoting and respecting PSID's talents can often be properly understood as a form of *caring* for them. In other words, fostering PSID's talents may sometimes primarily be a way to show proper concern for them, to duly recognize their needs, and to act upon it. An immediate objection to my suggestion will be that everyone wants to give "proper" concern and "due" recognition, but the whole question is to justify what counts as "proper" and "due." A follow-up objection is that any answer I could give would reintroduce the vicious redistributive paradigm that Silvers wishes to avoid (i.e., the one that casts PWD as the "worst off"). A third objection is that I cannot avoid reintroducing this negative stereotyping simply calling pity-like attitudes by more virtuous names (like love, concern, or care). A response to all three objections can be found in care ethics. For instance, Michael Slote, one of its influential proponents, holds that institutions are just when they are designed in a way that "reflect empathically caring motivation on the part of (enough of) those responsible for originating and maintaining them"[29] My point is not to explore care ethics in this chapter (and the familiar charges of improper paternalism and intuitionism that comes with it) but to emphasize that a properly empathetic or caring stance need not imply pity. Many people who care for PSID – from family members to friends, to teachers, and other professional caregivers – feel admiration and respect for them and their talents *through* a caring lens, rather through any kind of utilitarian reasoning. Distributive reasoning within politicized ethics of care need not entail the stereotypes that Silvers seeks to dismiss.

---

[28] At times, Silvers seems to conflate both kinds of talents which are, after all, all parts of someone's talent store. But our intuitions differ when someone can reach a "talent score" of 100 while someone else only has the potential to score a 50 (if we suppose for argument's sake that this scale is a proper way to talk about talents). To help both people to achieve 60 percent of their respective potentials seems unfair, as this goes far past a threshold that already respects people's basic needs to realize their talents, and seems more of a luxury (and support of privilege) than realizing other aspects of people's welfare.

[29] Michael Slote, *Moral Sentimentalism* (Oxford: Oxford University Press, 2010), at 125.

On the other hand, Silvers grounds her theory of "justice for talents" on two pillars that are different than caring, and even more different than compensation and charity.[30] First, she focuses on the fact that realizing people's talents "enabl[es] cooperative interaction among them,"[31] lets them participate in "productive cooperation," and does not exclude them from "collaborative human activities" where these strengths and talents can be put to use.[32] However, this conception of talent limits what kinds of talents would be supported for those who are in demand from a social point of view. There is a good side to this: it frames PSID as being "like the rest of us." We are all "selling" our talents intersubjectively, and part of Silvers's argument is that we should not think of PSID as having anything less to "sell." However, it is not obvious that all PSID do indeed have talents to "sell." Some PSID may have a number of gifts and their very existence may enrich the lives of those around them in many ways, but not in ways that have market value. Thus, the first pillar of Silvers's "justice for talents" argument connects social integration and talent in a way that seems unnecessary, limiting the notion of talents or the justifications for supporting talents.

Silvers's second pillar is oriented toward individuals rather than the common good: promoting someone's talents respects that person's autonomy and improves their self-esteem.[33] It is true that autonomy and the development of personal projects and talents is a prized outcome – not only in the social contract tradition but in modern moral and political philosophy writ large. However, it is not clear that supporting the talents of PSID as a matter of remediation or care should come before supporting their talents as a reward for exercising these talents. (Otherwise, as I will suggest, capping their talents in more restrictive ways would not seem as unfair.)

4.1.4 A Remediating Distributive Scheme or an Integrative Pro-Talents Scheme

In this section, I criticize the tendency, as illustrated by Silvers, to opt for a unique scheme or a unique justification to deal with PWD, as well as the tendency to generalize conclusions that apply to some cognitively disabled people to every person in the larger group of PWD. These reductionist or generalizing tendencies, though easily correctable, characterize a considerable amount of literature on disability and justice. I do not reject Silvers's position but instead I suggest that its reach needs to be curtailed.

---

[30] Some might suggest that there is a third pillar in Silvers's argument: that the development of talents, including exceptional talents, is the relevant social aim. However, I situate Silvers's position in the more conventional framework of setting social priorities by thinking about people's well-being.
[31] Silvers, "No Talent," at 198.
[32] Ibid. at 196.
[33] Ibid. at 192.

I agree with Silvers that integrative schemes are important in order to respect PSID. Further, I agree that conceptualizing PSID as non-reciprocating recipients of care is likely to feed (and feed on) prejudices about disabled people as "talentless and burdensome." In many cases, this conceptualization leads to insufficiently valuing the input of people with disabilities and our relationships with them, resulting in a loss for society. I do not agree, however, that a framework that focuses on compensation or remediation for the worst off is conceptually bound to cause this prejudicial impact. Silvers's claim that it inescapably[34] causes such an impact seems unjustified. In fact, this compensatory framework could be preserved, and its harmful social reception mitigated in practical ways that would not lead to its wholesale rejection.

Are there other reasons for considering PWD as autonomous beings to whom we owe integration as a matter of justice, rather than as vulnerable and dependent beings for whom justice requires us to compensate, remediate, and care? In addition to the reasons noted above, Silvers (and Francis, on this subject) note the advantages of having PSID remain within our mainstream political tradition and liberal commitments. These reasons justify promoting a conceptualization of PSID as social participants but I find that they do not compellingly justify why we should *not* conceptualize people with profound disabilities as "cared-for" – perhaps even the "worst off" – and deserving support and protection as a matter of justice. This one-sided characterization of PSID is also criticized in alternative theories that consider PSID to be primarily dependents, and only considers that they ought to be integrated or encouraged in order to develop their talents as a means of properly caring for them. There are two paradigms – both encompassing a conception of PSID – which form the basis for their subjecthood and of the duties of justice that are owed to them. The former nests obligations of care or protection within a more fundamental obligation to respect the autonomy of people with disabilities, whereas the latter nests the obligation to respect their autonomy within a more fundamental duty to care for them. A third option would be to accept a paradigm that reconciles both dimensions (caring and autonomy) by recognizing that PSID are at once autonomous and dependent, that these traits are ineliminable aspects of our shared humanity, and that both morality and justice should take this into account without trying to subsume one dimension into the other. This pluralist model implies that all human beings are dependent and vulnerable – as well as autonomous – to varying degrees at different times in their lives. Such a model avoids singling out PSID as a radically different category of political subjects who do not only contingently happen to have some greater needs in some particular social contexts but who are somehow "ontologically needy." I will return to this pluralist model in the concluding chapter.

It may be useful to contrast Silvers and Eva Kittay's personal experiences to make sense of their respective generalizations,[35] as they both use the category of

---

[34] Silvers, "Formal Justice," at 34.
[35] Silvers camps herself on the integration/autonomy side (*ibid.* at 38–39, 144).

"disability" in a way that requires more specific analysis. Professor Silvers was a wheelchair user and, like other wheelchair users, she had to cope with much exclusion and humiliation.[36] Despite this exclusion and humiliation being prejudiced and unfounded, it often costs wheelchair users the opportunity to exercise their entitlements and express their talents. It is understandable why exceptionally gifted people like Silvers are not interested in charity. They demand instead to be treated with decency and to be given the same opportunities as others in order to realize their conceptions of the good and to satisfy their tastes. Indeed, it is profoundly insulting for someone as capable as Silvers was to be socially imagined as a "burden," an image that is reinforced by the policies and theories that emphasize disabled people's needs over their talents, and distinguish their needs as somehow essentially different from those of others. A modified version of nineteenth-century feminist Sarah Grimké's famous statement would capture the stance that Silvers applies to disability: *I ask no favors for people with disabilities. I surrender not our claim to equality. All I ask of our fellow able-bodied citizens is, that they will take their feet from off our necks.*[37]

Professor Kittay, on the other hand, has a daughter, Sesha, who has congenital cerebral palsy and a severe mental disability. When I met Sesha she was expressive, pleasant, and welcoming, but she was unable to talk and it is unclear to me whether she would have recognized me if I had come to pay her a visit on the following day. Kittay has been Sesha's caregiver for her whole life and, like most parents of cognitively impaired people, has made sure that her daughter will be properly cared for when her parents can no longer carry out this work. It is perhaps unsurprising that much of Kittay's work has focused on the issue of the fair distribution of caring.[38]

I believe that such personal experiences enrich one's philosophical arguments, as they enrich the life of the philosopher and her moral insight. At the same time, while both Silvers and Kittay address valid problems in their writing, relying upon personal experiences may risk overgeneralizing. There is a danger that a philosopher, in wanting to make a forceful point about the category of persons with disabilities as a whole, neglects that alternative views may also hold in other cases, or in the same cases concurrently but to varying degrees.[39]

As obvious as this point might sound, Silvers and Kittay – like other authors – sometimes broaden the scope of their conclusions more than is necessary. The

---

[36] *Ibid.* at 1, 114–15.
[37] Sarah Grimké, *Letters on the Equality of the Sexes and the Condition of Woman*, Letter II (Boston, 1837). The original reads: "I ask no favors for my sex. I surrender not our claim to equality. All I ask of our brethren is, that they will take their feet from off our necks."
[38] Consider Eva Kittay, *Love's Labor: Essays on Women, Equality and Dependency* (New York: Routledge, 1999).
[39] On the issue of dealing philosophically with highly personal issues related to disability, see Eva Kittay, "The Personal Is Philosophical Is Political: A Philosopher and Mother of a Cognitively Disabled Person Sends Notes from the Battlefield" (2009) 40:3–4 Metaphilosophy 606.

category of "disabled people" cannot be equated with the category of the "PSID," nor can different individual PSID or their social contexts be conflated. For example, there are important moral differences between physical and mental disabilities, as well as between light and severe cognitive impairments, since they are associated with different needs and obstacles that can be met and overcome through different relationships. In the four essays by Silvers (one co-written with Francis), only one is about disability in general. The examples used in that particular essay[40] illustrate cases where conceptualizations of disabled individuals as objects of protection and care rather than as social participants have not been beneficial for all parties involved.[41] Silvers then seamlessly transposes many of her arguments and her core way of thinking into her three other essays that are focused on mental disability. However, this transposition becomes problematic when it is applied to PSID: it underestimates the number of PSID that this integrative theory and its liberal conceptual apparatus – no matter how broadly conceived – fails to plausibly capture, and it fails to properly express why we feel morally obligated to people with severe intellectual disabilities.

The solution is to make it clear that PSID constitute a unique case. This assertion should not alarm theorists who are inclined to detect theoretical moves that have socially outlying effects. I am not suggesting that PSID fall under a different status altogether. I believe that both paradigms of autonomy and dependence apply to all human beings, and that both frameworks apply alternately and to different extents at different times of our lives. Only narrow (and somewhat outlandish) understandings of autonomy, care, and dependency allow us to categorize people as *either* autonomous *or* dependent. Philosophical, political, and legal constructs that idealize reductionist categories do more harm than good. The fact that an individual might be extremely dependent and have almost inexistent autonomy should not fundamentally affect her moral and political status, even though the autonomy-based framework would apply to a very limited degree or, in some cases, not at all. The level of our autonomy does not necessarily correlate to our level of dependence in an inversely proportional way, except when both apply to the same role, relationship, or event, and where their simultaneous increase would be contradictory. To illustrate this, one can be highly autonomous and yet highly dependent on others, as is the case of people leading complex collective endeavors toward success. One's lack of autonomy in a particular respect, like feeding oneself, may more or less directly correlate to an augmented dependence (in this case, being fed) in that specific regard. It does not independently affect, however, that person's capacity to perform other roles (e.g., being a university professor).

[40] Silvers, "Formal Justice."
[41] I would still assert that, even in these cases, remediating frameworks should not be abandoned altogether, although I agree that they should recede when they become incompatible with more appropriate integrative frameworks, just as paternalist outlook and caring attitudes should make way for respecting autonomy when the context demands it.

This conciliatory or pluralist model would not reject the pertinence of social contract theory for describing moral obligations and duties of justice, but it would curtail it to certain relational aspects of PSID's lives (and to aspects of the lives of nondisabled people as well). By contrast, the exclusively contractual model insists that justice is fundamentally a matter of dealings with subjects who are autonomous and independent and that, while other traits (like vulnerability and dependence) might be ineliminable, they indirectly become considerations of justice only if the welfare of subjects with those traits is rationally discussed by contractors and conceived of in a variety of ways (which, ultimately, exclude PSID).

A pluralist model, if successful, would at least curtail contractualism's ambition to provide the grounds for a robust moral status. I start sketching out this model in Section 4.2.4 and in the concluding chapter of this book. The second portion of the current chapter addresses contractualist views that insist that PSID have what it takes to be contractors.

4.2 PSID'S CAPACITY FOR FORMULATING AND REALIZING A CONCEPTION OF THE GOOD

An important constructivist feature of social contract theory is the idea that a substantial notion of the "good" (pursued individually and collectively) should not precede (and determine) contractual procedure. Instead, a substantial notion of the good should: (1) be an outcome of, or inherent in, the developed contractual procedure and (2) be left for individuals to determine for themselves within certain (contractually determined) constraints.

It is therefore important for Silvers and Francis to show that PSID can have and express such a "will" – that is, that they can effectively author a conception of the good and, in so doing, place themselves among those actors who require a contractual scenario to avoid conflict and to maximize the possibility of realizing their conception of the good. Their aim, in this regard, is to show that PSID possess the powers or capacities necessary to be "full-fledged cooperators" within the social contract tradition. Silvers and Francis argue that PSID possess the three powers that traditionally characterize the connections between a moral agent and a conception of the good within contractualist thought (particularly the Rawlsian branch) – reciprocity, responsibility, and self-origination.

The power to *reciprocate* is the capacity to "[govern] one's self to benefit others in return for being benefited oneself."[42] Contrary to Rawls and Nussbaum who claim that reciprocity is foundational in traditional social contract theory, and similar to

---

[42] Leslie Francis and Anita Silvers, "Thinking about the Good: Reconfiguring Liberal Metaphysics (or Not) for People with Cognitive Disabilities" in Eva Feder Kittay and Licia Carlson, eds., *Cognitive Disability and Its Challenge to Moral Philosophy* (Malden, MA: Wiley-Blackwell, 2010), 237 at 249.

Christie Hartley, who suggests an alternative understanding of reciprocity to make social contract theory inclusive of PSID,[43] Silvers and Francis claim that the capacity to reciprocate is not required to obtain the "status of full participant in social cooperation."[44] In other words, they reject the requirement of reciprocity as meaning "abilities to strategize or to be of use to others,"[45] but would not reject it if it were reduced to meaning "mutually beneficial capacity to engage with one another."

Silvers and Francis's notion of *responsibility* correlates the capacity to control one's thoughts about a conception of the good with one's understanding of its feasibility. These capacities enable an agent to be in control of a conception of the good, rather than having this conception control her, and to be responsible "for pursuing and realizing that good."[46] PSID may not always be able to review the feasibility and propriety of their conception of the good but they may be assisted in doing so (and may also be assisted in elaborating on the conception itself, which is the third power).

The last moral power is the most fundamental: it is the capacity to be the author of a conception of the good. Put another way, it is the capacity to subjectively value one's self and one's goals rather than to simply endorse society's values. As we will see in our analysis of some of Christine Korsgaard's arguments in the following chapter, this is the Kantian idea that the ultimate, nonderivative source of value is found in a legislating act of the individual will. Value is not found in the world independently from the exercise of a capacity to "take [oneself] and [one's] personally embraced ideas of the good ... as the source of [one's] duties and obligations."[47] These powers of "self-origination" and "self-authentication" are endorsed by Rawls,[48] as well as by Silvers and Francis as the fundamental requirements of a full social participant.

4.2.1 Beyond the Independence Assumption

Silvers and Francis reinterpret the Rawlsian contractualist requirement that subjects of justice should possess these moral powers rather than discarding it or diminishing its centrality to a theory of justice. Employing the same strategy that they did in their "Justice Through Trust," they claim to explain it in its most plausible form. In this case, like all of their essays analyzed in this book, they do not depart from traditional liberal concepts but instead claim that these concepts have been misunderstood.

---

[43] See Section 4.2.2, "The Capacity to Engage."
[44] Francis and Silvers, "Thinking about the Good," at 250.
[45] Ibid. at 251.
[46] Ibid.
[47] Ibid. at 253.
[48] Ibid. at 240, 253; John Rawls, "Kantian Constructivism in Moral Theory" (1980) 77:9 J Phil 515 at 546.

Thus, they maintain that a proper understanding of these concepts – purged of myths and prejudices – would allow for the integration of PSID.

Part of their strategy is to question the "independence assumption" and the normative conception of the subject upon which it rests. The "independence assumption," at work in liberal theories including those of Rawls, postulates that people build their conception of the good "in abstraction from interaction with others. Ontologically, everyone is an island with respect to constructing conceptions of the good."[49] This assumption relies on a "deeply normative ... idealization of agency as insularly independent."[50]

Silvers and Francis distinguish between two aspects of constructing a theory of the good. The first is the idea that I have described as being central to the social contract theory and its metaphysical and political recentralization around the subject as the original source of value (*qua* valuer). The conception must be elaborated individually, personally, or subjectively so as to be the subject's own in a morally relevant way. The second aspect is that this elaboration must take place in abstraction of social relations. Silvers and Francis wish to preserve the first requirement and jettison the second.[51] This is in line with their focus on preserving the authorship of a conception of the good, autonomy, and self-origination of value, while accepting that support, dependence, social help, and social scripts are used in the process.

Their justification is that the independence assumption is mistaken. Drawing notably from feminist literature[52] and from Anthony Appiah's concept of social scripts (i.e., "narratives that people can use in shaping their projects and in telling their life stories"[53]), they argue that the exercise of autonomy must be understood – in ethical terms – as taking place within a matrix of relationships. Moreover, conceptions of the good, though they "must be tailored [to reflect] the individual's subjective experiences and personal characteristics" (i.e., the "individual" aspect), must also take into account social contexts, scripts, and roles.[54] Appiah conceives of individuality as a social rather than presocial notion: even though it is the product of a subjective creation, it must respond to our environment. This is a compelling view; the subjective input consists of the individual constructing her identity by responding to, endorsing, picking, and valuing elements of social scripts or narratives that are provided by collective identities.[55] The individual cannot elaborate her

---

[49] Francis and Silvers, "Thinking about the Good," at 480.
[50] Leslie Francis and Anita Silvers, "Liberalism and Individually Scripted Ideas of the Good: Meeting the Challenge of Dependent Agency" (2007) 33:2 Soc Theory & Prac 311 at 332.
[51] *Ibid.* at 311, 322, 332; Francis and Silvers, "Thinking about the Good," at 243–44, 254.
[52] For example, Catriona MacKenzie and Natalie Stoljar, eds., *Relational Autonomy: Feminist Perspectives on Autonomy, Agency, and the Social Self* (New York: Oxford University Press, 2000).
[53] Anthony Appiah, *The Ethics of Identity* (Princeton, NJ: Princeton University Press, 2007), at 22.
[54] Francis and Silvers, "Individually Scripted Ideas," at 322.
[55] For an account of human nature complementing Appiah's view of individuality, see Christian Smith, *Moral, Believing Animals: Human Personhood and Culture* (Oxford: Oxford University Press, 2003).

conception of the good *independently* from these cultural standards, though she can *autonomously* do so, which implies that she can reject these narratives instead of using them in "shaping [her] pursuits and telling [her] life stories."[56] Appiah, Silvers, and Francis therefore subscribe to the communitarian acknowledgment of the necessity to start from collective "scripts" when constructing one's personal identity and, more specifically, to employ social contract theory when elaborating a conception of the good.[57]

Going one step further, they introduce the idea of individuals receiving support when elaborating a conception of the good. Rejecting the "independence assumption" allows them not only to correct the mistaken belief that agents construct their conception of the good in abstraction of social scripts — and thus exercising their autonomy in a non-relational way — but also allows them to claim that agents reach their personalized conceptions of their good aided by others. Whether through parents teaching us about the many social narratives that are available to us, through colleagues inspiring us to adopt one narrative rather than another, through friends helping us to organize our narrative by calling our bluff or criticizing our quixotism, we constantly receive external input in building our conceptions of the good. Similarly, in response to Nicholas Southwood's acknowledgment of the important role that "advisors" play in our lives,[58] Silvers and Francis note: "[w]e commonly advise or urge or even intervene to induce unmindful or feckless individuals to shift plans or adopt different projects. Most of us do not build responsible aspirations independent of our responses to other people, nor are we expected to do so."[59]

Since we are all dependent to varying degrees upon some kind of advisorship, there is no need for a unique framework to apply in the case of PSID, whose trustees and/or collaborators should provide a mode of support that is tailored to their needs, assisting them in constructing and realizing subjective conceptions of the good.

Two elements of their argument cement this claim. First, they protect themselves from the criticism that their view implies a controversial, substantial conception of the person by denying that theorists who claim to provide a political rather than metaphysical account (like Rawls and Nussbaum) do not really succeed in doing so. The independence assumption is precisely the sort of metaphysical commitment that Rawls seeks to avoid: it relies on the ontological picture of people as independent self-validators who are bound and informed by reasonableness alone, which excludes the idea that "conceptions of the good are interactive and intersubjective

---

[56] Appiah, *The Ethics of Identity*, at 108.
[57] *Ibid.* at 22, 108; Silvers, "Formal Justice," at 102; Francis and Silvers, "Thinking about the Good," at 254; Francis and Silvers, "Individually Scripted Ideas," at 322, 331–32.
[58] Nicholas Southwood, *Contractualism and the Foundations of Morality* (Oxford: Oxford University Press, 2010), at 111ff.
[59] Francis and Silvers, "Thinking about the Good," at 251; see also Francis and Silvers, "Individually Scripted Ideas," at 325, 332–33.

products."[60] Second, they reject the idea that autonomy must be a non-scalar notion to play its role within social contract theory. Francis explains that autonomy is a bundle of various attributes – including the capacities to value, to be responsible, and to self-originate, as described above, as well as the capacities to act in accordance with categorical imperatives (by opposition to desires) – necessary to not be subject to coercion and to participate in the construction of justice.[61] Her point is to demonstrate that PSID possess enough of these attributes to be meaningfully described as autonomous.

The different arguments presented by Silvers and Francis in the essays that I explore here fit coherently together and amount to a compelling defence of a dependent contractual agency. I find this view hard to resist and I agree that our contractual agency is much more dependent and socially scripted than what the "independence assumption" suggests. However, I note that their characterization of the "independence assumption" is perhaps too bold or unfair to Rawls. For example, Charles Taylor's similar criticism of "atomism" – a theoretical posture characterizing social contract theories that is connected to the idea that an obligation to "belong to or sustain society" derives from, rather than precedes and shapes, the ascription of individual rights – does not imply that atomistic conceptions of the good must be arrived at both individually and in isolation of everyone else.[62] If anything, the fact that Rawls and other liberals would make some room for individuals to rely on others to elaborate their conception of the good supports, rather than undermines, Silvers and Francis's argument.

Unlike them, however, I do not think that this argument applies to all PSID. For some, a "proxy" does not seem able to successfully express PSID's powers of responsibility and self-origination – at least not to the extent relevant for social contract theory. Also, for some (if not all) PSID, and potentially even nondisabled people as well, a person's autonomy (or their cognitively assisted autonomy) does not completely explain why we are obligated to others in many circumstances, including as a matter of justice.

While I would expect theorists like Silvers and Francis to insist upon a more optimistic empirical assessment (and perhaps not to share my intuition that the contractualist framework fails to completely capture what we owe to PSID), I believe that the way to successfully escape the criticisms of their account of a proxy is to reduce their notion of "collaborators" to the notion of trustees speaking in PSID's interest, whether or not this speech translates PSID's actual will, desire, autonomy, or conception of the good. However, accepting this position would be a retreat from the theory of passive citizenship, which I will criticize in the next chapter for its

---

[60] Francis and Silvers, "Thinking about the Good," at 243.
[61] Leslie Francis, "Understanding Autonomy in Light of Intellectual Disability" in Brownlee and Cureton, eds., *Disability and Disadvantage*, at 200–202.
[62] Charles Taylor, *Philosophy and the Human Sciences: Philosophical Papers*, vol. 2 (Cambridge: Cambridge University Press, 1985), at 188.

inability to provide *contractual* grounds for granting such a fictional representation to beings who would not otherwise be incorporated into a contract-based society.

Before criticizing their account of cognitive prosthesis, I wish to consider an alternative to Silvers and Francis's (still relatively demanding) contractual requirements for the powers of autonomy, responsibility, and self-origination. Christie Hartley has suggested a more radical lowering or broadening of the cognitive requirements set by social contract theory to grant an individual robust moral status. Instead of capacities to autonomously elaborate a conception of the good as well as a second-order idea about its feasibility and desirability, Hartley suggests that all that is required is a capacity to engage.

4.2.2 The Capacity to Engage

Hartley argues that all that contractualism requires is the capacity to "make a *cooperative* contribution to a society based on mutual respect" for someone to be granted full membership as a subject of justice.[63] From there, she can deny the Rawlsian requirement that subjects of justice ought to possess the two powers of moral personality[64] to partake in the kind of social cooperation that lies at the heart of contractualism. She argues that almost all PSID fulfill this requirement.

Let me flesh out Hartley's key points and explain why I believe they either beg the question or rely on noncontractualist intuitions. That said, even though I do not think that her key points entirely succeed in integrating PSID as they purport to do, her argument has the merit of decisively bringing the Kantian thread that is woven into the contractualist tapestry to the forefront. Not all subjects of justice are (Rawlsian) philosophers, even though this is what the sophisticated requirements of social contract theory seem to imply. Theorists like Francis, highlighting how autonomy is multifaceted and that being a subject of contractualist justice does not require all of these facets, or theorists like Hartley, who say the same of social cooperation, are much-needed voices trying to make sense of the fact that subjects of justice are not equally cooperating; many of them receive more than they give or the other way around. As Hartley (and Korsgaard and Nussbaum) points out, "[c]ontractualists need not claim those to whom the principles of justice apply are the same as those who design the principles."[65] That is, not everyone needs to be a social designer of fair institutions. One could respond by noting that these statements confuse the ideal representation of subjects of justice and designers of social institutions with actual citizens like you and I but my point is rather that this ideal is not the right ideal. A contract-based society should not be idealized as an expansion

---

[63] Hartley, "Justice for the Disabled," at 28.
[64] "[T]he capacity for a sense of right and justice (the capacity to honor fair terms of cooperation and thus be reasonable), and the capacity for a conception of the good (and thus to be rational)" (Rawls, *Political Liberalism*, at 302).
[65] Hartley, "Justice for the Disabled," at 28.

of a one-to-one, tit-for-tat contract, but rather as a matrix of relations enabling "contractual relations"[66] to take place. As we saw, this idea is most forcefully expressed by Silvers and Francis. My criticism of Hartley is that, while she rightly extends the range of relations that, we intuitively think, should count to make one a full subject of justice, it is hard to see how these relations still qualify as contractual, even on her broad contractualist account.

Hartley uses contractualism's well-established commitments to reinterpret some of its notions that may otherwise exclude most of PSID. Notably, she understands the notion of social cooperation as (contractualist) reciprocity rather than as the notion of mutual advantage.[67] By that, she means that cooperators' contributions do not have to be "a net gain for society" and she shows that a Rawlsian understanding of reciprocity as mutuality may plausibly depart from a more contractarian understanding. Rawls conceives of reciprocity as: "a relation between citizens expressed by principles of justice that regulate a social world in which everyone benefits judged with respect to an appropriate benchmark of equality defined with respect to that world."[68] Further, he claims that "all who do their part as the recognized rules require are to benefit as specified by a public and agreed-upon standard."[69]

This understanding of reciprocity opens the door to what we may call "rule-contractualism," in the sense that the focus is not on whether a particular individual can partake of all social institutions as the "fullest possible" idealized participant of the social contract could, but whether she can participate in a contractualist society. Rule-contractualism displaces, rather than answers, the following question: what are the rules according to which individuals can act to be social cooperators? On contractualist accounts of the passive citizenship of PSID or on contractarian accounts of their robust moral status, this rule-contractualism may require only that their inclusion improves the conditions that make a contractual society operate well, even though they may only be passive subjects or objects. In contrast, Hartley answers that individuals are to be considered full subjects of justice if they take an active participatory role, which brings the notion of mutual respect to the forefront of what contractualism values and promotes.[70] However, as we will see, this could also be taken to mean that PSID are not active participants in the social contract, but only active participants in certain relations that are necessary for a contractualist society to operate well. In that case, they would not really be "active contractual subjects" but would instead be passive citizens or objects, which would hinder the

---

[66] Not in the ordinary sense of contract but in the sense of mutually benefitting and binding expressions of one's autonomous will.
[67] Hartley, "Justice for the Disabled," at 18–19.
[68] Rawls, *Political Liberalism*, at 17.
[69] John Rawls, *Justice as Fairness: A Restatement*, ed. Erin Kelly (Cambridge: Harvard University Press, 2001), at 6.
[70] Hartley, "Justice for the Disabled," at 28. "Contractualism concerns the establishment of mutual respect among members of society; this essentially has to do with individuals relating to each other in a certain kind of way" (at 29).

quality of their status, as we saw in the chapter on contractarianism and passive citizenship.

Hartley's next move is to distinguish herself from Cynthia Stark or Rawls who, while making room for a spectrum within which "how much individuals contribute is not important," remain mindful that certain individuals are not able to contribute to "all spheres of social life: the political realm, the family, civil society, and the economy."[71] Hartley suggests that the deepest commitment of contractualism (to reciprocity as social cooperation within a society that promotes mutual respect) does not "compare or evaluate the different contributions of members" and whether they are "able to contribute to each of the main institutions."[72]

This is how Hartley arrives at her desired conclusion that contractualism only requires a capacity to contribute cooperatively to *some* of the social institutions in a way that allows relations of mutual respect to take place. Hartley says that such relations include, for instance, relationships of care, which are relationships in which almost all PSID can meaningfully participate (at least at the receiving end). On her account, all they require is a capacity to engage, which she defines as:

> [T]he capacity to see another as a responsive, animate being and to recognize the ability of the other to be responsive to something she interprets as a communication to herself. It is the ability to recognize others in a certain kind of way and to attribute to them a certain kind of standing (the standing of a being with whom communication is possible), but it also involves the ability to make some kind of communication to another.[73]

It is at this point that Hartley's argument becomes problematic. First, it seems to make the value of relationships with PSID contingent upon that they factually improve the quality or number of mutually respectful relations. On this reading, I take her to say that many relationships in which PSID participate are only derivatively valuable. She says: "[c]ertain kinds of relationships among members of society such as mutually supportive companionate relationships and relationships based on mutual trust help make relationships based on respect possible."[74]

However, other passages raise a textual ambiguity and she could mean – instead, or also – that these relations are themselves an instance of mutually respectful relations. This raises: (a) the empirical question of whether PSID can indeed take part in relations of respect in the contractualist Kantian sense that she has been evoking. Or, alternatively, (b) if we defined respect more broadly or along a spectrum to apply in the case of PSID, it begs the question of what would be the basis for such respect.

---

[71] *Ibid.* at 24.
[72] *Ibid.* at 27.
[73] *Ibid.* at 28.
[74] *Ibid.* at 29.

Hartley writes that "the capacity for engagement makes possible certain sorts of cooperative relationships that fundamentally concern individuals relating to each other in a certain kind of way and are themselves important to contractualist society."[75] I am not sure in what "kind of way" these (say, passive, caring) relations would be important to a *contractualist* society (though I have no doubt that they matter to society and ground duties of justice on noncontractual grounds). If she means nothing other than the argument offered by Silvers and Francis in "Justice Through Trust" – that is, that such relations, by their very existence, create a beneficial climate of trust – then we have already examined the problems with this argument. If she means to give a meaningful role to PSID not as moral legislators, but as members within a community of moral legislators, thus giving them a role beyond passive citizenship, it is unclear how the value of the relations requiring a capacity to engage can be explained in such contractualist terms. Hartley refers to authors arguing outside the boundaries of Kantian contractualism, like Kittay, who grounds duties to care on care ethics and Silvers, who grounds them on trust and some contractarian assessment of the desirability of such trust. Now, it could be said that trust and caring are just two types of relationships that are "crucial to establishing a society based on mutual respect through their capacity for engagement"[76] – that is, a contractualist society. However, Hartley would have to explain who is owed mutual respect and why: she is not saying that trust or caring matter in and of themselves, but rather that they matter because they contribute to a contractualist society based on mutual respect. The membership to such a society is most likely based on some notion of special worth inhering in individuals, but the source of such a worth must be explained.

Such explanations should not be found in PSID's usefulness for society, if usefulness is understood in a way that is reminiscent of the contractarian instrumentalizing and self-interested tendencies that Hartley rejects.[77] Hartley sets out to argue that the relationships in which PSID are able to engage meaningfully are important to a contractualist theory of justice and important in a way that grants PSID full subjecthood. However, I find that the value of the relations in which many PSID engage cannot be explained by contractual terms. At best, she makes a case that they are derivatively valuable in the sense that they facilitate and promote the sort of mutually respectful relationships that do matter. In that sense, her reading of Rawls evokes what Kant says about our indirect duties toward animals.[78] Although she tries

---

[75] *Ibid.*
[76] *Ibid.* at 28.
[77] *Ibid.* at 18.
[78] For instance, when she says, "through relationships with others, individuals who lack the two moral powers can contribute to the family and civil society more generally by helping others develop values that are important for fair cooperation" (*ibid.* at 29). For Kant's view on our obligations toward animals, see his *Lectures on Ethics*, J. B. Schneewind, trans. and ed. Peter Heath (New York: Cambridge University Press, 1997), at 212.

to go further than saying that treating PSID well will improve our treatment of subjects of justice, I do not see how her additional arguments are contractualist, Kantian, or Rawlsian.

Hartley is right to focus on Rawls's view of justice as cooperation based on mutual respect, requiring citizens to "recognize the independent validity of the claims of others" instead of essentially as a (contractarian) "cooperative venture for mutual advantage."[79] But whereas Rawls bases the validity of his claim on individual moral powers, like Kant who grounds intrinsic moral consideration on moral agency, Hartley is stuck between a rock and a hard place. Either she grants derivative value to PSID on the basis that they can partake of relations which, in turn, serve relations that are truly valuable on a contractualist account, or she develops an account of the value of the relations in which PSID actually engage, which can hardly be contractualist.

This is a paradox or a tension in her argument. The contractualist seeks reasons for attributing full moral consideration to people on grounds that are not merely self-regarding – characteristics that call for respect in the person (i.e., their dignity) – whereas the contractarian looks for a self-serving benefit that stems from interacting with another person. Hartley explicitly endorses the contractualist view and rejects the contractarian one. But after presenting the contractualist view and a Kantian reading of Rawls focusing on mutually respectful (rather than beneficial) relations, she turns to a more instrumentalizing argument, in which she claims that PSID can engage in relations that ultimately serve society. In order to stay within the other-regarding argument she had previously been making, it seems that she has to explain why we value PSID for themselves, not because of their contribution. However, she may lack a theory to support this argument. She tries to use the Kantian or Rawlsian justifications, but they do not fit PSID and, as I have explained, it is not satisfactory to suggest (even if it were accurate) that these relations can help other, intrinsically valuable, relations to take place and flourish, for this simply introduce the aforementioned paradox or tension into her argument. What theory, then, can we supplement her argument with that would better fit PSID's actual capacities?

4.2.3 *Playing One's Part: Extending the Repertoire of Social Roles beyond Contractually Valuable Ones*

Rawls considers "part" to mostly mean "contribution," but it can also mean a "role," as in a part in a play. In Rawls's case, the pertinent "role" is that of the contributor, so both meanings are conflated, but Rawls is aware that humans can play many parts and that notions of personhood or human nature could be associated with the notions of *homo oeconomicus*, *homo faber*, or *homo politicus*. He writes: "Beginning with the ancient world, the concept of the person has been understood,

---

[79] Hartley, "Justice for the Disabled," at 19. Hartley is quoting Rawls' *A Theory of Justice*.

in both philosophy and law, as the concept of someone who can take part in, or who can play a role in, social life, and hence exercise and respect his various rights and duties."[80]

His commitment to conceiving of justice as a fair system of cooperation led him to focus on one particular part – that of contributor – defining a "person" as a "normal and fully cooperating [member] ... over a complete life."[81] Further, he claims that only those who benefit others can receive social benefits themselves: "all who do their part as the recognized rules require are to benefit as specified by a public and agreed-upon standard."[82]

Like Hartley, I believe that this definition does not limit the notions of "part" and "doing one's part" to paying back in a "tit-for-tat" contractarian way. However, unlike Hartley, I am not bound by the deep Kantian commitment of Rawlsian contractualism that found people's "inviolability" on a conception of persons as rational beings who are able to assess justifications.[83] Notably, this allows me to consider whether one could play a "part" in a way that would not involve cooperation or contribution. This concept begins to take shape when we reflect upon the "part" that PSID play in our society. If we start by asking which "role" – contractual or otherwise – PSID play in our society and by questioning the nature and potential value of the relations through which PSID effectively engage with others, we do not necessarily arrive at the Rawlsian inclusivist contractualist conclusion that these relations are cooperative and reciprocal (in a contractualist sense of cooperation and reciprocity).

Let us now take a closer look at the type of caring relations that qualify, according to Hartley – namely "mutually supportive relationships with family, friends, and caregivers."[84]

Often, we think of how those with severe mental disabilities are supported by and provided with companionship from others. We do not consider how those with mental disabilities also provide support to others. However, the capacity for engagement makes communication possible; and through communication, which need not be verbal, individuals with severe mental disabilities provide support and companionship [and love] to others.[85]

---

[80] Rawls, *Political Liberalism*, at 18. On the notion of "person" and its Latin origin *persona* meaning "mask, character, person in a play; one who plays or performs a part; a character, relation or capacity in which one acts," see Jenny Teichman, "The Definition of Person" (1985) 60:232 Philosophy 175 at 177; see also Peter Singer, *Practical Ethics*, 3rd ed. (New York: Cambridge University Press, 2011), at 73–75.
[81] Rawls, *Political Liberalism*, at 336.
[82] Rawls, *Justice as Fairness*, at 6.
[83] Hartley, "Justice for the Disabled," at 18; John Rawls, *A Theory of Justice*, rev. ed. (Cambridge: Harvard University Press, 1999), at 24–25; Immanuel Kant, *Groundwork of the Metaphysics of Morals*, trans. and ed. Mary Gregor (Cambridge: Cambridge University Press, 2012), at 433, 439.
[84] Hartley, "Justice for the Disabled," at 29 (emphasis removed).
[85] Ibid.

Looking for more ways in which PSID are not just passive recipients in such relations but are also *cooperators* in a *contractualist* sense, Hartley adds:

> Some individuals with mental disabilities are humble or kind in such a way that interaction with these individuals can help others better understand what is important in life and even their own humanity, its limitations, and its fragility. The humility of some, best appreciated through relationships with them, can humble the rest of us by countering arrogance, which threatens a society based on mutual respect.[86]

I could not agree more with this statement, based on my own experience of growing up and living with a brother with intellectual disabilities. However, I have already explained why I fail to see its contractual dimension.[87] The idea that PSID pay us in comfort, love, and self-realization is mistaken for many reasons: (1) The theoretical effort of looking for ways in which they could "pay us back" for love and care employs the contractarian logic of looking for a self-interested, mutually beneficial relationship that Hartley (rightfully, I believe, as I noted in Chapter 3) sets aside. (2) When we focus on features of the relationship itself – in this case, a relationship of care – I do not see how the Kantian framework of moral agency or its most extended version of simple "cooperative engagement" would apply to it, unless this engagement also applies to the vegetal and animal kingdoms. If we did, in fact, extend it to apply to animals and plants, we would fail to account for the particularity of relations with autonomous people as well as relations with PSID. (3) If, to avoid this conundrum, we valued the features of the noncontractual relations we have with PSID simply because they contingently serve relations which *are* valuable on a contractualist account, this would make the value of these noncontractual (probably caring) relationships and the status of PSID derivative. This would be unsatisfying according to both my and Hartley's goals because it would fail to capture the greater value that these noncontractual relations possess and offer.

One does not have to look far to find an alternative account: it is in view as soon as we stop insisting on framing it in a contractualist way. For example, we no longer see love as a "benefit," but as the precondition and the motivation for us to care for a PSID. Their support, friendship, companionship, and love are not benefits that

---

[86] Ibid.
[87] It is odd to suggest that we give PSID a robust moral status because they teach us about ourselves (e.g., about our vulnerability and the value of caring). We would not even let them sit at the negotiation table if that were the case, because what they teach us is partly how other-regarding we are and that we have pre-contractual duties toward them. To frame this as another kind of self-knowledge that can fit a contractual framework is incoherent. Perhaps it would make it clearer to distinguish between an "effective" and "ineffective" piece of knowledge, in the specific sense that it affects the knower's motivations. The contractarian framework assumes that the desire of what is traded by the party acquiring it, and the self-regarding attitudes of that bargaining party, will not be transfigured by this acquisition. However, my claim is that this sort of "effective good" (self-knowledge) cannot be traded like food and money, and cannot be made into an "ineffective" good.

people seek contractually. The idea is prima facie absurd: do we pay or contract for love? Can we, even as a conceptual matter, pay for such a thing? Do we not, in fact, corrupt the object or otherwise debase or degrade it by submitting it to contractual logic?

There is obviously background solidarity at work here which needs to be explored and theorized and which does not find its best expression in contractarian or contractualist accounts. Whatever ethical bond is at work, it justifies the belief that we all play parts and that it is fair that we should do what our parts – our roles, our relations – require of us, fair that we should be blamed if we fail to do what we must, and fair that we should not be considered less of a member of society because we cannot play a part that most people are expected to play – that is, that we cannot engage in contractarian or contractualist cooperative roles. These intuitions are familiar to us in a society filled with vulnerable and dependent people who are sometimes temporarily dependent on our care (and sometimes permanently so). One person's part may be to help others gracefully. Another person's part may be to be helped, and perhaps to show gratitude, love, or patience toward those who help them, even when this is a challenge (e.g., when a person who has great difficulty accepting support, having been highly autonomous throughout their whole life). Imagine a sinking ship. The role of the captain is to coordinate and delegate to others, perhaps at the cost of her life. Strong people in positions of authority must lower the rowboats, parents and caregivers must care for their children, and children must obey their parents and respond to their care in an appropriate way for their age. Beings that are not able to have self-aware responses, like babies and PSID, may not "help" in any way, and yet they must be helped. To abandon the ship and leave them behind would seem a particularly monstrous act because of the relationship of dependence that they have with us within the matrix of roles we all occupy in specific contexts.

It is hard to see, on the contractualist accounts explored up to now, how we can flesh out these familiar intuitions without appealing to more than the recognition of one's legislating will as a trait that confers a robust moral status. I conclude that many PSID cannot occupy robust moral status-granting contractualist roles any more than they could be fully cooperating members in a contractarian sense. They seem to play other social parts, but contractualism has trouble explaining the performance and normative consequences of these parts. This does not mean that Hartley's requirement of a capacity to engage could not lie at the basis of a noncontractual theory of justice. Hartley's arguments thus resemble those of Silvers, who (in frequent collaboration with Francis and occasional collaboration with Michael Stein) has also developed elements of a theory of inclusivist justice that does not focus so much on requirements for subjecthood or moral status. Instead, Hartley's theory is focused on "collaborative engagement" (though one may think that it introduces its own notion of a requirement – that of being able to take part in a collaborative engagement). This theory comes with appealing advantages and problems of its own. But these theories are not, strictly speaking, contractual ones, unless we reinterpret the social contract tradition in ways that are so radical that it would abandon its central commitments to the key cognitive capacities with which I take issue. Like Hartley's arguments, Silvers's anti-exclusivist conception of justice seems to rely on some sort of normative background solidarity (or another ethical concept like Levinas's responsiveness to otherness, Derrida's hospitality, Iris Murdoch's "loving gaze,"[88] or various other potential ethical bedrocks, such as empathy, care, and vulnerability) that goes beyond contractualist requirements.

4.2.4 Cognitive Surrogacy[89]

Silvers and Francis claim that PSID can meaningfully carry out the role of social cooperators, as understood in a contractualist account, with proper external support that amplifies, rather than supplants, their autonomy and conceptions of the good. They suggest that trustees should provide PSID with "prosthetic cognitive probing through a process of assistive thinking."[90] The key problem with their ingenious device is that such a cognitive prosthesis does not work in the most severe cases of mental disability. Jeff McMahan and David Wasserman conclude their assessment of this concept by stating that, in some cases, the presumption that human beings "have the potential to participate in human forms of life" is groundless.[91] Some PSID, they explain, simply cannot "take part in human social life through the assistance of other human beings."[92]

However, Silvers and Francis do not claim that the tool of mental prosthesis would work with the most severe cases of cognitive impairments. They recognize the distinction between "a prosthetic process that remains a simulation of a particular human capacity that the subject lacks and a prosthetic process that compensates with a different capacity."[93] For some PSID, there are simply no prostheses that could enhance, amplify, or adapt their limited cognitive capacities. The cognition of PSID is so limited or hard to decipher, build upon or extrapolate from, that one

---

[88] Iris Murdoch, *The Sovereignty of Good* (London: Routledge & Kegan Paul, 1970); Nancy E. Snow, "Iris Murdoch's Notion of a Loving Gaze" (2007) 39:3–4 J Value Inquiry 487.

[89] The words "trustees," "surrogates," "collaborators," and "proxy" are used more or less interchangeably in Silvers's and Francis's discussions. Apart from the basic distinction I will make between helping someone to speak and speaking in someone's interest (the key difference between the kind of trusteeship that is needed for active and passive citizenship, respectively), it is not necessary to elaborate a more sophisticated typology for my purposes here. I will also use these terms interchangeably.

[90] Francis and Silvers, "Thinking about the Good," at 490.

[91] David Wasserman and Jeff McMahan, "Cognitive Surrogacy, Assisted Participation, and Moral Status" in Rosamond Rhodes, Margaret P. Battin, and Anita Silvers, eds., *Medicine and Social Justice: Essays on the Distribution of Health Care*, 2nd ed. (New York: Oxford University Press, 2012), 325 at 332.

[92] Ibid.

[93] Francis and Silvers, "Thinking about the Good," at 486.

wonders how plausible the claim that PSID's authorship can be preserved is, and why this claim would justify undertaking a prosthetic endeavor in the first place if granting the robust moral status is conditional on its success.

In some cases, the personality, character, or social identity of a cognitively deficient individual is a purely social construction. Though such fictional social identities can arguably be morally meaningful within some social contexts,[94] they have an essentially relational basis and do not rely on the value of some internal capacities.[95] The moral status of a PSID would require that we fully integrate them into our political community in order, for instance, to have other people within our community respect them even though they are not related or otherwise connected to them. Yet the basis for this integration would not be found in the respect owed to their conception of the good that exists *in potentia*, waiting to be fully developed, expressed or "translated" through prosthetic means, nor in the respect of whatever kernel of autonomy a being who is somewhat able to engage with others and react has, on a broad account of autonomy.[96] The reasons for integrating PSID would lie elsewhere altogether, and would not be the contractual reasons that Silvers and Francis are considering.

The simple fact that collaborators are exclusively "inspired" by the PSID in question is suspicious; the notion of being "inspired" is clearly one step toward acts of creation or imagination and one step away from deferential reconstruction based on attentive empirical observations. I believe that these notions are best thought of as existing along a spectrum, with the individual expressing her own autonomy (relatively) independently on one end, and with trustees speaking entirely for her on the other. I also believe that a notion of co-authorship (of conceptions of the good and of contracting performances) should be envisaged by theorists of cognitive prosthesis but the normative impact of such a co-authorship is not very relevant here. Instead, I want to emphasize that, as we move from the autonomy end to the paternalistic end of the spectrum, the contractualist justification for trustees to intervene to provide a cognitive prosthesis gradually weakens, just as other justifications (e.g., paternalistic concern) start to place increasing weight on justifying and delineating the role of trustees.

There comes a point where the contractualist justification becomes either only incidentally relevant, or becomes nested within another kind of justification that takes priority or incorporates it. Conversely, a contractualist or autonomy-focused

---

[94] For instance, Kittay refers to anencephalic children ("At the Margins of Moral Personhood" [2008] 5:2–3 J Bioethical Inquiry 137).

[95] Although these disabled individuals' moral status could be based on internal (e.g., genetic) attributes, which take a moral signification relationally – such as their humanity or the fact that they are born to humans, or the special connection with their mother.

[96] See Hartley, "Justice for the Disabled," for her notion of engagement, as previously defined and, respectively, Francis, "Understanding Autonomy in Light" for her scalar, complex notion of autonomy.

theory can nest the caring or dependency concerns when we get close to the other end of the spectrum. How both kinds of justifications fade into, or are made secondary, to one another could be illustrated by the following figure, which can illustrate how many disagreements within the "care versus justice" debate[97] could be resolved by curtailing their overgeneralizing reach.

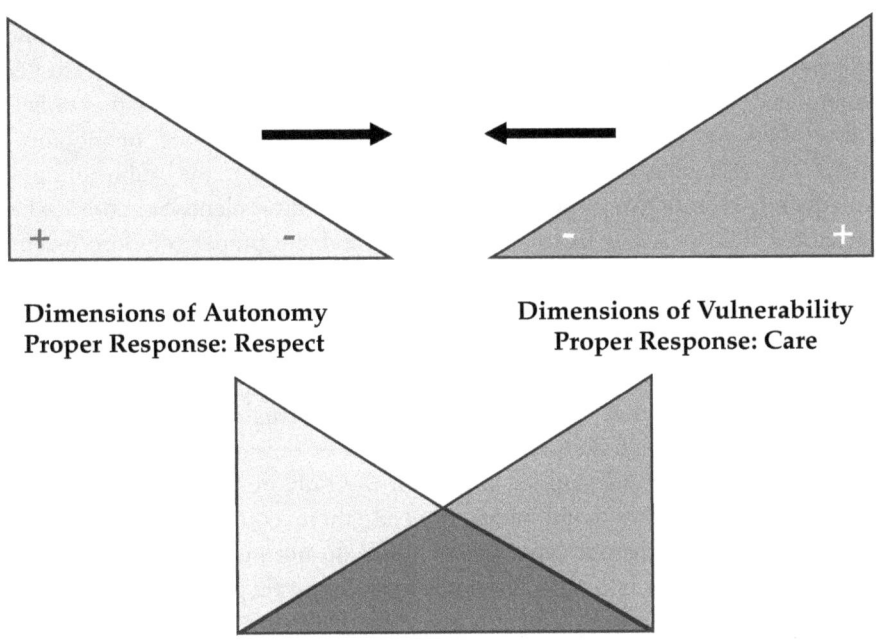

Dimensions of Autonomy
Proper Response: Respect

Dimensions of Vulnerability
Proper Response: Care

Scaling Dimensions of Autonomy and Vulnerability
Spectrum of Proper Responses

These overlapping spectrums of needs and capacities seem to illustrate a rather natural and plausible way to look at normal variations within our species – both in the sense of some individuals being more dependent or autonomous than others, and with a single lifespan being characterized by various states of autonomy and dependency. The figure above could be contrasted with another illustration, which would show two squares, as opposed to two triangles, denoting clear dichotomies between all-or-nothing statuses (i.e., inlier–outlier; capable–incapable; autonomous–dependent; able-bodied–disabled). Some policymakers and theorists think of human beings as inhabiting either one box or the other. They may therefore

---

[97] Consider, e.g., Anita Silvers, "Reconciling Equality to Difference: Caring (F)or Justice for People with Disabilities" (1995) 10:1 Hypatia 30; Eva Kittay, "When Caring Is Just and Justice Is Caring: Justice and Mental Retardation" (2001) 13:3 Public Culture 557.

fail to create social structures and laws that fit a complex reality. In turn, citizens must uncomfortably fit, assuming they can fit at all, the all-or-nothing regimes too commonly offered to them, or else be excluded entirely. Philosophers similarly risk excluding certain persons from the purview of their theories by resisting pluralist, nonideal, scalar models of justice. (This is not to say that pluralist theories do not pose problems of their own. We will come back to this in the concluding chapter.) In any case, the illustration above visually captures how I suggest we should think about trusteeship, as one of many tools used to operationalize theories of political participation for PSID. It would allow for a certain pluralism that better reflects human needs and aspirations and – most importantly – it would deny that only the contractualist end of the spectrum can inform a theory of justice, or morality in general. It also illustrates my discussion above, under the subheading "A Remediating Distributive Scheme *or* an Integrative Pro-Talents Scheme," where I suggested that we avoid theorizing disability and the proper response owed to persons with disabilities in an all-or-nothing way. Contractual theories should no more assume that the subject of justice ought to stand at one end of the spectrum than theorists of vulnerability or care ethicists should assume that the state ought to systematically subordinate respect for autonomy to a caring outlook.

Although it is true that, in some cases, the contractualist paradigm simply no longer plausibly applies, it is also true that, in many cases, along the aforementioned suggested spectrum, it still applies but is not the only or central justification for granting PSID a robust moral status. Indeed, there comes a point along this spectrum where the internal capacities of PSID do not justify adopting cognitive prostheses. When there is so little autonomy to represent via prosthetics, and perhaps so little value to realize in this regard, it is more likely that we are in fact valuing something else altogether. It is on the basis of this other, moral consideration that we seek to offer a prosthesis to discover PSID's autonomy.

Distinguishing the Capacity to Originate a Conception of the Good from the Capacity to Express This Conception

I conclude that, in some cases, cognitive prostheses are not justified on a contractualist basis, though they may be helpful and morally warranted on noncontractual grounds. I therefore wish to curtail my criticism to an extent. I believe that Francis and Silvers, like Wasserman and McMahan, should not lump the capacity required to produce a conception of the good with the capacity to perform certain activities that engage this individual conception of the good during the contractual process. They combine both capacities into a single activity which, they posit, either can or cannot be accomplished by way of an external support, preserving authorship. It would be more accurate to separately evaluate the authentic performance of originating a conception of the good from the performance of deploying, endorsing, or defending this conception within a contractualist account.

Even if PSID have sufficient capacities to be identified as the authentic authors or agents of their conceptions of the good – short of having "contracting capacities" that can be amplified – they can sometimes hardly be said to be the agents taking *contractual* steps to actualize this conception of the good and to realize their tastes. David Wasserman and Jeff McMahan put this point compellingly: "Moving someone's arm in a manner that she enjoys is not helping her to move her arm unless she contributes to, directs, or authorizes the movement."[98] In the context of evaluating the authorship of (idealized) contractual actions, the skills relevant to the "contracting act" go beyond the sole skill of authoring a conception of the good. Otherwise, how could Silvers and Francis say that collaborators do not *represent* PSID, but instead "[enable] their subjects to configure ideas so as to represent themselves while the [contractual] process unfolds through their use, via prosthetic functioning, of the trustees' cognitive and linguistic skills"?[99] These "contracting" cognitive and linguistic skills are central to the authorship of the "contracting" actions and cannot be supplemented without jeopardizing it.

Thus, my criticism of the tool of a cognitive prosthesis differs from that of Wasserman and McMahan, as they do not even consider that it can attribute the authorship of a conception of the good to PSID.[100] On the contrary, I believe that we can attribute a conception of the good to (at least) those PSID who sufficiently express their preferences to enable their collaborators to read their interests, and who accurately express PSID's conception of the good, without the collaborators becoming co- or sole authors of these conceptions. PSID's relative passivity only becomes a threat to authorship when this conception of the good is taken to mean more than a conception of the good *simpliciter*, but rather a conception of the good that justifies granting the person full moral status under a contractualist framework. That is, the problem arises when we seek to not only attribute to PSID a conception of the good, but go further to attribute the rational, deliberative, reasonable, and other agential capacities required to facilitate or enable the realization of this conception of the good through a political structure secured by a contractualist society-building process.

4.3 CONCLUSION

It appears that there is an unspoken moral background to the theories explored in this chapter. For example, why do theorists insist on interpreting, via prosthetics, the

---

[98] Wasserman and McMahan, "Cognitive Surrogacy, Assisted Participation, and Moral Status," at 331.
[99] Francis and Silvers, "Thinking about the Good," at 493.
[100] "[T]he subject could hardly be said to employ her trustee as a prosthesis unless she played a more active role than that of inspiring or informing the conceptualization of the good. A suit, however closely fitted, is made by the tailor, not the wearer. Even if the wearer indicates where the fit is too tight or loose, her role is far too passive to make her a co-creator" (Wasserman and McMahan, "Cognitive Surrogacy, Assisted Participation, and Moral Status," at 331).

capacities of a being who has so little to interpret? Why do they support recognizing the talents of a being who has so little talent? These strategies assume that PSID are already members of society, even though they all rely on PSID's supported capacities as the requirements for membership, either as a contractor or an active citizen. Accommodating or supportive social measures seem warranted on the basis that PSID *already* belong to our society and are entitled to equal consideration.[101] However, the grounds of this membership seem to be a prior concern which cannot be explained on contractual terms. If we analyze contractualist and contractarian strategies without taking this concern into account, they begin to look like conceptual stretches or dubious empirical wagers. No matter how severe a person's disability, these authors seem to assume that we must give her some concern as a *person* – that is, as a member of our society to whom robust duties are owed. In this sense, contractualist and contractarian thinkers may find it natural to frame PSID not only as persons but also as contractors. Otherwise, they must concede that the normative concept of "person" is not exhausted by that of a "contractor." In my concluding chapter, I suggest that this position may not, in fact, be as damaging to contractual theories.

---

[101] Or otherwise possess a kind of inherent worth that is not predicated on their intellectual or physical capacities and that would justify their social inclusion or the cultivation of their talents.

5

People with Severe Intellectual Disabilities as Passive Citizens

5.1 PSID AS PASSIVE CITIZENS OR INDIRECT PARTICIPANTS

Let us define passive citizenship as (1) a robust moral status (2) granted by "fully cooperating members of society" to individuals (3) who are not themselves "fully cooperating" parties (i.e., who do not have the capacities of a direct contractor). Presumably, passive citizens possess features other than direct contracting capacities or they are situated in noncontractual relationships with contractors. Either of these situations may justify granting passive citizens a robust moral status.

Securing this status through passive citizenship circumvents a major problem. The primary problem with constructing PSID as contractors is split into discrete areas of concern. First, we need to reconceptualize what it takes to cooperate or participate in a contract; second, we need to examine PSID's "contribution" from a new empirical standpoint; and third, we need a new conceptual framework to consider these issues in a different way. As we saw in previous chapters, some theorists – like Martha Nussbaum or David Gauthier – are skeptical about such endeavors. They say that trying to prove that PSID are, indeed, bringing something to the table is not the way to conceptualize the duties that we owe to them. However, some passive citizenship theorists refuse to give up on the social contract tradition and believe there is a way to include grounds for strong duties – even toward those who cannot cooperate – within social contract theory.

While circumventing the prima facie implausible claim that PSID can be reciprocal contributors, arguments about their passive citizenship face a potentially insurmountable problem. Granting a strong status to noncontractors on contractualist grounds seems nonsensical, at first glance. The challenge is to find arguments explaining why those who *are* contractors would grant a robust status to PSID. The immediate obstacle that arises is that, whatever grounds are suggested, one suspects it will either produce too contingent a moral status (i.e., by making it the mere product of contractors' desires) or it will not be rooted in contractualism (i.e., by grounding its necessity or robustness in a noncontractual constraint).

At any rate, passive citizenship, whether contract-based or not, enjoys an apparent advantage. Granting a robust moral status (including robust rights) to PSID by representing their interests rather than by imagining how they could represent themselves (or select delegates) may better reflect people's usual assumptions about what we owe to PSID. People in this group are commonly seen as unable to fend for themselves in a harsh and brutish world, to stand discursively for themselves (e.g., by negotiating, lobbying, or voting) nor to care for themselves in a more organized society. Giving people with profound disabilities a delegate to speak on their behalf – among other proposals compatible with the architectonic idea of having their interests robustly represented in public reasoning – seems to be the only option if we want to promote their welfare using the political instruments and structures at our disposal.

This popular view is controversial, given the shift away from substitute decision-making to supported decision-making urged by the U.N. *Convention on the Rights of Persons with Disabilities*. I am not suggesting that indirectly representing the interests of PSID through the design of social arrangements would necessarily provide them with indirect representation in their everyday lives, nor I am implying that substitute decision-makers cannot take PSID's expression of preferences into account. I am, however, starting from the premise that some human beings will sometimes benefit from indirect representation in contractual processes more than they would benefit from direct participation (which is the situation that we examined in the previous chapter).

I examined arguments attempting to bring PSID inside the purview of contractarianism in Chapters 2 and 3, so I will focus on versions of contractualism attempting to do the same in this chapter, mostly by evaluating the extent to which the contractors' legislature can provide satisfactory reasons for granting a robust moral status to PSID. I will nonetheless highlight when my comments apply to both traditions, especially when traces of both traditions can be found in a particular author (such as Rawls).

5.2 DISSOCIATING THE CONCEPTS OF MORAL LEGISLATORS AND MEMBERS OF THE MORAL COMMUNITY

To theorize the status of a passive citizen within a contractual theory, the first step is to detach two notions that are generally conflated: that of being a contract-maker and that of having a strong status under a contract – that is, those who can provide benefits and those who can receive them.[1]

---

[1] A jurist's reaction to the statement that a party to a contract can be separated from a beneficiary of it might be that this is more than a contingent conflation. Rather, it is a classic feature of contract – having a right under it is the same as being a party to it. A lawyer's first intuition might therefore be that extending the robust benefits of a contract to those who are not party to it is a non-contractual idea. However, this legal assumption is not justified when we analyze the

This is a (contractualist/contractarian) subset of a general conflation between beings able to confer value upon entities and entities with intrinsic or nonderivative value. An example of this could be moral agents, on one hand, and beings with full moral status, or who are a self-authenticating source of moral and political claims who cannot be instrumentalized, or who must be treated as ends rather than means, on the other. There are many ways to formulate this dichotomy because it has been made within various theoretical frameworks. A political focus – warranted by the political aspect of social contract theory – would make us privilege the Kantian term of "passive citizen" related to the political notion of citizenship. By contrast, a broader ethical focus would make us adopt the term "moral patient," notably used by Tom Regan to describe certain animals.[2] It does not matter which term is preferred, as it is associated with the possession of a robust moral status. This is not necessarily the case when people hold that a variety of nonrational, nonhuman moral patients have different moral statuses that call for different degrees of moral consideration based on different moral principles.

Cora Diamond has highlighted three possible groups that do not necessarily overlap when making moral evaluations. Her formulation considers that the *author* (x) of the moral evaluation, the *agent* evaluated (y), and the *object* of the agent's behaviors and attitudes (z) do not need to be the same group of beings: "[w]e xs assess together the character and conduct of us ys so far as it affects ourselves and our fellow zs."[3] Diamond's conceptual categorization is a useful insight as it helps us identify problematic conflations and better detect voices that have been left out of the discussion. PSID's evaluative standpoint is systematically excluded from group x, generally excluded from the group of contractors y, and sometimes even from the group of moral patients or passive citizens z.

However, in this chapter, the variable of the *author* of the moral evaluation is not problematized by those who would theorize the passive citizenship of PSID, nor would these authors problematize the group of the *agents* whose conduct is being

---

notion of contract. The legal doctrine of privity of contract, which would support the legal assumption, can be criticized on the account that, even though it may be beneficial to keep the contract between its parties, there is also virtue in preserving the parties' freedom and autonomy to contract in a way that benefits a third party. For one thing, not all legal systems have strict rules of privity. For another, one of the methods Anglo-American law has used to get around the privity doctrine is the legal category of a trust, which makes a third party to a contract a beneficiary of something like a right. When parties make a contract for the benefit of a third party, they create an express trust of the benefit of the contract for that party, who then has proprietary interest in the benefit of the contract. See, e.g., *Re Schebsman*, [1994] Ch 83 (CA); *Johns-Manville Canada Inc v. John Carlo Ltd*, [1980] OJ No 3084, 113 DLR (3d) 686.

[2] To be a moral patient according to Regan means that one is owed moral duties directly, notably that of respect. His criterion for granting these moral duties is not relevant to our contractual enquiry. See Tom Regan, *The Case for Animal Rights* (Berkeley: Berkeley University Press, 1983).

[3] Cora Diamond, "The Importance of Being Human" (1991) 29 Royal Institute Philo Supplement 35 at 37.

morally evaluated or prescribed.[4] Authors only want to extend the group of the *objects* of this conduct. Their basic idea is that PSID ought to benefit from the social contract (i.e., have their interests robustly considered at some stage of the process) without being part of the legislative group, the contractors. This confronts us with two (categories of) problems, which constitute the subjects of the two following subsections: problems with granting a robust moral status on a contractual basis to noncontractors and problems with the representation of PSID in the contractual process.

Let me start by explaining how and why the questions of (1) who can make a contract and (2) who can benefit from a strong moral status under that contract, are often conflated and why this conflation is not necessarily warranted.

5.2.1 *Why Contractees Are Often Thought to Be the Only Beneficiaries of the Contract*

It Is in the Nature of the Contract
Under the contractualist/Kantian tradition, the conflation is best understood by considering Kant's theory that only moral legislators – those able to enact the moral law – are owed nonderivative respect, that is, they are subjects of this moral law. To put this another way, only respecters need to be respected. A similar idea is found in Rawls's theory of justice when he says that only those able to give justice are owed justice. The basic contractualist logic behind this conflation is that the only beings worthy of intrinsic respect are persons *qua* enactors of the rational law. What is worth respecting in these persons is their embodiment of the moral law: their rational, autonomous self. Respect of autonomy is so central to this Kantian way of thinking that nothing else warrants granting a strong moral status when we think in terms of the status that members of a moral and political community have.[5]

Though this chapter is focused on contractualism, let me note that the same holds for contractarian logic. We make deals with people who are able to bring something worthwhile to the bargaining table. We have no reason to bargain with the weak, the poor, or those less gifted intellectually (and so on) because they have too little to contribute. This implies a selfish stance: a focus on self-interest and evaluation of a person's worth according to their instrumental worth for our private

---

[4] It is however a variable that is worth problematizing within the social contract tradition, especially when we want to challenge the most basic assumption made by an author. For instance, when "we" (x) wonder what "we" (y) owe to "each other" (z) as social contractees, the answer is likely to be different if the "we" includes the voices of PSID or their family members.

[5] Immanuel Kant, *Groundwork of the Metaphysics of Morals*, trans. and ed. Mary Gregor (Cambridge: Cambridge University Press, 2012), at 36–37, 42–43; *The Metaphysics of Morals*, trans. and ed. Mary Gregor (Cambridge: Cambridge University Press, 1996), at 91. See also Diamond, "The Importance of Being Human," at 35–36. I consider, however, an alternative reading of Kant by Christine Korsgaard below.

purposes. In its most radical form, there is no other distinctive value to be recognized. Hobbes wrote that those who have these capacities and refuse to consent to the social contract must "justly be destroyed by the rest."[6] It follows from this stance that what matters most when we reflect about our social arrangements is the ability to respect – and be accountable if we fail to respect – collective bargaining rules and the rules bargained for. As self-interested bargainers, we have no reason to grant a strong moral status to anyone else; those who cannot benefit, who threaten, or who cannot be bound by agreement are just a potential nuisance.

This explains why we may think that the central contractual beneficiary is a contractor, or why it may be easy to overlook other kinds of human relationships governed by contractual norms of justice. However, granting a robust moral status to beings that are unable to contract is not necessarily analytically incompatible with these positions.

On the contractualist account, instead of insisting on the "Kantian split" between Kantian reasonable and rational persons and "everything else in nature,"[7] one could explore the mechanism that underlies the attribution of value to see whether it could value PSID in a no less robust way than other contracting capacities. Christine Korsgaard provides us with such a position.

On the contractarian side, we could investigate how PSID are in fact useful to a community of contractors even though they do not have contracting capacities, as traditionally understood. If what is centrally normative on a contractarian account are the capacities to understand, negotiate, be bound by, keep, and to be held accountable to a contract, then exploring notions of trusteeship seems a plausible way to integrate PSID into our social contract. However, if what is centrally normative on a contractarian account is the fact that contractees bring benefit (or threats) to the table, and the philosophical focus is on the instrumental value of these elements rather than on the way that rational agents deal with them, then one would explore the value that PSID can bring to the table, regardless of their capacity to explain what they are doing. Yet in the first part of this book, I already have argued that such arguments are not promising.

There Is a Single Answer to Both Questions

These two questions:

(1) Who can make a contract?
(2) Who can receive the benefit of a robust moral status under that contract?

---

[6] William Molesworth, ed., *The English Works of Thomas Hobbes of Malmesbury*, vol. III: *Leviathan* (London: John Bohn, 1839–45), at 162.
[7] Martha Nussbaum, *Frontiers of Justice: Disability, Nationality, Species Membership* (Cambridge: Harvard University Press, 2006), at 138.

are subcategories of two more general questions that can also be conflated:

(1*) How are we to solve, politically, what seem like irreducible disagreements about the good in our society?
(2*) Who has a robust moral status?

Question (1) assumes that a contractual answer has already been provided to the more fundamental question (1*) and has moved on to identifying the conditions for participating in the contracting procedure.

Although questions (1*) and (2*) are distinct, it is possible that an answer to (1*) implies an answer (at least partially) to (2*). Contractualism gives such an answer. It claims that, *because* we can solve the social ineliminable disagreement on conceptions of the good life using a contractual procedure, we ought to recognize a special status to those beings able to participate in such a procedure.

If we answer, as Rawls does, questions (1*) and (2*) using a theory of the right rather than a theory of the good, it becomes hard to see the basis on which we would grant a robust moral status to PSID. Theorists of the passive citizenship of PSID assume that it is impossible if we take robust moral status to be possessed by a "primary subject of justice." PSID are not such subjects, so on what basis would we give them strong and equal rights? To remain within the contractual tradition, this basis would need to be contractual; that is, we must provide an answer to question (2) instead of an answer to the broader (2*). Whether we use a Rawlsian or a Hobbesian framework, it is easy to see that having the status of a contractor gives one a robust moral status (and how, therefore, (1) and (2) can have the same answer). The more controversial question is whether there are other contractual grounds for robust moral status, and theorists of passive citizenship maintain that there is. They argue that able contractors will decide to include PSID in the contractual process; therefore, PSID's status can be contractually based. This poses two apparent problems.

First, this decision would have to be the product of individual citizens' wills, who would need to agree that it is good to grant a robust moral status to PSID. This taints the kind of moral status that PSID would have with an apparent derivativeness or contingence. Second, social contract theory relies on a constructivist and proceduralist method, which puts the right before the good (i.e., because people disagree too much on the good but can still agree that there is a right way to settle their disagreement). Decisions that participants to the procedure make are constrained by the fairness of the procedure rather than in terms of a contentious conception of the good life (e.g., one's propensities to be charitable or to show solidarity with the vulnerable). Thus, on many contractual accounts – notably that of Rawls – a conception of the right dictates who has the fullest moral status. This causes not only the aforementioned problem of derivativeness. It also raises the problem that any such status can never be as axiologically important, or that we will integrate PSID too late in the process, structurally speaking.

Regarding the lesser ontological value of their status, Martha Nussbaum connects the statuses of "direct" contracting participants and of citizens under the contract (at least under Rawls). These participants are the "primary subjects of justice" and, therefore, one can legitimately wonder if it is conceptually possible to give non-contractors a robust moral status. Nussbaum's idea is that the direct participants to the contractual procedure – the primary subjects of justice – enjoy an intrinsically superior status, one that reflects the "Kantian split between the rational/reasonable person and everything else in nature."[8] If PSID are represented by trustees as passive citizens, the concern is that whatever status they are given will somehow be ontologically inferior.

Regarding the primacy of the right over the good, John Finnis has pointed out that selecting the right as the best way to solve the irreducible ethical pluralism affecting democratic, political discussions effectively deprives some human beings from a moral status altogether. The answer to the question "who has the capacities to participate in the right process?" inherently excludes people who cannot discuss or contract properly (notably PSID), but it also imposes content restriction on the discussants who can participate. It might be said that, as far as our identity (or at least our identity *qua* political participants) is concerned, rational and reasonable people are partly excluded. The resulting negotiation misses some key ethical features of what a public discussion could encompass, and may not fully recognize the discussants' autonomy, dignity, and integrity, as Habermas and Rawls suggest. The discussion is impoverished through its dismissal of unrefuted ethical arguments. For instance, views about the good are categorized as irrelevant to a discussion about basic principles of justice in a Rawlsian framework because they are too subject-relative and irrelevant to the moral discursive procedure. This constructed (and, Finnis says, mistaken) distinction between private conceptions of the good and public reasons, or between the ethical and the moral, cuts participants to this circumscribed discussion "from the very meaning of the discourse of his partners in discourse, or at least so radically misconceives their views that civil conversation with them is substantially obstructed."[9] Finnis wagers that a rich ethical discussion, though complex and messy, should guide our political deliberation about the principles of justice, as opposed to the wager that state neutrality through right processes is the only way to deal morally with ethical disagreements, which should be left out of the political discussion in the first place.

---

[8] *Ibid.* at 7, 138. This kind of assessment is challenged by Korsgaard, as we will see, although it probably remains that, on a Rawlsian account, it is likely that both questions have the same answer, anchored in a conception of fairness. However, (a) we can develop accounts of passive citizenship on non-Rawlsian contractual grounds and (b) it does not exclude another strategy to adapt a Rawlsian account to integrate PSID by extending a conception of the right. But this is not what this section contemplates, as here I assume that it cannot be done.

[9] John Finnis, *Reason in Action* (Oxford: Oxford University Press, 2011), at 56.

At least on a Rawlsian account of justice, the theorist of PSID's "passive citizen" status seems to be caught between a rock and a hard place. On one hand, conceptions of the good involving benevolence toward PSID cannot be integrated into the Rawlsian legislative contractual process. As Nussbaum says, "the present-time sort of trusteeship would require [the trustees in the original position] to know that they do have benevolence and how strong it is" which would go against Rawls's "commitment to parsimony of assumptions" about the parties in the original position.[10] On the other hand, if PSID are taken into account at a later stage of the legislative process when the veil of ignorance is lifted, the status of PSID seems to be less fundamentally anchored in the requirements of justice and to be more derivative upon individual preferences. Nonetheless, Cynthia Stark has argued that the latter solution confers an appropriately robust status upon PSID. Others argue that a contractually given robust moral status is as good of a status as one obtained through direct possession of contracting capacities. We will return to such arguments once we have considered a few more of the obstacles for a theory of passive citizenship for PSID.

Equality Requires It: PSID Are Too Unequal in Terms of Capacities to Be Granted an Equal Status

Another reason why people who are not moral agents cannot be granted the highest sort of moral status is a commitment to equality. The claim is that extending strong moral consideration to noncontract-makers is incompatible with this commitment because, whereas contract-making capacities can be a placeholder for (almost) universally equal grounds for moral consideration, the various properties of beings who are not moral agents, and the various relations we have with them, do not provide secure grounds to justify equal moral consideration.

For instance, both Kant and Hobbes, within their dramatically different conceptual frameworks of values, need to assume that people *equally* possess some properties in order to justify a strong and equal moral concern. Kant notes that civil equality, one of the attributes of a citizen, is "not recognizing among the people any superior with the moral capacity."[11] Hobbes claims in the *Leviathan* that "as to the strength of body, the weakest has strength enough to kill the strongest, either by secret machination or by confederacy with others, that are in the same danger with himself."[12]

This assumption of natural equality is reflected in an assumption of idealized equality or contingently required equality in Rawls's theory. Hobbes wagers that every Goliath has his David, who is feared enough to warrant a surrender of natural rights to the sovereign, is echoed in Rawls's circumstances of justice, where there can be no exceptionally gifted people who can dominate the rest if justice as fairness

---

[10] Nussbaum, *Frontiers of Justice*, at 136–37.
[11] Kant, *Metaphysics of Morals*, at 91 (emphasis removed).
[12] Molesworth, *Leviathan*, at 110.

is to be at all possible. Kant's assumption about the universality of the capacity for moral law is echoed in Rawls's notion of "range properties" that apply to the property of having moral powers.[13]

It would seem unfair, according to such contractual accounts, to grant equal moral status to PSID if they do not equally possess the capacities that ground this moral status. This view is committed to equality in two senses. First, it is committed to give moral salience with respect to the equality of physical and cognitive capacities. Second, it is committed to the equality of status within the political community.

The first commitment could be challenged on the grounds that equal treatment can be justified by a theory of justice or morality that does not require moral patients to actually possess equal natural capacities. Such a theory may not be contractual, however, unlike those of Hobbes, Kant, and Rawls.

Regarding the second commitment, it is noteworthy that this equality is not analytically required by the nature of contract-making or even social contract-making. When we make deals, powerful people will simply get the lion's share. Why would the one holding the more comfortable position agree to put himself in a lesser position? Would she want to imagine what the outcome of their bargain would be if things had been more equal? Potential reasons for putting oneself in this position evoke something beyond ordinary contracting. What shocks us about the idea of a social contract that gives various statuses to different citizens might have little to do with contracting *per se*. Perhaps, it is something historically contingent (i.e., a particular kind of political and social arrangement, such as democracy) that justifies the idea that people are all equally threatening to one another, or all equally gifted with reason or moral agency. In these circumstances, equality may be a fiction required by political or psychological needs rather than by empirical fact. We could imagine a social contract leading to unequal political statuses for unequal parties.[14]

---

[13] John Rawls, A *Theory of Justice*, rev. ed. (Cambridge: Harvard University Press, 1999), at 444–45.

[14] Some theorists, like Jeff McMahan, prefer a scalar way of thinking about status, as it better corresponds to the actual variation of properties that provide reasons for granting a moral status (Jeff McMahan, *The Ethics of Killing: Problems at the Margins of Life* [New York: Oxford University Press, 2002]). Although I agree that a scalar theory of moral status would be helpful to both moral and political theories, I note that it is helpful to distinguish a "moral status" from a "political status" (i.e., when the notion of "moral status" is used in the context of granting the status of a subject of justice). When we look at status from the point of view of the political community, it becomes obvious that there are good reasons for saying that citizens are equal even though their capacities differ greatly. For one thing, when we deal with political questions, the failure to consider intersubjective aspects of respect and moral consideration becomes problematic, if only because a political approach forces us to consider relations among members of a society. Abstract thought experiments, on the other hand, more easily adopt a non-relational point of view, making it less apparent that only analyzing internal properties may be missing something important. Incidentally, my view of moral status is not scalar in the simple sense of ranking people along a spectrum of moral considerability or importance. While some of its aspects are, indeed, scalar, my understanding of moral status is

However, no contemporary contractual theory (or more generally liberal political theory) would suggest creating a society in which some citizens have a lesser political status, where their voices and interests count for less in public reasoning. Similarly, there is little reason to challenge this commitment to equality. There is a simpler, less radical solution than to rethink the social contract tradition's conceptual attachment to equality.

A commitment to equality[15] of moral status within society could plausibly be maintained. Separating the question of "who is a moral agent" from the question of "who is a moral beneficiary," allows us to accept that moral beneficiaries can be granted an equally strong moral status on reasons other than their possessing equal physical and cognitive capacities (or capacities which, though unequal, enable them to make a sufficient contribution or threat to others).

It seems conceptually possible for beings who do not have contracting capacities – that is, neither the capacities to take part in a bargain, nor the capacities to sit at the negotiation table with moral legislators – to nonetheless be the beneficiaries of this contract. More precisely, it seems conceptually possible that these beings could have a robust moral status under it – the sort of status that contractees who did take part in the contractual process negotiated for themselves out of self-interest, or self and mutual respect.

While the aforementioned obstacles to this possibility have to do with the idea that the contractual *beneficiary* must absolutely be equated with the concept of a capable contractor, the next section will present problems having to do with the concept of *trusteeship* and, more precisely, with the possibility that the use of a trustee may prevent beneficiaries from this trusteeship from having as robust a moral status as other citizens.

5.3 PROBLEMS WITH BEING REPRESENTED BY A TRUSTEE IN THE CONTRACTUAL PROCESS

Another set of problems with granting a robust moral status to PSID comes from the fact that they must be represented by trustees – a kind of delegate who would occupy a more active or intrusive role than delegates for nondisabled citizens or contractees.[16]

---

multifaceted and would include various standings within different kinds of relations. I briefly describe this view in the concluding chapter.

[15] I am not invested in the issue of equality given my pluralist, relational view of what grounds moral attitudes, and I think that some form of basic, intrinsic concern happens to be equally given, as I will explain in the last section of this book. However, perhaps there are sound political reasons – probably having to do with the human need for social recognition and self-esteem – to consider equality important. Otherwise, I share Harry Frankfurt's skepticism about the intrinsic value of equality (Harry Frankfurt, "Equality and Respect" [1997] 64:1 Social Research 3).

[16] By contrast, the chapter on active citizenship emphasized a self-effaced sort of guardianship where the trustee/guardian is mostly conceived of as a "prosthesis" facilitating the expression of someone else's will and interests.

There are three kinds of arguments against trusteeship in the context of passive citizenship: metaphysical, epistemological, and structural. The first criticism is that we cannot grant a robust status to PSID because only value-givers merit this status, and it cannot be indirectly conferred to PSID by other members of their political community or by idealized contracting parties within a contractual process. That is the argument that I associated with Nussbaum in the previous section – that there is a "Kantian divide" between people with moral agency, on the one hand, and the rest of the world, on the other. As we will see, Korsgaard provides an argument against this position: being a value-giver does not necessarily make us more valuable. We can give as normatively stringent a value to nonrational beings as we give ourselves and other rational agents. If we hold the view that we give value to entities rather than detect it in them, this seems perfectly possible.

At a basic level, we can make this point by invoking commonsense beliefs about representation and passive representation, which support the idea that passive citizenship is not a second-rate status as some would assume. The idea that one is not well represented by, is excluded from, or is exploited by the political process because one is not a decision-maker, would, according to Nicholas Southwood, make

> [M]odern democratic politics ... a desperately non-inclusive affair in which the only individuals included (at all) in the agreements taking place in democratic legislatures would be the members of a tiny political elite; the vast majority of citizens would be straightforwardly excluded.[17]

In saying this, Southwood appears only to be criticizing the requirements of direct participation. But once we concede that it is acceptable to see simulacra of participation through other forms of indirect representation, we should not take issue with the indirectness, conceptual construction, or metaphorical character of the representation that is involved in passive citizenship. However, we can take issue with a different aspect of being a decision-maker. One reason why we value decision-makers as legitimizing state authority is not because we directly partake in the decision-making process, but rather because it enables us to ratify (perhaps indirectly) the norms imposed upon us as meeting certain standards of reasonableness. Passive citizens are unable to do this. They therefore fail to indirectly and conceptually justify state authority and to ensure that their autonomy is respected.

If we hold the position that the capacity to legitimize state authority (by theoretically consenting to it or assessing its reasonableness or fairness) is part and parcel of what gives active citizenship its metaphysical gilt edge, then we will think that passive citizenship is deprived of it. Yet, on a more paternalistic understanding of state authority – which gains its legitimacy by meeting citizens' needs – the

---

[17] Nicholas Southwood, *Contractualism and the Foundations of Morality* (Oxford: Oxford University Press, 2010), at 110.

difference between passive and active citizens is less relevant, insofar as we hold that the capacities for individually understanding the legitimacy of a norm serve not only to legitimize state power but also to ensure that the individual's basic need for control over her existence is not violated. If we took such a view, the fact that passive citizens cannot "ratify" the norms to which they are subjected does not harm them in a particular way that it would if they were autonomous. Even though it is a statement of proto-philosophical intuition rather than an articulated argument, these comments assuage two concerns that passive citizenship may be a second-rate status: because of the artificiality of the representation that it requires, and because its structure is not sensitive to the subject's autonomy.

There is a second (sociohistorical) comment that should preface the first argument we will examine in favor of granting PSID a "passive" robust moral status. This is the longstanding assumption that being disabled, and/or not meeting the culturally contingent benchmark of a "normal" person, and/or having difficulties performing social roles with the same degree of independence as most other people, all correlate to having an intrinsically inferior value. "In almost all places and among all people," Anita Silvers notes, "individuals with certain physical or intellectual anomalies are assumed to be, by the very nature of their condition, inferior."[18] Moreover, disability has not only been long assumed to be a terrible fate but also to be a somehow deserved one. Therefore, people with disabilities are not worthy of the sort of pity, compassion, or fair compensation that we would be inclined to give to the victims of sheer bad luck. "From antiquity, the traditional explanation for their disadvantage has supposed that there is some moral flaw, not necessarily theirs but perhaps that of their progenitors, for which failing they must suffer."[19] We must be aware of this underlying, though mutable, backdrop of disability history when we analyze philosophical arguments purporting to support people with disabilities.[20]

The epistemological issue is that the trustee may not be able to detect what is in the interest of PSID or be able to correctly balance whatever conception she has of PSID's interests with PSID's own expression of their desires. These epistemological difficulties are unavoidable when we deal with the best interests of beings who cannot express their opinion about what they want or who are otherwise not in a good position for doing so (like a child or someone under the influence of drugs). However, if the trustees are well-meaning and duly informed about the best course

---

[18] Anita Silvers, "Formal Justice" in Anita Silvers, David Wasserman, and Mary Mahowald, eds., *Disability, Difference, Discrimination* (Lanham, MD: Rowman & Littlefield, 1998), 13 at 56.

[19] Ibid. at 57.

[20] Worldviews may change, but the need to fault or blame disabled people for their state is perennial. Insofar as their fate is considered "bad" and we naturally tend to look for a culprit when badness occurs, it is all too tempting to take the "victim" who is experientially closest to the bad event as a scapegoat. Although this no longer takes the form of, say, the idea that people inherit the debt of their ancestors' sins, it surfaces in other forms. For instance, PSID are often conceived as a burden to others, and this burden is interpreted as an individual problem with biological, rather than social, causes.

of action to overcome epistemological obstacles, there is little else that can be required from them (or from their appointers) in a moral sense. Although this is too complicated an empirical matter to be solved by *a priori* assertions, one cannot help noting that, no matter how different people with severe disabilities are from nondisabled people, they share even more similarities being members of the same species. This obvious fact alone should make us optimistic about securing some reliable knowledge about how we can make their lives better. Finally, although epistemological obstacles would render the institution of trusteeship for PSID absurd if they were serious and insurmountable, less dramatic epistemological obstacles are more likely to affect the accuracy of the trustee's decisions, rather than to downgrade PSID's status. In other words, these obstacles would not justify, in and of themselves, to conclude that PSID's status is significantly politically inferior.

One of the structural issues is that, even though in theory trustees representing those unable to represent themselves ought to be guided by their beneficiaries' interests alone, some fear that "in a process of bargaining to a social contract trustees could not help but represent their own interests rather than the interests of the beneficiaries of the trust relationship."[21] This concern is shared by Kittay, Nussbaum, Silvers, and Francis, and this structural issue is made worse when it is connected to the epistemological one:

> [T]rustees or other stand-ins are parties to the contract and therefore would be bargaining in their own right as well. There would be conflicts of interest – their own interests against the interests of those whom they represent. The safeguard of selecting them as decision makers because they take an interest in their beneficiaries, as well as because they are in an epistemologically favorable position, could fall prey to such conflict. Worse still, if there is no independent way of understanding what the interests of the beneficiaries are, there is no way of judging whether the conflict has corrupted the contracting process.[22]

It seems that we need to refine the fundamental fear that a trustee would be partial to her own interests. First, the fear that delegates think about their own well-being and prioritize it in covert ways that go beyond their moral or legal ambit is not a problem that is unique to PSID's representatives. It can affect any political representation, though it is a plausible concern that the epistemological difficulties in the case of

---

[21] Leslie Francis and Anita Silvers, "Justice through Trust: Disability and the 'Outlier Problem' in Social Contract Theory" (2005) 116:1 Ethics 40 at 53. Note that Silvers and Francis refer to Martha Nussbaum's position in "Beyond the Social Contract: Toward Global Justice," Tanner Lectures on Human Values, Canberra (November 2002) and Cambridge (March 2003), tannerlectures.utah.edu/lectures/documents/volume24 /nussbaum_2003.pdf. Eva Kittay makes a similar point in questioning whether it is fair to expect the dependency worker to represent the needs of the other and her own when others represent only themselves – thus violating the position that each counts for one. See Eva Kittay, *Love's Labor: Essays on Women, Equality and Dependency* (New York: Routledge, 1999), at 110.

[22] Francis and Silvers, "Justice through Trust," at 53.

PSID may make it easier for a dishonest delegate to cover her tracks – though not as easy, perhaps, as Silvers and Francis suggest.

Second, the concern that trustees speaking for a PSID will be unduly influenced by their own interests is certainly plausible if we are talking about trustees in real-life politics, but it is possible, at least conceptually, to imagine a non-corrupted trustee. Indeed, this is an amendment to Rawls's original position that Adam Cureton has suggested: to appoint trustees in charge of speaking for PSID, and them alone.[23] However, this escape route through an ideal process may be a dead end if we consider that, sooner or later, a real person (like Rawls or you) needs to imagine what these idealized trustees would say about PSID's interests.

Another major structural issue is that PSID may be entitled to speak too little or too late in the contractual process of a trusteeship. Even supposing the trustee will know PSID's interests and put them before her own, her representation may not be sufficiently effective to promote PSID's interests. Why would the trustee be entitled to speak only too little or too late? On some contractual accounts (at least those we are considering in this section, which assume that PSID are only conferred a status as one of the outcomes of the social contract) PSID can only be integrated when some fundamental decisions about the order regulating our society (like Rawls's principles of justice) have already been made. In Rawls's theory, for instance, only primary subjects of justice would be entitled to participate in the early sequences of the contractual process.

PSID will also not be expected nor invited to speak about all subject matters. The social contract tradition generally limits what participants to the contract can say to things that will affect them. (In a way, the whole point of resorting to a contract is to avoid having the parties disagree about basic matters such as how the polity should organize itself or what objective teleological basis should direct the shape of our society.) Nonetheless, individuals have a vested interest in choosing certain procedural rules of justice, as well as other rules regulating collective endeavors that will affect them. Accounts conceptualizing PSID as passive beneficiaries can be expected to limit what PSID's trustees are entitled to say about social projects in which PSID do not actively participate. PSID are thought to only have an interest in projects insofar as they are not hurt by them and, otherwise, only have an interest in being cared for. If some projects have some negative impacts on PSID, then trustees may have grounds to voice their interests. However, by then, many fundamental rules and projects will have already been agreed to, and the trustees' intervention is, at best, going to provide some form of compensation rather than to fundamentally challenge what is harming PSID. As a result, the corrective or compensatory measures may prove unsatisfactory. Though thinking about disabled people in a compensatory way can be challenged by theorists of the active

---

[23] Adam Cureton, "A Rawlsian Perspective on Justice for the Disabled" (2008) 9:1 Essays in Philosophy.

citizenship of PSID – as we have seen in the previous chapter – it is much harder to imagine how to do so within the framework of passive citizenship.

This obstacle can interfere with PSID's access to both abstract and concrete kinds of social advantages and can affect all kinds of disabilities. For instance, deaf people may be given subtitles or interpreters to accompany movies but had they had more of a say, they might have asked their municipality to invest in an artistic center offering greater visual entertainment. This portion of the problem may not be structural. Perhaps people with disabilities are not asked to speak on certain matters simply because the way in which it will indirectly affect them has not been properly assessed. It need not be because there are justifications to neglect some of their interests. It remains, however, that when these interests require their trustees to represent them at a stage where only active citizens are expected to be heard, it is at least *likely* that their absence from the process will go unnoticed.

5.4 INDIRECTLY ACQUIRING DIRECT MORAL CONSIDERABILITY BECAUSE THE CONTRACTORS MAKE PROVISIONS FOR IT

In her Tanner Lecture, "Kantian Ethics and Our Duties to Animals," Christine Korsgaard made the argument that, on a (neo-)Kantian account, animals can be intrinsically valuable even though they are not the source of their own value. In other words, they would be intrinsic sources of moral claims though in an other-authenticating way, rather than in a self-authenticating way. Her argument replies to the metaphysical concern that the status of PSID as passive citizens is doomed to be too contingent and derivative in a way that makes it normatively weaker, less stringent, or otherwise inferior to the status of noncognitively disabled citizens. Although her argument is about animals, it applies, *mutatis mutandis*, to other nonrational beings as well.[24]

---

[24] Christine Korsgaard, "Fellow Creatures: Kantian Ethics and Our Duties to Animals," Tanner Lectures on Human Values, University of Michigan (2004), tannerlectures.utah.edu/_documents/a-to-z/k/korsgaard_2005.pdf. Early on, she generalizes the problem of exclusion from the "Kingdom of Ends" to all non-rational beings (at 81). She does add that people who "are at stages of their lives when reason is undeveloped, inert, or non-functional" still possess the standing of "rational beings under the Kantian conception" (at 82). This might point to the "nature of the kind" arguments – that is, arguments grounding moral status on the fact that a being belongs to a kind or a *genus*, but which might also be limited to humans who will at some point reach a rational stage. She also explicitly limits her project to non-human animals as "the one group" among many that does not constitute rational beings, which indicates that she does not see a problem in categorizing PSID as beings possessing the standing of "rational beings under a Kantian conception." I suspect that she focused on animals because, like most philosophers theorizing the rights of marginal cases and non-philosophers (but *contra* Peter Singer and many utilitarians), she assumes that the case of PSID is unproblematic. When she asks, "[w]hat about infants ... or the very old and demented ... the severely retarded and the incurably insane ... [and] non-human animals? Are none of these to be regarded as ends-in-themselves? And if not, does that mean that we are allowed to use them as mere means to our ends?" (at 81). The latter question only seems to apply, in practice, to animals. It is therefore

Andrew Cohen has offered a similar argument, although it would fall within the contractarian tradition.[25] Following Christopher Morris,[26] Cohen distinguishes between primary and secondary moral standing. The difference between them is that, in the first case, one has negotiated contractually to obtain one's *own* status; in the latter, one has contractually negotiated for a robust status to be given to an individual who is unable to make a contract. This implies (1) that the status did not preexist the contract (which implies a similar view of value to Korsgaard's) and (2) that it is not required for any other reason than the parties' wills to contract for that status.

5.4.1 *The Problem with Piggybacking Moral Statuses*

Cohen's strategy is to say that "the only difference [between primary and secondary moral standing] is in the genesis of the standing."[27] This genesis does not matter: the standing obtained is as metaphysically strong. First, one may answer that this standing is "as metaphysically weak" instead of "as metaphysically strong" as a status based on properties inhering in the status-holder. Cohen gives a scenario in which Peter extends "direct moral regard" to Emma because James makes this contractual demand on him. But James could change his mind and stop making demands of Peter. "Nontuist that he is," Cohen writes, the contractor (Peter) "would stop extending [Emma, the beneficiary party, who we may assume is a disabled child] any moral regard."[28]

The key problem with this, as Christopher Morris notes, is that we cannot satisfactorily explain on this (contractual relational) account (of status) why PSIDs or children would have a robust moral status vis-à-vis their protectors or parents. Morris concludes that "[i]t appears that someone need not have moral standing in relation to the agent(s) who is the vehicle for one's secondary moral standing."[29] This is an admission that a contractarian account cannot explain why parents should intervene contractually to protect their child rather than to negotiate in favor of any other entity (and secure, Cohen illustrates, a secondary moral status for neckties

---

possible that Korsgaard would disagree with my application of her argument to PSID given that she would have included PSID through a "nature of the kind" argument. I am not discussing the validity of this argument here, though I can mention that, like other variants of human exceptionalism, some, like Peter Singer, find it to be an insufficiently convincing way to justify the robust moral status of PSID.

[25] Andrew Cohen, "Contractarianism, Other-Regarding Attitudes, and the Moral Standing of Nonhuman Animals" (2007) 24:2 J Applied Phil 188.
[26] Christopher Morris, "Moral Standing and Rational-Choice Contractarianism" in Peter Vallentyne, ed., *Contractarianism and Rational Choice: Essays on David Gauthier's Morals by Agreement* (New York: Cambridge University Press, 1991), 76 at 89–90.
[27] Cohen, "Contractarianism," at 191.
[28] Ibid. at 194.
[29] Morris, "Moral Standing and Rational-Choice Contractarianism," at 95.

instead). "If that is their choice," Cohen concedes at one point, "so be it."[30] Yet, Cohen attempts to circumvent (if not solve) the problem of optionality in three ways. First, he suggests that there may be other non-optional grounds for moral standing outside of contractarianism,[31] which does not solve the issue of optionality from a contractarian point of view. Second, he makes the relatively familiar claim (among theorists working on the notion of the status of children and the disabled) that others will care for them if their parents are not. This is a descriptive rather than normative claim and therefore it does not explain why this concern is morally warranted or even stringent. His third argument borrows from Simon Blackburn's "projectivist quasi-realism" and suggests that "[c]ontractors *ought* to extend direct moral regard to any being with a particular characteristic(s) such as sentience or a distinct capacity to flourish."[32]

I agree with this view for reasons that need to be argued for on noncontractual grounds, which are made in my introduction to Korsgaard's argument. However, the term "contractor" in the previous quote is unnecessary: the obligation applies to all moral agents and is not rooted in contractarianism. Cohen would suggest that we should wed contractarianism and this theory about the robust status of animals. (His argument also applies to PSID; he actually refers to infants. Morris referred mostly to infants and the infirm and only mentioned animals passingly.) Cohen writes that "[c]ontractarianism is not committed to saying that it is permissible to torture animals if the contract ignores them."[33] He is repeating that there can be other grounds for moral standing external to contractarianism. Insofar as I take him to narrow the reach of contractarianism to a more limited domain of morality, I agree. However, I suspect that his marriage of quasi-realism to contractarianism aims more at narrowing the application of contractarian theory and would thus constrain it. People would be *wrong* to make certain contractual agreements or fail to make others.[34] Cohen assumes that critics like myself worry about the contractual/constructivist subjective view on the foundations of value. However, I do not; my own account is similar to his. What I worry about is the coherence of his argument when he calls this noncontractual account contractarian. If it constrains contractors normatively, then it subordinates the contractarian commitment to the parties' will to a greater good that ought to trump this contractual will. The contract metaphor would be reduced to a means of carrying out a theory of the good. In this sense, Cohen's suggestion that they are compatible and can be married seems unwarranted.

Korsgaard's contractualist standpoint allows her to make this marriage: she can explain why we ought to extend the contract to benefit PSID in a way that is not

---

[30] Cohen, "Contractarianism," at 193.
[31] Ibid. at 191, fn. 12.
[32] Ibid. at 197.
[33] Ibid. at 198.
[34] Ibid. at 197–98.

incompatible with (and indeed, emanates from) contractualist assumptions, even though this marriage is incompatible with contractarian ones.

5.4.2 Extending the Contract to All Intrinsically Valuable Beings and the Problem of Prioritization

Korsgaard's key idea is that a robust moral status or, rather, the kind of value which grounds it, is conferred by moral agents through certain acts of will. Therefore, the metaphysical criticism, which insists that moral agents have a special value based on their internal properties (that PSID do not have) and maintains that PSID's status is worth less because it is derivative and given to them by moral agents (and thus, one may add, contingent upon these agents happening to care for them) does not arise. All valuable beings have been given status by acts of will, not only PSID.

Instead of emanating directly from internal properties, value is conferred on people through a kind of interpersonal attribution. While it could still be said that moral agents can attribute this kind of value to themselves, while PSID depend upon moral agents conferring it upon them, PSID's characteristics still warrant direct moral consideration – a noncontingent, noninstrumental kind of consideration. There is simply no justification, on Korsgaard's account of how things are or come to be valuable, why a more indirect way of acquiring intrinsic value would make a being's moral status any less important or demanding.

This account of how beings acquire a special kind of value (including the robust moral status that interests us) does not mean that moral agents can confer value to anything they want, contractually or otherwise. We must, Korsgaard suggests, grant the special value we grant to ourselves to all who partake of our "natural good." This would encompass PSID, nonhuman animals, or any being that "matters to itself," in the sense that something that is good for this being is good from its point of view.[35]

Three elements of Korsgaard's arguments are important for our purposes: the Kantian theory of value that she uses and two conceptual distinctions that she draws that grant intrinsic value to certain nonrational beings (which Kant failed to do). At the outset, my conclusion notes that the problem with realizing that we, as contractors, share a flourishing nature with PSID, requiring us to recognize their moral status on grounds compatible with contractualism, is that we also share this nature with all living things. Korsgaard cannot provide a contractual criterion for prioritizing some intrinsically valuable beings over others. Although I can imagine some noncontractual criteria to do so, I cannot think of a contractual criterion that would preserve the kind of value that she secures for PSID. In fact, all that Korsgaard does (not that it is a small feat) is to show that Kantians can agree with the (accurate, I believe) idea that beings partaking of human goods are intrinsically valuable. This is in the sense that they are important "like us" instead of important "for us," or that

---

[35] Korsgaard, "Fellow Creatures," at 103, fn. 63.

5.4 Indirectly Acquiring Moral Considerability

they have the well-being of their own and ought to be regarded as such morally. This is the kind of conclusion that thinkers endorsing a "list of goods" theory (like Nussbaum) affirm with much less hesitation. To think anything else, Finnis simply said, is to be "buried in untruth."[36]

Korsgaard proceeds, through the Kantian psychological and moral route, to flesh out a case for this conclusion and, although I am personally attracted to psychological and moral explanations that rely on the notion of empathy (moral and psychological) to make this case, I find her Kantian metaethical case convincing.[37] Nonetheless, it faces the same problem as any of these other accounts: it gives reason to recognize the intrinsic value of a variety of nonrational (human and nonhuman) beings, but does not provide us with an account of how to prioritize some beings over others. In fact, even though Korsgaard refers to the Kantian notion of passive citizenship, she does so to make her point about the special *value* that animals have, rather than about their moral status.

The issue of why PSID would be contractually given a robust kind of *value* is solved, but the issue of why they would be given a robust moral and political *status* and set of rights is not, unless we assume that all beings sharing our "natural good" will have such status and rights, or we provide an account of the relative normative stringency of different moral statuses, or give an account of why and how certain intrinsically valuable beings make certain demands upon certain moral agents.[38]

In terms of the Kantian metaphysics of value – and how it relates to the notion of a moral community in which members owe obligations to one another in a way that could be understood within a contractualist framework – there are three key elements to understand Korsgaard's argument and its appeal: (1) the Kantian account is a "fitting attitude" account of value (2) which correlates a conception of moral agents as value-givers and as "ends-in-themselves" (3) and this comes with valuing constraints.

On a Kantian account, like in other accounts of value that reject value realism, moral legislators create value rather than detect it in the world. In Korsgaard's words, "we do not desire things because they are valuable; rather, we take them to be

---

[36] Finnis, *Reason in Action*, at 48.
[37] It would fall beyond the scope of this book to compare the merits of her case with available alternatives, notably because her argument can still be presented in a contractual framework.
[38] Or short of reaching over-pessimistic or odd conclusions, such as assuming that all living things ought to make stringent demands on all of us all the time, but that we are doomed to fail morally and no moral guidance can be found to make the best of this failure. The only *contractualist* way to justify why a PSID should be given water before a plant that Korsgaard points to is that moral agents happen to care more for PSID in ways that render them non-instrumentally valuable or valuable for their own sake – yet not the source of their own value, not "ends-in-themselves" (Korsgaard, "Fellow Creatures," at 88, fn. 24). However, this would not defeat the metaphysical criticism. Korsgaard's criterion for attributing intrinsic value (having a good for oneself/itself – i.e., well-being of one's own) defeats the metaphysical criticism, but at the cost of creating a politically unmanageable passive citizenship.

valuable because we desire them."³⁹ Korsgaard therefore rejects the idea that human beings "simply have intrinsic value."⁴⁰ She maintains that "[t]he decision to regard ourselves as the source of legitimate normative claims is the original act that brings the world of normative reasons and values into existence."⁴¹ Her lyrical concluding sentence perhaps makes a better case for her agent-emanating view of value than a rational argument could, as it invites the reader to share her proto-philosophical intuitions about the matter: "We are the only beings who ... can shake our fists at the uncaring universe, and declare that in spite of everything we *matter*."⁴² Implicitly, we humans can also assert the value of all beings sharing our mysterious fate or, more precisely, what we think is valuable about this fate.

The conception of ourselves as value-givers is fundamental in Kantian moral thought. It is part of our psychological makeup rather than a chosen, posited conception. It is a fact about us that we are "rational beings, who are conscious of our choices and [their] grounds" and that "we can pursue our ends only if we are satisfied that doing so is good – that is, that our ends are worthy of pursuit."⁴³ Value is the necessary implication of our rational nature: "[b]ecause we are rational, we cannot act without at least implicitly endorsing the principles upon which we act."⁴⁴ This particular way of desiring and valuing ends implies that we see ourselves as "sources of values" – "[w]hat matters to me ... really matters, and is worth pursuing, because *I* matter."⁴⁵ This conception of ourselves is what Kant refers to when he says that we are "ends-in-ourselves." This term serves to distinguish between things that are good *for something* and things that are good *in themselves*. The ends that we choose "are not good in themselves, but only relative to our own interests."⁴⁶ They are good for us but we, in turn, are not good for something else in the same way. This is not so much a statement about the value that we (or anything) have, but about how humans value things. It is implicit in our way of valuing that we must take ourselves to be ends-in-ourselves. This is why Korsgaard notes that "even the

---

³⁹ *Ibid.* at 93.
⁴⁰ *Ibid.* at 101, fn. 61.
⁴¹ *Ibid.* at 101; see also Christine Korsgaard, *The Sources of Normativity* (Cambridge: Cambridge University Press, 2000), at 161–64.
⁴² Korsgaard, "Fellow Creatures," at 109.
⁴³ *Ibid.* at 93.
⁴⁴ *Ibid.* at 95.
⁴⁵ *Ibid.* at 93. Similarly, J. David Velleman writes: "Of course, we assume that a person's good does matter. But we make this assumption only because we assume that people matter – that everyone has a value that makes him worth caring about ... [O]ur appreciation of value that accrues to someone depends on a prior appreciation of a value inhering in him" ("A Right to Self-Termination?" [1999] 109:3 *Ethics* 606 at 611). On the idea that the value of a good for a person is not a "categorical" value, to put it like Velleman, or that the value of such goods is not intrinsic to certain states of affairs but rather is nested in the intrinsic value possessed by the person experiencing such states, see Elizabeth Anderson, *Value in Ethics and Economics* (Cambridge: Harvard University Press, 1995), at ch. 1.
⁴⁶ Korsgaard, "Fellow Creatures," at 93.

special value of humanity as an end-in-itself comes from our own legislative acts" and that through "the very act of treating our own ends as good and worthy of pursuit, in spite of their lack of any inherent value, we in effect *confer* the status of end-in-itself on ourselves."[47]

However, it is not because valuing precedes value that valuers can confer any kind of value upon anything they wish. There are various constraints that render certain valuing attitudes fitting and others improper. We do not only value things in isolation of other valuers, but we are "moral legislators" in the sense that we are "sources of [legitimate] normative claims that are binding [on all rational agents]."[48] This is because all rational agents can recognize valid reasons and respond to "legislative acts" and the appropriate, natural stance that we adopt is one that can be shared by all rational agents. In the Kantian moral system, "that amounts to asking the question of the categorical imperative – whether the maxim 'I will do act-A for the sake of end-E' can function as a universal law."[49]

How do Kantian metaphysics of value relate to the notion of a moral community on a Kantian account? The result of considering that others are, like ourselves, ends-in-themselves – and that their autonomous choices (their ends) are valuable and should be promoted like ours – is a community of rational, autonomous beings who respect one another. Kant calls this the "Kingdom of Ends." Korsgaard defines it as a "notional community, constituted by the relations among human beings with a shared commitment to a conception of ourselves and each other as ends in ourselves."[50] More than a spiritual Kingdom, this is "a kind of constitutional democracy, in which each citizen has a legislative voice,"[51] by which they express moral laws, which are the laws of this notional community.

This counts as a kind of social contract theory. As we saw, the idea that moral laws are the product of the subjects' will, and that the legal subjects are lawmakers, is "the animating idea of contractualism."[52] This seems to inevitably exclude nonrational beings.

Two conceptual distinctions in Korsgaard's argument are significant: the first seeks to open a conceptual possibility that Kant seems to be closing when he creates a dichotomy between *persons* (rational beings) on the one hand, and *things* (the rest of nature) to be valued only as means instead of ends-in-themselves, on the other. Korsgaard maintains that this is incompatible with the way Kant holds that how we value "the ends we pursue in our actions."[53] Some things that we value, we value for

---

[47] Ibid. at 94–95. Of course, a value realist account may hold that we are mistaken in doing so and that our psychological inclinations to implicitly endorse a conception of ourselves as ends-in-ourselves are not where we should start.
[48] Ibid. at 93.
[49] Ibid. at 94.
[50] Ibid. at 81.
[51] Ibid.
[52] Stephen Darwall, *Contractarianism / Contractualism* (Malden, MA: Blackwell, 2003), at 5; see also Southwood, *Contractualism and the Foundations*, at ch. 3.
[53] Korsgaard, "Fellow Creatures," at 88, fn. 24.

their own sake – that is, as an end, though not an end-in-itself. A natural object may thus gain "the status of a relatively valuable end" if someone "happen[s] to care about it."[54] In other words, the ends–means pair does not necessarily correspond to the dichotomy between self-authenticatingly valuable and externally authenticatingly valuable. One's value as an end can be externally authenticated.

Korsgaard says that such a middle-ground status "could not be used as a general duty to animals" because of its contingency.[55] I am unsure, however, why this is the case. If there is no constraint on our valuing, this status would be contingent upon our whims. But it may not be the case that we can agree to the maxim that it is acceptable for us to disregard the welfare of animals (a position we could hold, for example, in relation to a decision not to take piano lessons). Indeed, this is the argument that Korsgaard will make. She may want to preserve a different conceptual space for ends like piano lessons, but I am not sure how these cases (piano lessons and animals) differ in terms of being conferred externally as the value of an end. Rather, they differ in terms of the kinds of constraints limiting the agent's option to confer on them this value or not.

Her second distinction tracks what makes the difference (or rather, what is mistakenly thought to make a difference) between the *kinds* of properties of a being that would justify a non-optional constraint to value that being as an end. It is the distinction between *being a source* of robust normative claims (i.e., "claims that must be recognized by all rational agents"[56]) and *having the capacity to confer* this robust normativity, where "robust" refers, in the Kantian account, to the final and self-authenticating character of value, as well as its agent-neutral normativity, which we explored in Section 5.3.

Korsgaard justifies the integration of nonrational beings to the moral community using this second distinction. She explains how we give value to nonrational beings just like we give value to ourselves. Her conclusion is that "we *legislate* that the natural good of a creature who matters to itself is the source of normative claims."[57] We do so because, when we take ourselves to be ends-in-ourselves, we do not only take our *autonomous nature* to be "the source of legitimate normative claims."[58] We do not only respect our autonomous choices but also "the content of those choices," and it is a constant choice that moral agents make to "choos[e] to pursue what [Korsgaard calls] our 'natural good.'"[59] On Korsgaard's account, any entity has a natural good in the sense of having what "enables it to function at all and to function well."[60] Living things, however, have a good of their own. When something is good

---

[54] Ibid., in contrast with Kant, *Groundwork*, at 36.
[55] Korsgaard, "Fellow Creatures," at 88, fn. 24.
[56] Ibid. at 95.
[57] Ibid. at 106.
[58] Ibid. at 93.
[59] Ibid. at 102.
[60] Ibid.

for a car, this is because it allows the car to perform its function which, in turn, serves the good of some entity other than the car. In contrast, when something is good for a living thing, we may be referring to what is good for this living thing itself, from its own point of view.[61] This is because living things have needs and well-being of their own. By identifying the pursuit of such a good in ourselves, we are effectively affirming or conferring a normative value to this kind of good in others. That is, we are legislating that "the kind of natural good characteristic of creatures who experience and pursue their own good ... is the source of normative claims."[62]

I believe that Korsgaard's account suffices to ground the intrinsic value of PSID. Her Kantian argument for recognizing that animals are ends-in-themselves is sound and can be applied to PSID. My criticism of her account is that, while it justifies the position that many beings have intrinsic value, it grants a robust value to such a large variety of beings without telling us how we should prioritize the claims that all these beings make on us. On this basis, it seems too abstract or ideal to be satisfactory as a contractualist account. I hold a view similar to Korsgaard concerning the criterion that a being has intrinsic value, but I think that we must, as a second step, resort to the normative content of various relations to explain what kind of duties weighs on who, toward whom, and to what degree. I cannot explain this sort of supplementary relational theory here, but it is not contractual. I do not see how her Kantian account could provide us with clearer instructions, except by developing an argument according to which moral agents can (contractually and legislatively) choose which beings to prioritize. However, if her account did this, it would resort to putting nonrational beings in the category of "relatively valuable [ends]," which she contemplates in her first distinction, where she grants that this is insufficient "to ground a general duty to [nonrational beings]."[63] I would add that this status is not only unsatisfactory because it lacks universality, but also because it does not provide a sufficiently robust status to PSID in the sense of being affected by optionality or contingence.

Thus, Korsgaard's account can plausibly justify that we ought to grant intrinsic moral considerability to nonrational beings such as animals and PSID. But is it sufficient to ground PSID's robust moral status? And can it do so on contractualist grounds?

From Intrinsic Value to Robust Moral Status
Rational agents can, *qua* legislators in the "Kingdom of Ends," contractually bestow a strong status on PSID, but this status would accomplish much less morally and politically than a contractualist theory expects a robust moral status to do. The problem is that the criterion of having a good for itself could include plants – not

---

[61] Ibid. at 104.
[62] Ibid. at 105.
[63] Ibid. at 88, fn. 24.

only animals, and not only PSID. I believe this broad range of intrinsically valuable beings is justified, but we cannot grant a robust status to all beings that are merely alive, unless "robust" is given a less meaningful definition to allow for more easily defeasible obligations. The mosquito and the lettuce cannot make a robust claim on me to continue their existence when their lives must be shortened for the good of my child. Something more needs to be said here. More precisely, I think, something needs to be clarified about the relations I have with all the entities involved, and their respective needs and forms of life.

This means that we have only granted intrinsic value to people with profound mental disabilities, but we have not established the sort of status this value would correlate to, and why. Korsgaard's theory of passive citizenship for fellow (nonrational) creatures succeeds in explaining why passive citizens are to be taken seriously – that is, why they are as intrinsically valuable as active citizens. But this conclusion comes at the cost of saying that all living things are also passive citizens. Korsgaard recognizes this problem: "Why shouldn't we have obligations to all living things? But if we do, how can we possibly meet our obligations?"[64]

She discusses the issue of whether "ought implies can," but her answer that Kantian moral standards are ideal and which we may not be able to reach – but toward which we must strive – does not help us organize the striving in a moral way (assuming, as contractual theories do, that morality has *something* to say to the less than ideal strivers that we are). Korsgaard's theory also does not answer urgent questions that need precise answers within a contractual framework, such as: Who has rights, and what is the nature of these rights? How are we to manage a massive conflict of rights and to prioritize between intrinsically valuable beings in a non-arbitrary way? How is this position to be formulated as a contractual theory? Korsgaard's exhortation that we should at least "do our best ... as far as we possibly can,"[65] starting with not hunting and eating our fellow passive citizens, is cold comfort for anyone worried about how the status of passive citizen is precarious, and that, in this account, it seems to be an explicitly second-rate kind of citizenship.

The question is not only whether we matter intrinsically, but whether we matter contractually – that is, in a way that calls for a specific series of society-governing principles and rights and that explains why it is important to give water to a PSID before watering a plant. The question of intrinsic value is only relevant if it can answer the contractual question, which it begins to answer. Yet, because it does not explain why and how passive citizens are as important as full citizens within the political or legal community, it does not provide a satisfactory contractual answer,[66]

---

[64] *Ibid.* at 107.
[65] *Ibid.* at 108.
[66] By suggesting that "we" should try not to eat passive citizens and certainly not hunt them for fun, Korsgaard is already inferring double standards by suggesting that active and passive citizens are not equal. Or at least, although they should *ideally* be equal citizens, in practice, they will benefit from less stringent rights. As I mentioned, contractualist thought would

unless we take the social contract tradition to a place where it has never been before and conceive of society as Nature and the social contract as a unilateral act of will. The problem with this is not only that we would have to reimagine many key concepts of the tradition (like reciprocity), but also that the social contract as a substantial or heuristic device to vehicle our moral intuitions would eventually break down. Whatever notion of community between moral agents and nature may emerge, it would be counterproductive to this (potentially enlightening) de-anthropocentric endeavor to express moral agents' complex (noncontractual) relations with their fellow creatures in terms of a paradigmatically human kind of interaction: a contract. Even contracts between very different beings (say, God and mankind) have not fictively posited the abilities of parties to the contract to understand its terms.

5.5 EXTENDING PASSIVE CITIZENSHIP TO PSID IN A RAWLSIAN FRAMEWORK

In the previous section, I dealt with a contractualist (and, briefly, contractarian) argument for passive citizenship. I showed that there was no problem in indirectly granting PSID a direct respect. The very fact of giving direct moral consideration to beings who cannot contract, value, or grant this moral consideration themselves is not of itself (metaphysically) problematic. Rather, I was concerned with whether this moral consideration led to a robust moral status. More precisely, I was concerned with the contingency of this standing (with regard to Cohen's argument), the low threshold to grant robust moral status, and the inability to prioritize between beings that pass this low threshold (with regard to Korsgaard's argument). My critique does not necessarily prove that it is impossible to come up with a contractualist or contractarian account of passive citizenship that would not overcome these structural problems. But it indicates that it is hard to imagine how one could, especially since the problems of contingency and overbreadth are (at least sometimes) connected. By hammering one problem down, we may cause the other to pop out.

In this section, I present a few more contractualist strategies from Rawlsian perspectives to explain why contractors ought to grant this passive citizenship to PSID. I will focus on Adam Cureton's and Cynthia Stark's proposals because they are detailed and promising, but also share problematic features, which are representative of the limitations of other contractual arguments (such as those of Thomas Scanlon, Nicholas Southwood, and Christine Korsgaard). Although these theorists make distinct points, their arguments, I suggest, ultimately gesture at some sort of

> generally hold that morality and justice provide us with more precise guidance than that. Otherwise, a more idealized brand of contractualism that has given up explaining how to morally prioritize between intrinsically valuable beings would be unappealing in comparison to alternative moral accounts.

normative relation/bond[67] or good that falls beyond the scope of the social contract tradition, although this bond can supplement it.

5.5.1 Considering PWD and PSID as Community Members for Whom Parties in the Original Position Design Principles of Justice

One of the most famous conceptual tools drawn from Rawls's theory of "justice as fairness" is the "original position" (OP), a thought experiment in which readers are asked to adopt a moral point of view characterized by impartiality-inducing features. One such feature is the "veil of ignorance" behind which every individual is made ignorant of:

> [H]is place in society, his class position or social status, nor does anyone know his fortune in the distribution of natural assets and abilities, his intelligence, strength, and the like. [We] shall even assume that the parties do not know their conceptions of the good or their special psychological propensities.[68]

The parties to the social contract under Rawls's theory of justice are imagined as standing in this original position when they choose the principles of justice that will govern society – that is, "the principles that free and rational persons concerned to further their own interests would accept" as equals in such a position.[69]

We may think about the veil of ignorance as applying directly to members of society who momentarily "do not know how the various alternatives [of principles of justice they can choose from] will affect their own particular case."[70] However, Rawls later specifies that persons in the OP are "representatives of free and equal citizens [and] act as trustees or guardians" – that is, they will seek principles of justice that best "secure the fundamental interests of those they represent."[71] We can keep both postures in mind – that is, imagining the parties in the OP as future citizens or as representatives of such citizens – as we assess plausible ways of integrating PSID within the purview of contractual justice. In the first case, one would argue that negotiating contractors should consider the possibility that they may turn out to have some kind of severe disability. In the second case, one would argue that the parties in the OP should represent PSID's interests. Initially, these two suggestions seem like the most intuitive contractualist strategies to ensure that the

---

[67] For instance, Scanlon refers to a "tie of birth"; Stark refers to a moral response to people's basic needs; Southwood refers to the significance of being affected by a contractual decision to which the affected party has not participated; Cureton implies a presumption of integration for all PWD; Korsgaard's recognizes that non-rational creatures are "like us" in some morally compelling way. I do not deny these starting points are intuitively compelling; I only question whether they are best fleshed out in a contractual idiom.

[68] Rawls, A Theory of Justice, at 11, 118–23.

[69] Ibid. at 10; see also John Rawls, Justice as Fairness: A Restatement, ed. Erin Kelly (Cambridge: Harvard University Press, 2001), at 15ff.

[70] Rawls, A Theory of Justice, at 118.

[71] Rawls, Justice as Fairness, at 84.

interests of PSID will be given fair consideration during the process of designing a society's principles of justice, constitution and laws. The underlying intuition is that it would be unfair to design a society that advantages or disadvantages some members on the basis of having a permanent and severe disability.

However, this intuition must be justified. On a Rawlsian account, the veil is justified because it expresses the moral claim that certain facts about people should not matter when setting up a system of distributive justice – their skin color or gender, for instance.[72] On a Rawlsian contractualist account, while parties behind the veil of ignorance can make provisions for the worst that could happen to the people they represent, they are limited by these parameters – that is, what could happen, precisely to the people they represent. These represented people are defined as fully cooperating throughout a lifetime and exclude PSID.[73] To circumvent this constraint without abandoning Rawlsian commitments to contractualist ideals is no small challenge, considering the "main idea" behind justice as fairness and the elaboration of principles of justice:

> [W]hen a number of persons engage in a mutually advantageous cooperative venture according to rules, and thus restrict their liberty in ways necessary to yield advantages for all, those who have submitted to these restrictions have a right to a similar acquiescence on the part of those who have benefited from their submission. We are not to gain from the cooperative labors of others without doing our fair share.[74]

The exclusion of "unusually expensive"[75] or "permanently dependent"[76] people seems to follow from such a premise. This is because PSID, amongst others who are unable to sufficiently reciprocate the benefits they would gain from belonging to society, "fall outside the bounds of social cooperation [and can even be denied] citizenship."[77] To place PSID in the OP seems to distort the nature of contractualist Rawlsian procedure, which is focused on particular kinds of relations – namely, those taking place between similarly capable strangers reasonably negotiating in a self-interested way. The contractual process cannot be reduced to asking ourselves, what should we make provisions for, or whom should we care about? Though the temptation to interpret it as such may reveal another moral pull, it has nothing to do with Rawlsian contractualism and it is incompatible with it insofar as it involves prioritizing the good over the right. As such, theorists considering the needs of those who are radically dependent and unable to engage in cooperation, and the importance of giving and responding to care, like Eva Kittay, or theorists emphasizing the

---

[72] Rawls, *A Theory of Justice*, at 118.
[73] John Rawls, *Political Liberalism*, expand. ed. (New York: Columbia University Press, 2005), at 20–21.
[74] Rawls, *A Theory of Justice*, at 96.
[75] Nussbaum, *Frontiers of Justice*, at 104.
[76] Kittay, *Love's Labor*, at 105.
[77] Ibid.

importance of partaking to certain basic human goods, like Martha Nussbaum, have sought foundations of justice outside of Rawlsian contractual thought.

Indeed, suggesting that parties in the OP imagine they might turn out to have grave disabilities once the veil of ignorance is lifted or asking them to represent the interests of PSID may be an academic distraction that does not tell us enough about the moral status of PSID or why they deserve it. Including PSID within the OP, or adding severe intellectual disability to the list of features that parties behind the veil of ignorance do not know about themselves, seems to presuppose obligations to PSID. But the question of whether we have obligations of justice toward PSID or whether they have moral status is precisely what is at issue. In other words, the motivations that parties in the OP have do not explain the contractualist integrationist drive as well as other moral norms would. Why even engage, then, with an impartiality-maximizing veil of ignorance? The one side trying to find fair principles has no need to convince the other of its reasonableness, as its grounds for respecting the PSID are already established. The status of PSID is not, therefore, explained by features inherent to the contractualist procedure, unlike the status of nondisabled citizens.

Three groups of individuals found within Rawls's "veil of ignorance" argument are useful to discuss passive citizenship: the constituents ("you and me"[78]), the parties (the artificial parties representing the constituents), and the beneficiaries (those whose fundamental interests the parties attempt to secure[79]). The reason why the constituents would create the parties to represent them is well fleshed out in Rawls's *A Theory of Justice*. However, if we consider that the constituents could want to construct parties attending PSID's interests, we must separate the three groups. To reformulate the doubt from the paragraph above more explicitly with these groups in mind: it is unclear why the constituents could not directly help the beneficiaries (PSID) and instead go through the artificial parties in the OP to do so.

In order to assuage this doubt, a philosopher who defends the hypothesis that the parties in the OP can and ought to represent PSID's interests must tell us:

(1) That it is conceptually possible within the Rawlsian framework within which she is working;
(2) why it is necessary; or, failing to prove necessity,
(3) why the constituents would be moved to create parties concerned with PSID's interests;
(4) whether the reason given in (3) is stable and categorical enough to constitute the basis for the robust moral status that we assume PSID are entitled to; and
(5) whether, if the reason given in (3) is robust enough, it is best served (or served at all) by a contractual procedure (e.g., by creating parties concerned with PSID's interests).

---

[78] Rawls, *Justice as Fairness*, at 87.
[79] Ibid. at 84–85.

Integrationist Rawlsians generally focus on questions (1) and (3), whereas the hypothesis of this book would press them to give compelling answers to the other questions as well.

For instance, in his article "A Rawlsian Perspective on Justice for the Disabled," Adam Cureton seeks to show that we can use a Rawlsian approach to help us justify that we have robust obligations of justice toward the disabled.[80] Much of his argument consists of showing that Rawls's theory of distributive justice is only a "limited project," but that this limited project rests on a Rawlsian framework that can be, according to Cureton, extended to the disabled.[81] In fact, even the "limited society" would include citizens with "hearing, visual, mobility, and cognitive impairments," as long as their disabilities would not prevent them from exercising their capacities for a conception of the good and for a sense of justice (referred to as "moral powers").[82] The limited society would, on the other hand, exclude severely and moderately cognitively impaired people (including the PSID) who permanently or temporarily lack these powers. The Rawlsian approach, however, would include everyone.[83]

I will consider some of Cureton's arguments for reaching these conclusions. He shows that integration is not precluded by some Rawlsian premises as often assumed. Arguing for this possibility does make progress toward integrating PWD within a Rawlsian framework, and the usefulness of this progress is questionable if reasons for the materialization of this possibility are themselves not explained by (or perhaps even incompatible with) a Rawlsian framework.

Distinguishing a Rawlsian Framework from a Theory of Justice as Fairness
Cureton distinguishes a Rawlsian framework from the limited project of a theory of justice and concludes that the former leaves the possibility of integrating PWD intact. Cureton concedes that PSID and other people lacking the moral powers would be excluded from Rawls's limited project of justice as fairness, but could be included under a broader Rawlsian approach:

> Once we relax [the] assumption [that society consists of people who are all fully cooperating citizens] and suppose that the parties know they are choosing principles of justice for a society that also includes radically and moderately cognitively impaired people, there is good reason for them to choose principles of justice that protect the interest of all people with disabilities.[84]

I will focus on four key themes that Cureton deals with in his argument – four elements of Rawls's theory that need to be amended or interpreted in a way that admits the integration of PSID – to assess the strength of his argument.

---

[80] Cureton, "A Rawlsian Perspective."
[81] Ibid. at §1.
[82] Ibid. at §6.
[83] Ibid. at §7.
[84] Ibid.

(1) LEAVING IMPORTANT THINGS FOR LATER Cureton argues that Rawls's project is not a holistic theory of social justice, but a limited project. We could call this the "limited project answer" to the problem of excluding PSID from the "fundamental question of political justice," which Rawls takes to be:

> [T]he most appropriate conception of justice for specifying the terms of social cooperation between citizens regarded as free and equal, and as normal and fully cooperating members of society over a complete life.[85]

Rawls does not deny that people become sick and disabled and that some are born with permanent severe mental disabilities. He grants that provisions for these "misfortunes" must be made, though he is unsure on which grounds and whether this falls within the sphere of justice.[86] If it does, it would be a problem of extension which he leaves for later discussion.[87] Rawls writes: "[i]f we can work out a theory that covers the fundamental case, we can try to extend it to other cases later. Plainly a theory that fails for the fundamental case is of no use at all."[88]

Cureton's response to this criticism – that focusing on central cases undermines the importance of PSID – is that dealing with central cases first does not necessarily entail that they are more important. Temporal priority does not imply a priority in importance.[89] This is true, logically speaking, though it does not speak to the issue of the contingent impact of Rawls's theory on political culture. That said, this "pragmatist critique" is addressed to the social reception of Rawls's theory of justice, and it should not be conflated with issues internal to the theory.

Indeed, Rawls does not say that we *must* think of disabilities as a matter of incremental extension to "justice as fairness," nor does he proffer that we should not think of the issue at all. He concedes that we may have to revise the answers already reached and that justice as fairness may turn out to be at fault – and a potentially grave one at that.[90]

Cureton also points out that Rawls's limited project is setting aside issues of "punishment, warfare, other nations, and nonbasic institutions," which "most of us would regard as fundamental and important issues of justice."[91] Surely, Rawls did not think that punitive justice is irrelevant. Still, one could note that issues of justice toward PWD include issues that are at the heart of justice as fairness, such as issues of distributive justice. Rawls's postponement of the case of disability does not only exclude a different sphere of justice (e.g., punitive justice) but subcategories of fields with which he is dealing. While Rawls's limited project could

---

[85] Rawls, *Political Liberalism*, at 20.
[86] Ibid. at 20–21.
[87] Ibid. at 20.
[88] John Rawls, "Kantian Constructivism in Moral Theory" (1980) 77:9 J Phil 515 at 546.
[89] Cureton, "A Rawlsian Perspective," at §2.
[90] Rawls, *Political Liberalism*, at 20–21.
[91] Cureton, "A Rawlsian Perspective," at §2.

also be said to exclude sub-fields, such selective exclusion makes it harder to ignore the pragmatist critique.

To be sure, there are good reasons to take the pragmatist criticism with a grain of salt. Generally speaking, authors are often leaving important things unsaid; it would be odd to start systematically holding them to have said that unexplored topics are of less importance. It would be equally naive, however, to deny that discrimination is widespread in intellectual history, see when authors remain silent about certain topics (regardless of good faith), particularly when these topics are closely related to the argument at hand. It is a truism that power is most effective when it acts in this hidden way.

Martha Nussbaum and Eva Kittay maintain that Rawls's prioritization or postponement is not "trivial"[92] nor "innocent"[93] and implies a "seriously misleading"[94] "[obliteration of] much that characterizes human life."[95] Their comments point to a more substantial problem in choosing a particular conception of person (as a cooperating member) and a particular conception of political justice as the most fitting starting points. Granted, the spiraling, back-and-forth of the Rawlsian reflective method that aims to reach an equilibrium between convictions at different levels of generality[96] may enable Rawlsians to integrate the fact of disability later in the process of designing a fair society. Nevertheless, "different starting points do not lead to the same conception of justice in reflective equilibrium."[97] What if our strongly held intuitions – the "considered judgments"[98] emanating from our sense of justice – differ significantly from those of Rawls?

For instance, Kittay and Nussbaum take dependency as an essential part of our starting assumptions, including the central case of persons and relations on which we build:

> Because dependency strongly affects our status as equal citizens (that is, as persons who, as equals, share the benefits and burdens of social cooperation), and because it affects all of us at one time or another, it is not an issue that can be set aside, much less avoided. Its consequences for social organization cannot be deferred until other traditional questions about the structure of society have been settled without distorting the character of a just social order. Dependency must be faced from the beginnings of any project in egalitarian theory that hopes to include *all* persons within its scope.[99]

---

[92] Kittay, *Love's Labor*, at 77.
[93] *Ibid.* at 88; Nussbaum, *Frontiers of Justice*, at 127.
[94] Kittay, *Love's Labor*, at 88.
[95] Nussbaum, *Frontiers of Justice*, at 127.
[96] Rawls, *Justice as Fairness*, at §10.
[97] Cureton, "A Rawlsian Perspective," at §2.
[98] *Ibid.*
[99] Kittay, *Love's Labor*, at 77. Kittay is referring to a different sort of equality than the one Rawls is referring to. This equal right to share in the benefits and burdens of social cooperation does not

Cureton succeeds at making the case that Rawls's failure – that is, to set up the assumptions of the ideal society and the establishment of the principles of justice in a way that would directly justify distributive structures responding to the needs of children, the severely disabled, and the elderly – does not necessarily imply that such structures cannot be later developed. However, it still seems likely that Kittay's and Nussbaum's concerns would be better assuaged if different starting points animated social design from the very beginning. Theories of justice beginning with vulnerability and dependency rather than cooperativeness, inclusiveness rather than profitability, concrete injustices of exclusion rather than idealized conceptions of personhood may yield benefits for PWD that "justice as fairness" may never provide, even once amended. Kittay argues, for instance, that "a theory of the political that excludes dependency concerns can be maintained only by the exploitation of those who do dependency work or by the neglect of the concerns of the dependents."[100]

(II) CIRCUMSTANCES OF JUSTICE The circumstances of justice are the "background conditions" that render justice "both possible and necessary."[101] *Objective* conditions have to do with the natural or social facts that are required to obtain justice. For instance, there must be some temporal and physical proximity between citizens to make cooperation possible. There must also be moderate scarcity – too many resources would conduce to an overabundant state of nature whereby parties do not need to engage in joint cooperative ventures, while too little would render these ventures unstable or not worthwhile. Rawls's more problematic objective condition invokes a kind of equality. The capacities of individuals in search of a beneficial social arrangement must be "comparable in that no one among them can dominate the rest. They are vulnerable to attack, and all are subject to having their plans blocked by the united force of others."[102]

The *subjective* conditions for justice are characteristics of the cooperating subject. Their needs and interests must be "roughly similar" or "in various ways complementary"[103] so that working together be mutually advantageous. However, they must also be making "conflicting claims on the natural and social resources available."[104] Otherwise, principles of justice regulating their social cooperation would be superfluous; they would all spontaneously work toward the same ends. What explains the conflict of interests is what Rawls calls the fact of reasonable pluralism – that is, "the fact that ... citizens affirm different, and indeed incommensurable and

> map on equality in capacities, but rather in an equal moral worth possessed by all human beings.

[100] *Ibid.*
[101] Rawls, *A Theory of Justice*, at 109.
[102] *Ibid.* at 110.
[103] *Ibid.*
[104] *Ibid.*

irreconcilable, though reasonable, comprehensive doctrines in the light of which they understand their conceptions of the good."[105]

The exclusion of the PSID (and, more generally, of people who are not roughly equal to others in terms of physical and mental powers) seems explicit in both the objective condition of rough equality and the subjective condition for individuals to "have their own plans of life."[106] PSID are neither cognitively roughly equal nor able, prima facie, to hold a conception of the good life.

Cureton argues (*contra* Nussbaum[107]) that the stipulation of these particular circumstances of justice does not imply that PWD ought to be excluded from the scope of justice from the outset, similar to how he argued that delaying the issue of disability does not imply that the issue is not important for a Rawlsian. He explains that the circumstances of justice, though they postulate capacities about the people inhabiting the idealized society for which principles of justice are to be enacted, do not require that *all* the members of society possess these capacities. There need only be *enough* members with these capacities to obtain justice in general. In other words, the goal of the notion of "circumstances of justice" is not to determine who has a robust moral status. As Cureton puts it, they "are not meant to pick out which members of a particular society are owed justice."[108] Instead, these circumstances are the "most minimal conditions" for cooperative social arrangements to take place.[109]

In terms of rough equality of capacities, Cureton notes that Rawls's focus is not on the weak and the vulnerable; after all these individuals can hardly prevent people with greater physical and cognitive capacities to establish a system of cooperation to regulate their social interactions. Indeed, it is the presence of superiorly gifted individuals who could potentially dominate the rest and prevent them from engaging in a system of cooperation that would prevent the realization of justice.[110] The same goes for a capacity to form a conception of the good life: "systems of social cooperation can [still] be mutually beneficial when some members of society lack a conception of the good."[111]

The idea that Rawlsian (or cooperative) justice between mentally and cognitively capable people can still be obtained in a moral community with severely disabled people is believable. The presence of PWD seems unlikely to prevent the "normally capable people" to establish principles of fair social interactions between them, no more than the presence of animals or plants would.[112] Let us call this idea the "they

---

[105] Rawls, *Justice as Fairness*, at 84.
[106] Rawls, *A Theory of Justice*, at 110.
[107] Nussbaum, *Frontiers of Justice*, at 27–28.
[108] Cureton, "A Rawlsian Perspective," at §3.
[109] Ibid.
[110] Rawls, *A Theory of Justice*, at 110.
[111] Cureton, "A Rawlsian Perspective," at §3.
[112] Unless we assume that we already owe something to PWD – something that Cureton seems to imply by saying that PWD with tremendously expensive problems may ruin us as a society and make it impossible to be a fair society. This is the kind of issue that surfaces when we do not

don't get in our way" strategy. If enough citizens are "roughly similar in physical and mental powers"[113] and have a conception of the good life, they can set up a successful system of fair cooperation, even if a number of PWD would take advantage of it – that is, even though some PWD who could not cooperate would be members of society.[114] However, what does "being part of a society" mean, then? On what grounds and in what sense would PWD be "members" of society? If it is on grounds unrelated to possessing roughly equal capacities, why would this membership be normative, and to what extent would it be?

I will call a membership granted on the basis that these members "don't get in the way" of normally cooperative persons "membership simpliciter" to distinguish it from membership to civil society or political community. The latter form of membership is synonymous with "citizenship." The community to which "members simpliciter" belong refers to an actual human society, in which we find attachments, dependency, and fluctuating universal displays of vulnerability of various kinds from various causes. As "natural" as it would feel to include PWD within such a society, the challenge we face is to properly justify this inclusion on moral or political grounds so as to explain the parameters and grounds of duties owed to PWD.

The fact that Rawls's theory of social justice does not deal directly with severe disabilities – or that the circumstances of justice take PSID out of the social picture when designing principles of justice in an idealized society – does not imply that it is impossible for PWD and PSID to be considered as subjects of justice on grounds yet to be given. Two questions remain: can such grounds be found within contractualism? And will these grounds respond to the revisionist challenge presented in Chapter 1 of this book?

(III) SOCIETY AS A FAIR SYSTEM OF COOPERATION The "fundamental organizing idea of justice as fairness" – that is, the system that other Rawlsian basic ideas must serve, "is that of society as a fair system of cooperation."[115] Naturally, such a fundamental and systemic understanding of a fair political society as a "mutually advantageous cooperative venture"[116] seems to prima facie exclude PSID, because they seem to be unable to take a reciprocating part in this social cooperation.[117] As we saw, many authors have challenged the idea that PSID cannot participate in a "society" defined by Rawls by reflecting on the nature and extension of participation or engagement, as well as reciprocity and mutual advantage. Nussbaum, for one, thinks that any defense of social contract theory trying to claim that PWD actually

---

explain why we ought to integrate PWD to our society as citizens rather than simply put forward the idea that doing so would not harm us.
[113] Rawls, *A Theory of Justice*, at 109–10.
[114] Cureton, "A Rawlsian Perspective," at §2, §4.
[115] Rawls, *Political Liberalism*, at 15.
[116] Rawls, *A Theory of Justice*, at 96.
[117] Kittay, *Love's Labor*, at 105.

5.5 Extending Passive Citizenship to PSID

play a contributive part to society is "doomed to failure,"[118] though she probably has in mind a narrow or contractarian sense of cooperation when she states:

> To include in the initial situation people who are unusually expensive or who can be expected to contribute far less than most to the well-being of the group ... would run contrary to the logic of the whole exercise."[119]

As for Cureton, he does not challenge the idea that PSID cannot participate as (underestimated) contributors in a "society" defined as a mutually beneficial system of cooperation. Instead, he repeats the "they don't get in our way" strategy: reciprocity can still obtain among roughly equally capable citizens if PWD and other less than fully cooperating people are "members simpliciter" of our society. He maintains that "[f]ully cooperating people can receive their fair share of the social surplus even when others around them have not fully participated, and even when these people receive some of the benefits of social cooperation themselves."[120]

The grounds and implications of a "membership simpliciter" remain unclear. Why would noncooperating beings be members – even honorary ones – of a cooperative venture? We may also worry that PSID are unobstructive to reciprocal cooperation because they will only get some limited benefits of this cooperation (which, presumably, they must not disrupt with significant demands affecting social structures if the "they don't get in the way" strategy is to work). If so, is that satisfactory for PSID?

(IV) THE ORIGINAL POSITION The parties in the OP are rational in the sense ordinarily understood in economics: they take "effective means to ends with unified expectations and objective interpretation of probability."[121] They also have two "moral powers":

(1) A capacity for a sense of justice, which is "the capacity to understand, to apply, and to act from the public conception of justice which characterizes the fair terms of social cooperation."[122] Rawls stresses that this is "a condition of human sociability"[123] and that conceptions of justice will be most stable if they build upon this natural, human capacity, similar to the tendency to reciprocate.[124]

(2) A capacity for a conception of the good, that is, "the capacity to form, to revise, and rationally to pursue a conception of one's rational advantage

---

[118] Nussbaum, *Frontiers of Justice*, at 105
[119] Ibid. at 104.
[120] Cureton, "A Rawlsian Perspective," at §4.
[121] Rawls, *A Theory of Justice*, at 127; see also Rawls, *Justice as Fairness*, at 87.
[122] Rawls, *Political Liberalism*, at 19.
[123] Rawls, *A Theory of Justice*, at 433.
[124] Ibid.

or good."¹²⁵ Forming and pursuing a conception of the good accounts for a person's motivation to strive for personal happiness. It is more individually oriented than having a sense of justice: "a person's good is determined by what is for him the most rational long-term plan of life."¹²⁶ Someone's good "normally consists of a more or less determinate scheme of final ends, that is, ends we want to realize for their own sake, as well as attachments to other persons and loyalties to various groups and associations."¹²⁷ Someone's "plan of life" is "designed to permit the harmonious satisfaction of [these] interests."¹²⁸

The parties are also mutually disinterested, not in the sense that they are selfish or that they view their constituents as only having interests in their own well-being. On the contrary, their constituents may well have "attachments and loyalties giv[ing] rise to [other-regarding] devotions and affections" as part of their conceptions of the good.¹²⁹ These conceptions, however, give rise to some of "the most intractable and deeply divisive [conflicts]"¹³⁰ and, like other disagreements about the good, make it reasonable to construct parties who will only be concerned with the interests (whether self- or other-regarding) of their constituents.

PSID (unlike the physically disabled) may not possess the two moral powers or be rational and, therefore, cannot be parties to the original choice situation. It could also be said that caring for them may be part of someone's plan of life and may morally be a good thing, but that the parties are designed to ignore such attachments or plans.

To mount his defense of Rawls, Cureton makes use of the notion of representation. He claims that the parties in the OP are distinct from the members of the society for whom principles of justice are being chosen. The former are representatives or trustees of the latter. The parties in the OP do not need to be idealized reflections of the constituents: "[W]e are free to place restrictions on the sort of people who can participate in the original position without also placing the same restrictions on the group for whom principles are to be chosen."¹³¹

The problem remains that Cureton does not provide us with a positive reason for including PSID in the "represented" group. He seems to take for granted that they are a part of our society. In a sense, this seems obvious – in what other societies could PSID be members? And yet, it needs to be explained; the only concept of society that Cureton is presenting, after Rawls, is a political one, where

---

¹²⁵ Rawls, *Political Liberalism*, at 19.
¹²⁶ Rawls, *A Theory of Justice*, at 79.
¹²⁷ Rawls, *Political Liberalism*, at 19.
¹²⁸ Rawls, *A Theory of Justice*, at 80.
¹²⁹ Rawls, *Political Liberalism*, at 19; see also Rawls, *A Theory of Justice*, at 111–12.
¹³⁰ Rawls, *Justice as Fairness*, at 85.
¹³¹ Cureton, "A Rawlsian Perspective," at §5.

"membership" means reciprocally cooperative citizenship rather than "membership simpliciter."

Cureton ultimately concedes that PSID should not be included in the original position. He insists, however, that they can be "included in the group for whom principles of justice are to be chosen."[132] Nothing should prevent the constituents, according to Cureton, from constructing parties who would represent the interests of PSID. As Rawls writes, "[r]emember it is up to us, you and me, who are setting up justice as fairness, to describe the parties ... as best suits our aims in developing a political conception of justice."[133] Also, while we must not assume shared values within a political society, we must assume that citizens all value their conception of the good, which itself is a kind of value or meta-value.[134] It makes it harder to radically discard the suggestion that no shared value should be assumed from the outset when discussing principles of justice, if some of these values – though not related to the Rawlsian political discursive ethics – seem universally shared.

If the parties are artificial persons, why could we (the constituents) not design them to defend PSID's interests if it corresponds to our judgments about what is *right*? Cureton has not provided an argument as to why it would be just to defend and advance the interests of PSID and, indeed, such an argument would be difficult to mount, given other Rawlsian commitments. When providing a justification for creating parties concerned with the PSID's interests, we are almost bound to end up invoking a conception of the *good* (in opposition to the *right*).

For instance, one may try to argue that it would be reasonable for the constituents to create parties who would represent PSID's interests, where reasonableness is associated with a sense of justice and, being a virtue tracking what is "right," it would respect Rawls's lexical priority of the right over the good.[135] Rawls does not define explicitly the concept of reasonableness other than by saying that "reasonable is viewed as a basic intuitive moral idea" and that we can rely on its use to understand it.[136] Ordinary use of the notion and Rawls's use of it[137] suggest that "reasonable" is not such a basic idea. The fact that we spontaneously find something reasonable (or not) does not exactly indicate that reasonableness is a basic intuitive moral idea. Rather, it indicates that the beliefs about the *entitlements' validity*

---

[132] *Ibid.*
[133] Rawls, *Justice as Fairness*, at 87.
[134] As Rawls seems to concede, though he would probably have resisted this characterization (*ibid.* at 20). As Michael Sandel notes of the Rawlsian/Kantian/liberal traditions, "[j]ustice is more than just another value. It provides the framework that *regulates* the play of competing values and ends; it must therefore have a sanction independent of those ends. But it is not obvious where such a sanction could be found" ("The Procedural Republic and the Unencumbered Self" [1984] 12:1 Political Theory 81 at 83).
[135] Rawls, *A Theory of Justice*, at 27–28. Rawls notes that "the principles of justice that are agreed to are lexically prior in their application in a well-ordered society to claims of the good" (*Collected Papers*, ed. Samuel Freeman [Cambridge: Harvard University Press, 1999]).
[136] Rawls, *Justice as Fairness*, at 82.
[137] *Ibid.* at 6–7.

underlying the claims being made are stable, or simply not (yet) questioned or brought to our awareness in a way that makes these beliefs susceptible to rational revision. To illustrate, when a child has a tantrum to obtain chocolate cake after dinner and will not stop stomping her feet until the parent gets up and starts baking, we immediately find it unreasonable because we know what a child is entitled to and we find that the claim she is making goes beyond this entitlement. Could it not be our intuitive belief, then, that PSID are entitled to have their interests represented in the OP? It might be the case if we consider that we are not entitled to our capacities. It seems intuitively unfair that, out of bad luck, PSID would end up excluded from the benefits of belonging to our political community. However, this intuition involves an other-regarding concern that can hardly be explained as a part of a conception of the right. Decisions about redistribution to noncontractors seem to be the sort of thing that should be the *outcome* of the contractual process. We cannot incorporate any particular good (like that of caring for vulnerable creatures, for instance) to guide the parties in the OP; we can only decide what kind of assumptions about contractors and the contracting situation are reasonable. If PSID are unable to be contractors, it is hard to see how they could come into the picture through any argument about the nature of the contractors and the contracting situation.

One may suggest we stop thinking about PSID as a category of individuals and instead think of profound disabilities as something that can affect constituents. This seems coherent with the Rawlsian claim that natural talents and abilities are a common or collective asset of society.[138] While it is an appealing suggestion to extend the veil of ignorance to cover permanent and severe cognitive disabilities, it misunderstands Rawlsian conceptions of society and political justice by ultimately resting on noncontractual ideals (like intraspecies solidarity or responsiveness to vulnerability and dependence) instead of contractual ones (like reciprocity).

Problems with "Membership Simpliciter"

Rawls's relational focus of "justice as fairness" is also inadequate in explaining why we should take PSID's interests into account when designing basic principles of justice. Rawls explicitly focuses on one kind of relation to the exclusion of others: the relation between parties with a sense of justice. The constituents create parties so that they can direct how these relations should be fairly regulated. This follows from what he takes to be the "fundamental question of political justice" – the terms of

---

[138] Rawls, A Theory of Justice, at 87, 156, 274. "The point then is simply that no one deserves to be born with greater or less innate intelligence or ability, greater or less strength and health, or greater or less beauty or physical attractiveness, charm, and so on, than anyone else. This is different from saying that no one deserves or owns his/her natural features" (Samuel Freeman, *Justice and the Social Contract: Essays on Rawlsian Political Philosophy* [New York: Oxford University Press, 2007], at 116). See also Andrew Kernohan, "Rawls and the Collective Ownership of Natural Abilities" (1990) 20:1 Can J Phil 19.

social cooperation between reasonable and rational people.[139] Other kinds of relations are simply outside of this primary "focus," as they are not the basis for gaining the standing of citizen within the political society.[140] Thus, we should not think of the political society as being cemented or normatively regulated by any other kind of relation.

This is why gesturing at a notion of membership simpliciter would likely not fit the Rawlsian account. Whatever community to which PSID would be members simpliciter – which would involve a kind of (yet to be argued) background solidarity – could not be taken to provide the parameters of the political society. As Rawls explains, "[i]t is a serious error not to distinguish between the idea of a democratic political society and the idea of community,"[141] the latter meaning a group, the members of which "are united in pursuing certain shared values and ends ... that lead them to support the association and in part bind them to it."[142] A political society, on the other hand, is presented as distinct from the relations, associations, and communities "within it and across it."[143] The aforementioned moral powers (as opposed to other relational capacities or particular shared values) are the justification for being a part of it. "In justice as fairness," Rawls maintains, "a democratic political society has no such shared values and ends apart from those falling under or connected with the political conception of justice itself."[144]

These cooperative members – who are able to respond to reasonableness and be reasonable themselves – may indeed become very disabled out of brute luck, but their status of contractor is already secured. But some individuals are unable to cooperate for their whole lives, and thus they cannot at any point have the status of contractor. The party in the OP can ask herself, "what if the constituent I am representing is among the most severely disabled?" only if the severely disabled has the status of a constituent. In a way, the parties are no more entitled to ask themselves "what if I were representing a PSID" than "what if I were representing a giraffe or a plant." Such questions might actually be enlightening counterfactuals that hone in on the moral insights that human empathy and other-regarding concern could provide. But the initial choice situation is not designed to express such an other-regarding concern or to capitalize on such an empathy.[145] It is not unimaginable for a strong normative status to be granted to PSID (and even giraffes and plants) on the basis of participation to kinds of communities, or to kinds of relations, but not on the basis of participation to the specific contractual relation that Rawls has in mind. Short of broadening what is meant by social cooperation (which

---

[139] Rawls, *Political Liberalism*, at 20.
[140] Ibid.
[141] Rawls, *Justice as Fairness*, at 21.
[142] Ibid. at 20.
[143] Ibid.
[144] Ibid.
[145] Ibid. at 84–85.

is the strategy pursued by other contractualists), there seems to be no (Rawlsian contractualist) grounds for the parties in the OP to be concerned for PSID. The revisionist challenge presented in Chapter 1 reminds us why this is so.

(V) THE REVISIONIST OBJECTION TO REPRESENT ALL HUMAN BEINGS IN THE OP The assumption that PSID should (if they can) be integrated into the contractual process on the grounds of their noncontractually based robust moral status would be a contingent move, unless we explain why it is necessary that a noncontractually based robust moral status translates into a contractual one. One such explanation could be a species-based argument for status – that PSID are contractors, or deserve the moral status equivalent to that of contractors, on the basis that they belong to a *genus* of beings who normally develop the necessary features to be contractors. On this account, a contractually based robust moral status would not be given to particular individuals on a case-by-case basis but rather to the *genus* as a whole. However, this is not, *per se*, a contractual argument. It is a separate "nature of the kind" argument about how status should be attributed to beings and it stands separate to the argument that explains how this contractual status would actually promote the welfare of PSID.

The anti-speciesist philosophical movement denounces the apparent arbitrariness of the frontiers of the "we" or the "everybody" mentioned above.[146] If "everybody" gets represented, then why deprive entities like lakes, flowers, insects, or nonhuman animals of representation?

If parties in the OP are asked to take into account the possibility of being PSID, why not take into account the possibility they might be chickens, trees, or rivers? This calls for the following response: "I can imagine myself as a human being with all kinds of grave impairments and disabilities made worse in this or that social context. Rawls assumes that parties behind the veil of ignorance will promote the interests of the citizens they represent, like trustees represent the interests of beneficiaries. I can think of many contingent, undesirable possibilities that could make a human life go poorly – such as being Jewish, gay, or disabled in Nazi Germany. Being a giraffe or a fern or a rock is beyond the scope of what I can imagine."

The answer to this is that the objector is talking about imagination, identity, and other things that are unrelated to Rawls's political concerns. Parties behind the veil of ignorance are not asked to assess *all* risks inherent to a human life. They are asked to assess the risks that would affect the lives of the persons they represent. And while the parties behind the veil of ignorance know very little about the persons they represent, they know that they are "persons" able to cooperate in a mutually beneficial way, which necessarily implies they have sufficiently similar needs, capacities, vulnerabilities. This excludes ferns, giraffes, and (at least some) PSID.

---

[146] Finnis and Regan have also made this challenge. See "Discourse, Truth and Friendship" in Finnis, *Reason in Action* as well as Regan, *The Case for Animal Rights*.

The objector does make a morally compelling point by referring to obligations she intuits toward PSID. Those intuitions could provide noncontractual reasons to include humans who do not have the potential to develop contracting capacities, can provide justifications for not applying these reasons to nonhuman entities, or can prioritize the needs of certain beings over given the resources that are available. Yet none of these justifications are contractual arguments.

The foregoing analysis suggests that relations or bonds with PWD within our community are difficult to articulate in Rawlsian terms. Cureton seems to assume that there is a "society simpliciter." As such, the parties will choose principles of justice by idealizing what Rawls means by "political society," and that these principles *can* still apply to the society simpliciter. His argument is that they can, not that they should. The very presence of PSID as members of the society simpliciter does not prevent the obtainment and application of principles of justice.[147] Short of giving a stronger normative content to the "association" with PWD, their integration within the realm of contractual justice remains too morally optional, in contrast with an *a priori* requirement of justice. The idea of a membership simpliciter not only fails to provide an adequate answer to the revisionist challenge but also to ensure that PSID's membership will not be a second-rate kind of citizenship, especially if what is owed to them as a matter of justice is to be decided at later stages of designing political society, from a paternalistic standpoint.[148] In this sense, their very presence is conceptually superfluous in the basic vision of justice. This is problematic given the history of PWD's social exclusion. As Kittay says, "although nothing in the construction of the OP prevents a representative in the hypothetical situation of the OP from thinking about her or himself as a dependent or a dependency worker, nothing assures it and so these concerns will not necessarily be represented."[149] To be sure, this status is better than nothing, but it is doubly problematic given its contingence and because of the kind of respect that it entails.

5.5.2 Granting PSID a Passive Citizenship on the Basis of the Normativity of Basic Needs

Cynthia Stark argues that a "suitably modified" Rawlsian contractualism can "provide grounds for meeting the needs of people who are not able to contribute to the production of the goods necessary to sustain them."[150] Stark and Southwood deploy a similar strategy: they both integrate PSID for broad and appealing reasons. For

---

[147] Integrating PWD in society will not prevent "a social system of cooperation *as a whole* [to] succeed" (Cureton, "A Rawlsian Perspective," at §3), that is, to make all of society's members "including its disabled ones, better off than if no such arrangements existed" (*ibid.* at §4).
[148] *Ibid.* at §7.
[149] Kittay, *Love's Labor*, at 89.
[150] Cynthia Stark, "How to Include the Severely Disabled in a Contractarian Theory of Justice" (2007) 15:2 J Political Phil 127 at 127.

Southwood, PSID are "affected" by the decisions, while Stark holds that PSID have basic needs. These conclusions seem intuitively right, however, we will see that they fall beyond the scope of the contractual frameworks they use (Southwood uses his own, while Stark uses a Rawlsian one). Southwood's and Stark's arguments build on one of the most important justifications that can be given for granting passive citizenship to PSID: their needs. Yet having needs only takes us halfway to a contractual justification. One must also have capacities to fulfill other people's needs or to possess intellectual capacities that the Kantian strand of contractual thought associates with dignity. In this last section, I consider different needs-based justifications for granting a robust moral status to people who do not possess such capacities and explore whether they are compatible with Rawlsian or other contractualist commitments.

Stark only suggests that we consider PSID's interests at a later stage of the contractualist Rawlsian constructivist process, and some worry that her account does not yield a sufficiently good status for PSID. These concerns relate to the contingency of this status and the possibility of structural exclusion. We have covered some of these grounds when introducing prima facie objections to passive citizenship and when dealing with theorists of active citizenship who do not believe that passive citizenship is sufficient or the most morally appropriate way to conceptualize PSID's status. Stark argues for a kind of passive citizenship for PSID, insofar as passive citizenship is defined as (1) not correlating to the capacities of a contractor (or a "fully cooperating party"), but (2) implying a robust moral status. Her account suggests that the needs of noncooperating PSID in terms of "shelter, food, clothing, transportation, utilities, and the like" would be minimally met, and this minimum would be "high" and "comprehensive."[151] Moreover, like other passive citizenship theorists, Stark is not trying to construct the severely disabled (at least those who are noncooperating) as fully cooperating parties by reconceptualizing the standards of cooperation. She believes room can be made for grounding strong duties toward the noncooperative within Rawlsian theory. She finds these grounds in "Rawls's scattered remarks about a guaranteed social minimum."[152] The problem is that this minimum is designed for the fully cooperating. She argues that it need not be.

The scholars who have responded to Stark's article (namely, Christie Hartley and Sophia Wong) disagree with her that PSID cannot be considered normal contractors, as opposed to passive citizens (to use my terms). That is, they disagree that the first definitional element of passive citizenship should hold with regard to PSID. Hartley argues that Stark does not have a correct view of the social product[153] and Wong argues that it is not possible to distinguish between cooperating and

---

[151] Ibid. at 138.
[152] Ibid. at 129.
[153] Christie Hartley, "Justice for the Disabled: A Contractualist Approach" (2009) 40:1 J Soc Phil 17 at 32.

noncooperating as Stark assumes it is.¹⁵⁴ In contrast to these critiques, I accept the position (for the sake of the argument) that PSID are not contractors, and rather take issue with whether the robust status that Stark carves out for PSID coheres with her contractualist framework.

The grounds she suggests for PSID's passive citizenship is the plausible idea that "being a non-contributor and simply having needs, especially unusual needs, is also a reason for being owed a particular share of the social product."¹⁵⁵ I will call this the "General Need Principle" to distinguish it from three other "need principles." At first glance, this principle does not seem required by a contractual relation if it is based on the mere fact of having needs, as opposed to occupying some contractual role *and* having such needs. Therefore, whether Stark suggests grounds that are part and parcel of a contractualist theory must be examined. Here, Stark faces the same sort of challenge as Korsgaard. Like Korsgaard, she nests her needs-based argument in a contractualist framework (Rawls's instead of Kant's). Her proposed interpretation does not really undermine core contractualist commitments, but it seems to be driven by concerns that are not really contractualist. She would need to explain why it is structurally required, rather than assuming it simply "fits," so to speak.¹⁵⁶

I suggest that Stark's use of Rawlsian contractualist notions does not justify the placement of the "General Need Principle" within the contractualist framework, so much as it technically allows it. This lack of justification makes this allowance seem arbitrary or *ad hoc*. What accomplishes the real justificatory work is not really discussed: it could be benevolence.¹⁵⁷ Korsgaard's argument, in contrast, made the case that it was conceptually necessary for some nonrational beings to have intrinsic

---

¹⁵⁴ Sophia Isako Wong, "Duties of Justice to Citizens with Cognitive Disabilities" in Eva Feder Kittay and Licia Carlson, eds., *Cognitive Disability and Its Challenge to Moral Philosophy* (Malden, MA: Wiley-Blackwell, 2010), 127 at 132–34.

¹⁵⁵ Stark, "How to Include the Severely Disabled," at 135.

¹⁵⁶ If that were her line of argument (which it is not), she would face the sort of challenges that I would raise against Adam Cureton (Cureton, "A Rawlsian Perspective").

¹⁵⁷ I say benevolence because nothing excludes it in her article. I am struggling to understand the source of normativity for including PSID in her account, other than the same "commonsense" position that motivates Rawls to say that, of course, we owe "a duty towards all human beings however severely handicapped," which Stark ("How to Include the Severely Disabled," at 130) quotes from Rawls, *Justice as Fairness*, at 176, fn. 59. But the existence of needs is not, in my opinion, the source. We contemplate needs and try to fulfill them because something else, X, requires us to do so. Detecting and fulfilling needs becomes a means of accomplishing X. Whereas X is well-defined in the case of non-disabled people within the social contract tradition, it is often referred to as unarticulated evidence by authors who try to integrate disabled people into the social contract through passive citizenship. Rawls's and Stark's comments on the nature of this X illustrate this and support the idea that they may not feel compelled to say much about it, precisely because it falls outside of a contractualist framework.

Besides, within a Rawlsian framework influenced by Kant, it seems plausible that this sort of general duty toward all human beings correlates to the kind of imperfect duty that we generally have in mind when we refer to "benevolence." (See Rawls's open-ended comments, Rawls, *Justice as Fairness*, at 176, fn. 59.) While Stark's suggested framework to deal with PSID is not supererogatory, it is possible to think of stringent obligations of benevolence insofar as we do

value. However, the argument did not translate a sufficiently explicit and complete contractualist account of a robust moral status or explain how to prioritize all these duties. Stark's suggestion, on the other hand, yields a well-defined (though potentially second-rate) status for PSID within a contractualist account. But one is left wondering whether her approach necessarily follows from the Rawlsian framework and cannot otherwise be explained by nonjustice duties like benevolence and charity.

Balancing Three Valuable Principles

Stark's article aims to achieve a balance between three potentially conflicting principles capturing different valuable grounds for owing robust duties within a Rawlsian contractualist framework. I will refer to them as (1) the Cooperation Principle, (2) the Justifiability Principle, and (3) the General Needs Principle.

(1) The Cooperation Principle

The Cooperation Principle recognizes the importance of individual cooperation to the social product in a theory of distributive justice. In Rawls' account, this principle is fundamental. Society is essentially "a cooperative venture for mutual advantage"[158] and a just society is "a fair system of cooperation over time, from one generation to the next."[159] As we saw, it is the fundamental organizing idea of justice as fairness, meaning that the other ideas must be "systematically connected" in a way that fits within the cooperation principle.

Within a Rawlsian framework, this value is recognized through terms of reciprocity: "all who are engaged in cooperation and who do their part as the rules and procedure require, are to benefit in an appropriate way as assessed by a suitable benchmark of comparison."[160] This appropriate benefit or compensation takes the form of having one's interests represented during the process that determines the basic structure of society in a principled way. This will "specify basic rights and duties within its main institutions and regulate the arrangements of background justice over time."[161]

Stark agrees that it is important to exclude the noncooperative from the early stages of designing a fair society. The (noncooperating) PSID would be excluded from the original position. In contrast with being white, male, "tall enough to slam dunk," or atheist, the fact of having participated in the production of the social product is a "legitimate reason for being owed a particular share" of it and fundamental principles of distributive justice should reflect this.[162]

---

not incorporate the notion of optionality within benevolence, but rather mean "other-regarding."
[158] Rawls, *A Theory of Justice*, at 4.
[159] Rawls, *Political Liberalism*, at 15.
[160] Ibid. at 16.
[161] Ibid.
[162] Stark, "How to Include the Severely Disabled," at 135.

(2) The Justifiability Principle

The Justifiability Principle requires that a theory of justice provides subjects with a justification that they find reasonable and fair (even though they may disagree with it) for the exercise of power over them. Rational people can justify the external exercise of power over them in a way that is compatible with their autonomy, as they are able to recognize the desirability of the power/norm for themselves. Valuing autonomy, the Justifiability Principle identifies how autonomy is exercised both within a society governed by norms and in more interpersonal situations, that is, the way in which moral agents provide and respond to reasons, and how they have higher order desires that reflect a particularly meaningful exercise of their autonomy. The moral will is one such kind of desire, and reasonable justifications speak to such a will.[163]

Rawls calls the Justifiability Principle the "liberal principle of legitimacy"[164] and he connects it with the "constitutional stage" of his contractualist constructivist process. Let me distinguish the sequence of these stages, as Stark makes use of their distinctiveness. Rawls's "four-stage sequence" describes four "appropriate point[s] of view from which certain kinds of questions are considered."[165] The veil of ignorance is gradually lifted along the four legislative stages so that the two fundamental principles of justice[166] that frame the basic structure of a fair society decided during the first stage – the original position – can be concretely applied. (And of course, for the sequence to be meaningful, the norms established at an earlier level cannot be modified at a later one.) The three following stages are constitutional, legislative, and judicial/administrative. Whereas in the OP, the parties know only "the principles of social theory," at the constitutional stage, they are given "general facts about their society, that is, its natural circumstances and resources, its level of economic advance and political culture, and so on."[167] The constitution is meant to "design a system for the constitutional powers of government and the basic rights of citizens."[168] At the

---

[163] This principle is echoed in the work of Rawls, Habermas, Scanlon, and other liberal constructivists. The general adoption of this principle indicates the great importance that the liberal tradition grants to the need of having our autonomy (before other human needs) respected. One gets a better sense of this when we see the Justifiability Principle as a tribute to the "nature of citizens ... as capable of being justified" (Cynthia Stark, "Respecting Human Dignity: Contract versus Capabilities" in Kittay and Carlson, eds., *Cognitive Disability*, 111 at 111) rather than a tribute to an abstract state of affairs where individual autonomy is being realized.

[164] Rawls, *Political Liberalism*, at 137. This legitimation is accomplished by subordinating state power to constitutional requirements: "the essentials of which all citizens as free and equal may reasonably be expected to endorse in the light of principles and ideals acceptable to their common human reason" (*ibid.*). Like Stark, I prefer the term "justifiability" because it focuses on what makes political principles, legal norms, and other exercises of power legitimate – namely, through justification.

[165] Rawls, *A Theory of Justice*, at 172.

[166] For the statement of principles in Rawls' work, see Rawls, *Political Liberalism*, at 291.

[167] Rawls, *A Theory of Justice*, at 172–73.

[168] *Ibid.* at 172.

legislative stage, the parties design particular laws and policies, compatible with the previously enacted constitution, on the basis of their further knowledge of "the full range of general economic and social facts."[169] Rawls constructs the constitutional stage to implement the first principle (the "equal liberty" principle) and the legislative stage to implement the second principle (which includes the principle of equal opportunity and the difference principle).[170] The fourth stage is the judicial and administrative application of laws and policies to particular cases, which implies that all facts about people's characteristics and circumstances are known.[171]

Recall, Stark says that possessing the two moral powers is not enough to be considered a cooperant. This view, along with the distinction between the Justifiability Principle and the Cooperation Principle, enables us (as cooperants) to tell people who cannot be cooperating members of our society that "we are sure you understand, as reasonable and rational beings, why we have excluded your interests (and your existence as subjects of justice) from the original position." Although Stark argues that we can avoid this conclusion, we might then add: "you must also understand why the Constitution, laws and policies were made without you in mind (or perhaps considering you only as a natural burden upon some citizens)." Like us, you must be responsive to the importance of the Cooperation Principle. We show you respect by justifying our decision to exclude you, and our justification for this exclusion is that we must "guarantee that members of society have similar claims on a share of socially produced goods, namely one that is influenced by their engaging in social cooperation."[172] This last quote is reminiscent of ostensible (but false) assertions of equality between people with physical disabilities, that is, by stating that someone in a wheelchair is equally entitled to walk up the stairs to a court of justice. One response to this is that one may well be rational and reasonable and still assume that, despite one's inability to cooperate, one is entitled to be considered a subject of justice when the basic institutions of a fair society – or the principles upon which they will be built – are being designed. As Stark correctly concedes, this position is fundamentally incompatible with Rawlsian contractualism. Her strategy to overcome this, as we will explore, is to suggest that allowing the constitutional conventioneers to represent the noncooperating, as well as the cooperating, is compatible with Rawlsian contractualism.[173]

---

[169] Ibid. at 175.
[170] "[The first principle's] main requirements are that the fundamental liberties of the person and liberty of conscience and freedom of thought be protected and that the political process as a whole be a just procedure.... The second principle comes into play at the stage of the legislature. It dictates that social and economic policies be aimed at maximizing the long-term expectations of the least advantaged under conditions of fair equality of opportunity, subject to the equal liberties being maintained" (ibid. at 174–75).
[171] Ibid. at 175.
[172] Stark, "How to Include the Severely Disabled," at 138.
[173] Ibid.

(3) The General Needs Principle

According to Stark, the General Needs Principle is the basis for including severely disabled individuals within Rawlsian contractualism, according to which "simply having needs [is] a reason for being owed a particular share of the social product."[174] This raises two issues. First, does that share correspond to a sufficiently robust moral status? Second, assuming that it does, can this truly be justified within Rawlsian contractualism – that is, (a) will a Rawlsian "Need Principle" extend to PSID, and (b) if it does extend to PSID, is this compatible with Rawlsian contractualism?

Indeed, Stark answers "yes" to these questions. To better analyze how the General Needs Principle works and whether it succeeds to fit within Rawls's account of justice, we can divide it into three variants: (a) the Humanity Principle, (b) the Basic Needs Principle, and (c) the Social Minimum Principle.

(a) *The Humanity Principle*

The "Humanity Principle" is based on a powerful and widely shared intuition that we owe moral obligations to all human beings. Yet, it is unclear what duties it implies. Such an idea has been developed to justify PSID's moral status and define its extent and implications. However, I do not think it provides a complete picture of PSID's moral status, because (at least a variant of) it focuses on what moral agents owe to "naked" human beings. The most promising variant of the Principle focuses on the relations between human moral agents and all human beings, *qua* human beings and nothing more. The problem with this is that we are rarely as metaphorically "naked" as this standpoint requires us to imagine. Indeed, we are part of many relations which entitle us to claim some rights and privileges. I believe that the very fact of being human provides a person with intrinsic value and a relatively strong – if not "robust" in the political sense of the term that we have been using – moral status. But I also believe that there are other relations that play such an important role in explaining what we owe to PSID, such that the basic rights stemming from their "naked" humanity are rendered superfluous. Instead, people with profound mental disabilities benefit more from the extensive and stringent rights vested in other relations. If anything, our duty to people *qua* human beings might be to place them (back) within relations that would benefit them. Given the social and relational nature of human beings, this is not an implausible claim. An orphan child may be placed within a host family. A stateless individual may be given citizenship. In this sense, moral agents' contribution to the welfare of the "naked human" may be better exercised by placing her within a relational framework rather than relating to her personally. Though we could try and bestow benefits through our personal relations, I suggest that, in many cases, what will most help the "naked human" is to place them in some kind of relationship that responds to her nature and needs. For

---
[174] *Ibid.* at 135.

instance, PSID may be placed in fiduciary relationships to protect their well-being. The Humanity Principle should not be overlooked because it is too basic. It can in fact act as the last wall between human decency and barbarity when essential relational frameworks break down.

The vagueness of the Humanity Principle is clear from Rawls's definition: "I take it as obvious, and accepted by common sense, that we have a duty towards all human beings, however severely handicapped. The question concerns the weight of these duties when they conflict with other basic claims."[175] Rawls does not flesh out this "self-evident" duty, and nor does he claim that it can fit within his contractualist framework. It could yield fairly minimal obligations like the basic moral requirement of preventing something really awful from happening to someone else "if you are the person in the best position [to do so] and it won't cost you much," that is, the rights implied by Anthony Appiah's "emergency principle."[176] It could also yield a comprehensive set of rights, notably if the fact of being human is seen to provide a claim to citizenship equal to the "fully cooperating" person. Therefore, it is not clear that the humanity principle yields the kind of robust status for PSID that we are trying to justify on the basis of the social contract tradition. Stark notes that Rawls "does not tell us whether these are duties of *justice*."[177] Indeed, Rawls leaves it open as to whether the principle of humanity grounds duties of justice, duties of justice as fairness, or other kinds of moral duties.[178]

When Rawls writes that "[a]t some point, then, we must see whether justice as fairness can be extended to provide guidelines for [the case of the noncooperating],"[179] we are tempted to think that such guidelines are not so much an extension of the theory of justice as fairness, but rather a way to structure the theory of justice so as to make it hospitable to some external, presumably noncontractual theory. Indeed, not all strategies of extension on contractualist grounds are prima facie implausible. On the contrary, all the authors explored in this book extend contractual notions, criteria, or grounds. These strategies are different from attempting to show that a principle of humanity can derive from contractualist grounds. Reconciling such a principle with Rawlsian contractualism is quite a challenge – one that Stark does not take up, preferring to focus instead on the notion of a social minimum – but a challenge which makes her reliance on the humanity principle[180] seems out of kilter with her argument. The reason why this reconciliation is prima facie implausible is due to the apparent incompatibility between the variety of bases the Humanity Principle could have, as well as the

---

[175] Rawls, *Justice as Fairness*, at 176, fn. 59.
[176] Anthony Appiah, *Cosmopolitanism: Ethics in a World of Strangers* (London: W.W. Norton, 2006), at 161–62.
[177] Stark, "How to Include the Severely Disabled," at 130, fn. 10.
[178] Rawls, *Political Liberalism*, at 21.
[179] Rawls, *Justice as Fairness*, at 176, fn. 59.
[180] Stark, "How to Include the Severely Disabled," at 130.

essential Rawlsian contractualist commitment to working out "fair terms of cooperation when society is viewed as a system of cooperation between citizens regarded as free and equal persons, and as normal and fully cooperating members of society over a complete life."[181]

(b) *The Basic Needs Principle*

Rawls's "Basic Needs Principle" is as follows:

> [T]he first principle covering the equal basic rights and liberties may easily be preceded by a lexically prior principle requiring that citizens' basic needs be met, at least insofar as their being met is necessary for citizens to understand and to be able fruitfully to exercise those rights and liberties.[182]

Given Rawls's definition above, the Basic Needs Principle is justified within his contractualist framework. However, it would not benefit noncooperating, noncitizen beings that the first principle entitles to exercise rights and liberties.

Wong proposes that this "Principle of Need suggests that the structure of society should be changed to make it more inclusive," because it would justify enabling citizens to enjoy the primary goods that the two principles of justice are meant to distribute.[183] However, we see that not all PSID can be enabled to partake of these rights and liberties. If, on the other hand, we assume that the rights and liberties in question will necessarily fit people with disabilities because they have been tailored for them, then this implies that the fully cooperating assumption has been lifted in the original position. The principles of justice are meant to fit and benefit fully cooperating people who can reciprocally benefit one another. The Basic Needs Principle offers plausible grounds for enabling nondisabled people to enjoy the goods secured by the principles of justice and for that enjoyment to extend to disabled people as well, but only insofar as disabled people become fully cooperating members. To conclude otherwise would unfairly and inaccurately deny the social aspect of certain disabilities. Stark and I have bracketed this category of PSID as unproblematic for the present discussion in order to focus only on those people who we can classify as truly noncooperating.

(c) *The Social Minimum Principle*

Stark relies on this third version of a general need principle: "Rawls believes that claims of need, among other things, should be addressed by means of a guaranteed social minimum. Since the claims of nonparticipants are claims of need, their claims should be met, on Rawls's account, under the auspices of the social minimum."[184] Stark's definition of the notion of a social minimum is as follows:

---

[181] Rawls, *Justice as Fairness*, at 176, fn. 59.
[182] Rawls, *Political Liberalism*, at 7; see also *ibid.* at 44, fn. 7; 46–48.
[183] Wong, "Duties of Justice to Citizens," at 137.
[184] Stark, "How to Include the Severely Disabled," at 137.

[T]he funds collected through transfers (income or consumption taxes) that are necessary to e.g., sustain an active and productive work force, rear and educate children, provide for the retired, establish a national defense, ensure savings for future generations, provide healthcare for the fully cooperating and meet the basic needs of all (fully cooperating) citizens.[185]

As Waldron writes, we could fix the social minimum "cardinally," that is, "on the basis of an assessment of the resources that basic human needs require."[186] Social wealth could also be distributed ordinally, in the sense that "nobody's share should be greater than anybody else's."[187] In the former case, the social minimum would be determined according to what human beings need "to lead decent and tolerable lives" and that this determination will not go up simply because the average social wealth rises.[188] In the latter case, the social minimum would be characterized by an egalitarian commitment that makes the social minimum a kind of "social dividend."[189] Rawls's approach belongs to the second case. It does not matter whether we refer to the relative levels of *persons'* wealth or *persons'* basic needs. The question is simply whether PSID are such persons. Neither justifications do (in principle) cover PSID, as both only address the fully cooperating. Furthermore, if the "cardinal" approach to fixing the social minimum refers to "human needs" full stop, then it exposes itself to the criticisms that apply to the Humanity Principle and the Basic Needs Principle.

Stark's proposal is "to retain the fully cooperating assumption in the original position but to drop it at the constitutional stage of the theory."[190] If she proposed that PSID benefit from the social minimum as established for the fully cooperating, on the basis that their needs are similar and overlap, this would not correlate to a sufficiently robust status for PSID, whose "social minimum" is particular. In addition, this approach seems arbitrary because, even if PSID's needs were easily integrated, it is unclear why we would integrate them in the first place. However, Stark claims that the constitutional conventioneers ought to imagine they might be disabled. But it is not clear why and how that position fits within Rawlsian contractualist commitments. First, if it is based on any form of personal doctrine held by the conventioneers (such as believing that we should care for PSID), this doctrine cannot be used as valid public reasons.[191] Second, the principles of justice that have been decided in the OP must be functionally implemented at this stage. Therefore, integrating PSID at this later stage is to do indirectly what could not be done directly. The constitutional stage is not the time to decide fundamental

---

[185] Ibid.
[186] Jeremy Waldron, "John Rawls and the Social Minimum" (1986) 3:1 J Applied Phil 21 at 22.
[187] Ibid.
[188] Ibid. at 21.
[189] Ibid. (emphasis removed).
[190] Stark, "How to Include the Severely Disabled," at 138.
[191] Rawls, *Political Liberalism*, at 225–26.

questions such as who should be a subject of justice. Rather it is the stage in which to work out the principles that are already decided and to plan for their application in practice.

Another difficulty with lifting the fully cooperating requirement at the constitutional stage is that it seems to be an arbitrary, *ad hoc* strategy to recognize both the value of cooperation and the moral pull of human needs, without first explaining why these two considerations *must* be balanced within contractualism. Rawls's structure does not provide explanations as to why it is best that the "full cooperation" assumption be lifted (if ever) at the constitutional stage. On the contrary, the constitutional conventioneers designing the social minimum are "subject to the constraints of the principles of justice already chosen"[192] which, as Brian Barry writes, "leaves precious little to the convention exception points of details."[193]

Ultimately, Stark seems to say that her solution is the only way to satisfy the Cooperation Principle and the General Need Principle, but that only the former principle is compatible with Rawlsian contractualism. The General Need Principle is only justified by Rawlsian contractualism when it refers to the needs of the "fully cooperating." When it refers to PSID's needs, it seems disjointed and incompatible with Rawlsian contractualism. I struggle to find in Stark's argument (or to imagine on my own) a justification that would not be a target of this criticism. Stark provides excellent contractualist reasons for excluding PSID at the OP stage, but fails to provide a positive reason for "removing the fully cooperating assumption at the constitutional stage" other than that it "allows for the adoption of a comprehensive social minimum that is compatible with the norm of reciprocity mandating adequate compensation to full contributors."[194] This resembles Cureton's argument, which assumes that we *want* to include PSID and *should* include them if to do so is not incompatible with contractualism. I do not think that this compatibility has been established, but even if it were, Rawlsian thinkers seeking to include PSID within the purview of contractualist justice should not only show this compatibility but also show that the basis for the General Need Principles would be best understood in contractual terms (as opposed to through noncontractual ethical frameworks). As we have seen, it cannot be found in Rawls's version of the Humanity Principle, which stands outside of his contractualist theory of justice, and may even threaten its credibility.[195]

---

[192] Rawls, A *Theory of Justice*, at 172.
[193] Brian Barry, *The Liberal Theory of Justice. A Critical Examination of the Principal Doctrines in A Theory of Justice by John Rawls* (Oxford: Clarendon Press, 1973), at 138.
[194] Stark, "How to Include the Severely Disabled," at 139.
[195] Rawls, *Justice as Fairness*, at 176, fn. 59. For similar reasons, philosophers like Adam Cureton and Henry Richardson may well be right to point out that Rawlsian conceptual resources do exist to make sense of the duties we owe to PSID. Richardson mentions the ideals of empathy and equality ("Rawlsian Social-Contract Theory and the Severely Disabled" [2006] 10:4 J Ethics 419 at 429) and Cureton mentions the importance of paternalistic principles to protect those unable to care for themselves (Cureton, "A Rawlsian Perspective," at §7). However, these

5.6 CONCLUSION

I do not think that attempts to integrate PSID at a later stage of the contractual process of institution-building overcome the contingency of their status, unless we invoke other justifications that do not fit a contractualist logic. This supports the conclusion that theories of the passive citizenship of PSID cannot succeed on contractualist grounds. (And further, as we have seen, nor can these theories succeed on contractarian grounds.) It remains arguable that PSID could be integrated at an earlier legislative stage of the contractual process, or that (on the basis of non-Rawlsian contractual theories) PSID could be active contractors rather than passive citizens. On a contractarian account, this would mean that PSID would benefit us more than traditional contractarian accounts have assumed. On a contractualist account, it means that people with profound disabilities could take part in the sort of "Kantian reciprocity"[196] to a greater degree than traditional contractualist accounts have assumed. However, we have seen in previous chapters that arguments to that effect tend to be either implausible or to leave relevant questions unanswered.

Ultimately, my conclusion is that social contract theorists who argue for the status of passive citizens for PSID are caught between the devil and the deep blue sea. On the one hand, they can integrate PSID at a later stage of the contractual process of building the rules for society. Indeed, they can even leave it to the citizens of a society to decree that PSID shall enjoy a political status that is equal to theirs. Yet, conceptually, this leads to a fragile, possibly paradoxical posture. Despite Korsgaard's and Cohen's metaphysical reassurances about the capacity of "full" citizens to confer intrinsic value onto PSID, we notice that these full citizens would only grant the status of full citizenship to PSID because they value them. Presumably, these value-giving citizens make this assessment on the basis of their conception of the good. Insofar as social contract theory puts the right before the good, there is something paradoxical in indirectly granting a status to PSID that was not able to be directly granted. In any case, practically speaking, this decree comes too late and is contingent upon a specific desire of full citizens rather than a structural requirement of our society.

On the other hand, we may think that it does not matter whether full status is given to PSID early or late in the society-building process, as it is grounded on the stringent moral pull that they have on full citizens (and presocial human beings) – which can be based on their needs, or simply because they are affected by fully capable people's actions. However, that kind of moral status would not be granted on a contractual basis. This does not refute the more general hypothesis that we

dimensions of Rawls's political theory may not properly belong to – or be best explained in terms of – his contractual apparatus.

[196] Term used by Nussbaum to qualify a Rawlsian understanding of justice as taking place between people with the "Kantian moral capacities" (Nussbaum, *Frontiers of Justice*, at 137).

could conceptualize PSID as honorary guests, fictitious members, or passive citizens of our political community on grounds other than contractualist or contractarian ones. However, my claim is that any such account, contractual or not, misconceives the nature of human society and the life that we share with PSID. In this misconceived view of our social world, we imagine "society" and "subjects of justice" according to a reductionist conception of the autonomous self, from which we begin all ethical investigation and social design, and by reference to which we define how to accommodate marginal cases within the spectrum of humanity.

6

Other-Regarding Concern and Exploitation

6.1 SITUATING THE CHAPTER

She was intensely sympathetic. She was immensely charming. She was utterly unselfish. She excelled in the difficult arts of family life. She sacrificed herself daily. If there was chicken, she took the leg; if there was a draught she sat in it – in short she was so constituted that she never had a mind or a wish of her own, but preferred to sympathize always with the minds and wishes of others.... Killing the Angel in the House was part of the occupation of a woman writer.

Virginia Woolf, *Professions for Women*

Many social contract theorists, whether contractualists or contractarians, advance a self-interested point of view on morality, eliminating other-regarding concerns from their theories of morality and justice. Some insist that they are not developing a self-oriented morality, because the fact of recognizing others as bargainers or consenting beings, and of negotiating with these beings in ways that respect their capacity to bargain or consent, constitutes a sort of moral respect. However, this sort of "moral respect" is not other-regarding in a significant sense. While these social contract theories do recognize certain traits in others that encourage beneficial social cooperation, they do not draw their normative strength from other-regarding concern. On the contrary, contractarians generally suggest an instrumental use of this recognition to better determine what social arrangements or interactions most benefit an individual contractee.

As we have seen in previous chapters, this exclusion of other-regarding concern by some social contract theorists is problematic because such authors explicitly claim that relations with PSID fall outside the province of justice and morality. One way to challenge this exclusion of other-regarding concern is to think of relationships that are clearly underpinned by other-regarding concern and are generally thought to have a moral dimension, such as many intimate relationships. Social contract theorists may answer this challenge either by denying that private, intimate, or personal relationships should be evaluated morally or by separating the moral dimension of such relations from their other-regarding aspects.

My goal in this chapter is to respond to the latter answer by showing that it rests upon a substantive conception of the person that presumes self-regarding concern to be a condition of morality. I do so by examining the work of those authors who explicitly exclude other-regarding concern from the heart of morality and justice: Susan Dimock and Jean Hampton.[1] I will argue that, without explicitly engaging with other-regarding concern, even the authors we examined in earlier chapters cannot fully succeed in explaining why we owe the sort of robust concern to PSID that I believe we owe them as a matter of morality and justice. On this basis, social contract thinkers who try to include PSID as full members of a contractual society only truly succeed insofar as they integrate other-regarding concern within their contractual apparatus or imagery.

6.2 HAMPTON AND DIMOCK'S FEMINIST CONTRACTARIANISM

6.2.1 *Stating the Problem: Exploitation*

Exploitation is equated with the absence of mutual benefit, and it characterizes a (or the) central feature of an unjust relation. In other words, nonexploitation is a necessary condition for a relation to be just.[2]

Hampton and Dimock offer two arguments for rejecting the moral significance of other-regarding concern. First, they claim that their self-interested evaluative framework can be applied to private relationships and that this framework circumscribes the relevant matters of justice or morality. Second, they argue that other-regarding attitudes not only undermine justice and moral obligations but also give rise to injustice and exploitation. This second claim reflects a legitimate concern that many philosophers in the field have noted: exploitation emerges when we privilege caring, other-concerned attitudes and define our own interests in terms of other people's welfare.

The problem that feminist contractarians are attacking can be stated from a private or public point of view. From the private standpoint, certain individuals (typically women) in intimate relationships are expected to contribute more to the other person's (e.g., a husband's) welfare or to a common project (e.g., child-rearing). This imposes unfair demands, maintains the *status quo* of domination, grants social recognition only to those individuals who take pride in their self-effacing feat, and

---

[1] The two essays that serve as the focus of this chapter are Susan Dimock, "Why All Feminists Should Be Contractarians" (2008) 47:2 Dialogue: Can Phil Rev 273 and Jean Hampton, "Feminist Contractarianism" in Jean Hampton, *The Intrinsic Worth of Persons: Contractarianism in Moral and Political Philosophy*, ed. Daniel Farnham (New York: Cambridge University Press, 2007).

[2] See, e.g., Hampton, "Feminist Contractarianism," at 20.

curtails the freedom of women who wish to showcase other self-empowering virtues.[3] From a public standpoint, a group of individuals can come to be expected to carry out certain types of work for what may well be a collective burden (such as women's traditional unpaid care work) and institutions and distributive patterns can be designed to reflect this inequity. However, contractarians do not conceptualize the kind of exploitation happening in private relations differently from the institutional setting.[4] I agree that the institutionalization of exploitation and private exploitative expectations are likely to mutually reinforce one another. However, to insist on a single conception of exploitation to account for both domains is problematic. It mistakenly assumes that every instance of an imbalance of benefits is to be evaluated identically and independently of the relational context.

Three Illustrations
I would like to illustrate the problem revealed by feminist contractarians with three examples. The first is taken from Carol Gilligan's work on gendered moral development, where she attributes an ethic of justice to men and of an ethic of care to women. I use Gilligan's illustration to respond to Hampton, who also relies on her work. The second example is a commonplace scenario, and the third is a literary example that is adapted to the concerns I discuss in this chapter.

(1) AMY AND JAKE Jake and Amy, two eleven-year-old children, were asked "when responsibility to oneself and responsibility to others conflict, how should one choose?" Jake said succinctly "you go about one-fourth to the others and three-fourths to yourself." Amy's more convoluted answer was

> Well, it really depends on the situation. If you have a responsibility with somebody else, then you should keep it to a certain extent, but to the extent that it is really going to hurt you or stop you from doing something that you really, really want, then I think maybe you should put yourself first. But if it is your responsibility to somebody really close to you, you've just got to decide in that situation which is more important, yourself or that person, and like I said, it really depends on what kind of person you are and how you feel about the other person or persons involved.[5]

Many feminists have relied on Gilligan's findings to vindicate the view that, contrary to what was previously assumed by a male-dominated perspective on moral

---

[3] *Ibid.* at 29–30. See also Ruth Sample's analysis of the work of Catherine MacKinnon in "Why Feminist Contractarianism?" (2002) 33:2 J Soc Phil 257 at 261.
[4] "Contractarians do not recognize any in principle distinction between the public and private, or any natural division of labour between the sexes. Both the public and private involve situations where mutual benefit is attainable but only through cooperation and trustworthiness, and any justified division of labour will be such that it provides mutual benefit" (Dimock, "Why All Feminists Should Be Contractarians," at 282).
[5] Amy's and Jake's interview abstracts are from Carol Gilligan, *In a Different Voice: Psychological Theory and Women's Development* (Cambridge: Harvard University Press, 1993), at 35–36.

development,[6] a woman's "moral voice" was indeed "moral," and was no less mature when voiced as a child, or wiser when voiced as an adult. A woman's moral voice was simply different: other-regarding, nurturing/caring, anchored into concrete situations and relational, instead of self-regarding, impartial, transcendent, and universalizing. However, contrary to those thinkers who argue that Amy's "caring" moral voice was actually preferable to Jake's, Hampton is not so adamant. She considers that Amy's inclination to meet other people's needs "borders on outright servility":[7]

> In their archetypal forms, I hear the voice of a child who is preparing to be a member of a dominating group and the voice of another who is preparing to be a member of the group that is dominated.[8]

(II) THE DEVOTED HUSBAND Let us consider the case of a man who takes great care of his wife. She acts in an irascible way and does not do her share of domestic tasks, even though she could. She had some health issues, which quickly became a pretext for her to be served by her husband. It becomes clear that she considers him to fulfill the role of a domestic servant. However, her relationship to him is arguably more dominating than the servant–master relationship, as she does not pay her spouse and insults him routinely in a way that she would not insult a domestic servant or a stranger.

(III) LE GRAND CAHIER ("THE NOTEBOOK") Agota Kristof's first novel, which earned her the European Prize for Literature, tells the tale of the development (including moral development) of a pair of twins in the midst of war. Their mother leaves them in the care of their grandmother, a cruel and greedy woman who accepts the children very reluctantly and exploits them more than she cares for them. As the twins grow older, wiser, and stronger, their wits earn them freedom from their grandmother's rule; they threaten to have her killed if she doesn't behave in a certain way (and, it should be noted, they require her to behave in a moral way). The novel presents a chilling set of illustrations of caring and relating to people in need of care. The twins are both (at different times) cared-for and caregivers, and in many cases, they suffer and engage in abuse and exploitation that seems monstrous. I suggest that their relationships are valuable in ways feminist contractarianism cannot capture.

6.2.2 *The Feminist Contractarian Solution*

Hampton and Dimock anchor their position on the Hobbesian insight that "morality should not be understood to require that we make ourselves the prey of

---

[6] As illustrated in Lawrence Kohlberg's work, to which Gilligan was responding.
[7] Hampton, "Feminist Contractarianism," at 5–6.
[8] *Ibid.* at 8.

others"[9] and David Gauthier's contractarian claim that "[sociability] becomes a source of exploitation if it induces persons to acquiesce in institutions and practices that but for their fellow-feelings would be costly to them."[10]

Dimock endorses a contractarian theory of both justice and morality. Morality requires that we act in our self-interest, and that the relations in which we participate be beneficial; that is, they leave us better off than if we had not partaken in them. Speaking for contractarians, Dimock argues that relationships are moral when they are "governed by norms and exemplify dispositions that make possible mutual benefit."[11]

Hampton's contractarian "test," which also applies to intimate relationships, is equivalent.[12] In this test, she incites us to ask:

> Given the fact that we are in this relationship, could both of us reasonably accept the distribution of costs and benefits ... if it were the subject of an informed, unforced agreement in which we think of ourselves as motivated solely by self-interest?[13]

In both cases, the costs and benefits are "not themselves side effects of any affective or duty-based tie between [parties to the relationship],"[14] which therefore excludes any vicarious enjoyment of another's happiness.

Whether or not a relation is mutually beneficial provides the contractarian standard against which to evaluate the morality of any relationship, even personal and intimate ones. Feminist contractarians can (and do) make two sorts of claims about the morality of relations that are not mutually beneficial. The stronger claim is that such a relation is necessarily entirely morally bad. The weaker claim is that the relation is morally bad in only one dimension – its fairness/justness.[15]

It seems that any plausible feminist contractarian account must deal with the fact that, even if one accepts that relationships must be mutually advantageous to be moral and fair, there is some value in these relationships that cannot be simply explained by a concern for justice. Hampton eloquently makes this point:

> None of us fosters a friendship with another out of a concern to be fair. Joining a church or a charity organization, volunteering in one's community, organizing

---

[9] Hampton, "Feminist Contractarianism," at 29.
[10] David Gauthier, *Morals by Agreement* (Oxford: Oxford University Press, 1987), at 11.
[11] Dimock, "Why All Feminists Should Be Contractarians," at 282.
[12] Although, as Janice Richardson notes, "only the party exploited is behaving irrationally" in a Hobbesian account, by contrast to Hampton's Kantian commitments ("On Not Making Ourselves the Prey of Others: Jean Hampton's Feminist Contractarianism" [2007] 15:1 Fem Legal Stud 33 at 37).
[13] Hampton, "Feminist Contractarianism," at 21.
[14] *Ibid.* at 21.
[15] However, one may hold that the morality of at least certain types of relations is dependent upon their fairness (even without considering that the "justice" of a relation exhausts its moral dimensions). If so, the weaker contractarian claim would, in practice, not be very different from holding the stronger claim.

charities for people in other countries, committing oneself in the manner of Mother Theresa to the needs of the desperately poor, are ways of creating a role for oneself that are prompted by interests that may have a good deal to do with honoring the worth of these individuals but perhaps have much more to do with the love one feels toward others.[16]

Hampton also seems to recognize that some relationships, like a friendship, have some special value of their own that cannot be exhausted by justice. She says that love and distributive justice "are not opposing responses,"[17] contrary to what philosophers assume when they reject the application of contractual thinking to intimate relations. However, as I will explain, her view is that this "special value" is nonmoral. Dimock goes further in rejecting the idea that noncontractarian aspects of these relations are valuable for other reasons, proposing an "all the way down" contractarian account of the value of such relations. The fact that those within some intimate relations will need to have certain drives, traits, or attitudes (such as the need to be "caring, patient, and emotionally open"[18] to raise a child) is mentioned only as an afterthought and is considered to have no moral weight. No moral theory underlies these personal traits or preferences: one could value caring patiently for a child just as one could value eating cakes voraciously. The picture that emerges is one where anything goes within an intimate relationship as long as it is mutually beneficial. The moral guidance is reduced to this: "make sure your relationship is not exploitative of anyone and, for the rest, do whatever you wish. There is no morally better or worse way to go and there are no substantial moral constraints to occupying the role of a friend, a lover, etc." In the contractarian mindset, it could not be otherwise, for mutual benefit ensures that nothing can really go wrong. On the other hand, nothing can go well, absent mutual benefits. To paraphrase Hampton, love is only possible if distributive justice prevails.[19]

This last assertion indicates that Hampton sees justice as a necessary condition for love, friendship and other intimate relations (or rather, *non-corrupted* versions of these relations), but that justice may not be sufficient to account for the special value that we ordinarily detect in private, personal relations and roles. Hampton concludes that this "special appreciation" that moral agents have corresponds to "particular nonmoral value[s]."[20] These values are "impressive and important"[21] and they make beings *worthy* of partial attitudes. Indeed, attitudes and behaviors responding to these values will not only be "permissible" but, at times, will even be "appropriate."[22] Intimate ties can be "healthy" and "worthy of praise" (although, only insofar as they

---

[16] Hampton, "Feminist Contractarianism," at 37.
[17] Ibid. at 31.
[18] Dimock, "Why All Feminists Should Be Contractarians," at 287.
[19] Hampton, "Feminist Contractarianism," at 31.
[20] Ibid. at 38.
[21] Ibid.
[22] Ibid. at 33.

allow for reciprocal benefit).[23] They can also be "morally acceptable" (because they meet *other* criteria).[24] Yet, they are not "moral," to place Hampton's own quotes around her strictly contractarian notion of morality.[25] Hampton, it turns out, like Dimock, does not recognize noncontractarian moral value in personal relations (or any noncontractarian moral value, for that matter).

However, Hampton does not go as far as Dimock in terms of denying the value of certain things that cannot be properly explained in contractarian terms. Dimock does not entirely dismiss the (nonmoral) value of relations, but the Hobbesian stance she endorses is committed to a subjective theory of value,[26] according to which what is good for a person is simply that which she desires. Therefore, she gives little (if any) substantial ethical guidance at the subjective level. Hobbesian ethics only becomes normative when it deals with "morality" – that is, when it offers a test to the morality of a normative source (e.g., a relation, a rule, or a contract) or whether a normative source "maximizes the expected utility (preference satisfaction) of the person."[27] Therefore, whatever nonmoral, subjective, noncontractarian value Dimock leaves intact is very small. She also claims that relations that cannot yield mutual benefit are not normative,[28] which further reduces her understanding of noncontractarian ethics to optional, subjective, and nonnormative preferences. In contrast, Hampton seems to leave more space for noncontractarian values, identified as elements that have a substantial, life-enhancing, normative value that relies on more than simply being desired and rationally bargained for. She allows for the fact that, though these values are "nonmoral," this need not imply that they are also not ethical.[29]

It follows that not all PSID will be owed anything as a matter of justice or morality. Severely cognitively disabled individuals, for example, may not be able to engage in mutually beneficial cooperation with others and are thus analogous to infants who depend on others for care. Hampton writes that, in this way, infants do not exploit their mothers, any more than a man dying by the side of the road is exploiting the Good Samaritan who stops for him. In these cases, a beneficiary does not "tak[e] advantage of the benefactor's affection for or feeling of duty toward him in order to receive the service."[30] Could we not say that the baby is (passively) taking advantage of the mother's emotions, in the sense that she benefits from her attention without being able to reciprocate? If we understood mutual benefit as a matter of objective results, where the absence of any such results indicates exploitation, that

---

[23] *Ibid.* at 21.
[24] *Ibid.*
[25] *Ibid.* at 38.
[26] Dimock, "Why All Feminists Should Be Contractarians," at 281.
[27] *Ibid.* at 278.
[28] *Ibid.* at 285.
[29] See Section 6.6, on "nonmoral values."
[30] Hampton, "Feminist Contractarianism," at 33–34.

6.2 Hampton and Dimock's Feminist Contractarianism

would seem to be the case. However, in Hampton's account (which reflects the Kantian dimension of her "contractarianism") injustice and exploitation (which are closely connected, if not reducible to one another, in feminist contractarian accounts[31]) involve the failure to acknowledge the exploited party's worth.[32] And infants can neither recognize nor fail to recognize their mother's personal worth. In this sense, the infant–mother relationship is neither fair nor unfair. According to Hampton, "fairness cannot exist between individuals whose powers and capacities are so unequal."[33] She explains:

> There is something absurd about inquiring into the morality of the relationship between, say, a mother and her newborn infant by asking, "What services could each agree to? What would they be unreasonable to reject?" For, so long as this radical inequality prevails, such a relationship is outside the province of distributive justice – in part because an infant or anyone severely infirm is incapable of reciprocating the benefit, making it ridiculous for any moral theory to require it, and in part because such people are not manipulating the situation to extract "free care" from others.[34]

It also follows from Dimock's strict Hobbesian contractarian logic that relationships that do not allow for mutual benefits should be considered to be morally neutral, at best. Dimock says that, in such cases, "perhaps we are beyond the realm of morality, because we are beyond the realm of interaction and so beyond the realm of normativity."[35] Dimock insists that few human relationships meet this threshold. In this category are "those between infants and mothers, or the completely infirm and their caregivers."[36] I think it is misleading to consider parent–infant relations as a rare exception. Rather, it seems to be the other way around – few human beings have *not* been raised by caregivers.[37] Regardless, whether exceptional or not, these relationships are located outside the margins of both justice and morality. Dimock and Hampton agree that to qualify a mother nurturing a defenseless child, or a person caring for a friend who has become profoundly mentally impaired, as "moral" is "evaluatively inept."[38]

This exclusion of cognitively and physically limited people from the province of justice and morality appears to contradict Hampton's claim that "[i]t seems to be a feature of our moral life that we regard a human being, whether or not she is

---

[31] See Section 6.3.1, "An Excessive Focus on Exploitation."
[32] Hampton, "Feminist Contractarianism," at 20, 33.
[33] Ibid. at 21.
[34] Ibid. at 32–33.
[35] Dimock, "Why All Feminists Should Be Contractarians," at 285.
[36] Ibid.
[37] Dimock must have meant few in kind rather than in number. But, even then, I fail to see the sort of weight that her argument is meant to have, other than indirectly stating that the human relationships that cannot be potentially mutually beneficial from a self-interested perspective are unimportant.
[38] Hampton, "Feminist Contractarianism," at 38.

instrumentally valuable, as always intrinsically valuable."[39] Hampton seems to hold that a plausible moral theory should integrate all human beings. At any rate, she rejects Hobbesian contractarianism on the grounds that it relativizes and instrumentalizes everything, including human beings. Instead, she adheres to a Kantian version of the "contract image,"[40] which captures a particular conception of the person and of human worth, and she holds that justice requires that "each party's worth [be] properly acknowledged."[41]

Hampton avoids the contradiction by implying that outliers, such as infants and PSID, have no intrinsic *moral* value. This follows from her concession that contractarianism tells us only how to relate *morally* to other people, but not how to relate in general terms. Morality is too "limp"[42] to explain the rich texture of human interactions. She maintains that "[t]he intrinsic value morality tells us to respect in our dealings with other persons is probably not the only kind of value each of us has."[43] Contractarian theorizing tells us how to morally respect others, and how to honor their intrinsic worth. However, it does not tell us how to form various relationships, or what they are for.[44] "[H]ow we should relate to our fellow human beings" is beyond morality, although Hampton suggests that moral respect is a necessary condition for many intimate relations/bonds/emotions (like love) to exist.[45]

We will return to the question of whether a nonmoral account of the value of some disabled people is promising or not. However, we should first make clear that Hampton's contractarian conclusion is that PSID possess neither instrumental nor intrinsic value or, in Hampton's terminology, dignity – that is, a value that stands beyond instrumentalization and pricing according to how others subjectively value it.[46]

This exclusion of the PSID is based on Hampton's conception of the person, and more particularly of the first component of this conception: human worth.[47] She uses the Kantian conception of human worth, according to which being a moral legislator makes us the sort of beings that deserve moral respect. Such worth is acknowledged by a "Kantian contractarian" (which others would term a "contractualist") account, as its idealized contractual process requires every participant to agree to it. Indeed, Hampton sees her version of the Kantian contract as incompatible with the instrumentalization of others. She concedes that, unlike Rawls, her contractual test is not a "morally neutral device" but is rather "an image fed by normative ideas that one is ultimately relying on when using the test to make

[39] Ibid. at 12–13.
[40] Ibid. at 25.
[41] Ibid. at 33.
[42] Ibid. at 37.
[43] Ibid. at 38.
[44] Ibid.
[45] Ibid.
[46] Ibid. at 38. Again, Hampton does not deny that PSID have another kind of value, but it is important to stress that they do not possess intrinsic value within her account of morality.
[47] Ibid. at 22.

moral evaluations."[48] In particular, she gives key normative weight to the ability to consent. Hampton is thus limited in her assessment of *human worth*, although her assessments of *legitimate interests* are much broader, for which she gestures toward a more comprehensive theory of human goods, before constraining it by only counting the legitimate interests of those deemed *worthy* on her Kantian-contractarian account.[49] Short of having the capacity to consent, therefore, human beings are *not* the sort of beings from whom it is fitting to obtain consent, and therefore the sort of beings that ought to be idealized are equal participants with equal bargaining powers to this contract.[50]

Thus, the feminist contractarian conception of personhood immunizes persons from exploitation at a cost. At first glance, it appears that this cost is assumed by those less able to dispute this conception. Ironically, those excluded from this powerful anti-exploitative protection are those who many of us believe we owe the highest duty to protect from exploitation. These disquieting thoughts should prompt us to problematize how this anti-exploitation contractarian philosophical campaign is carried out.

6.3 A RESPONSE

6.3.1 *An Excessive Focus on Exploitation*

Dimock and Hampton's task seems daunting; they claim to reduce the whole of human morality to the question of whether interactions are mutually beneficial. Before engaging with the foundational premises of the feminist contractarian argument (i.e., those relations can only be moral if they are mutually beneficial to self-interested parties), I want to discuss the merits of the apparent objective of their project: the need to design a theory of morality that is "exploitation-proof."

Dimock and Hampton reject all moral justifications that prescribe, value, or make room for relationships or actions that are exploitative. This rejection depends on the premise that there is no possibility of goodness or rightness in an exploitative relation or action. I want to challenge the feminist contractarian idea that exploitation is so bad that it outweighs or cancels out any other potential sources of good. Indeed, Dimock and Hampton's contractarian feminism gives insufficient (if any) weight to noncontractarian values within morality that trump exploitativeness.

I also want to emphasize that all the phenomena that Dimock and Hampton define as "exploitative" would not deserve this pejorative epithet on an ordinary understanding of exploitation as well as on alternative philosophical understandings of it. It is not my intention to offer a defense of exploitation (which is indubitably bad). Rather, I suggest that many relations in which a party does not take a self-

---

[48] *Ibid.* at 26.
[49] *Ibid.* at 22, 27–28.
[50] *Ibid.* at 26–27. Her conclusion thus further illustrates my discussion in Chapter 5 about the limits of contractualism.

interested contractarian stance (and in which she gives more than she gets, if we consider the bargain from that perspective) are far from obviously exploitative.

It is understandable for exploitation to play a major role within the liberal moral tradition, if not more generally in modern thought. Exploitation shackles the exercise of a value central to these traditions – namely, autonomy. However, the contractarian framework at hand goes as far as making exploitation the only substantial moral problem. However, if we consult our ordinary intuitions about exploitation, do we find that it is the central feature of (if not a synonym for) injustice and immorality? Surely, we have reasons to respond to a situation by saying "this is unfair" and "this is immoral," other than because we are victims of exploitation. Hampton and Dimock disagree, and their particular criticism of exploitation entails a broad rejection of other-regarding morality, including even in the context of personal relations, which are fueled by other-regarding concern.

6.3.2 Their Conclusions Overreach

My main problem with Dimock and Hampton's argument is that their conclusions overreach by rejecting the noncontractual dimensions of the morality of intimate relationships while simultaneously attacking the problem of exploitation that sometimes comes with these relations. Their attempts to reject the moral relevance of relational concepts like love and care fails to be convincing. Indeed, what they have made a compelling case for is how these relations can be corrupted and how some components of these relations can be fertile grounds for exploitation.[51] Yet, they do not show that noncontractarian grounds of morality of intimate relationships are unconvincing – one cannot reject these grounds only because these relationships have the *potential* to be dramatically exploitative and harmful. Contractarians still need to supply the (counterintuitive) argument that the moral significance of personal relations is best understood as a contract. In other words, they need to demonstrate that exploitation is bad because it fails to meet contractarian standards, rather than, for example, because exploitation evidences a lack of care for the other, or imperfectly realizes the good of friendship or love.

---

[51] Their reference to external sources (like Hobbes or Gauthier) does not buttress their claims. Dimock spells out her understanding of morality sufficiently for the reader to disagree with it. The only grounds for her argument that she leaves out of her paper is her defense of non-tuism, which she includes in another paper: Susan Dimock, "Defending Non-Tuism" (1999) 29:2 Can J Phil 251. However, I have not found in this other paper anything less axiomatic than in her piece on feminist contractarianism. Dimock can use bedrock assumptions, but it is equally acceptable for people to disagree with them. For her part, Hampton disagrees with non-tuism and does not condition the acceptability of her view on the correctness of another moral theory, only on her explanation of the correctness of a conception of human worth, which readers could find lacking. In any case, if their arguments clash with our considered judgment, connecting them with higher ground theories highlights the limitations of such theories.

Hampton does maintain that the fair contractual dimension to these relations acts as a moral component to the condition for the relation to exist.[52] Dimock more explicitly embraces the idea that contract-like thinking informs and constitutes these personal relations. Dimock's "constitutivist" position is not intuitively compelling and the contractual picture of intimate relations that emerges from this account is chilling. When I am told that this picture only accounts for the morality of these relations (but that there are other socially and psychologically important aspects to these relationships) I am more, not less, skeptical of the argument. I will deal with this argument later in this chapter, but for now my point is that, should this argument fail, Dimock and Hampton cannot fall back on their powerful criticism of exploitation to make their reductionist case in favor of contractarianism. It is insufficient to merely point out the fact that intimate relations can be exploitative.

Equally, it is insufficient for Dimock and Hampton to show how well their non-tuistic "mutual benefit test" works to prevent exploitation, unless they assume there is no other way to insure individuals against exploitation, and that exploitation is indeed the only thing that morality and justice should be concerned about. This position needs to be argued, and compellingly so, for it is far from obvious that there is a lack of resources within the cognitive, conative, and affective structure of intimate relations to deal with the harm caused by exploitation. For instance, it seems fundamental that what it means to properly love or care for someone requires us not to exploit that individual. However, contractarians do not take the complex structure of these intimate relations seriously; they do not grant much weight to the value of other dimensions of these relations apart from their justness.

Of course, we need to protect people against exploitation, but that does not mean that we should throw the baby (other-regarding concern) out with the bathwater (inappropriate self-abnegation). As it stands, Dimock and Hampton's argument does not support their elimination of noncontractarian elements from morality. It only entitles them to suggest that a contractarian test could *inform* the complex moral assessment of intimate relationships. This brings me to specify the extent to which I believe their criticism is informative and could be used as *part* of an anti-exploitative check on the moral relationships that we have with vulnerable people. Such a check is not only relevant in cases of people who are susceptible to emotional exploitation but is especially relevant in the case of PSID.

6.3.3 How Contractual Thinking Can Inform a Moral Assessment of Intimate Relations?

The mutual benefit test proposed by Dimock and Hampton is informative, even if I disagree with them that it exhausts all moral evaluation. It allows parties to a relationship to be *aware* that they are giving more than they are receiving or that

---

[52] Hampton, "Feminist Contractarianism," at 38, 31.

they are receiving more than they are giving. This awareness can routinely slip the minds of both parties to a potentially exploitative relationship. The exploited person forgets that she was ever entitled not to be exploited, and the exploiter forgets that she is doing something wrong, likely due in part to moral weakness and opportunism, or to the fact that the corrupted relationship has become the *status quo*, which justifies the exploitation. These explanations are mutually reinforcing. For instance, out of opportunism, the exploiter can rationalize her behavior by (ill-advisedly) invoking the moral weight of the relation.

From my noncontractarian standpoint, exploitation is not established merely because a relationship fails the test of mutual benefit. A party who takes part in a relationship that does not make her better off is not necessarily being exploited. I will elaborate later about why there is more to being exploited than failing to receive a sufficient benefit. For now, I only want to say that if the mere realization that one is giving more than one is receiving does not necessarily imply exploitation, it does inform the parties of the existence of a symptom of exploitation, and invites them to carefully evaluate the context, the imbalance, and whether it is exploitative. The parties (or anyone assessing their relationship) can then reach two different conclusions. Yet, both will differ from the conclusion that contractarian feminists like Dimock and Hampton assume they would reach.

The Insight That the Relationship Would Be Morally Lacking Were It a Contract between Mutually Disinterested Parties

The moral evaluation of an intimate relationship as a *contract* can indicate that certain moral dimensions that would prevail in a relationship between strangers (and that should generally exist within these private relationships) are absent. Feminist contractarians (or at least Dimock, who claims to speak for them) do not acknowledge the private/public distinction. However, rather than using a moral framework that genuinely transcends this distinction, they use a public framework that prevails between *strangers* (or at least strangers coexisting within an ethical community). The contractarian moral relational model is typically that of a relationship between strangers who bargain with one another. At the heart of this account is an insistence on the self-interested contractual standpoint, self-interested motivations, and a self-concerned perspective.[53] My suggestion that this standpoint is typical of a relational model between strangers is hardly provocative.[54] Of course, Hampton and Dimock would disagree with me and insist that their contractarian model applies equally well (indeed, better) to intimate relations. Nevertheless, they are not proposing a different private moral model or framework, so much as they are making the case that the public framework is applicable to (and indeed, is the only framework that can morally illuminate) private relations.

---

[53] *Ibid.* at 21, 29.
[54] In fact, they concede that their attempt to show the contrary is innovative, e.g., *ibid.* at 31.

Even if I set aside my disagreement and consider that this public relational model can explain the morality of intimate relationships by itself, I also do not think that emphasizing the criterion of mutual benefit makes the best case for it. Instead, as Hampton suggests, one should emphasize what the requirement of mutual benefit stands for – that is, the more fundamental notion of mutual respect, or recognition of the other's particular (Kantian) value (*qua* moral legislator). As such, one can emphasize the characteristics (apart from profitability) that should be a part of relations between strangers. Think of how we generally behave toward strangers, including those with whom we bargain. We abide by rules of civility relating to showing tact, kindness, and patience. These moral aspects of what I take to be the public model – and which contractarians seek to apply to all relations – reflect the contractualist idea of mutual respect as being part of the costs and benefits that one expects from a relationship, and I think Dimock would accept Hampton's position on this issue.

It should now be easy to understand that thinking about a private relationship as though it were an interaction between disinterested strangers can allow us to see how far an intimate relation has forgone some of the basic relational virtues (such as kindness, respect, tact, politeness, and patience) that we would expect people to demonstrate. We could imagine, for instance, a dispute between a mother and daughter, during which the mother says: "No one has ever treated me with such little respect!" Equally, we could imagine a young woman entering her boyfriend's apartment, keeping her snow boots on, throwing her books and handbag on the couch, and, without offering any greeting, declaring: "I'm too tired to be polite. I've been polite to everyone all day at work. Feed me."

I diverge from Dimock and Hampton here because I do not hold that these failures to demonstrate virtues are necessarily immoral (although in the examples above, they probably are to a degree), as these are failures of a contractual relationship. However, the mother–daughter or boyfriend–girlfriend relationship is *not* a contractual relationship.[55] Contractarian feminists hold that they *are*, although not in the ordinary sense of contractual relationships. They hold that such relationships are contracts in the sense of involving costs and benefits and reflecting our roles of bargainers and moral legislators. At any rate, they hold that these relations are only moral or immoral and just or unjust, insofar as they can be assessed in those terms. In other words, morality and justice have nothing to say if and when relations cannot be explained in those terms.

I think that this contract-like (exclusively "public") model is useful but it only partly informs our moral assessment. These thought experiments provide us (and the people immersed within a relationship) with a healthy intellectual distance from which to assess particular situations. From this distance, the mother, from the example above, might realize that she would not endure this level of disrespect

---

[55] And can, therefore, potentially be made acceptable within a noncontractual framework.

from anyone else, and would take stock of how disrespectful her daughter has become. Equally, the daughter can counterfactually think of her mother as a stranger (like a bus driver or a waiter), which might help her realize that she is not behaving appropriately toward her mother, something that she may not be able to see clearly otherwise. Her filial relationship encumbers her relational understanding vis-à-vis her mother with so many other moral and nonmoral elements. Indeed, asking a child to project herself onto different roles and relationships is a normal part of her moral education, and an effective way of developing empathy. This is especially the case if the daughter can imaginatively extend behaving morally to other relationships, so as to realize that this moral approach should be applied in still other relationships. Equally, the boyfriend can come to realize that he is putting up with someone who does not deserve his patience and respond with a cliché like "I do not need this," a response which singularly echoes a cost–benefit assessment.

Such an assessment can usefully supplement our moral evaluation of intimate relationships, but only if we extend our imaginative resources. It cannot, *contra* Hampton and Dimock, wholly supplant that moral evaluation. In fact, I would go further and say that the contract-like assessment (or the "public model" or relation-between-strangers model) provides us with mere insight, as opposed to a normative element. Once we realize that our intimate relation is missing the kindness, tact, or politeness that we would show to strangers, we are inclined to ask whether or not this is morally acceptable *from within the moral framework that is applicable to the relation*, be that the parent–daughter relational framework or the boyfriend–girlfriend framework. We may discover that these traits are equally applicable in both frameworks. However, we may also find that the particular structure of an intimate relationship makes this trait more or less important than it would be for a stranger. For instance, the nature of a particular relationship may require much more kindness than is required in our relationships with strangers. By the same token, the same intimate relationship may make a lack of tact or gentleness less of an issue. Although we have to thank the contractual thought experiment for elucidating this realization, it does not logically lead to a second realization that a contractual component is missing from these intimate relationships. Rather, we realize that a normative element inherent to the structure of the intimate relationship is not being properly actualized or acknowledged. This brings me to the second way that a contractarian outlook on intimate relations can be morally informative.

A Plurality of Morally Normative Relations
A contractual element may indeed be missing, but rather than indicating a defective intimate relationship, it indicates that another type of relationship between the same parties would be defective. To accept this position, one must accept the simple and obvious idea that human beings stand in different relations toward different beings while also accepting the compelling but controversial idea that these different relations imply different duties understood within different "normative relational

codes." This helps us to conceptualize the fact that we have different duties toward different people (or entities of all sorts) without struggling with the plurality of these duties and the irregularity of how these duties weigh on different agents.[56] Thinking in terms of relations (and roles within these relations) makes it unnecessary to eliminate the private/public or the Jake/Amy dichotomy – as Hampton and Dimock suggest we do – because we make room for the possibility that there are different "relational normative codes" or, as value pluralists put it, there are different values and different ways to fittingly relate to them.[57] Indeed, some relations place a crucial weight on mutual benefit, while others place very little emphasis on it. This perspective coheres better with the ordinary understanding we have of many relations that are not centrally focused on self-concerned mutual benefit and with our intuition that these relations are morally important for noncontractual reasons.

To explain this position more concretely, the girlfriend in our example above might realize that she is not treating her boyfriend with the same degree of respect that she would treat a colleague or friend. It may also be that some of the relations in which we stand with others have nothing to do with our intimate relationship with them. For example, a father who kills his son out of anger has not only failed to properly play the role of a father or caregiver, he has also failed as a human being who owes an obligation to all other humans to not harm them gratuitously. Similarly, I may owe it to my sister to pay her on time for repairing my car and to not take advantage of the fact that her business is doing poorly by underpaying her. This obligation is understood within a bargaining relation. However, I may say "hi" to her, just as good neighbors should. I may also help her by moving her sofa into her apartment, as good brothers should. All of these obligations can be linked to different roles and relations.

We wear many different moral hats and occupy different moral roles, and moral theory must define the variety of relational moral codes and balance between conflicting roles. A particular relationship can supplant another if those relationships are conceptually incompatible or if one relationship makes it acceptable to mitigate or suspend the obligations that derive from the other. For example, I can fail my sister in many ways – as a fellow bargainer, as a brother, as a friend – but not as a stranger in my community, for she is not a stranger to me. Certain relations will endure more than others: it will always be possible for me to fail my sister *qua* "fellow human."

In sum, this role-based way of looking at purely self-interested relationships concedes to the point of feminist contractarians that evaluating whether a relation

---

[56] I will sketch a relational or "role-based" view of morality in the concluding chapter. However, recognizing the merits of these noncontractual frameworks does not require one to commit to a relational view of morality, only to accept that some things other than mutual benefit matter.

[57] For theoretical support for such a position, see, e.g., Elizabeth Anderson, *Value in Ethics and Economics* (Cambridge: Harvard University Press, 1995); Mary Anne Warren, *Moral Status: Obligations to Persons and Other Living Things* (Oxford: Oxford University Press, 2000).

is self-serving can be morally enlightening. The closer the relationship is to a contract, the more enlightening this evaluation can be. However, if we accept that there is more than one type of moral relationship, we can start thinking about the notion of "exploitation" within other relational frameworks in a way that would probably be richer and more accurate.[58] What counts as exploitation in one relationship may count as an acceptable – indeed, perhaps a socially expected – sacrifice in another. I will return to the idea that certain relations give rise to kinds of phenomena that we commonly think of as "exploitation" but that the contractarian "self-interest" test would simply not detect. It would seem more productive to ask, "am I being exploited?" once we have a richer, relational understanding of exploitation, rather than to apply the "self-interest test," which may fail to detect instances of exploitation or may incorrectly condemn a relation as immoral.

What this relational way of looking at morality suggests – against the view of feminist contractarians – is that we occupy many *moral* roles other than a "contractual" one and that we may fail someone *qua* "contractee" while still relating to that person appropriately within other relational frameworks. Some of these moral frameworks may (although not necessarily) excuse the former failure. However, contractarian feminists have a conception of the person that implies that the only relational duty that matters morally is to reciprocate benefits that are received.

6.3.4 *The Contractarian Conception of the Person*

There are many angles from which one can disagree with contractarian feminists. For example, I doubt that the idealized model of non-tuist interpersonal relations, associated with a model of relations between strangers, will exhaust the moral roles that people play. Different angles of criticism are interconnected – that is, the contractarian focus on one sort of value, the contractarian conception of personhood, the contractarian relational model, and the general contractarian understanding of the frontiers of justice and morality all rest on one another. Still, the most central point of disagreement is arguably the conception of the person, if only because Hampton presents it as such:

> As I understand [the conception of the person], in a successful contractarian theory the contract is a (mere) device that, if used in the right circumstances, will call to mind and organize these concepts in a way that will enable us to apply them to diagnose successfully the presence of injustice in a relationship.[59]

Hampton holds that "distributive justice is a species of moral concern generally, which I define as *treating people consistent with the contractarian conception of the*

---

[58] There may or may not be a single, unifying concept of exploitation, but the way it plays out in diverse relations vary and, at any rate, the contractarian "self-interest test" is no such unifying concept.

[59] Hampton, "Feminist Contractarianism," at 22.

person."[60] Concern for the justice in a relationship is a concern "that each party's worth is properly acknowledged,"[61] where worth is understood as the conception of human worth, which is one of two normative aspects of the contractarian understanding of the person. What is this worth? As I mentioned before, Hampton uses "the Kantian idea that people have *intrinsic, noninstrumental value*"[62] but limits the holders of this value to the sort of beings who are able to consent, and excluding beings whose wills can be supplanted, dominated, and frustrated in a way that makes exploitation possible. Above all, Hampton insists that the parties to a relationship or a social contract take a self-interested, self-concerned perspective, so as not to make themselves prey to others.[63] Hampton's and Dimock's tests assume self-interested motivations, and indeed make them a central part of an idealized bargaining situation.[64]

Hampton and Dimock conceive of persons as beings able to consent and negotiate,[65] and the non-tuist assumption adds that contractarians should not have "sufficiently robust preferences for the well-being of others that they would act morally just because doing so realizes good for others."[66] The first assumption seems to incompletely represent (and the second, non-tuist assumption seems at odds with) the reality of what human beings are – both factually and in an idealized sense – and the way in which we conceptualize what needs, desires, and capacities a person should be entitled to actualize. People exist within a matrix of relationships and values that are important to their communities, and some of these relationships involve making sacrifices for others or putting someone else's happiness before our own. To postulate that these relations should be subtracted from our moral evaluation (for instance, by imagining a bargaining situation where they are not factored in) assumes a conception of the person that needs to be thoroughly defended.

Ultimately, however, this conception of the person is assumed rather than argued for. It faces the sort of communitarian challenge that Michael Sandel addresses to Rawls. Referring to this criticism (of an "implausible metaphysical conception of the person"[67]), Hampton writes that, contrary to Rawls, she does not claim to present a strictly political rather than metaphysical conception of the person. Rather, her metaphysical claims are not an embarrassment to contractarian theory; in fact, they are an indication of its strength. This assertion – similar to how feminist contractarians highlight exploitation – is explained by the powerful idea that we,

---

[60] *Ibid.* at 30.
[61] *Ibid.* at 33.
[62] *Ibid.* at 25.
[63] *Ibid.* at 29.
[64] *Ibid.* at 21; Dimock, "Why All Feminists Should Be Contractarians," at 279.
[65] Here, "person" is used in the normative sense of the term – the sense that entails moral obligations that are proper responses to a conception of human worth and human legitimate interests.
[66] Dimock, "Why All Feminists Should Be Contractarians," at 279.
[67] Hampton, "Feminist Contractarianism," at 35.

as human beings, are only morally important *qua* autonomous beings. My view is that autonomy is only one of the morally significant traits that human beings have. It is central to only some of the roles that we occupy and is not the only way to justify the morality of all our relations.[68] Hampton does not deny that these other traits have some value and that our species is deeply sociable but she insists that we should only make use of this natural characteristic in a strategic sense when designing the structure of a fair society to better teach its members that we are beings of equal intrinsic worth. The only "self" that we have the moral duty to actualize is the autonomous portion of our own self.[69]

A good way to challenge such philosophical starting points is to consider whether the way they play out complements our strongly held moral intuitions. Consider Hampton's example that it is not the case that "anything goes" as long as the relation is contract-like and mutually beneficial under Kantian contractarianism (which I have called contractualism), as opposed to Hobbesian contractarianism:

> Before a group of people could even consider the question, "What terms could we reasonably accept for our surrogacy contract?" they would have to ask the question, "Is the very idea of a surrogacy contract something that each of us could reasonably accept?" ... Remember that both Kant and Rawls have argued that the contract idea, when invoked, precludes certain institutional structures and social practices ... that are degrading; similarly [the contract test should forbid] a variety of social arrangements that are demeaning – that is, inconsistent with the worth of all the parties involved.[70]

The worth she is referring to here is the intrinsic, noninstrumental value that inheres in autonomous beings, or in humans *qua* autonomous beings, as "people equally situated and motivated to secure their legitimate interests."[71] Of course, she makes a good case that these parties – "in particular, the prospective surrogate mother"[72] – may still find that the commodification of wombs/mothering is degrading. But there are two limitations to this argument.

First, the commodification of mothering is degrading only because the prospective parties agree that it is. Whenever theorists committed to contractual proceduralism try to argue that it is not the case that *any* contract-like, mutually beneficial agreement is fine (i.e., by claiming that contracting parties would not agree to this or that), their opponents can still insist on the contingency of such an agreement. On this account, commodifying the womb is not intrinsically worse than commodifying

---

[68] See section "A Plurality of Morally Normative Relations."
[69] Hampton, "Feminist Contractarianism," at 35–36. I am not saying that Hampton (or Kant) and Dimock are *hostile* to affects, partiality, and other-regarding concern, or that they deny that other-regarding concern can be motivating; only that they deprive these elements from having any moral consequence.
[70] Ibid. at 26.
[71] Ibid.
[72] Ibid.

ice cream, as people's autonomy could be contractually exercised to agree or disagree with the commodification of both items. Unless there is something intrinsically autonomy-demeaning in a certain activity, it is my understanding that Hampton and other contractarians still want to be able to make an argument when faced with things that seem wrong, but they cannot point to exploitation to explain this wrongness.

Second, and more importantly, since some PSID will not be among the equally situated contracting parties – the "us" in the question of "can each of us reasonably accept this?" – they would be excluded from the benefits of an anti-surrogacy policy. Or at least (and this is an important distinction) if they were to fall under such a policy, it would not be because surrogacy degrades or demeans them, as they would lack the "noninstrumental and equal" worth possessed by autonomous beings.[73] In turn, the devastating idea of "female PSID womb-farming" would not be intrinsically morally wrong within a fair feminist contractarian society.

Why does it matter that PSID benefit from protective measures for the right reasons? First, it matters simply because we would be getting policy wrong if we were to do otherwise. Second, it matters because people with disabilities are not protected even when the (wrong) reasons do not apply. Consider again Hampton's example of the Good Samaritan who helps someone bleeding by the roadside. She holds that the Good Samaritan is commendable because the person being helped, in receiving this service, does not take advantage of the Samaritan's duty toward her.[74] I have trouble seeing how Hampton expects intuitive support for her position from this illustration because I cannot think of a better example to illustrate what is missing from the contractarian picture of morality. The fact that the bleeding, dying person is not *exploiting* the Good Samaritan is marginal; in fact, it is the last thing any ordinary person would have on their mind when commending the Good Samaritan's actions. Rather, we think that the Good Samaritan acted morally (not just in a way that promoted, as Hampton suggests, some special nonmoral values[75]) because of her attitude, the moral value of her action, or the result of those actions. Whether one conceives of morality as residing primarily in consequences, duties, characters, or relations, it is not the absence of exploitation that will centrally explain the moral value of the Good Samaritan's attitudes or behaviors. If anything, the absence of exploitation is more likely to *not* vitiate this value. It does not constitute a substantial explanation of why we would prize the Good Samaritan's actions. In fact, short of elevating other-regarding concern as morally significant grounds or criteria of actions, we cannot commend the Good Samaritan's actions, at least no more than we could commend her choice to buy an ice cream for a reasonable, nonexploitative price.

The fact that these contractarian implications do not tally with our moral intuitions weighs against the credibility of the contractarian conception of the person. By

---

[73] Ibid. at 36.
[74] Ibid. at 33–34
[75] Ibid. at 33, 37–38.

contrast, Michael Sandel and Elizabeth Anderson[76] have argued that certain goods should not be sold, not just because of the traditional argument against the possibility of exploitation but because it would corrupt certain relations, like mothering in the case of surrogacy contracts. This implies an acknowledgment that *relations themselves* – not just autonomous *beings* – ought not to be degraded. Yet it could also be connected to a conception of the person as enmeshed with, or fundamentally needing, certain kinds of relations to flourish. Furthermore, it could be based on the welfare of the future infant, rather than on the surrogate's welfare or on motherhood. Surrogates and babies who are unable to exercise or develop autonomy may have other aspects of their welfare that other accounts of personhood would take into account. This is not to say that surrogate contracts would be deemed moral or immoral on certain grounds – contractarian or otherwise. Rather, I suggest that our moral assessment of this question is incomplete on the strictly contractarian grounds proposed by Hampton. Or, at least, those uncomfortable with being unable to morally condemn PSID womb-farming will suspect that this is the case. By reflecting on what prompts this discomfort, they may reach alternative conceptions of personhood that better cohere with our most firmly held moral intuitions.

One can transpose the narrowness of contractarian notions of exploitation and personhood to the narrowness of the framework that contractarians use for their moral evaluation. Proper evaluative frameworks, as I have suggested, and as I will further illustrate in the following section, are likely to be morally richer and more complex than a non-tuist test of mutual benefit. Two uncertainties that exist in Dimock's and Hampton's arguments facilitate their rejection of these alternative frameworks (and the conviction that the contractarian focus on self-interestedness is a metaphysical strength of their accounts). These uncertainties will be developed in the following two sections.

6.3.5 Other-Regarding Frameworks Need Not Facilitate Exploitation

In her comment on Jake's and Amy's respective paradigmatic moral outlooks, Hampton claims that

> Jake is susceptible to a brand of moral immaturity that manifests itself in an insensitivity to the needs of others and a failure to see himself as a fellow caretaker in a relationship.[77]

and that

> Amy is susceptible to a moral perspective that makes her too sensitive to other people, and her concern to meet their needs borders on outright servility.[78]

---

[76] Anderson, *Value in Ethics and Economics*; Michael Sandel, "What Money Shouldn't Buy" (2003) 5:2 Hedgehog Review.
[77] Hampton, "Feminist Contractarianism," at 5.
[78] Ibid. at 5–6.

This is part of the contractarian feminist argument that the "female" other-regarding moral outlook is more likely to lead to exploitation than the "male" self-regarding moral outlook.[79] However, I challenge both the idea that a self-regarding outlook is immune from exploitation and the idea that an other-regarding outlook is conducive to exploitation. The correlation or connection between these respective outlooks and exploitation can be conceptual or statistical and there are reasons to question both positions. That is, even assuming that exploitation, defined in contractarian terms, is the central issue of justice, it is unclear that a self-regarding stance on morality is either conceptually incompatible with exploitation, or inherently more likely to reduce it than would an alternative framework that incorporates some other-regarding elements.

To assume that exploitation is the central issue of justice and morality conflates two dichotomies. The first pits a *self-regarding* (as well as impartial and detached) outlook on morality against an *other-regarding* (as well as concrete, situational, or role-based) outlook. The second opposition is between a set of self-regarding virtues and vices (self-love, self-respect, selfishness) and a set of other-regarding virtues and vices (altruism, self-effacingness, servility). However, these two sets do not necessarily correspond to one another. The virtues and vices listed can be possessed by both Jake and Amy; that is, they can be associated with both other- and self-regarding outlooks on morality. Jake's and Amy's views can be formulated in more or less altruistic forms. If Jake were more altruistic, he might have said "half for me and half for others." If Amy had been more selfish, she might have said the words "maybe" and "really" less often when qualifying how important her own goals would have to be in order to trump other-regarding concern.

Jake and Amy are caricatures who invite us to qualify one of them as good and the other as bad. Since they do not exhaust the possible combinations of moral views, virtues, and vices, it may be more informative to depolarize the kind of relations in which they take part and recognize a continuum of normative bonds – from the most distant (such as one's relationship with a credit card company) to the most intimate (the relationship we have with our parents).

---

[79] Hampton does say that "[n]either of these voices should be allowed to inform our moral theorizing" (*ibid.* at 8). But it is clear that the contractarian mutual benefit test corresponds to Jake's self-regarding outlook, although (1) it is less greedy, for it requires one to be better off, not to be *very much better* off, as in Jake's balance of three-quarters for himself and one-quarter for the rest (*ibid.* at 3). In fact, Dimock's account explicitly entails a non-tuist stance, meaning that the bargainers will not compare themselves with others; they will evaluate whether they are better off without considering if the other side is getting an even better deal. (2) Hampton's emphasis on the Kantian roots of her version of the contractarian test also involves a recognition of the contractarian person's intrinsic, noninstrumental worth or dignity that is not *necessarily* present in Jake's moral voice, although there is a possibility that his voice could be formalized in a Hobbesian or Kantian way. In any case, given that Hampton's interpretation of the Kantian social contract as demanding a central emphasis on self-regarding concern, it still matches Jake's self-regarding outlook. I also note how both Hampton (*ibid.* at 29–30) and Dimock ("Why All Feminists Should Be Contractarians," at 284–85) criticize Amy-like "feminine" virtues as opposed to "masculine" ones, both associating the former with exploitation.

There is no necessary connection between care, other-regarding and other so-called mothering or nurturing ethics and exploitation. Amy's self-abnegation does not have to be an integral aspect of the moral position she gestures toward. It *could* be explained by her gender and some social and psychological factors that are gender-related. She may even have reached the moral position she favors because of social and psychological tendencies that make her eager to be altruistic. However, this does not mean that, once this moral position is reached, it cannot stand on its own (like any other rational position) independently from whatever irrational elements (fears, nonmoral emotions, pressures, and/or neuroses) that may or may not motivate any particular individual's choice.

However, there certainly is a *factual* connection between exploitation and gender, and experts in history, psychology, and sociology should continue to add to the critical literature on (notably) women's exploitation and the factors that facilitate it. My point is that these factors are not part and parcel of these noncontractarian/feminist/nurturing ethics, *contra* Hampton, Dimock, and their followers. It has not been proven that these issues cannot be rectified from within these theories.

As I argued in Chapter 3 with respect to a trust-based social contract theory, a self-regarding outlook does not conceptually preclude exploitation. One can be entirely self-interested and still be exploited simply because exploitation is not necessarily self-imposed. (Indeed, feminist contractarians would be more successful if they limited their criticism to that kind of exploitation, but they do not.) We can think of the examples of children or slaves. One can recognize people's particular abilities to negotiate, bargain, and consent, but then employ these traits as part of an exploitative strategy.

In fact, one could argue that a self-regarding moral outlook is *more* likely to yield exploitation. This becomes apparent when we consider what a society would look like if self-regarding or other-regarding attitudes were systematically fostered within the social structure. A society of Amys, where moral agents consider other people's welfare instead of pursuing their own selfish endeavors, may well be less exploitative than a counterpart society composed of individualistic, self-interested Jakes. A society in which everyone's primary concern is to not make oneself prey to others may in fact produce more exploitation than a society where everyone adopts observant, other-regarding attitudes. Rather than dwelling on the empirical merits of such a hypothesis, I merely suggest that its prima facie plausibility is sufficient to counterbalance the plausibility of the contrary hypothesis. We can see that Hampton and Dimock's contractarianism cannot get a lot of mileage out of the statistical suggestion that exploitation would diminish in a society that incentivized individuals to adopt a self-regarding negotiating stance.

Indeed, in practice, systematic exploitation does not happen as frequently in situations where people are self-effacing (although it *is* a particular and grave type of exploitation that frequently happens in intimate relationships). Generalized exploitation happens because of active exploiters, not simply because of the attitudes of the exploited. Arguably, a moral theory that focuses on the attitudes of potential exploiters may do more to prevent exploitation than a moral theory that focuses on the attitudes of the potential exploited group. Of course, we do need to look at the particular type of exploitation occurring within intimate relations. However, Hampton and Dimock ignore the most general cases of exploitation and not only public ones. To give one example of exploitation that occurs within private relations and that does not correspond to self-denying "female" attitudes, let us consider the case of children. Exploited children do not subject themselves to exploitation or render themselves open to emotional manipulation. They are just actively exploited, and their vulnerability and exploitation are not satisfactorily explained by the fact that, as children, they take on an other-regarding point of view.

6.3.6 Failing the Costs–Benefits Test

Another reason that feminist contractarians dismiss other-regarding relational frameworks to evaluate the morality or fairness of relations is that these frameworks take into account kinds of costs and benefits that cannot be distributed, and are therefore "outside the province of justice."[80] Hampton calls these *affective* costs and benefits. They include (1) the pleasant and unpleasant emotions that one feels when in a relationship, as well as (2) the personal investment in a relation that has to be maintained through some effort, the persistence/extinction or blooming/withering of which can be perceived as motivational costs and benefits. Hampton also excludes the costs and benefits associated with (3) the duties toward the other parties to the relationship (or, I may add, the relationship itself) and to (4) non-self-interested motivations.[81]

First, I want to challenge the idea that these other-regarding, affective, or vicarious costs and benefits cannot and should not be calculated as part of the costs and benefits that one gets from a relationship considered from the contractarian standpoint (i.e., from within Hampton's and Dimock's own contractarian tests). Second, I think that Hampton puts too much weight on the problem of incommensurability between affective and non-affective costs, or at least I fail to see why this problem would plausibly exclude affective costs from the sphere of morality. It seems that, in order to reply to these two criticisms, contractarian feminists must fall back on their postulated (idealized and normative) conception of the person, which begs the question of the value of that conception. Third, given this response, I will highlight the shortcomings of their narrow conception of the person when applied to cases of intimate relationships (and while I do not propose an alternative, I pave the way for such an alternative proposal). I will demonstrate that Hampton and Dimock's

---

[80] Hampton, "Feminist Contractarianism," at 21.
[81] *Ibid.* at 21–22.

approach to relational justice/morality does not align with our ordinary intuitions on the matter; in fact, it invites us to jettison some of our most sincerely and seriously held beliefs. These beliefs are not only important for nonmoral or nonobviously moral reasons,[82] but eliminating them from morality would make morality odd or alien to us. These intuitions are so central to our set of ordinary moral beliefs that we might think of them as the sole beliefs that endure once our ordinary concrete "considered judgments" – to use Rawls's terms – are "duly pruned and adjusted."[83]

Why Would Other-Regarding or Affective Benefits Not Count?
Why would these affective benefits not count as part of the relational costs and benefits to be reasonably distributed within a relationship?[84] Are they not enjoyable goods that parties may wish to contract for? What is it about these goods that makes them unfit to enter the contractarian calculation? The logic of a mutually beneficial contract seems insufficient, of itself, to justify this exclusion. After all, if exploitation is, as Gauthier says, "the outcome for the person whose supposed partner defects from the joint strategy on which he bases his action,"[85] it could not have happened merely because the parties agreed to a joint strategy that maximized some other-regarding benefits. Feminist contractarians need to appeal to their particular conception of contractees to explain why allowing them to bargain for such goods would infringe on their dignity (or their noninstrumental worth) – that is, that contractees need to be exclusively self-concerned. Since this conception is contestable, it seems plausible to argue that, from a contractarian standpoint (if not a non-tuist one), vicarious happiness or affective benefits of many kinds can be weighed in the balance when assessing whether one is being exploited because one gives more than one receives.

For instance, let us consider the case of a devoted husband and father who is proud of being a *paterfamilias*. He invests more time in the multipartite "family relation" and in his roles of father and husband than the other members of his household. Yet, the satisfaction that he draws from the success of his family, including the happiness of family members, is such that (to him) it more than compensates his efforts. If the father is truly happier when his daughter is doing well and sadder when she is doing poorly, why would these real (but affective) costs and benefits not be considered when we evaluate whether his daughter is exploiting him? Maybe the family unit simply matters more to the father than to other members of his family. This situation does sound like it *may* give rise to exploitation but it does not necessarily involve exploitation.

---

[82] For instance, because they may be conditions of a moral agent's integrity, or be conditions allowing the agent to accept her moral duties or embrace them subjectively, or be conditions for her to do anything at all, moral or not.
[83] John Rawls, *A Theory of Justice*, rev. ed. (Cambridge: Harvard University Press, 1999), at 18.
[84] Hampton, "Feminist Contractarianism," at 21.
[85] Gauthier, *Morals by Agreement*, at 175.

However, exploitation happens all too commonly, and philosophers can help better understand and reduce its occurrence by conceptualizing the ways in which underreported and undetected forms of exploitation occur. But contractarianism seems ill-equipped to take on this conceptualization. It only detects exploitation as the result of *some* kinds of costs and benefits in this calculus. If one disagrees with a contractarian normative conception of the person and considers that there is no reason to reject affective and vicarious enjoyments from our moral evaluation, one might think that contractarians are casting too wide or narrow a net. More precisely, if we need to weigh the moral implications of affective and vicarious benefits, we would probably have to distinguish between "good" and "bad" benefits. We would need to define those benefits that should count (and those that should not count) because they do not really contribute to the person's happiness. Rather, they are based on confusion or fear – say, the desperate attempts of someone to preserve her relationship because she is pathologically afraid of being alone. Contractarians cannot really evaluate whether and how the *relation* is corrupted, as they do not look at most of the characteristics that make up intimate relations. They qualify them (at best) as special but nonmorally valuable, but do not take them into their account of the moral health of the relation, which is artificially and reductively idealized into a bargain between mutually indifferent strangers. The person who gives "more than her share" to this bargain may reap affective or vicarious benefits that makes her share bigger than one would think, if we look only at one kind of benefit (say, the way that a couple distributes salaries and house chores). Similarly, the person doing less than her share may be incurring some other costs that need compensating.

Such possibilities show that someone who recommends evaluating the moral health of a relationship by calculating costs and benefits should not ignore these other costs and benefits. They should be taken into account because they are real and they are relevant for mutually disinterested agents considering the relation from a selfish distance, as the contractarian test requires. Such weighing is common and may even happen "within the agent" herself and have nothing to do with concrete exchanges between the parties. However, these costs and benefits do not constitute the whole moral picture of a relationship and may fail to account for what is corrupted and "morally unhealthy" in other ways, just as consideration of the relationship on these cost–benefit terms may wrongly classify it as unfair or immoral by failing to perceive the worth of other-regarding, affective, or vicarious benefits.[86]

Contractarians may maintain that we ought to think of persons as fundamentally self-concerned but we may simply disagree with this assumption. However, an argument that contractarians cannot make, which rejects the consideration of

---

[86] I will illustrate how noncontractual elements can be morally significant in the section on noncontractarian evaluative frameworks. See also the last chapter of this book on the value of caring and fiduciary relations.

other-regarding affective benefits, is that vicarious enjoyment or affective benefits should not be taken into account because they are disrespectful, degrading, or undignified (regardless of one's conception of the person) and they are necessarily a sign of exploitation.

6.3.7 Vicarious or Affective Benefits Are Not Necessarily Exploitative

First, let me distinguish between "vicarious" and "affective" costs. In the present context, enjoying a benefit "vicariously" entails that one considers someone else's benefit as one's own. This is different from personally receiving benefits in that someone else gets a distinct benefit. This latter "affective" benefit is the one that Hampton and Dimock focus on.

In the case of a vicarious cost or benefit, a parent considers her child's benefit as her own as a contractual matter, rather than as a metaphysical matter. This means that, when the parent "contracts" with her child, or with other people regarding the child, she puts (at least some of) her child's benefit alongside what *she herself* gains from this bargain. This does not mean that if the child is getting a good education, the parent herself gets a good education.

In the case of affective costs or benefits, not only is the parent's cost/benefit not the same as the child's (like in the case of vicarious benefit) but if it (improbably) became the object of a contractual agreement regarding the child, its weight would not correspond to the weight of the cost/benefit provided to the child. The parent's and child's cost or benefit need not be proportional at all, even though they are causally related. For example, a parent may incur an emotional cost of sadness and anguish because her child is taking drugs, even though the child is very happy herself. Although Hampton and Dimock do not use the notion of vicarious enjoyment/benefits/costs, their position implies that these cannot be counted as a benefit or cost within their "exploitation test" since these costs/benefits essentially involve an other-regarding stance.

It is easy to show that being "paid" in affective or vicarious benefits is not necessarily a form of exploitation, provided we do not begin from the position that such payment is exploitation, as the contractarian conception of the person does. A volunteer social worker who says "my efforts to improve the quality of a person's life are repaid ten times over" is not exploited simply because she does not receive monetary payment for her work. The social worker *could* be exploited – for example, if her client threatened to engage in dangerous or violent behavior toward himself if she didn't help him in a way that is above and beyond what she is able to give. However, in other circumstances, the social worker could take real satisfaction in her client becoming a more accomplished, happier person. On any conception of the person that does not exclude the moral significance of other-regarding relations (*qua* constitutive of one's personal identity or *qua* morally relevant personal commitments), and of other-interested motivations influencing one's assessment of a relationship's costs and benefits, such satisfaction can be a benefit worthy of pursuit.

In sum, the risk of exploitation that results from considering affective or vicarious benefits is not sufficient to justify rejecting such benefits from the contractarian test of a relation's moral health. I should point out that Hampton and Dimock do not explicitly deny this position. They even say that the "influence of affection or duty" is only "*potentially* blinding."[87] However, they do not mitigate their exclusion of this influence, as they already assume that this influence can only be blinding, but never morally enlightening. They say that we should suspend such influence "for purposes of testing the moral health of the relationship"[88] because they assume that a morally informative test of exploitation can only be about whether one party is losing out to the other party. This assumption cannot then be used to prove moral disrespect or disregard for the intrinsic value of the party who is "losing out" – Hampton implies that no affection, duty-related, or vicarious benefits count as a benefit to compensate for this loss.[89]

Hampton and Dimock make strong assumptions. Dimock, in particular, "begin[s] with the assumption that all human beings are utility-maximizers, who, when acting rationally, act in ways they expect will maximize the satisfaction or fulfillment of their preferences (for utility is just a measure of preference)" and therefore that "only those norms that maximize utility would be agreed to."[90] These preferences are subjective, in the sense that "something becomes our end [or preference] just because we care about it" and therefore, nothing precludes "affection, emotion, and attachments" from being the preferences/ends of a particular human being.[91] This seems to support the point I made previously: that, in itself, contractarianism does not preclude putting such relational benefits on the bargaining table. However, Dimock also embraces an "assumption of non-tuism"[92] that is identical to Hampton's assumption of self-interested motivations. This is the assumption that "the utility functions of each person do not make direct reference to the utility function of the others" for the purposes of the contractarian test of justifying the division of costs and benefits within a relationship.[93] This creates a tension in Dimock's position: if we allow these relational (tuistic) benefits to have weight within a contractarian justification, we cannot at the same time disallow other-regarding concern.[94]

---

[87] Hampton, "Feminist Contractarianism," at 21 (emphasis added).
[88] Ibid.
[89] Ibid. 21, 26.
[90] Dimock, "Why All Feminists Should Be Contractarians," at 275.
[91] Ibid. at 280.
[92] Ibid. at 279.
[93] Ibid. at 283. I have found nothing among the "technical reasons" for this assumption that would make it less of an assumption (see Dimock, "Defending Non-Tuism").
[94] Dimock could (although she does not) specify that she is only referring to those benefits that derive from affection and attachment and that are strictly self-regarding, which raises a different

Like Dimock, Hampton assumes that only strictly self-regarding losses and benefits matter morally. Dimock explicitly states that her conception of the person, which includes a conception of the person's (source of) worth, is doing the "moral work" within her view of moral contractual agreements, as said contracts are only a "heuristic device useful for picturing or suggesting this conception [of the person]."[95] She also says that her contract test is not a "morally neutral device" but rather "an image fed by normative ideas that one is ultimately relying on when using the test to make moral evaluations."[96]

It is clear from both these accounts that we should apply a non-tuist contractarian test of exploitation to all relations – including intimate ones – because we endorse the contractarian conception of the person. Therefore, Hampton cannot write, strictly speaking, that she is *arguing* for what she is *assuming*.[97] Given that both she and Dimock spend a considerable part of their articles *illustrating* how people can be exploited within intimate relations, I need to make clear that these illustrations, while otherwise valuable, cannot support the contractarian conception of the person or the necessity of a non-tuist contract test without falling into circularity.

6.3.8 *Nontransferable Costs and Benefits Can Still Be the Object of Distributive Justice*

Another reason that Hampton claims that costs and benefits "that come from the affection or duty holding the parties together in the relationship" fall "outside the province of justice" is that they "cannot be distributed."[98] According to her, it is not practically possible to balance the costs and benefits between parties so that one party does not lose out to the other, and justice be done.[99] Hampton's argument takes the form of an illustration: "[o]ne cannot distribute the pain that a parent feels when her teenage child gets into trouble, the happiness felt by someone because of the accomplishments of her friend, the suffering of a woman because of the illness of a parent."[100]

This is true, but it is insufficient to support her claim. The sense in which she means "distribute" here is limited. It is trite to say that we cannot distribute feelings among the population. Affective or vicarious benefits are typically personal – that is, they cannot be enjoyed by (or transferred to) anyone else in the same way that a task or an object can. Obviously, we cannot bring a deceased person back to life or return

kind of problem that I deal with in the next subsection. (See my analogy with drug addiction, below.)
[95] Hampton, "Feminist Contractarianism," at 24.
[96] Ibid. at 26.
[97] Ibid. at 21.
[98] Ibid.
[99] Ibid.
[100] Ibid.

a person's amputated leg in the same way that we can release her from her mortgage or give her money. In that sense, Hampton is right to say that such affective states cannot be distributed.

However, I disagree that these affective or vicarious benefits cannot be the object of (re)distribution in another sense that would make them an object of justice. Even though the loss or gain *itself* is nontransferable, these are still costs or benefits that can give rise to the distribution of other costs and benefits, if not these very same ones. The idea that justice should allow us to help people who incur unfair personal costs or encourage people who received unfair personal benefits to redistribute them is simple to grasp, and its intuitive appeal is not prima facie affected by the conceptual difference between compensation and reparation. (The employee who loses her leg at work should be properly compensated, even though the "cost" incurred cannot be cancelled out by giving her back her leg.) Indeed, in practice, legal norms generally allow for trading between kinds of gains and losses. Litigants often translate their harms and losses into monetary amounts. More fundamentally, it is a common belief of many liberal theorists of justice that people are not entitled to the advantages conferred on them by their natural talents. Such a belief is also at work within contractarian theories that idealize parties to the social contract as having equal bargaining powers, such as those of Hampton[101] and Rawls.[102] This belief only makes sense if we agree that justice can take factors into consideration that cannot be traded or transferred directly or in kind (e.g., intelligence or strength cannot be (re)distributed).

How do these ordinary intuitions and assumptions about distributive justice apply to Hampton's examples? While, of course, we cannot *transfer* the pain that someone feels for her child's difficulties or her parent's illness, we can compensate for it by offering some social services, such as a publicly funded support group for parents with sick children. A union might negotiate with an employer after a serious workplace accident so that employees have time off to seek psychiatric support and recover emotionally.

The claim that goods that cannot be distributed fall outside the province of justice might be implausible, but the exclusion of affective benefits from the province of justice seems justifiable since affective benefits are not clearly distributable. However, even if we accepted this claim, we could question whether all the costs and benefits that feminist contractarians would consider relevant for their moral assessment are distributable. For example, Hampton says that "one can distribute the burden of caring for an infant or running a household."[103] While any competent babysitter may change a baby's diaper, some other caring tasks may not be so easily – if at all – transferable to a third party, such as telling a child that they are loved.

---

[101] *Ibid.* at 26–27.
[102] Rawls, *A Theory of Justice*, at 87–88.
[103] Hampton, "Feminist Contractarianism," at 21–22.

Children may come to doubt the word of a nanny who continuously tells them that their father loves them very much when their father is almost always absent. This is because the appropriate way to relate to another person within an intimate relationship requires some personal, nontransferable involvement.

Besides, it would be strange if transferable acts of care (such as giving a ride to school or changing diapers) were more central to the moral dimension of childcare than acts of personal, nontransferable involvement (such as expressing affection and love). It also seems odd that Hampton would focus on the *affective* dimension of the costs and benefits since, in itself, there is nothing relevant about the fact that it is affective/emotional that makes a benefit fall beyond the scope of a contract. Indeed, people often contract to obtain various states of emotional satisfaction.

On can fairly infer that Hampton's real issue with these states is that the realm of affective costs and benefits is also where exploitation is bred. She rejects affection-based duties not because they cannot be transferred or distributed *per se*, but because her conception of distributive justice (and her conception of personhood underlying it) already excludes some goods from being taken into consideration when figuring out how costs and benefits ought to be distributed.

6.3.9 The Corruption of Certain Moral Practices When Considering Them as Distributable Goods

Another important criticism (in the same vein as the previous one, but coming from care ethicists rather than from feminist theorists of justice)[104] is that redistributing care serves to dishonor it, because redistribution treats it as a nonmoral good instead of a virtue, as a social good instead of a moral practice, and as an activity that makes a moral claim on us.[105]

It would be a mistake, when considering "dishonoring" care, to treat it as a good to be strategically traded as opposed to a moral practice. Yet, not all distributions of caring activities are incompatible with recognizing care as a moral practice. Of course, people who are asked to perform an act and who will receive payment (or a fine if they fail to comply with that directive) will comply in order to get paid (or avoid the fine). However, that sort of problem can be said to apply to many, if not all, omission- or action-imposing rules, and not particularly to care. In these cases, the general answer is that we do not live in a society of saints; not all people are moral all the time. This is why many rules are framed within a system that comes with self-regarding incentives. However, this is not, in itself, incompatible with the fact that

---

[104] Where justice is understood in the impartial, Jake-like sense of the term – that is, where it is reduced to the morality of relations between strangers of equal power. This is paradigmatically exemplified, in Annette Baier's words, by "minimal moral traffic rules, designed to restrict close encounters between autonomous persons to self-chosen ones" (*Moral Prejudices: Essays on Ethics* [Cambridge: Harvard University Press, 1995], at 116).

[105] See Sample, "Why Feminist Contractarianism?" at 261.

certain rules were initially designed with other-regarding concern in mind, even if they are ultimately performed out of self-regard. The criticism really is that this may *generally* be the case, but that some activities, like caring, constitute an exception.

First, I repeat that, while an action might only be truly moral if it is performed for the right reasons, the reality is that we do not live in a society of systematically moral people. It would be just as wrong for someone to act purely motivated by financial gain, as it would be to avoid committing fraud out of a fear of going to jail, rather than showing respect for one's fellow bargainer, at least within a Hampton-like contractarian account. Granted, this would not be the case on a Dimock-like Hobbesian account. On such an account, the exploiter is not acting immorally if she can exploit someone and there is no risk of punishment if she does. This position does not point to the particularity of care ethics but rather conforms to Hobbesian morality, which happens to adopt self-regarding motivations as grounds for morality, just as legislators and policymakers adopt it as their best strategy to get people to do good things. So, performing our duties to care for others may be done for the wrong reasons, but these "wrong reasons" may then motivate people to carry out many necessary duties, including in their personal relations.

Second, to treat certain caring duties as transferable tasks to be performed for self-regarding motives is not only compatible with caring but may be required by it. A mother who contracts with a cook to provide meals for her family while she works and picks up her sons from kindergarten is enabling herself to be a better caregiver, even though the cook has no caring sentiments toward the family.

This might be seen to dodge the question: what about those activities that must be performed personally? What if the cook actually feeds the baby? What if there is a specialized nurse who cleans and feeds a severely disabled child who is too heavy for the mother to lift? Putting a price on these services, while running a *risk* of commodifying them to some extent, may not necessarily do so conceptually or statistically. Care work is generally underpaid and not socially prestigious and may attract people who do it for the "right reasons" so that the money they earn is not a primary incentive, but rather a way to enable them to do this work.

Not everyone is cut out to be a careworker, but those who find it rewarding may well see it as a vocation instead of a job. I have found this to be the case in my personal experience, particularly when talking to people who work at L'Arche – an organization that creates homes and provides support services for the disabled – about their relationships with the people they are paid to care for. For example, one employee insisted that he worked there because he just needed the job, yet he appeared to display genuine fondness, kindness, caring, and friendship toward people with cognitive disabilities. These kinds of interactions are underlaid by the sort of motivations that have nothing to do with pay, at least when a person is performing the caring task. This careworker insisted that he tried to maintain boundaries between himself and the people he cared for because he wanted to limit the pain a "cared-for" person would feel when he would be transferred to a different foyer. However, I interpreted this interest in boundaries (given the reality that L'Arche is a community but not, strictly speaking, a family) as an indication of his other-regarding concern more than anything else.

6.3.10 Summing Up the Argument So Far

Thus far, I have questioned Hampton and Dimock's rejection of non-directly transferable affective benefits, other-regarding benefits, and vicarious benefits from within the contractarian evaluative framework measuring whether each party to a relationship is made better off (1) in terms of costs and benefits and (2) from a non-tuist perspective.

In order to make this argument, I have dissociated positions (1) and (2) and underlined that (1) need not be understood in non-tuist terms. That is, a contractor may still be made subjectively better off by an agreement for other-regarding reasons, such as agreeing to the "terms" of a relationship in order to gain benefits based on their affection for the other party. However, it seems hard to account for the "moral acceptability" and "praise-worthiness" of a parent–child relationship using the feminist contractarian test. Hampton and Dimock want to discard this possibility, on the grounds that it does not tell us much about the fairness (and morality) of a relationship. They make this claim due to their assumptions about morality and fairness, which include determining what a person is owed, which in turn depends on their conceptions of the person and human worth.[106] Yet these assumptions are not supported by the contractual logic of calculating costs and benefits from a subjective point of view. In other words, position (2) is not supported by (1).

Hampton seems to suggest that (2) is really at the heart of her moral theory and that "contract talk [is] only a heuristic device useful for picturing or suggesting this conception."[107] She also says that "there is not enough in the notion of a contract to constitute an adequate moral reasoning procedure in and of itself."[108] While I have no doubt that (2) is at the heart of her theory, I question the suggestion that (1) points to, suggests or pictures position (2), if by this claim she infers a causal link that works from (1) to (2) rather than from (2) to (1). While a non-tuist perspective can easily take a contractual form, it is simply not the case that a contractual bargain needs to take a non-tuist form. This allows us to conclude that the non-tuist assumption is, by Hampton and Dimock's own admission,[109] only an *assumption* justified by their conception of the person. By this reasoning, nothing prevents us from considering whether alternative conceptions of the person could be more appealing.

---

[106] Hampton, "Feminist Contractarianism," at 21–22.
[107] Ibid. at 24.
[108] Ibid. at 25.
[109] Ibid. at 21, Dimock, "Why All Feminists Should Be Contractarians," at 279.

However, Hampton is right to highlight that a view of morality as a contractual bargain fits comfortably with her conception of the person – that is, as the sort of entity that cannot be instrumentalized like a tool, but rather as one who must give their *consent*.[110] The very fact of thinking in terms of contractually acceptable costs and benefits limits the ways in which one can conceptualize and explain one's moral obligations. Hampton and Dimock do not mind (and indeed, seek support from) these limitations, since their own moral position lies within them. I now turn to (1) – this contractual logic of costs and benefits – which is secondary to Hampton's moral position, but still central to its imagery, and which limits the sort of other-regarding concern that we may take into account when evaluating the morality or fairness of a relation.

6.4 PROBLEMATIZING CONTRACTARIAN ASSESSMENTS OF COSTS AND BENEFITS

6.4.1 *Only a Matter of Costs and Benefits?*

It seems surprising to argue that moral obligations within relationships should necessarily aim to secure certain costs and benefits. Especially in the case of an intimate relation, we would expect that only some aspects of the relation entail a regard for costs and benefits. In this section, I do not seek to challenge consequentialism (or moral egoism) in general. Rather, my starting point is narrower and more concrete: that the moral health of a relation does not depend exclusively on a balance of costs and benefits.

My issue with Hampton's argument is not only that benefits based on affection or relational duties could, in theory, enter into the calculation of self-interested, autonomous, and reasonable agents considering "what's in it for them." I also think she mischaracterizes the position(s) that she attacks by presenting a moral evaluative framework based on *other-regarding costs and benefits* as the only alternative to a moral evaluative framework based on *self-regarding costs and benefits*. In comparison, I want to argue that the affection- and duty-based costs and benefits that she refers to are unlikely to be used to calculate costs and benefits at all. Plausible theories that use them will instead develop moral evaluative frameworks that do not (at least not primarily)[111] engage in such consequentialist calculi.

I noted that Hampton explicitly excludes the costs and benefits that come from duty or affection. There is a potential conceptual confusion here. While it is easy to see how a positive emotion could be a benefit one could self-interestedly pursue, it

---

[110] Hampton, "Feminist Contractarianism," at 26.
[111] By this, I mean that the intrinsic value, or ultimate reason for acting, will not be found in the consequences of an action, even though moral agents might, in some cases, take the consequences of their actions into account.

may be impossible to apply the "cost–benefit" contractarian evaluative framework to some duties. People who perform certain actions out of *duty* toward an individual or a relationship, or as a way to virtuously occupy the role they have within a relationship, may well have no regard for consequential costs and benefits. To reject the (duty- and virtue-based) moral considerations of these people on the grounds that these considerations do not translate well into costs and benefits (or into the sort of costs and benefits that contractarianism deem morally relevant) assumes that the contractarian framework is the only valid one to apply.

In the same way, the self-regarding contractarian framework has been assumed rather than proven when Hampton considers that partial *affection* would only motivate someone out of affective benefits (such as feeling good or bad when someone we love is doing well or poorly). Such a motivational explanation will seem bizarre to anyone who is involved in partial relations. What Hampton calls affective benefits are not benefits at all. They are emotional/affective symptoms. A person is happy or sad because of their child's success or their parent's sickness, but how they relate to their child and parent is not motivated by – and ought not to attempt to maximize – their personal emotional states. I suggest that it is more plausible that these people are motivated by concern for their child or their parent, and the normative relational framework in which they stand with each of them will guide how this concern materializes. Indeed, it is natural for us to think of someone as a bad caregiver if their action is ultimately aimed at their own (rather than the cared-for's) happiness. To say that parents feed their teenagers or that a devoted boyfriend repairs his partner's furniture only because their loved ones' happiness makes *them* happy is akin to characterizing the parents and boyfriend as drug addicts pursuing an (affective) thrill. For example, a mother who does not want her son to leave home because she wants to continue to enjoy the affective thrill of having him close to her may prevent him from attending a better university out of town, thus jeopardizing his education and future. She would fit the model of the affective drug addict, which clashes with the image of what we think a good parent ought to do.

Of course, this explanation is incompatible with the non-tuist assumption. The value of the relationship (and/or of the parent or child to whom the moral agent relates) cannot be articulated within the feminist contractarian account, which then pushes this value outside of the realm of morality and claims it to have, at best, a "special" "nonmoral value."[112] However, if we take the particular nature of the relationship that parents have with their children out of the moral picture and ask parents to account for the morality and fairness of their nurturing relations in terms of cost and benefits, many would be at a loss. The stripped moral account that remains will be, at best, a marginal explanation of whatever moral dimension the intimate relation has. The same applies to a relationship with this person's siblings, parents, lovers, friends, and partners. This is the case, even though partnership

---

[112] Hampton, "Feminist Contractarianism," at 38.

relations – in which people are typically more able to reciprocate – leave more room for discussion of contractual dealings. But it is difficult to see how these dealings would constitute the core, including the *moral* core, of the relation.

My two disagreements with a feminist contractarian approach to value and the way it compels moral agents to act are that (1) people *can* morally agree to the terms of a relation even if they are not trying to maximize the satisfaction of their own preferences or their benefits because the value of other beings calls for it and (2) that the way in which they *must* relate to other entities is not necessarily (or primarily) dependent on maximizing any benefits or minimizing any costs.

Point (1) has to do with the idea that our actions can, and sometimes should, be driven by a concern for others. This is why Dimock's attempt to save contractarianism from the traditional feminist attack (according to which "contractarians render all relations and actions as of merely instrumental value"[113]) by saying that people can still value the object of their own subjective preferences "intrinsically and not merely instrumentally"[114] does not address the heart of the criticism. Dimock's approach would still not be the proper way to relate to the entity in question, because our concern for the other party would ultimately be nested in concern for ourselves and for our own preferences.

Point (2) is that there are many ways to relate to an entity, and many would say that maximizing a beneficial state of affairs is not always the most fitting approach – morally speaking – especially when they take into account the complex moral reality of intimate relations.

In case we assume that both (1) and (2) claim that the proper way to relate to others is not necessarily by conducting a cost/benefit analysis, let me make clear that (1) prescribes certain proper motivations and reasons, whereas (2) prescribes the kinds of attitudes that we should hold toward certain entities – that is, it denotes the mode of valuing rather than reasons for valuing.

Elizabeth Anderson and Thomas Scanlon[115] have argued that the ways to appropriately relate to valuable things go beyond maximizing attitudes or actions. Consider the case of art (which we will assume has value for the purposes of this argument). Relating to art by making more of it, or by being a patron of the arts, certainly do not constitute the whole picture of how we can and should relate to it. In fact, the best way to relate to art is probably by engaging with it personally. This engagement or kind of "relation" with a painting cannot be understood in terms of "maximizing" the art itself; we cannot "maximize" a painting like we can maximize revenues. Maybe we could say that we are maximizing a state of affairs, namely the relation/engagement we have with this painting. However, when we say that we

---

[113] Dimock, "Why All Feminists Should Be Contractarians," at 280.
[114] *Ibid.* at 281.
[115] Anderson, *Value in Ethics and Economics*, at ch. 1; Thomas Scanlon, *What We Owe to Each Other* (Cambridge: Harvard University Press, 1998), at ch. 2.

want to "maximize" certain non-maximizing behaviors because they are what really matters, this sounds too convoluted a formulation to constitute a substantial, rather than semantic, difference.

The same that holds for art, leisure, and scientific inquiry also holds for human beings. Here, I assume that, in order to relate properly to different entities, we must take into account their nature, the sort of value, and utility they possess, the kind of entity they are, their potential, and so on. What they are includes their internal and relational characteristics. Human beings, like paintings, have their own particularities. Art cannot flourish, at least not in the special way that humans, animals, and other living entities can. Could it be said that we want to maximize states of affairs in which human lives better flourish – that is, maximizing their opportunities to partake of goods that will improve their lives?

I concede that we must sometimes consider the states of affairs that our actions may bring about in order to intelligently carry out our obligations that are grounded outside of these states *per se*. Consider the case of a friend. One thing that pieces of art and friends have in common is that they are unique entities, and their uniqueness matters. Someone who has never contemplated a painting but who signs large checks to buy paintings cannot be said to relate to art in the fullest way. Similarly, a person who encourages the value of friendship by, say, creating a "friends center" whereby people looking for friends can meet, treats friendship abstractly and anonymously.[116] She is not relating properly to the uniqueness that characterizes friends, and she is not befriending someone herself. Again, while these particularized obligations can be restated in "maximizing" terms, this matters little, for (1) the importance of the maximization of a friend's happiness is nested in the importance of the friend; and (2) some of the obligations we have toward our friends are not best understood (or maybe even comprehensible) in terms of maximizing some states of affairs. For instance, spending quality time with friends and empathizing with them when they experience hardship are considered to be integral parts of a good friendship. Supposing that this is correct, we might restate this conclusion as an *a posteriori*, consequentialist and detached observation of how something good was maximized, by claiming that we are "maximizing" our quantity of empathetic moments or moments of friendly socialization. However, this conclusion, while not incoherent, clashes with the way the good friend thinks of her own motivations and her moral duties toward her friend.

The primary moral guidance comes from (a) some theory of flourishing/goods (i.e., what the being we are concerned for needs in order to flourish) and (b) some relational normative framework that explains who owes what to whom. It is of no great substantial moral significance that moral agents formulate their courses of action in terms of maximizing costs and benefits for their friends. Such reasoning is

---

[116] This example is from Scanlon, *What We Owe*, at 88–89.

not, however, senseless; it just does not reflect the primary moral and motivational drivers that support friendship.

Therefore, there are costs and benefits within intimate relations, but they are not the emotional symptoms that Hampton suggests (such as the person's displeasure at hearing about her parent's sickness). Within relations that fittingly include other-regarding concern, and other-interested attitudes and behaviors, the costs and benefits may well be the happiness or unhappiness (flourishing or non-flourishing) of the people with whom we are in a relationship. However, these costs and benefits are very different from those within the contractarian account. Although benefits are pursued in these relations, they are not what intrinsically matters. That is, they are not what fundamentally drives agents or explains the morality of their drive, attitudes, or actions. This is contrary to what contractarianism suggests in looking at the beneficial consequences produced.

Now, contractarian logic still applies when the other-regarding partner to a relationship is negotiating with parties *outside* of this relation (like a parent buying bread from a third party to feed her teenage son). When she negotiates with the baker, she thinks of the "benefit" as her son's flourishing. The idea is that, even though we could describe her action of buying bread as the action of a trustee or an act of care for her son, the fact that she is wearing the "hat" of caregiver is only in the background of her mind while she occupies the contractual role of a bread-buyer and dealing with a bread-seller. In other words, the fact that she represents the interests of a third party (her son) does not really occur to her. Between herself and the baker, the benefit to her is the bread (which represents her son's benefit, if we assume, for example, that she cannot eat bread) and the benefit to the baker is the money that changes hands. In a trite sense, under the terms of this bread-selling agreement, the evident, contractual benefit belongs to the parent. However, this alone is not enough to conclude that the vicarious benefit is hers in a stronger sense (or sufficiently strong to count it as hers if we apply a looser version of the contractarian test that would relinquish the non-tuistic criterion). This then raises the question of whether vicarious benefits are possible. I will offer the beginning of a positive answer to that question below.

6.4.2 Are Vicarious "Benefits" Necessarily False or Exploitative "Benefits"?

According to a contractarian account, if an exploited party (such as the devoted husband) can count as his *own* benefit the fact that the other parties benefit from the contract, then he is no longer exploited. Hampton and Dimock point out that the devoted husband would endorse the benefit enjoyed by the other party not because the benefit has actually become his own, but because of his preference to satisfy the preferences of others – sometimes over his own – on the basis of affection or relational duty. They claim that the reasons for his endorsement of the benefit are not morally relevant – in fact, they are potentially blinding emotions – and further that, in practice, it is these emotions that are traded in exchange for services.

However, I disagree; I think they ought to say that these emotions are what *allows* the devoted husband to count as his own the benefits that accrue to his loved ones. Nevertheless, Hampton and Dimock insist that this is an emotionally exploitative trade. They want the parties to the relation to see this by stepping outside of their own emotions and looking at the relation from a detached (i.e., one's self-abnegation-inducing emotions) and self-interested point of view. I have already conceded that this strategy of adopting a counterfactually, strictly self-concerned outlook on one's relation is potentially informative, but that this perspective does not require us to subtract the sorts of vicarious benefits that Hampton and Dimock would like to preclude. To say that parties can legitimately care about themselves is insufficient, as such caring is not *incompatible* with caring about others and vicariously enjoying the successes and happiness of their loved ones.

The existence of vicarious benefits or happiness is too common to deny, but are these phenomena moral? They are as morally justified as the affection or relational duties that make them possible. In other words, they can spring from a healthy normative relational framework, from a corrupted one, from a fitting affective response, or from harmful emotional manipulation. It seems evident that to deny that someone can benefit vicariously from other people's happiness – and that others' happiness may genuinely increase their own – is misguided. However, it seems just as evident that there is such a thing as excessive self-abnegation (especially, historically speaking, in the case of women) and this, at least in some of its manifestations, is undesirable. What is more contentious is where to draw the line between normal and extreme self-abnegation.

Here, I only seek to point out that vicarious benefits are at least *sometimes* part of a morally healthy relationship (to use Hampton's terms), and I take the view that every relation has its own rules about how much other-regardingness and vicarious endorsing of another's benefits is appropriate. However, I should distinguish criticisms of typically false or corrupted vicarious benefits from more subtle criticisms, which may not be aimed so much at individual exploitation, but at a substantive view about what is worth investing oneself in.

First, consider the case of the self-abnegating woman who feels conflicted about her role as a wife and mother and who is remorseful – at once for not having been something else in her life other than a wife and a mother, for having given up career paths and projects, and because she does not, as a good wife and mother should, embrace her role of ensuring the happiness of others. This is an example where a certain role has been imposed upon a woman (by society, by her loved ones and perhaps by her own conscience) and she is socially required to grant that role a greater weight than one may think she should.

Contrast this with the case of the woman who has internalized and embraced her familial role, and is truly happy for her husband and son's happiness. In this second scenario, the person sacrifices and invests herself willingly and is a fuller, happier person for it. In the former example, she is socially expected to embrace her role, and there are pressures for her to perform it in certain ways. Even if these pressures are internalized, they do not correspond to vicarious, affection-related or relational duty-related happiness. The woman is unhappy (although, it may be part of her role to lie about her degree of happiness and the causes for it).

We can imagine other criticisms of this second scenario, such as a critical view of the values that are imposed by society, or of the presuppositions of an objective hierarchy of values, according to which the mother misses out, even though she is unaware of this and nevertheless feels fulfilled. We can argue by counterfactuals that the mother would be happier if she had had a different life altogether and had been taught different values.

I will not further explore these potential arguments here. For one thing, they are not as critically important for the questions on which I would like to focus. These questions are: have these hypothetical women truly chosen this role? Have they been put in charge of balancing the roles in their lives? And have they fully consented to the associated sacrifices, if sacrifices were made? Has this role really enriched their lives, or have they merely told themselves that this was the case? Have they preserved their integrity as they, in good faith, construct it and perceive it to be? These questions – linked to contractarian *consent* (following Hampton's test) – are more likely to do good in the short term for people suffering from relational exploitation than the greater metaphysical question of whether this consent is truly theirs or is truly in their best interests.

6.5 NONCONTRACTARIAN FRAMEWORKS

As previously discussed, I believe that the (kinds of) duties that moral agents have toward various entities depend on the nature of their relationship with these entities and their role within these relationships. This is why I have noted that contractarian feminists, like many moral theorists, tend to explain moral obligations, their stringency, and who owes them to whom, in terms of a single relation. This relation is the sort of mutually disinterested contractual relation that would most likely happen between two strangers in a social context that provides them with a level of comfort, safety, and equality to bargain. While I believe that the normative framework of a contractarian relation is useful, I doubt that it allows us to understand the most fundamental sort of relations that take place between the members of an ethical community, and even less so to understand intimate relations. As providing a satisfactory account of all the relations Hampton and Dimock are referring to would require me to replace their one-size-fits-all contractarian framework with many complex relational frameworks, I will only do a deep analysis of some aspects of the relational frameworks that I think best apply to, and make sense of, the moral obligations we have toward PSID. Therefore, in this section, I offer only a few examples and make a prima facie case that their moral complexity cannot be grasped from a strictly contractarian point of view.

Hampton and Dimock could fairly respond to my criticism by saying that they do not doubt that their contractarian account imposes a fictional, idealized, reductivist evaluative framework upon a complex reality, but that their account is only concerned with the *moral* aspect of this reality, not its remaining complexity, which is best left to psychologists. I concede that I cannot assert that many noncontractarian aspects of these relations are moral, no more than Hampton and Dimock may assert that all contractarian aspects are moral. Like Hampton, I must leave it to the reader to decide whether the contractarian framework suffices to explain (1) what is moral in these relations and (2) if these relations are corrupted or immoral, whether this can be entirely and satisfactorily explained in terms of exploitation (as understood by contractarians). My suggestion is that some morally relevant, relational, and other-regarding elements are being left out of a contractarian picture.

Let me return to two of my previous examples. In the case of the devoted husband, the relation was exploitative and therefore, immoral according to a contractarian account. This conclusion would not be changed if his wife's love for him was such that she would sacrifice her life to save his. This added context would not allow contractarians to translate the devoted husband's story into a contractarian framework, to evaluate whether there was exploitation, and to weigh the two decades of servanthood in exchange of twenty more years of life. These are not the sorts of obligations that could be negotiated within a contractarian framework. Self-imposed servanthood and giving one's own life are not things that contractarians could fathom putting on the negotiation table. These are not the sort of gifts, commitments, or duties that can be traded within, say, the normative framework of loving relationships (at least not in the contractarian sense of "trade").

It remains to say that, to most of us, sacrificing oneself to save others is admirable, and admirable in at least some *moral* way. While contractarians require the parties to a relation to ask "what's in it for me?" to test the morality of the relation, many other relational evaluative frameworks consider that this question drains the action of its moral value. (Consider relations that seem to conceptually require self-effacement or sacrifice, like parenthood.) Sacrifices do not fit the contractarian vocabulary and Hampton-like conceptions of the person. Good Samaritans are, at best, not immoral (they can be moral, but not *because* of their good deeds). The contractarian feminists' counterintuitive conclusion is that persons such as Mother Theresa or Jesus, or figures such as good parents, are not moral.[117] Their relationships these figures have with the people they care about are neither fair nor moral, because they are not profitable.

This illustration of the devoted husband may seem unhelpful, as the relation he has with his wife would probably not be deemed moral by any noncontractarian

---

[117] Hampton, "Feminist Contractarianism," at 37.

relational framework. However, I suggest that one may better detect what has gone awry in the relationship by using these frameworks and by referring to theories on love and friendship (for example) rather than by stepping outside of one's personal emotions, attachment, and relations and looking at each other *qua* strangers. We are not dealing here with a relationship between strangers; the woman is not treating her husband badly *qua* bargainer but is treating him poorly *qua* wife. For example, we usually think that household tasks must be shared according to everyone's capacities (rather than equally). A contractarian account could not explain the ways in which the relationship has been corrupted, other than by identifying exploitation. The devoted husband could be corrupting the relationship by infantilizing his wife in a way that is degrading for her, and by taking his revenge on her through small cruelties. But a contractarian account could not explain that the husband facilitates his wife's lack of certain virtues, for it is not committed to such virtues. Nor could it satisfactorily explain the immorality of cruelty (even as a cost for the wife, since these small cruelties are what allows the husband to endure the relationship), because this cruelty can only be understood as happening between beings who are mutually interested.

Contractarian feminists could also not understand how a relationship could become exploitative through taking advantage of another person's virtue, except by re-characterizing the virtue in question as some sort of disability or vulnerability, which is a distortion of the facts. One way of exploiting people is by taking advantage of their weaknesses or vulnerabilities, but another is to take advantage of their good nature, and contractarians do not have an account of good nature that stands independently of the results of a contract. This suggests that Hampton and Dimock trade on a very narrow idea of what counts as exploitation. It may be necessary to better understand the goodness or virtues of good people to fully understand and address their exploitation.

6.5.1 *What Do Contractarian Saints Look Like?*

Let me return to Agota Kristof's *The Notebook*. The "caring relationship" that takes place between the grandmother and the twins seems morally unhealthy, since the grandmother forces her grandsons work while mistreating them, sometimes out of sheer cruelty. This cruelty is all the more obvious when contrasted with the way she treats a girl she is hosting. She is distant to the girl, yet apparently respectful, and feeds her adequately. She may not love or care for her as she cares for the twins, but the contractarian thinks little of her relationship with the twins anyway. Surely, it is better for the girl that the grandmother does not relate to her affectively, in the same way as she relates to the twins? Agota Kristof makes us doubt it through the following story.

An old man brings a teenage girl whose life is in danger to the grandmother's house and asks the grandmother to take her in and pass her off as her own granddaughter. The man's connection to the elderly woman remains undisclosed, but it seems clear that she owes him nothing. The man begs her to have pity on the girl, and when that does not seem to convince the grandmother, he adds, "here is all the money and jewels that her parents possess. Everything is yours if you save her." Such are the terms of this contract-like deal. We see that begging for compassion, pity, and shared trust (mostly) failed. In the end, a monetary payment made sure the grandmother was not "exploited" by emotion. What the girl is unaware of is that the grandmother thinks of her – as good Hobbesian contractarians do – in purely instrumental terms.

Later in the tale, the grandmother is afraid that the jewels will be taken from her after the war. The girl's parents are dead (and, at this point, so is the old man), and the grandmother is certain the girl will reclaim the jewels. The grandmother cannot let that happen; she plans to poison the girl, muttering her plans to herself, while the twins listen from the attic. Of course, resorting to murder to secure one's gain is not part of any morally healthy relationship from any moral point of view, contractarian included. But in this imagined Eastern European country ravaged by war, where the rule of law is uncertain, *not* killing someone to prevent theft is not something that mutually indifferent strangers owe to one another, at least not on a Hobbesian account.[118] These circumstances dramatically situate the question: do we only want to think of fairness and morality of relations in terms of what self-interested strangers would opt for, thereby deliberately suspending any other-regarding concern?

On the other hand, the twins are asked by the old man – a stranger to them – to watch over the girl (also a stranger) and to call her "cousin." The chapter ends with the old man telling them that he trusts them. The twins take on this responsibility without seeking payment of any kind. They give the spot where they sleep to the girl and move to the attic. They spy on their grandmother, learn about her plans, and write to the village priest to let him know. They tell the grandmother that nothing is to happen to them or to their "cousin" because they have promised the old man to watch over their "cousin."

What I make of this story is that the twins take better care of their adopted cousin than their grandmother, even though this relationship is not mutually beneficial. A third party has paid the grandmother to make her relationship with the girl mutually beneficial, but the self-interested logic of this dealing opens the door to the possibility of instrumentalizing others, on the basis that this might better secure one's own welfare. Indeed, the grandmother adopts Hobbesian logic by seeking to murder the girl. She has no guarantee that the "contract" will be enforced, and therefore it is acceptable to do whatever she can to progress her own interests and not to renounce her right to anything, including to the jewels and to killing. Of course, the grandmother's relationship with the girl is not tainted by abuse, unlike

---

[118] Which echoes Hobbes's assumption that morality cannot exist in a state of nature.

her relationship with the twins; she does not hit, insult, or enslave her. But, when all is said and done, the grandmother's only hint of goodness will be expressed toward the twins, and the fact that she did not exploit the girl did not result in goodness, for she was about to murder her. By contrast, the twins' relation to the girl – based purely on a promise, on trust, and on fellow-feelings – amounts to successful caring.

Obviously, most of us would prefer to be cared for by the twins than by the grandmother. Most of us would think that a relation of protection or care is morally exemplified by the twins, regardless of the fact that it is not mutually beneficial. We would also consider that the grandmother's caring relation to the twins is more moral than her caring relation to the girl, even though the grandmother exploits (in a contractarian's sense) the twins but not the girl.

Hampton may fall back on her Good Samaritan exception to explain why the twins are not being exploited (and I agree) but she cannot explain why they are moral. Indeed, on her account, their unilateral commitment to the girl is not moral.[119] Hampton is aware that "we commend the caregivers precisely because they unselfishly provide care for the needy person, without thinking of any benefits for themselves," but this unselfish care is not something that contractarian feminists *morally* value.[120]

I want to highlight the difficulty with Hampton's idea that the Good Samaritan's services are only commendable because the benefitted party has not "tak[en] advantage of the benefactor's affection for or feeling of duty toward him."[121] Good Samaritans (or, on my more general account, moral agents) are *always* moved by their other-regarding concern. Hampton makes the important concession that, in some cases, other-regarding motivations leading to nonmutually beneficial deals will not correlate to exploitation. How is she to distinguish cases where other-regarding concern implies a violation of the benefactor's dignity from the cases where it does not? Her Kantian commitments simply require that the benefactor's self-interested moral standpoint not be tainted by other-regarding, self-effacing motivations. But that would exclude *all* Good Samaritan cases. Thus, her Good Samaritan exception seems to contradict her main holdings. Her response justifying this exception would

---

[119] It is not *immoral* but it cannot be a morally commended relation on her contractarian test. One may object that the Kantian elements in Hampton's thought would prompt her to say that the twins are acting morally by protecting the girl's intrinsic worth. However, Hampton's account is not a Kantian one. She would insist that one must be the protector of one's own intrinsic worth first. In fact, she would insist that one embarks upon self-benefitting deals and never forgets to put oneself first. According to her, it is *in this way* that one respects one's own intrinsic worth. In turn, Kant's account of what constitutes a moral action is not identical to Hampton's contractarian test.

[120] Hampton, "Feminist Contractarianism," at 33. It is "commendable" but not in a moral sense. I will note difficulties with Hampton's notion of nonmoral values in the penultimate section of this chapter.

[121] Ibid. at 33–34.

probably be (to take a concrete example) that the twins clearly are not being exploited. Thanks to their wit, they have the power to get whatever they want (and, indeed, they get away with murder). They exemplify an ideal moral agent, applying Hampton's reasoning, for they put themselves first at all times and will not flinch at using their father's death to escape, and neither will they instrumentalize their father to achieve their escape. Rather, they make sure he has fully consented to taking a risk, from which they (secretly) know they will benefit. They are, like Hampton's theory, at once Kantian and Hobbesian, for they also threaten everyone with murder but respect their dignity in doing so (at least from a contractarian feminist perspective). They protect at least four vulnerable individuals, and yet let them choose their death without mourning them. They offer vital care to their "cousin" but also make it clear that she will die if she enters their secret attic, and they make sure that – given her intelligence and their respect for her – she understands how serious this threat is. They both have a sense of the Kantian (consent- or autonomy-based) noninstrumental value that human beings have, and a Hobbesian sense of the way in which dealings operate. They always put themselves first, as contractarian feminists say moral agents should, thus recognizing their own worth. It is impossible to assert, relying on a contractarian or any other account, that the twins are exploited by their "cousin."

Hampton's exception requires that the "benefitted" does not take advantage of the "benefactor's affection for or feeling of duty toward"[122] those who are benefitted. The twins are not affectionate, but they do act out of duty. However, this duty is not personally attached to the "cousin" in that they do not feel dutifully bound to this girl. Rather, they are young men who keep their promise, in a way best understood within a deontological framework. The nuance is important, for it means their actions do not rest upon their other-regarding concern for the girl, and allows Hampton's Good Samaritan exception to be understood as not being an exception after all, and not contradicting her main holdings. By the same token, we come to see that her *moral* Good Samaritans are very peculiar Good Samaritans indeed, to the point that they are atypical, and that she would reject the morality of Good Samaritans' actions when these benefactors abandon their self-interested, self-concerned standpoint. It is misleading of her to talk about Mother Theresa (or of any saint-like figure) as not being exploited due to feelings of (other-regarding) duties outweighing self-concern or interest. The feminist contractarian saint-like (and Good Samaritan) figures are the twins. Any evaluation of the credibility of feminist contractarianism should consider how monstrous or admirable the twins are, rather than Mother Theresa or Jesus.

In any case, rather than acting morally by saving their cousin, they just do not act immorally. Good Samaritan cases are no different from situations of radical natural inequality (say, between a moral agent and a severely cognitively limited individual).

[122] *Ibid.* at 34.

They both fall outside morality and justice. Contractarians might say that morality would be possible if the situation were different – for example, if the "cousin" could pay the twins – but that, as things stand, we cannot expect anything from them *morally*.[123]

Many would rather think that we remain morally accountable because of another sort of relation in which we stand with fellow human beings, which *morally* constrains what we can do to others. Paraphrasing Michael Walzer, even where contractarian agreements cannot be established, social limitations or limitations on parties' capacities make it possible to be more or less humane and to pursue our own private preferences with more or less restraint. "We must try to understand how this can be so."[124] It is clear from the novel that the grandmother's only "moral" behavior lay in her attitudes toward her grandchildren, no matter how terribly she treated them. Asking her to put herself in the shoes of an indifferent stranger would have been much worse. In the case of the "cousin," it would have meant her death. In a context in which resources are so limited and the social context so precarious, we cannot afford to ignore what relational *moral* obligations, other than those incurred by a self-interested bargainer, could save the cousin's life.

While the importance of recognizing that relational evaluative frameworks may successfully supplant the contractarian one is clear in such dramatic cases, it is also revealed when we consider how impoverished our views of relations would be in more ordinary cases. For instance, one might be ambivalent about (apparently) psychologically healthy couples who treat each other like tactful and respectful strangers. They may succeed in treating their partners with the kindness, patience, and concern that people sometimes offer to strangers, but fail to display in their treatment of their loved ones. They may fail to properly fulfill the roles that their relationship requires of them. It may be emotionally easier for someone to choose the quiet, controlled, self-respect of a love modeled after relations between strangers, but this may simply not constitute love. The ambivalence one feels when contemplating parents or couples who politely but firmly put their own personal needs first comes from the intuition that they are failing to seize and partake of the important values of human life. Some would argue that we ought to make ourselves vulnerable to others (a much less pejorative word than "prey"), or at least that to do so does not render a relationship immoral. Some would say that, because vulnerability is ineliminable from the notion of love,[125] this makes love essentially immoral. Imagine that, because of fear of being exploited, the devoted husband refused to

---

[123] The twins' generosity, however, can be seen as exemplarily ethical, which is what truly makes them "saints" in Hampton's judgment. However, in Dimock's account, they stand closer to being exploited, which makes them less than ideal moral agents.

[124] "Even in hell, it is possible to be more or less humane, to fight with more or less restraint. We must try to understand how this can be so" (Michael Walzer, *Just and Unjust Wars: A Moral Argument with Historical Illustrations* [New York: Basic Books, 1977], at 33).

[125] See, e.g., J. David Velleman, "Love as a Moral Emotion" (1999) 109:2 Ethics 338.

get married. Maybe he would have missed out on many great moments in his life, like his relationship with his children, his romance with his wife until she became sick, and the admiration of relatives who praise the husband's patience and caring.

In these sorts of cases, Janice Richardson, siding with Hampton, points out that: "[Hampton's] test illustrates that exploitation is occurring but that the woman does not feel that there are any alternatives, at that time, because of social and economic structures."[126] As I said, this is only the case if a woman feels that she is expected to have a family life but does not genuinely count this benefit as her own.

Consider a final example: Jacques Brel's song "Ne me quitte pas" (Don't Leave Me). The poet implores a woman not to leave him, repeating "don't leave me" along with hopeful promises, which sound like bargaining offers. The poet says:

> I will offer you pearls of rain, coming from countries where it doesn't rain. I will dig the dirt until after my death to cover your body of gold and dust.... I will invent senseless words for you ... Let me become the shadow of your shadow, the shadow of your hand, the shadow of your dog.[127]

The poet's offer is a metaphorical surrendering of his entire self. He expresses and promises commitment and adoration. The woman will be the queen of his (kingdom of) love. Elsewhere in the song, he says that scorched earth has given wheat, and old volcanoes have ruptured again. These create metaphors for their potentially blooming love. What he puts on the table is hardly a "benefit" in the traditional contractarian sense. No time and money are put on the table, although their presence may be indirectly implied.

As in the case of the devoted husband, to translate this offer of love into concrete objects would mischaracterize the nature of what is actually at the negotiating table. While concrete objects of value may be reasonably enjoyed by anyone projecting herself in a relationship, the value of love *qua* benefit must be understood personally and relationally. It depends on the respective identity (in particular, the needs and affective makeup) of the parties and to the relationship itself. It becomes obvious that we cannot understand the poet to be offering objects in a nonpersonal sense – that is, in a way that could be weighed by mutually disinterested agents – for the real offer is the symbolism of love that is inherent to the indirect offer of concrete gifts. The proof of this is that while a detached outsider would value these goods, the loved one would reject them. The last thing she wants is to accept (or rather respond to, by accepting) his love, for which these objects stand.

In sum, a contractarian account fails to give moral weight to what is centrally being given in this example (love) and, if they translated this love into non-affective, concrete benefits, they would fail to explain why it would be wrong for the wife to

---

[126] Richardson, "On Not Making Ourselves the Prey of Others," at 52.
[127] Jacques Brel, *Ne me quitte pas* (Philips Records, 1959) (translation by author).

accept these benefits.[128] They would, however, correctly deem the relationship to be morally unhealthy if the woman did accept the concrete gifts without reciprocating in some way. But they would, I suggest, not take this position for the right reason. They would not be able to explain why the relation is truly morally unhealthy, because this immorality *is not based on exploitation, but on the corruption of key relational aspects of the personal relation of love* (which contractarians do not consider to be morally relevant). Indeed, contractarians only hypothesize that there is exploitation by ignoring certain kinds of benefits. The poet is willing to give his lover everything he has and more and asks for nothing in return, except to let him stand in her dog's shadow and to stare at her. However, the benefit for him is huge, and being in a relationship with her is worth more than all he can offer, in his eyes at least.

The contractarian does not get into the twisted logic of this debased romanticism and looks at it from the point of view of strangers bargaining for their own self-benefit. She calls it immoral because it is not mutually beneficial. A theorist of the moral aspects of loving relations calls it immoral because it is a corrupted sort of love. Of course, it may be corrupted because the loving party lets the loved one exploit him, but the wrongness of the exploitation is explained in terms of the expectations one has from a loving – and not a bargaining – relationship.

In fact, if the contractarian account was Hobbesian rather than Kantian (i.e., closer to Dimock's than to Hampton's), there would be fewer constraints on the preferences for which a party may choose to negotiate. The Hobbesian contractarian would not even detect the exploitation if the woman accepted the poet's self-degrading offer. If the poet benefits from it, that is all that is required.[129] Contrary to an infant or a severely mentally disabled person, the poet can consent, and just happens to greatly value the affective benefits of the woman's love.

Hampton's Kantian account would even fail to detect the type of exploitation at hand if the woman's love was translated into concrete benefits (like sexual favors).[130] To be fair though, such a relation would probably not pass Hampton's test, because it is unlikely that the thrills of the woman's presence could *reasonably* be thought to be worth all of the poet's pennies, as well as standing in her dog's shadow, given Hampton's conception of a person's legitimate interests.[131]

However, it does not seem that the immorality of the self-effacing relationship the poet desires can be fully explained by a lack of non-tuist benefits on his side. It seems that to fully explain the immorality of his self-debasement, the corruption of this

---

[128] It may be worth noting that, in some jurisdictions, being in love can be treated as a mental state that vitiates consent. See, e.g., *Louth v. Diprose*, (1992) 175 CLR 621 (High Court of Australia).

[129] If we take the "drug addict," self-regarding view of the sort of benefits that the husband would anticipate.

[130] Of course, this raises again the problem that it may be impossible to even conceptualize intimate, personal benefits of certain kinds as a benefit for strictly self-regarding parties.

[131] Hampton, "Feminist Contractarianism," at 22, 26–28

relationship, and his desire (and consent) for it, we need to refer to two factors that are not considered by contractarians: the nature of the intimate relation and affective benefits.

Thus, as the cases of the devoted husband and *The Notebook* illustrate, the contractarian evaluative framework fails to detect what most of us would think of as positive value within a relationship. Conversely, the song "Ne me quitte pas" illustrates a case in which the contractarian evaluative framework fails to detect what most of us would think of as a negative value.

These examples suggest that the contractarian evaluative framework cannot deal with the *moral* complexity of relations involving other-regarding attitudes. Intimate relations have a complex logic of their own and are just as much part of human moral life as contractual relations. The reader must wonder how plausible it is to reduce their moral significance to a contractarian framework, to claim that all moral relations are contractarian relations, and to seek support in the criticisms of non-contractarian frameworks (or deny their moral dimension) by evoking problems that matter much more within a contractarian framework.

6.6 OTHER FAILURES IN ACCOUNTING FOR THE SPECIAL VALUE OF "OUTLIERS"

In its most unapologetic form, contractarianism assumes that the party bargaining self-interestedly grants instrumental value to everything and everyone but herself. The content of Hobbesian morality is determined by what people could reasonably agree to in order to protect their self-interests. Their relationships are ultimately nested within a concern for themselves, and the concept of "reason" is purely instrumental: "norms are justified just in case following them maximizes the expected utility (preference satisfaction) of the person whose agreement we are supposing would be forthcoming."[132] Importantly, what has value is simply what is preferred, whether the object is human life or ice cream. This is the Hobbesian commitment to a "subjective theory of value."[133]

Dimock's Hobbesian contractarianism fails to account for the intrinsic, noninstrumental value of "outliers" (at least, of people in situations of radical inequality) as well as of any contractee. Dimock responds that Hobbesian contractarians can value things *noninstrumentally*. What is ineliminably instrumental is their reason, which is deployed to bring this value about and to maximize the satisfaction of their preferences. "We must believe the having, being, doing, or achieving of some things to be valuable in themselves if instrumental rationality is to have anything over which it can operate."[134] That is compatible with the Hobbesian subjective theory of value

---

[132] Dimock, "Why All Feminists Should Be Contractarians," at 278.
[133] *Ibid.* at 281.
[134] *Ibid.*

which "sees morality as a human invention" rather than as "the moral truth 'out there'" that we somehow detect.[135]

This response is unsatisfactory as it does not address the criticism that Hobbesian contractarianism fails to recognize the special intrinsic value that other people, and even other bargainers, have. Among other things,[136] to say that the agent herself values an object intrinsically only qualifies the concerns or values of this particular agent, and does not mean that the object is valued intrinsically by anyone else. Indeed, this would be too heavy a metaphysical prescription for contractarianism and would be incompatible with its subjective theory of value.

Hampton's Kantian contractarian account, by contrast, does recognize an intrinsic, noninstrumental value to other parties to the contract (or contract-like relations). However, those people who are not able to contribute to a reciprocally beneficial relation in terms of self-interested costs and benefits do not have such a value. Whatever "value" they (and a relationship with them) may have falls outside morality and normativity because they fall short of being the locus of instrumental cooperation.[137]

Who are these outliers? First, let me point out that their number may be greater than Hampton suggests. She insists that they are only those between whom a "radical inequality" of powers and capacities prevail, like infants or those who are "severely infirm."[138] However, it is not obvious why the outliers should be limited to the severely infirm. In fact, according to Hampton's contractarian test, it would make sense to not be in a relationship with people who are unable to provide me with as many benefits as I am giving them. Indeed, ending this relation would be the moral thing to do.[139] If Hampton agrees that it would be "ridiculous for any moral theory to require"[140] infants or infirm people to reciprocate the benefits they receive, why is it any less ridiculous to require more able – but still less capable than average – adults to reciprocate the benefits that they receive? Indeed, it is the same sort of factual impossibility that makes negotiating with babies absurd or ridiculous.

Like other contractualists, Hampton must appeal to the distinction between *idealized* and concrete agreements.[141] The problem is that we proceed to this idealization on grounds that are distinct from, and in tension with, some

---

[135] Hampton, "Feminist Contractarianism," at 11.
[136] In addition, one could also note that the regression argument to establish the existence of intrinsic value does not necessarily work (Robert Nozick, *Philosophical Explanations* [Cambridge: Harvard University Press, 1981], at 414) and that Dimock is confusing the notion of noninstrumental and nonfinal value (Christine Korsgaard, "Two Distinctions in Goodness" [1983] 92:2 Philosophical Review 169).
[137] Hampton, "Feminist Contractarianism," at 21, 33; Dimock, "Why All Feminists Should Be Contractarians," at 285.
[138] Hampton, "Feminist Contractarianism," at 33.
[139] *Ibid.* at 21.
[140] *Ibid.* at 33.
[141] *Ibid.* at 26.

fundamental contractarian commitments (even though one can also draw, as Hampton does, intellectual connections between both).

Hampton clearly adopts the Kantian idea that people have "*intrinsic, noninstrumental value.*"[142] She describes it as "a feature of our moral life that we regard a human being ... as always intrinsically valuable."[143] Yet, while the Kantian idea of an "end in oneself" or "intrinsic, noninstrumental value" is familiar enough, it is important to note that Hampton constrains its application and that only those who are able to consent will be counterfactually "idealized" into an "equal participant in the agreement process [possessing] equal bargaining powers."[144] Why? Hampton's answer seems to point to an axiom rather than an argument: they are the sort of beings who require consent. Although we have already reviewed the conception of the person which underlies this position, let me note that it is not clear how Hampton escapes the intuitionism that she seeks to avoid,[145] and that it is not obvious why only the capacity to consent matters. She claims that the frustration of that particular human need, rather than many others, calls for a morally stringent response from moral agents. However, I do not see any compelling reason to draw the line there and to only recognize that people are noninstrumentally, intrinsically valuable from a contractual perspective. Nor does it make sense to limit the recognition of Kantian intrinsic moral value – if one, like Hampton, endorses it – to the endorsement of *one's own* intrinsic moral value. Of course, the self-interested perspective of her contractarian theory/test allows the moral agent to legitimately value herself, her projects and interests. But what about the value of others?

Her answer would surely be that "others" must be their own advocates. Indeed, her more or less fortunate marriage of contractarian and contractualist commitments is justified through the idea that we must be "tenacious advocates of ourselves."[146] Other contractualists, and Hampton herself, would add that we can stand in the shoes of other self-advocates to evaluate the fairness of an agreement, but to account for it morally, we can still only look at the relationship from the point of view of so-called tenacious self-advocates. I agree that considering the point of view of self-advocates (other than ourselves) reflects the sort of "intrinsic, noninstrumental value" that Hampton evokes. However, I do not see why it would exhaust the recognition or response required by this value.

To sum up, first, Hampton must once again fall back on her assumed conception of the person, which prompts me to repeat that one can simply disagree with it. Second, as I have explained, the Hobbesian limitations (i.e., the contractarian test's focus on self-interest) imposed on her idea that people have "intrinsic, noninstrumental value" seem to suggest that many more people than the severely inapt would

---

[142] *Ibid.* at 25.
[143] *Ibid.* at 12–13, 23, 25.
[144] *Ibid.* at 26–27.
[145] *Ibid.* at 25.
[146] *Ibid.* at 29.

be outliers. Third, and most importantly, these outliers would be deprived of this "intrinsic, noninstrumental value" in a way that flies in the face of her claim that it is part of our human moral makeup to think of other humans as intrinsically valuable. Taking this position made her reject traditional Hobbesian morality.[147] The only value that she leaves for outliers and the relations that we have with them is the sort of "special nonmoral value" I described when I presented her position at the beginning of this chapter.

Like Dimock, she says that no *ethical* theory – perhaps apart from the Aristotelian one – can account for fellow-feelings and other-regarding values. She says that the concepts of *justice* and *morality* are "too limp"[148] to guide us, but it seems more plausible to me that it is her concept of justice and morality that are too limited. I agree with her when she says that it is absurd to inquire into the nature of morality by asking only "what services could each agree to?" when talking about a mother and her child,[149] but it is not necessarily absurd to inquire into the nature of the morality of the relationship between a mother and a child. It just means that contractarianism would limit itself to asking such absurd questions, and therefore it prefers to ask none.

Hampton's notion of *nonmoral values* (values that would guide our interpersonal relationships without falling within the realm of morality) is interesting but remains undeveloped. I want to avoid the question of whether normative elements can be nonmoral. It is my understanding that morality should provide guidance for our actions. It is one thing to say, "morality fails us, so let us rely on nonmoral interests, let us make war, etc." It is another to say, "morality fails us, so let us look for normative guidance in nonmoral standards or criteria that seems to warrant legitimacy and social approval (and other good things that look like morality)." In the latter case, it seems plausible to me that such standards and criteria are just other moral concepts that theorists have failed to fit within their preferred theory, but that they do not want to discard. I would take the intuitive ethical pull that they have on us as an indication that we have to rethink the province of morality, rather than creating outlying "morality-esque suburbs" that do not count as morality *per se*, but clearly share some of its key normative attributes. When philosophers plead that moral agents should be entitled to enough leeway to maintain their integrity, and that being a moral saint may not be all there is to human life, I find it natural to ask why that leeway should not be considered a part of morality. For one thing, bringing different (e.g., self-regarding and other-regarding) values under the same normative umbrella can facilitate an ethical discussion of what individuals and communities could or should do when they clash.

---

[147] *Ibid.* at 12–13.
[148] *Ibid.* at 37.
[149] *Ibid.* at 33.

Hampton, like Dimock, concludes that people who have too little power fall outside the province of justice and morality and have no intrinsic value. I am not comforted by the admission that something is (blatantly) missing,[150] or the suggestion that these people may have some other sort of special nonmoral value. Creating a kind of second-rate value or morality seems like a messy and harmful endeavor. More importantly, for the purpose of this book, it seems more philosophically plausible to say that we have not properly understood the moral value that these people possess.

Lastly, I note that Hampton and Dimock provide no argument that supports their view that no response required of intimate relationships is demanded by *morality* or *fairness* unless it is framed by an exclusively self-interested, mutually beneficial bargain. Hampton's assertion that calling such responses "moral" is "evaluatively inept"[151] does not satisfy most moral agents – philosophers or otherwise – who would not share her sophisticated, but counterintuitive, assumptions. I do not hold this against her: it may be impossible to argue beyond certain basic axioms and intuitions (at least apart from illustrations that try to make a reader adopt one's way of looking at the issue and, in turn, one's underlying intuitions). Indeed, I mention this to limit the objections that one may have concerning my argument in favor of noncontractarian grounds.

6.7 IS HAMPTON'S "KANTIAN CONTRACTARIANISM" NOT OTHER-REGARDING?

Hampton's "Kantian contractarianism" requires moral respect that is not merely prudential – that is, it does not only recognize that others have the power to help or harm me. It implies a realization of some *concern* that I have for them, and that this concern corresponds to moral obligations. Hampton's Kantian commitments prevent her from saying that her contractarian account benefits from the metaphysical leanness and no-nonsensicality that she is associated with the Hobbesian theory of value.[152] She admits to the substantial Kantian normative ideas that feed (through a contractual prism) her conception of human worth, which is in turn framed by the (mostly heuristic) notion of a contract.[153] This makes it difficult for her to get much (if any) mileage out of the fact that the normative assumptions guiding her moral evaluation would be widely, if not universally, shared. Such was a central concern of Hobbes, who feared the social consequences of moral disagreement. It also makes it impossible for her to endorse the long-standing liberal aspiration to moral

---

[150] *Ibid.* at 37–38.
[151] *Ibid.* at 38.
[152] *Ibid.* at 11.
[153] *Ibid.* at 24.

6.7 Hampton's "Kantian Contractarianism" 269

neutrality.[154] Contrary to Rawls, Hampton "do[es] not regard the contract test as a morally neutral device."[155]

However, while embracing some more substantial moral assumptions, she does not extend them very far, which prompts me to ask why she stops where she does, given that she has opened the door to a normatively charged conception of the person. This includes (1) a conception of human worth; (2) a conception of legitimate interests; and (3) a claim that the morality of our relations with others may not be explained just in terms of domination, prudence, brute force, and dumb luck. Why not admit that, if I am willing to put myself in the shoes of other "tenacious self-advocates," I am in fact recognizing that "each person matters"[156] in a way that implies some other-regarding concern? Why stop short of extending this concern to other aspects of others' welfare?

In other words, when we recognize the moral pull in the realization that others are "like us" in some ways, we have already crossed the line of making substantial moral assumptions. This does not mean that we have no good reasons to make some moral assumptions and not others, but our reasons for doing so can hardly be said to rest on a fear of moral disagreement. Indeed, we have already suggested that we ought to agree on some moral premises.

This may be more obvious in other areas under moral investigation. Consider the theorization of aid owed to foreign countries or their citizens. Theorists who construe our relationship with them as exploitative, in order to show that we owe it to them to establish a fairer situation, already assume that we ought not to exploit these people even though we could and have done so for a long time. We are not helping them out of charity, which is the typical moral currency associated with other-regarding concern, but out of a duty of (transnational) justice. The idea that we are simply repairing the harm from having exploited them is far from morally neutral. Why should we not make a profit off of them? It is not the act of benefitting from or enjoying the instrumentalization of some objects that stops us. Instead, it is because the *sort of beings that these strangers are* ought not to be exploited. And this is due to certain traits that they possess – for instance, their capacity to consent speaks to us and makes it unacceptable to us to exploit them. Surely people's vulnerability and capacity to suffer speaks to us in ways that make it similarly unacceptable for us to not care for them to some extent. Once we formulate the moral question in this way, it becomes much less obvious for the theorist to say "yes" to the normativity of the expression of autonomy, but "no" to the normativity of other aspects of people's

---

[154] In any case, the ideal of liberal neutrality has never fully recovered from the criticisms addressed to liberal versions of this ideals after the 1980s. These criticisms argued that liberal neutrality was itself a position in the debate over conceptions of the good life as opposed to a way to circumvent said debate (Patrick Neal, *Liberalism and Its Discontents* [Washington Square: New York University Press, 1999]).

[155] Hampton, "Feminist Contractarianism," at 26.

[156] *Ibid.* at 24.

welfare. The long-standing appeal in liberalism to the fact that the former trait is more easily universally agreed upon (and thus can be a better foundation for a universally accepted, durable, and stable political arrangement) becomes less convincing,[157] at least, not once we have clearly stripped it of its pretension of moral neutrality, or of its Hobbes-like exclusive appeal to prudence.

Given her core emphasis on how other-regarding attitudes facilitate exploitation, Hampton would probably want to avoid recognizing that any kind of other-regarding concern grounds the moral respect that she presents, although I would add that this other-regarding concern should not preclude a self-regarding concern. Agreeing to a structure where one can be a tenacious advocate for oneself, while recognizing that others are entitled to be the same not out of *prudence* but because they merit it, does not have to be explained in terms of other-regarding concern.[158] I think that it is the most plausible explanation and the one that best coheres with both our ordinary moral intuitions and our judgments on the fairness and morality of the structures that entrench these intuitions.

More importantly, I think that this is a plausible reading of Hampton. She believes that when someone is able to consent, it becomes fair to make sure that this person is reciprocally benefitted. As she writes, "I don't get you to paint my house simply by whistling and pointing to the paint, as if you were some kind of automated paint machine. I believe that to get you to paint my house I must get your *consent* to do so, and I also believe (if I think our contractual relation is ideal and hence just) that I can get your consent only if you are sure that I am not asking you to bear the costs of doing so without any reciprocating benefit from me to you."[159] What really counters exploitation is not the contractual process *per se*, but the moral agent's capacity to recognize and acknowledge other agent's special worth. Therefore, the sort of proposal that I make would not depart from this fundamental moral claim; it would simply suggest that contractarian feminists do not have a complete understanding of this special worth.

6.8 CONCLUSION

The general conclusions from my analysis of Hampton's and Dimock's arguments are that it is incorrect to say that (1) other-regarding concern as a source of moral obligation necessarily leads to exploitation or (2) contractual thinking necessarily

---

[157] It can still be argued that the value of autonomy is more important in some ways, but not that it fundamentally stands above all other values. See, e.g., Daniel Callahan, "Autonomy: A Moral Good, Not a Moral Obsession" (1984) 14:5 Hastings Center Report 40.
[158] For instance, it could be explained by a respect for some transcending universal law that particular legislators express.
[159] Hampton, "Feminist Contractarianism," at 26.

prevents other-regarding concern. This leaves room to argue for the importance of other-regarding concern, and other normative dimensions of relations that do not meet Hampton's test or Dimock's requirement, but can still be appropriate criteria of justice and morality. The importance of these other normative aspects remains to be developed, but I hope to have provided arguments against both a long-standing concern that such evaluative frameworks of morality and justice are so inherently laced with exploitation as to be worthless, as well as some sufficiently disquieting indications that what Hampton calls (rightly, within limits) "the wisdom of the egoist"[160] is not the only moral wisdom. As Baier puts it, "[i]t does not ... seem at all plausible, once we think about actual moral relations in all their sad or splendid variety, to model all of them on one rather special one, the relation between promissor to promisee."[161] Since neither Baier nor contractarians can do much more than suggesting the superior plausibility of their intuitions, and since it would be too simplistic to discard the contractarian position on the grounds that it is evidently missing something, I had to consider how insightful feminist theories could miss this "evidence." I find that they miss it because of their exclusive and uncompromising commitment to the normative conception of the person as autonomous as well as an overreaching rejection of (only potentially exploitative) other-regarding considerations as justifications for the fairness and morality of a relation.

In theory, feminist contractarians could reduce justice to mutual benefit without reducing it to the whole of morality, including the morality that would apply to any kind of partial/intimate relations and to mutual benefits as well.

If they limited their claim to justice, their position would be stronger, since it would come closer to acknowledging that there are some important moral dimensions that cannot be explained from the point of view of mutually beneficial cooperative endeavors. Such a claim would, however, create tensions between demands of justice and other demands of morality. Consider the case of a friend who calls you and asks you to keep her company because she is sad. You remember that, a year ago, you asked the same of her. If you think about this situation from a contractual perspective, however awkward it might seem, it appears that you owe her the service of keeping her company and that it would be unfair if you refuse. It does not seem absurd to say that your refusal would be unfair, but this contractual unfairness does not exhaust the wrongness of hanging up on your friend. In addition to challenging the idea that the *wrongness* of hanging up on your friend (and a human being in need) is wholly explained by a "contractual failure," we could also challenge the idea that the *unfairness* of such an action can only be explained in contractual terms.

---

[160] Jean Hampton, "The Wisdom of the Egoist: The Moral and Political Implications of Valuing the Self" (1997) 14:1 Social Phil & Pol'y at 21.
[161] Baier, *Moral Prejudices*, at 117.

The insistence of feminist contractarians to look at personal relationships through a lens historically and intuitively better suited to relationships between strangers reveals a key shortcoming of contractual thought that attempts to provide a moral theory applying indiscriminately to all human relations. This shortcoming invites us to consider how an alternative, pluralist model of relations could inform moral and political theory.

7

Beyond Contractual Relations

7.1 WHY CONTRACTUALISM OR CONTRACTARIANISM CANNOT FULLY INTEGRATE ALL PEOPLE WITH SEVERE INTELLECTUAL DISABILITIES

Contractual justice is far from a broken idea; it is simply a narrow one intended to deal with a limited variety of interpersonal relations. The idea is so intuitively compelling, so traditionally important in philosophy, and such a natural fit for a capitalist bargaining ethos, that it has unsurprisingly overreached and yet fallen short of meeting the demands of disability policy. Other moral and political theories could better guide our never-ending social endeavor to conceptualize bodies and minds that defy norms commonly used by scholars and policymakers. In this chapter, I propose that a "role-based" or "relational" account may fare better than a contractual one in explaining the robust moral status of PSID.

In this book, we have seen three main strategies that social contract theorists could adopt to either include PSID specifically (and PWD more generally) in the category of full subjects of justice or to confer a robust moral status upon them:

(1) Observing that they do possess the requisite contracting capacities, contrary to what has been assumed. This takes the form of an empirical argument that focuses either on PSID's actual capacities, or on the social structures that prevent or fail to facilitate people with disabilities from exercising the necessary contracting capacities.
(2) More clearly explaining, reinterpreting, broadening, or conceptually modifying the nature of these contracting capacities – or the values underlying them – so as to explain why people with profound mental disabilities actually possess these capacities.
(3) Conceding that PSID do not have the required capacities to contract, but maintaining that there are other reasons to justify their representation in contractual procedures. The argument is that these reasons

support a case for conferring a robust moral status upon this group and comply with contractual assumptions inherent to these contracting procedures.

Some arguments that may suffice to integrate PWD within the realms of contractual morality and justice cannot accomplish the same for PSID. PSID serve not only as a "hard case" that shows the limits of contractual thought; the distinct challenge they pose to moral and political theory can inform criticisms and insights that extend to PWD more generally and, indeed, everyone within the diverse biological spectrum of physical and cognitive capacities as well as the varied shapes that human societies take.

We have explored various difficulties and tensions within these inclusivist contractual theories. Their two main shortcomings are that (1) they cannot convincingly ground a robust moral status for PSID and (2) they do so at the cost of making this status merely derivative or contingent.

As regards to the first shortcoming, the conceptual adjustments made to integrate PSID into the social contract sometimes seem arbitrary or questionable, which suggests that implicit noncontractual justifications (e.g., species-based preferences, affective responses, partial attachments, values, goods, and virtues, such as caring or responsiveness to vulnerability) are at work. The reconceptualization of the scope of contracting capacities – or how and why PSID can take part in a contract-based mutually beneficial "joint venture" – stretches these concepts beyond the scope of social contract theory. Feminists have foreseen this conclusion: in many cases, it is wrongheaded to insist on normalizing PSID to fit within contractual frameworks. For instance, Virginia Held wrote that "[i]t stretches credulity even further than most philosophers can tolerate to imagine babies as little rational calculators contracting with their mothers for care."[1] Eva Kittay argues that, if her own daughter (who is profoundly disabled) could be sufficiently supported by living in a group home with round-the-clock support, this might be called "independent living," and if her daughter was then "made to partake in one tiny step in an assembly line production, and [was] given some practical compensation, we [could] call this 'working' and being 'productive.'"[2] However, she holds that "[t]o so stretch these concepts both empties them of meaning and undermines the possibility that dignity is compatible with lifelong dependency."[3]

My analysis of contractual inclusivist arguments gives me little hope that further conceptual tinkering would dispel their implausibility or the derivativeness of their

---

[1] Virginia Held, "Non-Contractual Society: A Feminist View" (1987) 13:suppl. 1 Can J Phil 111 at 120. See also Jean Hampton, *The Intrinsic Worth of Persons: Contractarianism in Moral and Political Philosophy*, ed. Daniel Farnham (New York: Cambridge University Press, 2007), at 21.
[2] Eva Feder Kittay, "When Caring Is Just and Justice Is Caring: Justice and Mental Retardation" in Eva Feder Kittay and Ellen K. Feder, eds., *The Subject of Care: Feminist Perspectives on Dependency* (Lanham, MD: Rowman & Littlefield), at 267.
[3] Ibid. See also Held, "Non-Contractual Society," at 114.

results. However, I find it promising to observe that these social contract theorists can sometimes be interpreted as implicitly appealing to a foundational, moral concern that lies beyond the social contract tradition.

As for the second shortcoming, we should be critical of conferring a moral status that is too derivative or contingent, because:

(1) This status has a potentially harmful impact on PSID. This potential harm is not only amplified by particular social contexts; it is also an inherent feature of contractual structures and the ways in which agents act within these structures.[4]

(2) This derivative status is less robust than that of other citizens. This is a problem if we assume that citizens should have equal moral status. As I have said, I am not concerned about equality for equality's sake, but it would be surprising to argue that an unequal status is sufficiently robust. The social contract tradition would not allow for inequality between different classes of status unless it accepted that some statuses have a lesser value than others. This would be incompatible with the liberal aversion to the notion of second-rate status or citizenship.[5]

(3) This argument gets morality wrong. This claim ultimately depends on the success of an alternative theory or (at least) of us discovering how starkly this derivativeness clashes with our strongly held moral beliefs.

If the social contract tradition cannot make room for people with disabilities, especially severe intellectual disabilities, what do we do now? There are three possible options:

(1) The failure to justify a robust status for PSID is bad news for social contract theory, which has proven its limits and must be at least partially

---

[4] See, e.g., Nussbaum's and Silvers's arguments in Chapters 4 and 5. Eva Kittay also notes that if "thinking [based on an indirect status] is the basis for providing aid, the aid will, of necessity, be a low priority in any public distribution of resources. It will tend to be minimal, except in cases in which individual acts of generosity surface" (Kittay, "When Caring Is Just," at 272). I also refer to Peter Byrne's quote that I put in the epigraph; Byrne claims that PSID's lack of contracting capacities (notably autonomy) or the derivative character of their "participation" necessarily correlates to a lower moral status. Even though contractualist and contractarian thinkers have suggested that the indirectness or derivativeness of PWD's contractual moral status does not affect its robustness, I have found that it does.

[5] As we have seen, a criticism of this "second-rate" status can take a metaphysical or practical form. For instance, if we bestow great social value on autonomy, then we see that PSID are less likely to hold or gain this value. Even if, through the autonomy of other agents, they gain a strong moral status, the fact that they are twice removed from the source of the value (autonomy) may make them "twice-removed" citizens. While such an argument is only convincing as a description of prejudices, these prejudices are still harmful. This problem is not as connected to the theory itself as to its application, though the fact that the theory fails to address this application may be regarded as a problem of the theory itself. However, more directly relevant to the structure of the theory is the fact that some capacities, such as autonomy, allow for autonomous individuals' needs to be given priority over others within a theory of justice.

rejected. The integration of a vast spectrum of human abilities into a moral or political theory would be a key criterion for its success.

(2) This failure is bad news for PSID, who must be excluded from the sphere of justice and perhaps of morality altogether, despite common intuitions that this would be wrong. The social contract tradition would invite us to revisit our intuitions and consider whether they are not mere prejudices or other nonmoral kinds of responses.

(3) Accept the limits and coexistence of particular moral theories that have to compromise with other moral frameworks to fit certain relations that we see as imposing robust obligations, but that still do not fit the contractual mold. Here, the work to be done is not to replace social contract thought, but rather to supplement it. Indeed, the social contract tradition succeeds in integrating the most "capable" or "cooperating" people among PWD and partially explains the integration of those PSID who can be normalized and participate in contract-like relationships, although they also (and perhaps more often) participate in noncontractual relationships. Therefore, we must (1) develop alternative moral frameworks to explain the significance of these relationships, such as fiduciary or caring relationships and (2) reflect on how to solve conflicts between these frameworks.

My conclusions do not encourage me to reject social contract theory altogether, nor suggest that an alternative theory to explain our duties toward PSID (like care ethics) should be expanded to the whole of society (like some care ethicists have suggested). On the contrary, my findings only urge different moral theories to stay within the boundaries of the relationships, people, and circumstances to which they apply, and to refrain from claiming that they cover all morality and to expel other normative sources to its "margins," or beyond its "frontiers,"[6] into the realm of the supererogatory and (nonmoral) emotions.

This claim strikes me as the most plausible and constructive way of criticizing the social contract tradition in terms of its failure to provide a complete and satisfactory account of PSID's moral and political status. The argument that it points to would require (1) defending a relational or role-based theory of morality and (2) defending the position that the moral relationships that our community has with PSID are not primarily contractual, but are instead (at first glance) fiduciary or caring relationships. I cannot deal with these undertakings in depth here, but I want to advance their prima facie plausibility. If I assume (rather than argue) that caring relationships are as morally significant as contractual ones to the interests of justice and morality,

---

[6] It is not a surprise that Kittay's and Nussbaum's criticisms of the exclusion of PWD are entitled, respectively, Eva Feder Kittay, "At the Margins of Moral Personhood" (2008) 5:2–3 J Bioethical Inquiry 137 and Martha Nussbaum, *Frontiers of Justice: Disability, Nationality, Species Membership* (Cambridge: Harvard University Press, 2006).

I can then go on to consider a preliminary objection to this hypothesis, namely: how do we adjudicate between the competing claims or values that derive from these relationships?

Therefore, this concluding chapter is exploratory. My choice of alternative solutions (i.e., caring relations) to explain the robust moral status of PSID and to deal with related problems, such as the compatibility of morally robust demanding relations, is motivated by my intuitions about the kind of moral account that makes room for both contractual and noncontractual alternatives and for the strong moral commitments that underlie both. In this conclusion, I suggest not only that social contract theories fail to some extent, but also that this is not necessarily bad news for either PSID or the social contract tradition.

While this book does not reject the social contract tradition wholesale, it agrees with many theorists that the myth of the autonomous, independent, fully cooperating subject who lies at the heart of the social contract fails to take into account the reality of vulnerability[7] and dependency[8] that characterizes the human condition. The social contract tradition is also inevitably complicit in the construction of the "disabled subject" and lacks the conceptual resources to self-criticize in that regard. The philosophical discourses asking what is owed to PSID are simultaneously narratives that construct "PSID" and assert specific personal characteristics (e.g., a sense of justice) and social relations (e.g., mutually beneficial bargaining) as natural starting points. If we took a different starting point – for instance, the social model of disability – we would not ask "what is owed to people with disabilities as a matter of fairness?" but rather, "what are the elements that socially disable them in the first place?" A "systemic turn" heralded by political theorists like Iris Marion Young[9] is becoming increasingly fashionable in legal and political parlance seeking to redress the roots, not only the symptoms, of injustice.[10] This systemic turn gives disability theorists the agenda of detecting structurally oppressive dimensions of societies, including the very problems constructed by liberals intending to redress them with the best of intentions.

---

[7] Recent philosophical accounts of vulnerability include: M. A. Fineman, "The Vulnerable Subject: Anchoring Equality in the Human Condition" (2008) 20:1 Yale JL & Feminism 1; M. A. Fineman, "The Vulnerable Subject and the Responsive State" (2010) 60:2 Emory LJ 251; Catriona Mackenzie, Wendy Rogers, and Susan Dodds, eds., *Vulnerability: New Essays in Ethics and Feminist Philosophy* (New York: Oxford University Press, 2013).

[8] See Eva Kittay, *Love's Labor: Essays on Women, Equality and Dependency* (New York: Routledge, 1999); Alasdair MacIntyre, *Dependent Rational Animals: Why Human Beings Need the Virtues* (Chicago: Open Court, 1999).

[9] In particular, her *Justice and the Politics of Difference* (Princeton: Princeton University Press, 1990) and *Responsibility for Justice* (New York: Oxford University Press, 2011).

[10] Consider, for example, its influence on the concept of "substantive equality" (as opposed to mere formal equality, which does not attend to the social context in which equality is sought) in legal scholarship. See Fay Faraday, Margaret Denike, and M. Kate Stephenson, eds., *Making Equality Rights Real: Securing Substantive Equality under the Charter* (Toronto: Irwin Law, 2006).

Whether or not a role-based solution is the most promising replacement, I contend that the social contract has exhausted its resources to help societies treat PSID and other disabled people fairly. To be sure, the influence of contractual ideas in our culture is palpable, and this includes the marginalization and "dis-citizenship"[11] of PSID. As Michael Sandel noted in response to Rawlsian proceduralism, "despite its philosophical failure, this liberal vision is the one by which we live."[12] *Hotel California*, the Eagles song about material excess, written five years after Rawls's *A Theory of Justice* was published, may say it more colorfully: "We are all just prisoners here, of our own device."[13] Let us explore how alternative devices, then, could better explain the moral standing of PSID.

7.2 TAKING RELATIONS SERIOUSLY

Chapter 6 explored noncontractual aspects of relationships and illustrated their importance to moral thought. The basic idea behind "relational" or "role-based" moral and political frameworks is simple: every situation where a moral issue arises can be presented relationally, and every moral dilemma can be solved by having an understanding of what is morally fitting for an agent occupying a certain role, within certain relationships, and in certain circumstances.[14] This structure of morality coheres with a compelling view of human nature according to which people develop their identity, individuality, and integrity by choosing to endorse (or not) certain roles.[15]

An approach that attends to the roles and relations from which agents emerge, and in which agents constantly find and define themselves, could be represented by a drawing: a moral agent on the right side, the object of her moral concerns on the

---

[11] See Chapter 1 for a discussion of this notion.
[12] Michael Sandel, "The Procedural Republic and the Unencumbered Self" (1984) 12:1 Political Theory 81 at 82.
[13] Bruce Young, *Hotel California* (Vancouver: Good Earth, 1979).
[14] An objection to this view is that not all moral dilemmas involve a "relation." For instance, when I hesitate between ordering ice cream and making healthy choices, it seems odd to say that I have conflicting relations between ice cream and with myself! Yet, these types of "relations" are extremely common. The former is an instrumental relation, perhaps nested in a relationship to ourselves, and the latter – the relation to ourselves – must assume that we can think about ourselves from an "outsider's perspective." I cannot offer a defense of these views here. I only mention them and would add that they do not involve, at first glance, any far-fetched metaphysical assumption. We often tell people to take a good look at themselves or to take care of themselves, as though the "I" we are addressing could direct its attention (as a subject) to the interlocutor (as an object). (The shared identity of the subject and object will affect the nature of this attention but does not prevent its possibility.)
[15] Consider, for instance, how we identify ourselves when we put on various existential, social, and moral hats, how we earn admiration and blame through adopting these choices, or how our identity or integrity are threatened when these identities are taken from us. I am also tempted to think that we do not see ourselves so much as holding values x, y, z as we conceive ourselves as disposed to act in x, y, z ways when confronted with varying relational demands.

left side, and an arrow between both, illustrating attitudes or actions connecting the agent to her concerns. A relational approach would pay primary attention to the *arrow*. In contrast, some moral theories focus on the moral agents (such as virtue ethics and deontology), while others focus on the object of her moral endeavors (such as utilitarianism). Part of taking role ethics seriously is resisting reductionist objections that would suggest that the arrow is directly or indirectly considered in all other normative theories, or that it can and should be fundamentally explained in terms of the subject or the object of her moral concerns. A relational view would claim that the arrow can be a fundamental or primary locus of our moral investigation, whether because relations and roles are axiomatically valuable or because articulating moral reflections around them is more informative or helpful.

Role ethics probably finds its most mature formulation in Confucian ethics, which commands the cultivation of virtues through the practice of rituals.[16] As Roger T. Ames and Henry Rosemont Jr. explain,

> [F]or the Confucian each situation requires the moral imagination necessary to put oneself in the place of the other [...], and then a determination to do one's utmost [...] to achieve what is optimally appropriate [...] under the circumstances. Confucians do not seek the universal, but concentrate on the particular; they do not see abstract autonomous individuals, but rather concrete persons standing in a multiplicity of role relations with one another; they do not focus exclusively on either intentions or consequences (agents or their actions), but on the virtuosity and productivity of the relations themselves. In the Confucian sensibility the appeal is to these particular persons in this particular family, defined by these specific relations. Mothers and daughters become such by virtue of their relations to each other. Indeed, persons *are* what they mean for each other.[17]

In order to understand Confucian ethics, Western readers must extricate themselves from "the basic conception of what it is to be a human being in Western civilization ... individualism."[18] This individualist prism, epitomized in the social contract tradition, defines human beings abstractly as autonomous and (typically) self-interested beings, and predicates their worth upon their potential to achieve autonomy, rationality, and capacities to enjoy freedom.[19] Needless to say, in this individualist picture, PSID's worth and humanity are threatened.

At the very least, focusing on the normative content of roles and relations (i.e., the arrow) and on how people come to endorse and perform them properly from a relational perspective would draw philosophical attention away from the notion of individual freedom, which has been paramount to Western modernity when

---

[16] David Wong, "Chinese Ethics," *The Stanford Encyclopedia of Philosophy* (September 2018), plato.stanford.edu/archives/fall2018/entries/ethics-chinese/.
[17] *The Chinese Classic of Family Reverence: A Philosophical Translation of the Xiaojing* (Honolulu: University of Hawaii Press, 2009), at 38.
[18] *Ibid.* at 36 (emphasis removed).
[19] *Ibid.* at 38.

discussing morality and justice. Instead, it brings us toward the most pressing (relational, role-based) questions people must figure out on a daily basis.

To distinguish a role-based ethics from other normative kinds of ethics, consider the case of a football player. A consequentialist would value the player on the basis of the number of points she scores. A deontologist would pay particular attention to whether the player respects the rules of the game and does not cheat. Sports aficionados are quick to point out that their favorite players not only score many points but also play *well* – with "sportsmanship" – that is, performing the facets of this "ritual" in an exemplary way. Virtue ethics may well overlap with (Confucian) role ethics insofar as they both focus on a player's virtues. But "Confucian virtues" are inherently relational, and so a role-based assessment of the player would not only examine her individual performance, but how she acted in relation to other players.[20]

I mention Confucianism as an illustration of role ethics because of its venerable history rather than to advocate it as a superior kind of ethics to deal with the social inclusion of PWD. Although, on the one hand, it would be a radical antidote to our post-Enlightenment sclerosed dogmas about individualism and independence, on the other hand, it may be hard to reconcile with the values of autonomy and the normative language predominant in our political culture. Many theorists and schools in the West also have noted the artificiality and oppressive impact of the "atomistic"[21] conception of the subject within liberal thought. Most of these criticisms have implied that a more relational stance was necessary, for instance, to better reflect the human condition and human societies, and to redress oppression that has been abstracted away from "atomistic" conceptions of justice. These criticisms are in great part articulated as answers to Rawls's mainstreaming of a Kantian conception of the person and of the kind of justice it calls for.

For instance, feminist philosophers in the West have attacked the concept of autonomy, calling it:

> [I]nherently masculinist, that it is inextricably bound up with masculine character ideals, with assumptions about selfhood and agency that are metaphysically, epistemologically, and ethically problematic from a feminist perspective, and with

---

[20] On the overlap between virtue ethics and Confucian "role ethics," see Wong, "Chinese Ethics."

[21] Charles Taylor used the term "atomism" to "characterize the doctrines of social contract theory which arose in the seventeenth century and also successor doctrines which may not have made use of the notion of social contract but which inherited a vision of society as in some sense constituted by individuals for the fulfillment of ends which were primarily individual. Certain forms of utilitarianism are successor doctrines in this sense. The term is also applied to contemporary doctrines which hark back to social contract theory, or which try to defend in some sense the priority of the individual and his rights over society, or which present a purely instrumental view of society" (*Philosophy and the Human Sciences: Philosophical Papers*, vol. 2 [Cambridge: Cambridge University Press, 1985], at 187).

political traditions that historically have been hostile to women's interests and freedom.[22]

While some feminist thinkers have come to doubt that autonomy is redeemable, and have proposed alternative ethical foundations for rights and justice,[23] others have worked toward rehabilitating the concept of autonomy as *relational*. The latter group of theorists shares the following conviction:

> [T]hat persons are socially embedded and that agents' identities are formed within the context of social relationships and shaped by a complex of intersecting social determinants, such as race, class, gender, and ethnicity. Thus the focus of relational approaches is to analyze the implications of the intersubjective and social dimensions of selfhood and identity for conceptions of individual autonomy and moral and political agency.[24]

The other value at the heart of liberalism – equality – has undergone a similar relational critique. Relational egalitarians claim that:

> Each of us is situated in a complex network of relationships that structures our lives, experiences, and perspectives in diverse ways. It would seem, then, that an account of relationships and the perspectives of those who are in oppressive relationships would be relevant to an analysis of the conditions needed to achieve equality. Yet liberal theory, which has been the focal point around which theorists have examined equality as a concept and as a goal, has not paid much attention to relationships.... By taking the sociality and interdependence of human beings as the starting point for theorizing about conditions for treating people with equal concern and respect, relational theory challenges traditional liberal conceptions of personhood and of what is needed to achieve equality.[25]

Relational approaches to liberal values have become increasingly successful in (especially feminist) academic circles, particularly in philosophy, law, and bioethical literature.[26]

---

[22] Catriona Mackenzie and Natalie Stoljar, eds., *Relational Autonomy: Feminist Perspectives on Autonomy, Agency, and the Social Self* (New York: Oxford University Press, 2000), at 3.

[23] Consider the work of legal scholar Martha Fineman, particularly "Anchoring Equality" and "Responsive State."

[24] MacKenzie and Stoljar, *Relational Autonomy*, at 4.

[25] Christine M. Koggel, *Perspectives on Equality: Constructing a Relational Theory* (Lanham, MA: Rowman & Littlefield, 1998), at xi. For an introduction to Relational Egalitarianism, see Kasper Lippert-Rasmussen, *Relational Egalitarianism: Living as Equals* (Cambridge: Cambridge University Press, 2018). For a discussion between theorists of relational autonomy and theorists of relational equality, see Natalie Stoljar and Kristin Voigt, *Autonomy and Equality: Relational Approaches* (in press).

[26] Influential works in the field include MacKenzie and Stoljar, *Relational Autonomy*; Jennifer Nedelsky, *Law's Relations: A Relational Theory of Self, Autonomy and Law* (Oxford: Oxford University Press, 2011). The mingling of these philosophical discourses with feminist bioethics and health law is well illustrated by Jocelyn Grant Downie and Jennifer J. Llewellyn, *Being Relational: Reflections on Relational Theory and Health Law* (Vancouver: UBC Press, 2012).

Other relational approaches to morality within, or akin to, feminist scholarship include care ethics and moral sentimentalism.[27] These affective and relational models of morality emphasize the importance of a relational prism in their discussion on how the self is defined and relates to the world, and how moral knowledge is acquired. For instance, much of Michael Slote's recent work has deflated the importance of rationality and reason, and suggests that relational practices of receptivity, caring, and empathy toward others are more morally informative, and can in fact shed light on why values central to the liberal tradition (like autonomy and equality) matter.[28] Eva Kittay writes that "being a person" – and therefore a subject of justice as per her account – "has little to do with rationality and everything to do with *relationships* – to our world and to those in it."[29] Explaining models of the self as defined through separation and connection as symbolized by Jake's (mainstream, masculine) voice and Amy's (relational, feminine) voice, Carol Gilligan writes:

> Describing himself as distinct by locating his particular position in the world, Jake sets himself apart from that world by his abilities, his beliefs, and his height. Although Amy also enumerates her likes, her wants, and her beliefs, she locates herself in relation to the world, describing herself through actions that bring her into connection with others, elaborating ties through her ability to provide help. To Jake's ideal of perfection, against which he measures the worth of himself, Amy counterposes an ideal of care, against which she measures the worth of her activity. While she places herself in relation to the world and chooses to help others through sciences, he places the world in relation to himself as it defines his character, his position, and the quality of his life.[30]

For overlapping reasons, these scholars are skeptical of projects that propose to transcend socialization in order to gain moral or political insight. How far they go in defining the self in function of its community (and the social scripts guiding the roles and relations within it) varies. For instance, amongst other famous critics of Rawlsian proceduralism, Sandel notes that this Rawlsian strand of liberalism offered the "exhilarating promise" of transcending social roles and determinants.[31] Thus, it bases itself on fictions of "unencumbered selves" and purports to apply to an equally fictitious society, or to stipulate the non-citizenship of certain of its members. Rawls's liberalism is therefore not only "the fullest expression of the

---

[27] For an introduction of these fields, see Virginia Held, *The Ethics of Care: Personal, Political, Global* (Oxford: Oxford University Press, 2006), and Michael Slote, *Moral Sentimentalism* (Oxford: Oxford University Press, 2010).
[28] Michael Slote, *From Enlightenment to Receptivity: Rethinking Our Values* (New York: Oxford University Press, 2013).
[29] Kittay, "When Caring Is Just," at 266.
[30] Carol Gilligan, *In a Different Voice: Psychological Theory and Women's Development* (Cambridge: Harvard University Press, 1993), at 35.
[31] Sandel, "The Procedural Republic," at 87.

Enlightenment's quest for the self-defining subject" but also of its futility.[32] Sandel writes that "despite its philosophical force, the claim for the priority of the right over the good ultimately fails."[33]

If such relational conceptions of identities and agents are correct, moral and political accounts of social and personal interactions should, according to Kenneth J. Gergen:

> [R]eplace the presumption of bounded selves with a vision of relationship. I do not mean relationships between otherwise separate selves, but rather, a process of coordination that precedes the very concept of the self.... [V]irtually all intelligible action is born, sustained, and/or extinguished within the ongoing process of relationship. From this standpoint there is no isolated self or fully private experience. Rather, we exist in a world of co-constitution. We are always already emerging from relationship; we cannot step out of relationship; even in our most private moments we are never alone.[34]

Communitarianism (and metaphysical views akin to Gergen's) is sometimes distinguished from relational theory (as defined above) on the basis that it conceptualizes the self as emerging from unchosen relationships, and risks "preserving or replicating existing relationships."[35] Relational theorists, on the other hand, focus on the relational situation of the self in order to reveal what stands in the way of an agent's ability to define – and not only discover – her ends. In defense of communitarians and other strands of relational ethics, conceptualizing the self as constituted by community roles and values "all the way down" need not make freedom or free will impossible. Besides, even if agencies were constituted and maintained in ways that constrained a (perhaps unrealizable) ideal of autonomy, acknowledging this state of affairs would not limit our freedom. On the contrary, it would point us in the direction of making the best out of the freedom that we do possess. Relational thinkers may not only answer the charge of determinism in a defensive way – that is, by pointing out that they are not ultimately undermining autonomy – but also with a counterattack emphasizing the downsides of an alternative ideal of bounded self. This individualist, one may say poetically, metaphysically lonely view of the self:

> [P]ervades our schools and organizations, where individual evaluation haunts our steps from the first moment we step into a classroom to our ultimate retirement. And thus we compete, tooth and claw, for ascendance over others. Self-esteem continuously hangs in the balance; the possibility of failure and depression is always at the doorstep. Under these conditions, what is the value of other people? Are they

---

[32] Ibid.
[33] Ibid. at 82.
[34] Kenneth Gergen, *Relational Being: Beyond Self and Community* (New York: Oxford University Press, 2015), at xv.
[35] Downie and Llewellyn, *Being Relational*, at 8.

not primarily instruments for our own pleasure or self-gain? If they do not contribute to our well-being, should we not avoid or abandon them?[36]

Relationists could also emphasize that taking social roles and relations seriously does not imply that one must never criticize oppressive or otherwise unfair ones. To this end, Samuel Scheffler writes:

> [T]he relationships that generate responsibilities for an individual are those relationships that the individual has reason to value. No claims at all arise from relations that are degrading or demeaning, or which serve to undermine rather than to enhance human flourishing. In other words, the alternative to an exaggerated voluntarism is not an exaggerated communitarianism or historicism. In recognizing that the significance of our social relationships does not stem exclusively from our choices, we do not consign ourselves to a form of social bondage. In surrendering the fantasy that our own wills are the source of all our special responsibilities, we do not leave ourselves defenceless against the contingencies of the social world.[37]

Another prominent instance of role-based ethics is found in professional ethics, which governs the behaviors of people who act in particular professional roles which are likely to raise ethical conflicts, as these people may be legitimately excused from ordinary morality. Professional ethics concern a kind of "special obligations," which, as Diane Jeske writes, "are obligations owed to some subset of persons, in contrast to natural duties that are owed to all persons simply *qua* persons."[38] The idea that all of us wear a multitude of moral hats is an under-examined challenge in moral and political theory, which tends to focus on a particular kind of relation (between persons *qua* person) and relegate "special," agent-relative obligations to the margins. The implication behind a role-based or relational approach to ethics is to take agent-relative obligations as the central case of moral obligations.[39] This view challenges the exceptionalism found within a common version of role morality by suggesting that ordinary morality is itself to be understood in this role-based way. While many role morality theorists would carve out a moral space that is differentiated from ordinary morality in order to make sense of people's particular social roles (like that

---

[36] Gergen, *Relational Being*, at xiv.
[37] Samuel Scheffler, *Boundaries and Allegiances: Problems of Justice and Responsibility in Liberal Thought* (New York: Oxford University Press, 2003), at 106. Sociological theories of roles also teach us that oppressive roles – including "master statuses" – "stick" to some social groups, but this need not count against a relational ethics. On the contrary, its relational focus enables it to detect and denounce how roles and relations can be harmful or immorally distributed. On role theory and disability as a "master status," see Sharon N. Barnartt, "Using Role Theory to Describe Disability" in Sharon N. Barnartt and Barbara M. Altman, eds., *Exploring Theories and Expanding Methodologies: Where We Are and Where We Need to Go* (Bingley: Emerald Group, 2001).
[38] Diane Jeske, "Special Obligations," *The Stanford Encyclopedia of Philosophy* (August 2019), plato.stanford.edu/entries/special-obligations/.
[39] As such, it would face the challenges that special obligations face, such as distributive and voluntarist objections (*ibid.*; Scheffler, *Boundaries and Allegiances*, at ch. 6).

of a lawyer or a medical doctor) and the way they conflict with ordinary moral expectations, here I am taking a relational view of ordinary morality.[40]

This is not to say that reasons applying universally to all moral agents – such as "a reason for anyone to do or want something that it would reduce the amount of wretchedness in the world,"[41] or concepts like "natural duties" (i.e., "owed by all persons to all others [irrespective of status or acts performed]"[42]) – would have no foothold within role-based ethics. Instead, a role-based ethics would invite us to pay attention to the nature of the community, roles, and relations involved in obligations that may seem to transcend community, roles, or relations. A universal obligation may, for instance, apply to all moral agents *qua* humans, so that one is prompted to reflect on the moral relevance, if any, of being a member of this species, or of relating to beings susceptible to peculiar kinds of vulnerability, attachment, pain, flourishing, etc.[43]

This approach may turn out to yield emancipatory power if it helps subordinated groups to reveal ways that so-called impartial or natural obligations disadvantaging them can, in fact, be relativized within oppressive social structures. The adage that "whoever invokes humanity wants to cheat"[44] is not out of place when attacking accounts of human rights, morality, and justice that purport to use an insufficiently relationally situated conception of personhood. A closer inspection of the obligations that we owe to each other *qua* persons reveals that the notion of "person" is contested. Contractual theories, as we saw, are no exception. Once correctly stated as more specific kinds of obligations (e.g., between similarly situated, capable, and independent strangers), it seems that all social obligations become, in a sense, agent-relative. The social contract tradition has generally put forward conceptions of moral personhood and subject of justice that could "cheat" PSID out of an opportunity to challenge its universal scope.

7.2.1 Resisting Reductionism

It is possible to reduce a role-based ethics to alternative ethical approaches that would consider roles and relations in a more secondary or instrumental way. For instance, rituals involved in roles and relations could be seen as a way to develop certain individualist virtues which are, in the end, what really matters. Or, paying attention to the matrix of relations that forms and maintains one's agency may

---

[40] See Judith Andre, "Role Morality as a Complex Instance of Ordinary Morality" (1991) 28:1 Am Phil Q 73.
[41] Thomas Nagel, *The View from Nowhere* (New York: Oxford University Press, 1986), at 152–53.
[42] A. J. Simmons, *Moral Principles and Political Obligations* (Princeton: Princeton University Press, 1979), at 13.
[43] This is only an illustration, not a speciesist stand; one may just as well examine the kinds of shared and distinct relationships and communities that human and nonhuman animals share.
[44] Carl Schmitt, *The Concept of the Political*, expand. ed. (Chicago: University of Chicago Press, 2007), at 54 (paraphrasing Pierre-Joseph Proudhon).

be a way to secure personal autonomy. Let me expand on this instance of reductionism.

Even theories that attend to the relational texture of autonomy more closely than atomistic theories can differ in subtle but meaningful ways. For instance, the aforementioned relational approaches to autonomy and equality are distinct from Confucian ethics. Consider Peter Hershock and Roger Ames's statement that "Confucian selfhood ... is defined in a network of relations, and moral autonomy is to be achieved through virtuosity in those relations."[45] Contrast it with feminist philosopher Diana Meyers's view of autonomy. She looks at the importance of socialization in understanding how personal autonomy is formed and maintained as a kind of competency. She criticizes mainstream accounts of personal autonomy for assuming "autonomy will be unintelligible unless a free agent can be found" and pursuing methods of "socialization-transcendence" that are doomed to fail.[46] Consider, in the same relational vein, Christine Koggel, who writes "a relational approach to equality asks what moral persons embedded and interacting in relationships of interdependency need to flourish and develop."[47] A number of relational theorists may ultimately strive for achieving substantial, meaningful, "real" equality (or ending the oppression of certain social groups, in the name of equality) or substantial autonomy. But those goals are still articulated as individual ideals, and "virtuosity" in relations becomes a means for personal achievement. Relational approaches thus give particular importance to personal autonomy or a personal dignified state of being recognized as an equal as the key achievement that the theory is concerned to secure. Confucian approaches view the roles and relations as repository of moral wisdom and would resist presenting them simply as means for individual achievement of personal goods. Of course, no one denies that human beings are both "free" and uniquely "autonomous" on the one hand, and part of a matrix of relations, on the other. But how theories approach these characteristics can lead to very different results. The ingredients may be present in different theories, but the order in which they are connected (baked!) will yield different results (cakes!).

Reductionism (i.e., explaining why relations and roles matter in terms of some abstract good or value) is an attractive move. Reaching a higher level of abstraction may help us revise, explain, and solve conflicts between messy rituals and norms constituting social scripts. Thus, although "we do in fact cite our relationships to other people in explaining why we have special responsibilities to them, many philosophers have been reluctant to take these citations at face value."[48]

---

[45] Peter Hershock and Roger Ames, *Confucian Cultures of Authority* (Albany: State University of New York Press, 2006), at xiii.
[46] Diana T. Meyers, *Self, Society and Personal Choice* (New York: Columbia University Press, 1989), at 41–42.
[47] Christine Koggel, *Perspectives on Equality: Constructing a Relational Theory* (Lanham: Rowman & Littlefield, 1998).

Often, the relational dimension of a moral problem fades into the background of a philosophical investigation. For example, in caring relations, one may focus on the vulnerability of dependents[49] or the injustice endured by unsupported caregivers.[50] This can become a problem if one loses sight of the relational context within which these values come to matter. It would be like staring very closely at an impressionist painting in order to study its meticulous craft. It could be informative as long as analysts do not forget that it is meant to be enjoyed – and only makes sense – from a greater distance. A relational stance may not just hold that maximizing the happiness of someone matters because that person matters, but also that this person matters to an individual because of the relation that individual has with this person. In other widely shared relations – such as a common solidarity between human beings, or a generalized respect for one's dignity – the idea of "relation" may be taken for granted because of its universality, standardized aspect, or minimalist content. That is, it is so present that it becomes invisible. It has become natural to focus, instead, on a particular good (like quality of life, to be maximized) or value (like autonomy, to be respected) instead of the relation itself.

Another kind of reductionism can happen within a relational approach: a "relationist" could reduce the moral relevance of various kinds of relations to a single kind of relation. The role ethics I have in mind, in contrast, would be pluralist, so that a diversity of relations would matter for reasons that would not be helpfully[51] reduced to one another. The social contract tradition could be interpreted in a relational way, as focusing on specific kinds of relations (e.g., tit-for-tat bargaining) between specific people (e.g., rational strangers contracting to maximize their preferences). Similarly, some may hold that the only morally relevant relations are those through which individuals exercise their capacity to consent. People holding this "voluntarist" view would then judge other relations accordingly – for instance, they would find unchosen relations unfair if they impose costs or confer benefits that do not stem from autonomous choices.[52]

Feminist models of relational morality may also choose a reductionist path. For instance, they may assume that the "masculine" moral voice is not relational. Such theories often import the unspoken assumption that there can be no meaningful "relation" other than relations that are characterized by other-regarding concern, such as the central case of parental nurturing, which is the wellspring for a significant amount of this literature. Commenting on Michael Slote's book on

---

[49] See, e.g., Robert Goodin, *Protecting the Vulnerable: A Reanalysis of Our Social Responsibilities* (Chicago: University of Chicago Press, 1985).
[50] See, e.g., Kittay, *Love's Labor*.
[51] I say "helpfully" because I intuit these relations could well all be explained in terms of some fundamental moral idea, like "concern," but this fundamental "moral fuel" would not help us solve common ethical issues that societies and individuals must confront. We need to grapple with the distinct normative texture of a variety of relations.
[52] Scheffler, *Boundaries and Allegiances*, at 97–98.

the ethics of care and empathy, Carol Gilligan notes that Slote "argues for a Copernican revolution in moral philosophy, moving empathy and relationship from the periphery to the center of an ethical universe."[53] However, contractual relations – which are very different from other relations of care or love – are still relations, no matter the difference in the moral capacities and attitudes involved. Slote's efforts, like Gilligan's and other feminist writers, to emphasize the moral weight of some relations thought to have little or no moral significance does not need to imply that very different relations should be marginalized (e.g., relations characterized by self-interest that take place between strangers in a way that makes the "relational currency" fungible and universal, making the personal identities of the people involved a secondary concern).[54] "[W]e need more than empathy to do justice to morality," Annette Baier writes, criticizing Slote's empathy-based account of morality, adding "[i]f allied with stupidity, impatience, and foolhardiness, empathy will achieve little."[55] From the point of view of virtue ethics, this criticism means that we need to cultivate a multiplicity of virtues. From the point of view of a role-based ethics, it means that we need to understand how one becomes a virtuoso at endorsing the roles that define one.

In addition to the charge of historicism, the main objection to such a broad relational understanding of morality is that the idea of relation either adds nothing to a moral investigation or it makes relationality trivial. That is, it can be seen as a semantic way to formulate problems that are not primarily about relations. This is the challenge that a full defense of role-based ethics would have to confront. In this conclusion, I can only state that the position that all moral conflicts can be expressed in terms of relational conflict holds the promise of (1) allowing us to give effect to the moral significance of a plurality of relations, moral capacities, and attitudes and (2) finding a way to prioritize these relations and effectively deal with conflicts between them, and to be realistic about situations where principled morality does not provide us with an answer.

Perhaps the best way to suggest that a relational approach to morality is promising – apart from the existing literature supporting variants of it, its theoretical

---

[53] Carol Gilligan, front matter, in Michael Slote, *The Ethics of Care and Empathy* (London: Routledge, 2007).

[54] The case that empathy is at the very root of our human moral responses is a different sort of claim. Though I endorse a similar view, I need not imply that relations that are characterized by other-regarding concern, partiality, and direct attitudinal attachment – while chronologically prior in terms of moral development – have to be considered as more central to the moral universe than the types of relations featured by impartialist and universalist traditions. Similarly, the fact that some actions necessitate primarily relational capacities (e.g., trust or love) while others call for primarily internal or individually exercised ones (e.g., a capacity to elaborate a conception of the good) does not mean that the latter kind of actions are not relational or that moral problems arising from them cannot be termed relationally.

[55] Annette Baier, "Is Empathy All We Need?" (2010) Abstracta (Special Issue) V 28 at 41.

potential, and its ability to solve some of the tensions noted in this book – is by pointing out how closely it maps our common way of approaching all kinds of beings with all kinds of capacities in our everyday lives. When we interact with different people, we immediately think of their identities – that is, of the social and cultural groups/communities they belong to. We then decide how to act, taking into account the following: (1) their identity, (2) our identity, (3) how to act in a way that does not artificially construct the person (a) as an anonymous container of properties and (b) as a detached and impartial moral agent, (4) the macro and micro social context (i.e., the social norms and scripts that regulate these encounters given the particular circumstances of each agent in this relation), and (5) our inclinations (to act properly or not).

Economists, psychologists, and philosophers are interested in different aspects of this process. What is puzzling – given how naturally we think in relational terms – is the fact that moral philosophers would *not* adopt this focus, pushing relational pluralism to the background once they have chosen a particular kind of relation to focus on, such as the contractual one. A likely response is that this is a choice philosophers make based on a reasoned belief that they are tracking a specific value, and they should therefore ignore relations, either because they have no value, or because they do not have the special kind of value that one is concerned with. We should be skeptical of this answer and suspect that some of these theories simply focus too closely on a single kind of value (like autonomy or survival found in variants of contractualism and contractarianism) or type of relation (such as a contractual one between self-interested agents fending for themselves) to the detriment of others. Once these valuable capacities, states of affairs or relations have been embedded in a unified theory, it is tempting to simply dismiss competing values rather than meeting their challenge. The fear of pluralism or the appeal of generalization is far from a trivial suspicion. Annette Baier, among other feminists, insists on the fact that most philosophers were men, too busy with certain kinds of relations (at work, in politics, in their clubs) to be concerned with others and, indeed, were probably contemptuous of these other, "lesser" endeavors, such as caring for and raising children. Thus, the assumption that these philosophers would model justice – or anything related to morality that is worth their consideration – on these particular relations and on the social scripts/norms that they spent most of their time understanding and analyzing, is hardly far-fetched. Susan Moller Okin wrote of Rawls that his "discussion of rational plans of life and primary goods might be focused more on relationships and less exclusively on the complex activities that he values most highly, if it were to take account of … traditionally more female contributions to human life."[56]

Of course, I can only gesture at what a role-based approach to morality may look like in this conclusion. I am suggesting that, when we consider what each of us,

---

[56] Susan Moller Okin, *Justice, Gender, and the Family* (New York: Basic Books, 1989), at 107–108.

individually and collectively, owe to PSID, we should think about our relations with people with disabilities and try to determine what is morally salient about these relations, all while being willing to revise these beliefs. It seems evident, from a commonsense perspective, that relations involving PSID matter – and not because of their capacity to engage or not in contractual roles. It seems, instead, that relations driven by other-regarding concern will best explain their robust moral status.

7.3 TAKING RELATIONS OF OTHER-REGARDING CONCERN SERIOUSLY

My position is that some of the faults and problems exhibited in the contractual variants could be overcome if the contract idiom – and the values underlying it – was replaced by a relational account that makes room for other-regarding concern.

This position stems from reflecting upon the relations that we have with PSID and that we would ordinarily think of as morally stringent. These relations would generally be considered to be fiduciary relationships or relationships of care – that is, relations in which a caregiver or trustee is in charge of promoting the welfare of a beneficiary or a cared-for person. These relations are grounded on some affective responses or dispositions on the part of the caregiver and involve other-regarding moral attitudes.

To give weighty moral significance to some special relations with PSID is not only more compatible with our deeply held beliefs about why we are stringently obliged to them (apart from a contractual explanation) but it also reflects our common understanding that these beliefs have a *moral* component, and should correspond to a robust moral status. For example, some care ethicists, notably Nel Noddings, place the value of a kind of special relation – caring – at the very center of morality. Noddings argues that "[h]uman caring and the memory of being cared for ... form the foundation of ethical response."[57] She suggests caring and being cared for are not only things that human beings naturally want but are also morally important of themselves,[58] in part because she locates the source of morality in some of the natural, affective responses of agents and their pursuit of an ideal ethical self.[59] This is a view that could be framed to favor a relational morality whereby agents realize themselves by assuming or endorsing certain roles. Yet, even though the reality of human vulnerability and dependency are so central to human life and to many moral relations in which we participate from birth to death, these aspects have been excluded, as Alasdair MacIntyre boldly suggests, from the history of Western philosophy, which has been dominated by the values of self-sufficiency and autonomy.[60]

---

[57] Nel Noddings, *Caring: A Feminine Approach to Ethics & Moral Education* (Berkeley: University of California Press, 1984), at 1.
[58] Ibid. at 7.
[59] Ibid. at 43, 48–51.
[60] Alasdair MacIntyre, *Dependent Rational Animals: Why Human Beings Need the Virtues* (Chicago: Open Court, 1999), at ch. 1.

I do not claim that care ethics is definitively the best alternative that should be pursued instead of, or in addition to, a contractual approach. I only use it here because it is probably the best available example of a theoretical trend that gives a serious ethical and metaethical weight to relations with dependent human beings.[61] The difficulties this trend faces when theorists adopt it into a theory of justice illustrate the danger of only recognizing the central value of *one* kind of relation, as I mentioned in the previous section. Some theorists of care and empathy purport to replace justice with care, or to put these attitudes at the heart of justice and dismiss those other attitudes that are usually taken to play a greater role (typically in a contractual framework), a move that drew Baier's criticism of the recent work of Michael Slote, mentioned above. Similarly, reviewing Virginia Held's recent expansion of the ethics of care into the political domain, Carla Bagnoli writes:

> How exactly [Held] sees [the integration of care and justice], however, remains highly problematic. At times Held suggests that they pertain to different domains, and that they should be allowed priority in their respective spheres of competence. At other times, she claims that care may "provide the wider and deeper ethics within which justice should be sought," questions the priority of justice, and argues for the priority of care.... But then Held admits that "the ethics of care may not itself provide adequate theoretical resources for dealing with issues of justice."[62]

The challenge resides, I suggest, in developing a pluralist and relational account of morality able to deal with conflicts between competing roles. Almost twenty years ago, Virginia Held was already both attracted by and unsure of such an account. In her essay "Non-Contractual Society," she writes: "I doubt that we should take any one relation as paradigmatic for all the others. And I doubt that morality should be based on any one type of human relation."[63] Here, she refers to her book *Rights and Goods*,[64] in which she "argue[s] for different moral approaches for different contexts, and [tries] to map out which approaches are suitable for which contexts" while adding that she may change her mind and "eventually suppose that relations between mothers and children should be thought of as primary, as the sort of human relation all other human relations should resemble or reflect."[65] On the

---

[61] For a different approach, consider for instance MacIntyre's argument to expand virtue ethics in a way that accounts for human beings' animal nature, in particular our vulnerable and dependent nature. In order to flourish, we need to pursue "genuinely common goods," such as a "network of relationships of giving and receiving" (*ibid.* at 108, 118). MacIntyre offers a list of the "virtues of acknowledged dependence" which are the qualities required to properly participate in these networks (*ibid.* at ch. 10). See also Nussbaum, *Frontiers of Justice*.

[62] Carol Bagnoli, "Book Review of *The Ethics of Care: Personal, Political, Global* by Virginia Held," *Notre Dame Phil Rev* (June 4, 2006), ndpr.nd.edu/news/25040-the-ethics-of-care-personal-political-global/ (citations removed).

[63] Held, "Non-Contractual Society," at 114.

[64] Virginia Held, *Rights and Goods: Justifying Social Actions* (Chicago: University of Chicago Press, 1984).

[65] Held, "Non-Contractual Society," at 114–15.

other hand, she also wrote that, although she may come to think that such a "nurturing" relationship should be primary or central to morality, she is "inclined at this point to think that we will continue to need conceptions of different types of relations for different domains, such as the domains of law, of economic activity, and of the family."[66] Her most recent book is still affected by the tension between pluralism and monism of moral grounds.[67]

I suspect that even when Held, Noddings, or Slote would grant the importance of moral pluralism to assess certain problems, they have a hard time letting go of the centrality of other-regarding attitudes like care and empathy because they sense the fundamental motivational, affective, and epistemological importance of these attitudes. My own view is that such a key, other-regarding element (which I tend to think of as "concern") does indeed occupy a foundational role in moral human life, but that it operates at a deeper level. When we arrive at a later stage of practical reasoning, other-regarding attitudes (e.g., concern) play a significant role in some relations (such as those that are perhaps unduly summarized as "caring") but not in others (such as those perhaps unduly categorized as "justice" or "contractual relations"). However, at this later stage of moral reflection, the shared similarity between a foundational concern or empathy (at the most basic level) and some caring relations (at a more applied level) need not give these latter relations a superior status. Rather, I suggest we pursue Held's earlier insight on the need to develop an account of morality that would recognize the plurality of human relations.

7.4 A RELATIONAL PLURALIST VIEW: CARE, CONTRACT, AND BEYOND

Taking a relational pluralist approach, we can more easily see that the social contract tradition (like other moral systems or theories) may provide a good analysis of the moral significance and implication of *one* kind of relation (i.e., contractual). We can also better detect when some variants of this tradition take *that* relation to be the *central* case of moral relations, and accordingly take the capacities or properties required for that relation to occur to be the properties that matter for gaining a robust moral status. Looking at the relations moral agents[68] have with PSID in various social contexts, we can reflect upon what is salient about these relations. As I suggested, once liberated from the contractual idiom and its conceptual constraints, we intuitively find that, in many cases, the relation is characterized by

---

[66] *Ibid.* at 115.
[67] Held, *Ethics of Care*.
[68] I leave it open whether some PSID have moral agency themselves or not. Certainly, PWD do, and only the most severely intellectually disabled people may not have it.

caring and dependence, and that the properties such as our ability to care and the reality of vulnerability are much more central to explaining our relational obligations than the presence of any contract-like features.

As the previous chapters indicate, the social contract tradition can hardly put this type of fiduciary relation at the center of its theory without challenging some of its key assumptions. Yet, we can imagine that both types of relations (i.e., contractual and caring) can trigger robust moral obligations, even without being reducible to one another. As stated in the introduction, I assumed that PWD and PSID had a robust moral status for the purpose of this book, and I add here that a full defense of the robust moral status of PSID would be more promisingly done on noncontractual grounds.[69] The philosophy of disability has been expanding exponentially in recent years,[70] but it is still an emerging field, and negotiating the moral status of PSID is still an important objective within this field.

To be sure, a pluralist relational account would still face daunting objections: First, if drives to endorse a role or to participate in a relation would be partially explained by emotions toward others, it would grant undue moral weight to psychological phenomena, such as affective dispositions or responses. Second, even if we allow that the psychological facts central to fiduciary relations are morally relevant, they may not be relevant to justice. Third, the value of these fiduciary relations can be nested in, or explained by, another account, such as a traditional autonomy-based or contractual account of morality.

Here are a few answers that could be given to these criticisms, and which would make room for caring relations: (1) While this theory would imply some substantial agreement about the good and human nature, so do contractual theories. (2) This theory does not disrespect autonomy; sometimes dependency and vulnerability require another moral response, and sometimes we can both care and respect a person to varying appropriate degrees. (3) Pluralist grounds for robust moral status are not that problematic and the social contract tradition should not indulge in normalizing PSID for simplicity's sake. Morality can, unfortunately, be messy. (4) The notion of "concern" may help to deal with conflict occasioned by this pluralism and to balance the acts of caring and respect. Furthermore, (5) particular relations and roles come with their own normative bundle of rules and, while some relations and roles are optional, leaving PSID alone altogether is not due to some basic relations able-bodied people have with them, the nature of which cannot be properly characterized as centrally contractual. Finally, (6) relations are not necessarily hostage to emotional or psychological states. We may think of choosing a relational status as choosing any privately enjoyable good (e.g., chocolate). This may

---

[69] Consider, e.g., John Vorhaus, *Valuing Profoundly Disabled People: Fellowship, Community and Ties of Birth* (New York: Routledge, 2018).

[70] For a recent survey of the field, see David Wasserman and Adam Cureton, eds., *The Oxford Handbook of Philosophy and Disability* (New York: Oxford University Press, 2019).

render relations volatile, and certain relations surely are. But we can also think of relations as communally defined phenomena in which agents already find themselves, or that somehow precede our choosing them, and we can think of roles as phenomena through which agents learn to feel, emote, and form preferences, rather than exclusively as the object of such preferences or emotions.

A role-based or relational account may still, in the end, not be preferable. If so, our examination of contractual thought still leads us to conclude that alternative accounts of morality and politics must go beyond normalizing people with disabilities into existing philosophical structures. Although this has been the strategy (successfully) deployed by philosophers and lobbyists to vindicate the rights of traditionally marginalized groups, and although incremental changes to mainstream moral philosophy and political thought are less radical, this book supports the claim that this strategy fails, at least in the case of people with severe intellectual disabilities. We must instead question mainstream assumptions about the metaethical starting point(s) of moral investigations – such as a requirement for an impartial, universal, and a-relational stance – as well as the fundamental criteria for society to be just and for a being to be a subject of justice.

Let me at least begin to address one challenge posed by a relational theory of morality that insists on taking the normative codes associated with various roles/relations seriously, as opposed to reducing them to a more fundamental principle expected to offer guidance. This challenge flags the difficulty in deciding which relational obligation shall trump in case of a conflict of duties. Sometimes a contractual relational framework is warranted to interrogate certain aspects of the way we relate to a person, and sometimes other frameworks are needed. Sometimes these frameworks conflict and sometimes they overlap, especially if they are addressing different dimensions of a person's needs, capacities, or roles. For example, instead of opting to respect someone's autonomy *or* caring for someone's vulnerabilities, we probably must do both, to various degrees. How are we to know, then, which role to endorse or which moral hat to wear?

Instead of feeling overwhelmed with the daunting prospect of moral pluralism, let us remember that we, as moral agents, are constantly called upon to make adjudication in cases of conflicting obligations. We say "sorry, I'll be late for the game, I must pick up my kid from school." We find these judgments entrenched in the law, for instance, when witnesses cannot be called to testify against family members in criminal cases. On an interpersonal level, we are tormented by the choice of giving someone paternalistic, potentially condescending advice or respecting her independence by letting her "learn the hard way." On a more immediate level, we are caught in a pleasing conundrum between living in the world of literary characters by reading our bedside novel or choosing to play with our cat. Though we rely on a relatively steady hierarchy of relational obligations, we rarely give absolute priority to a particular type of relation or to a particular person we relate to.

We are blamed or congratulated by ourselves and our peers when we endorse different roles in a way that suggests that (1) there is a right and a wrong way to strike a balance between the relational obligations we owe to ourselves and to different individuals and groups; (2) some relations are more valuable than others and some roles make more stringent demands than others; and (3) it is morally or ethically optional for moral agents to endorse a role or to choose between conflicting relational duties depending on the nature of the relation (and the circumstances in which this relation plays out).

If there is some higher moral gauge that helps us to decide which response is most appropriate, it may be something like solicitude or concern, Iris Murdoch's (loving) "attention," or Aristotle's virtue of practical wisdom (*phronesis*). This moral gauge would not necessarily offer us practical guidance in a situation of normative conflict. Rather, it may be a form of practical-epistemological wisdom – an insight that helps recognize the morally salient features of the situation we find ourselves in (and, if a relational account can help to clarify this process, to associate the situation with a relation) and choose which roles to prioritize. While we may not need such a basic meta-notion to balance between different relational obligations, I believe that the complex notion of concern could play this role, if we properly develop its affective, conative, and cognitive dimensions. Such views would no longer be "pluralist" if they ultimately reduce competing values to a single one. However, as James Griffin argues, "[c]ommensurability does not require monism,"[71] and it seems plausible that certain architectonic or scaling concepts can help people negotiate clashes between values while remaining separate from these values.

I have painted, in very broad, intuitive brushstrokes, the multileveled axiological components of what a relational theory of morality could look like. I believe that this broad account makes sense of the various relations we have with PSID. It seems that the most salient and stringent of these relations is caring. Taking caring roles and relations seriously may take some of the weight off of humanist philosophers producing non-relational justifications for caring for beings who lack capacities traditionally prized within Western philosophy. I think that understanding the social script and normative codes associated with caring relations, as well as appreciating their substance as a matter of morality and justice, is where the bulk of the work in understanding the robust moral status of PSID lies. PWD with less severe disabilities, on the other hand, are likely to benefit (sometimes more so) from a contractual understanding of relations between citizens. Importantly, not all relations "stick" to a certain group of people all the time, nor do they always hold between particular people (though perhaps some do, such as kinds of love or family ties). We may relate to an individual – disabled or not – both as a cared-for person or as a contractor, depending on the context. Not all of us may be autonomous and rational in a way that is required of subjects of justice and moral patients in the social contract tradition, but all of us are vulnerable and dependent.

---

[71] James Griffin, *Well-Being: Its Meaning, Measurement and Moral Importance* (Oxford: Oxford University Press, 1988), at 90.

People with the most severe disabilities may contribute to our understanding of our vulnerability and of the importance of caring relations in human life. They may lighten our existential burdens by playing their role, even though the roles they have been assigned to play in our "human comedy" are often not those of bargainers, soldiers, or moral philosophers, and even though their "contribution" hardly makes sense in the contractual idiom of mutual advantage or mutual justifiability. Reducing the morality of human relations to their contractual aspects is a mistake, though it is a promising political strategy of procedural reconciliation between disagreeing strangers. Social contract theorists should thank people with severe intellectual disabilities for guiding us toward a conclusion that improves our self-understanding as individuals and as a society. Indeed, we must recognize the value of people with disabilities, whether we thank them or not.

Bibliography

SECONDARY SOURCES

American Psychiatric Association, *Diagnostic and Statistical Manual of Mental Disorders: DSM-5*, 5th ed. (Arlington, VA: APA, 2013).
Ames, Roger T. and Henry Rosemont Jr., *The Chinese Classic of Family Reverence: A Philosophical Translation of the Xiaojing* (Honolulu: University of Hawaii Press, 2009).
Anderson, Elizabeth, *Value in Ethics and Economics* (Cambridge: Harvard University Press, 1995).
Anderson, Elizabeth, "What Is the Point of Equality?" (1999) 109:2 *Ethics* 287.
Andre, Judith, "Role Morality as a Complex Instance of Ordinary Morality" (1991) 28:1 *Am Phil Q* 73.
Appiah, Anthony, *Cosmopolitanism: Ethics in a World of Strangers* (London: W. W. Norton, 2006).
Appiah, Anthony, *The Ethics of Identity* (Princeton, NJ: Princeton University Press, 2007).
Aragona, Massimiliano, "The Concept of Mental Disorder and the DSM-V" (2009) 2:1 *Dial Phil Ment & Neuro Sci* 1.
Arendt, Hannah, *The Origins of Totalitarianism* (New York: Meridian Books, 1958).
Bagnoli, Carol, "Book Review of *The Ethics of Care: Personal, Political, Global* by Virginia Held," *Notre Dame Phil Rev* (June 4, 2006), ndpr.nd.edu/news/25040-the-ethics- of-care-personal-political-global/.
Baier, Annette, "Trust and Antitrust" (1986) 96:2 *Ethics* 231.
Baier, Annette, "Trust," Tanner Lectures on Human Values, Princeton University (March 1991), tannerlectures.utah.edu/_documents/a-to-z/b/baier92.pdf.
Baier, Annette, "Trusting People" (1992) 6 *Ethics* 137.
Baier, Annette, *Moral Prejudices: Essays on Ethics* (Cambridge: Harvard University Press, 1995).
Baier, Annette, "Is Empathy All We Need?" (2010) *Abstracta* (Special Issue) V 28.
Barclay, Linda, "Cognitive Impairment and the Right to Vote: A Strategic Approach" (2013) 30:2 *J Appl Phil* 146.
Barnartt, Sharon N., "Using Role Theory to Describe Disability" in Sharon N. Barnartt and Barbara M. Altman, eds., *Exploring Theories and Expanding Methodologies: Where We Are and Where We Need to Go* (Bingley: Emerald Group, 2001), at 53–75.

Barnes, Colin, "A Working Social Model? Disability, Work and Disability Politics in the 21st Century" (2000) 20:4 *Critical Soc Pol'y* 441.
Barnes, Elizabeth, *The Minority Body* (Oxford: Oxford University Press, 2016).
Barry, Brian, *The Liberal Theory of Justice. A Critical Examination of the Principal Doctrines in a Theory of Justice by John Rawls* (Oxford: Clarendon Press, 1973).
Beaudry, Jonas-Sébastien, "Of Apes and Men" in John Huss, ed., *Planet of the Apes and Philosophy: Great Apes Think Alike* (Chicago: Open Court, 2013), at 83–96.
Beaudry, Jonas-Sébastien, "From Autonomy to Habeas Corpus: Animal Rights Activists Take the Parameters of Legal Personhood to Court" (2016) 1 *Global J Animal L* 3.
Beaudry, Jonas-Sébastien, "Beyond (Models of) Disability?" (2016) 41:2 *J Med & Phil* 210.
Beaudry, Jonas-Sébastien, "The Vanishing Body of Disability Law: Power and the Making of the Impaired Subject" (2018) 31:1 *Can J Fam L* 7.
Beaudry, Jonas-Sébastien, "Welcoming Monsters: Disability as a Liminal Legal Concept" (2018) 29:2 *Yale JL & Human* 291.
Beaudry, Jonas-Sébastien, "Are Animals Persons? Why Ask?" (2019) 9:1 *J Animal Ethics* 6.
Beaudry, Jonas-Sébastien, "Theoretical Strategies to Define Disability" in David Wasserman and Adam Cureton, eds., *The Oxford Handbook of Philosophy and Disability* (New York: Oxford University Press, 2019).
Becker, Lawrence, "Reciprocity, Justice, and Disability" (2005) 116:1 *Ethics* 9.
Bird, Alexander and Emma Tobin, "Natural Kinds," *The Stanford Encyclopedia of Philosophy* (February 2017), plato.stanford.edu/archives/spr2018/entries/natural-kinds/.
Blackburn, Simon, *Oxford Dictionary of Philosophy*, 2nd ed. (Oxford: Oxford University Press, 2008), *sub verbo* social contract.
Brel, Jacques, *Ne me quitte pas* (Philips Records, 1959).
British Psychological Society, "Response to the American Psychiatric Association: DSM-5 Development," The British Psychological Society (2011), at 2, www1.bps.org.uk/system/files/consultationpapers/responses/DSM-5%202011%20-%20BPS%20 response.pdf.
Buchanan, Allen, "Justice as Reciprocity versus Subject-Centered Justice" (1990) 19:3 *Phil & Pub Aff* 227.
Byrne, Peter, *Philosophical and Ethical Problems in Mental Handicap* (New York: St Martin's Press, 2000).
Callahan, Daniel, "Autonomy: A Moral Good, Not a Moral Obsession" (1984) 14:5 *Hastings Center Report* 40.
Callicott, J. Baird, "Intrinsic Value in Nature: A Metaethical Analysis" (1995) 3 *Electronic J Analytic Phil*.
Carlson, Licia, *The Faces of Intellectual Disability* (Bloomington: Indiana University Press, 2010).
Cohen, Andrew, "Contractarianism, Other-Regarding Attitudes, and the Moral Standing of Nonhuman Animals" (2007) 24:2 *J Appl Phil* 188.
Cudd, Ann, "Contractarians," *The Stanford Encyclopedia of Philosophy* (August 2012), plato.stanford.edu/archives/fall2012/entries/contractarianism/.
Cureton, Adam, "A Rawlsian Perspective on Justice for the Disabled" (2008) 9:1 *Essays Phil*.
Daily, Donna K., Holly H. Ardinger, and Grace E. Holmes, "Identification and Evaluation of Mental Retardation" (2000) 61:4 *Am Fam Phys* 1059.
Darwall, Stephen, *Contractarianism / Contractualism* (Malden, MA: Blackwell, 2003).
Davis, Lennard J., *Enforcing Normalcy: Disability, Deafness and the Body* (London: Verso, 1995).
de Jasay, Anthony, *Social Contract, Free Ride: A Study of the Public Goods Problem* (Indianapolis: Liberty Fund, 2008).

Debes, Remy, ed., *Dignity: A History* (New York: Oxford University Press, 2017).
Diamond, Cora, "Eating Meat and Eating People" (1978) 53:206 *Philosophy* 465.
Diamond, Cora, "The Importance of Being Human" (1991) 29 *Royal Institute Phil Supplements* 35.
Dimock, Susan, "Defending Non-Tuism" (1999) 29:2 *Can J Phil* 251.
Dimock, Susan, "Why All Feminists Should Be Contractarians" (2008) 47:2 *Dialogue: Can Phil Rev* 273.
Donaldson, Sue and Will Kymlicka, *Zoopolis: A Political Theory of Animal Rights* (Oxford: Oxford University Press, 2011).
Downie, Jocelyn Grant and Jennifer J. Llewellyn, *Being Relational: Reflections on Relational Theory and Health Law* (Vancouver: UBC Press, 2012).
Dumas, Alexander, *The Count of Monte Cristo* (Open Road Media, 2014; originally published 1844).
Dworkin, Ronald, *Taking Rights Seriously* (London: Bloomsbury Academic, 2013).
Faraday, Fay, Margaret Denike, and M. Kate Stephenson, eds., *Making Equality Rights Real: Securing Substantive Equality under the Charter* (Toronto: Irwin Law, 2006).
Fineman, M. A., "The Vulnerable Subject: Anchoring Equality in the Human Condition" (2008) 20:1 *Yale JL & Feminism* 1.
Fineman, M. A., "The Vulnerable Subject and the Responsive State" (2010) 60:2 *Emory LJ* 251.
Finnis, John, *Reason in Action* (Oxford: Oxford University Press, 2011).
Francis, Leslie, "Understanding Autonomy in Light of Intellectual Disability" in Kimberley Brownlee and Adam Cureton, eds., *Disability and Disadvantage* (Oxford: Oxford University Press, 2009), at 200–16.
Francis, Leslie and Anita Silvers, "Justice through Trust: Disability and the 'Outlier Problem' in Social Contract Theory" (2005) 116:1 *Ethics* 40.
Francis, Leslie and Anita Silvers, "Liberalism and Individually Scripted Ideas of the Good: Meeting the Challenge of Dependent Agency" (2007) 33:2 *Soc Theory & Prac* 311.
Francis, Leslie and Anita Silvers, "Thinking about the Good: Reconfiguring Liberal Metaphysics (or Not) for People with Cognitive Disabilities" in Eva Feder Kittay and Licia Carlson, eds., *Cognitive Disability and Its Challenge to Moral Philosophy* (Malden, MA: Wiley-Blackwell, 2010), 237.
Frankfurt, Harry, "Equality and Respect" (1997) 64:1 *Social Research* 3.
Fraser, Nancy, "Rethinking Recognition" (2000) 3 *New Left Review* 107.
Freeman, Samuel, *Justice and the Social Contract: Essays on Rawlsian Political Philosophy* (New York: Oxford University Press, 2007).
Gauthier, David, *Morals by Agreement* (Oxford: Oxford University Press, 1987).
Gergen, Kenneth J., *Relational Being: Beyond Self and Community* (New York: Oxford University Press, 2015)
Gilligan, Carol, *In a Different Voice: Psychological Theory and Women's Development* (Cambridge: Harvard University Press, 1993).
Goodin, Robert, *Protecting the Vulnerable: A Reanalysis of Our Social Responsibilities* (Chicago: University of Chicago Press, 1985).
Griffin, James, *Well-Being: Its Meaning, Measurement and Moral Importance* (Oxford: Oxford University Press, 1988)
Grimké, Sarah, *Letters on the Equality of the Sexes and the Condition of Woman*, Letter II (Boston, 1837).
Hampton, Jean, "The Wisdom of the Egoist: The Moral and Political Implications of Valuing the Self" (1997) 14:1 *Social Phil & Pol'y* 21.

Hampton, Jean, *The Intrinsic Worth of Persons: Contractarianism in Moral and Political Philosophy*, ed. Daniel Farnham (New York: Cambridge University Press, 2007).
Harrison, Paul *et al.*, *Shorter Oxford Textbook of Psychiatry* (Oxford: Oxford University Press, 2017).
Hartley, Christie, "Justice for the Disabled: A Contractualist Approach" (2009) 40:1 *J Soc Phil* 17.
Held, Virginia, *Rights and Goods: Justifying Social Actions* (Chicago: University of Chicago Press, 1984).
Held, Virginia, "Non-Contractual Society: A Feminist View" (1987) 13: sup1 *Can J Phil* 111.
Held, Virginia, *The Ethics of Care: Personal, Political, Global* (Oxford: Oxford University Press, 2006).
Hershock, Peter and Roger Ames, *Confucian Cultures of Authority* (Albany: State University of New York Press, 2006).
Holmes, Oliver Wendall, "The Path of the Law" (1897) 10 *Harv L Rev* 457.
Jaworska, Agnieszka, "Caring and Full Moral Standing" (2007) 117:3 *Ethics* 460.
Jeske, Diane, "Special Obligations," *The Stanford Encyclopedia of Philosophy* (August 2019), plato.stanford.edu/entries/special-obligations/.
Johnson, Harriet McBryde, "Unspeakable Conversations," *The New York Times* (February 16, 2003), www.nytimes.com/2003/02/16/magazine/unspeakable- conversations.html.
Kant, Immanuel, *The Metaphysics of Morals*, trans. and ed. Mary Gregor (Cambridge: Cambridge University Press, 1996).
Kant, Immanuel, *Lectures on Ethics*, ed. J. B. Schneewind, trans. Peter Heath (New York: Cambridge University Press, 1997).
Kant, Immanuel, *Groundwork of the Metaphysics of Morals*, trans. and ed. Mary Gregor (Cambridge: Cambridge University Press, 2012).
Kernohan, Andrew, "Rawls and the Collective Ownership of Natural Abilities" (1990) 20:1 *Can J Phil* 19.
Kinghorn, Warren, "The Biopolitics of Defining 'Mental Disorder'" in Joel Paris and James Phillips, eds., *Making the DSM-5: Concepts and Controversies* (New York: Springer, 2013), 47.
Kittay, Eva Feder, *Love's Labor: Essays on Women, Equality and Dependency* (New York: Routledge, 1999).
Kittay, Eva Feder, "At the Margins of Moral Personhood" (2008) 5:2–3 *J Bioethical Inquiry* 137–56.
Kittay, Eva Feder, "The Personal Is Philosophical Is Political: A Philosopher and a Mother of a Cognitively Disabled Person Send Notes from the Battlefield" (2009) 40:3–4 *Metaphilosophy* 606.
Kittay, Eva Feder, "When Caring Is Just and Justice Is Caring: Justice and Mental Retardation" in Eva Feder Kittay and Ellen K. Feder, eds., *The Subject of Care: Feminist Perspectives on Dependency* (Lanham, MD: Rowman & Littlefield, 2012), at 257–76.
Kittay, Eva Feder and Licia Carlson, *Cognitive Disability and Its Challenge to Moral Philosophy* (Malden, MA: Wiley-Blackwell, 2010).
Koggel, Christine M., *Perspectives on Equality: Constructing a Relational Theory* (Lanham MA: Rowman & Littlefield, 1998).
Korsgaard, Christine, "Two Distinctions in Goodness" (1983) 92:2 *Philosophical Review* 169.
Korsgaard, Christine, *The Sources of Normativity* (Cambridge: Cambridge University Press, 2000).
Korsgaard, Christine, "Fellow Creatures: Kantian Ethics and Our Duties to Animals," Tanner Lectures on Human Values, University of Michigan (2004), tannerlectures.utah.edu/_documents/a-to-z/k/korsgaard_2005.pdf.

Le Méné, Jean-Marie, *La trisomie est une tragédie grecque* (Paris: Salvator, 2009).
Lippert-Rasmussen, Kasper, *Relational Egalitarianism: Living as Equals* (Cambridge: Cambridge University Press, 2018).
Lomasky, Loren E., *Persons, Rights, and the Moral Community* (New York: Oxford University Press, 1997).
Luhmann, Niklas, "Familiarity, Confidence, Trust: Problems and Alternatives" in Diego Gambetta, ed., *Trust: Making and Breaking Cooperative Relations* (New York: Basic Blackwell, 1988), at 94–107.
Machan, Tibor, *Putting Humans First: Why We Are Nature's Favorite* (Lanham, MD: Rowman & Littlefield, 2004).
MacIntyre, Alasdair, *Dependent Rational Animals: Why Human Beings Need the Virtues* (Chicago: Open Court, 1999).
MacKenzie, Catriona and Natalie Stoljar, eds., *Relational Autonomy: Feminist Perspectives on Autonomy, Agency, and the Social Self* (New York: Oxford University Press, 2000).
MacKenzie, Catriona, Wendy Rogers, and Susan Dodds, eds., *Vulnerability: New Essays in Ethics and Feminist Philosophy* (New York: Oxford University Press, 2013).
Malpas, Jeff and Norelle Lickiss, eds., *Perspectives on Human Dignity: A Conversation* (Dordrecht: Springer, 2007).
Mbembe, J.-A., "Necropolitics" (2003) 15:1 *Pub Culture* 11.
McAfee, Noëlle Claire, "Book Review of *Love's Labor: Essays on Women, Equality and Dependency* by Eva Feder Kittay" (2001) 32:3 *Metaphilosophy* 344.
McMahan, Jeff, "Cognitive Disability, Misfortune, and Justice" (1996) 25:1 *Phil & Pub Aff* 3.
McMahan, Jeff, *The Ethics of Killing: Problems at the Margins of Life* (New York: Oxford University Press, 2002).
McMahan, Jeff, "Our Fellow Creatures" (2005) 9:3–4 *J Ethics* 353.
McMahan, Jeff, "Challenges to Human Equality" (2008) 12:1 *J Ethics* 81.
Meyers, Diana T., *Self, Society and Personal Choice* (New York: Columbia University Press, 1989).
Mills, Charles, *The Racial Contract* (Ithaca: Cornell University Press, 1997).
Minow, Martha, *Making All the Difference: Inclusion, Exclusion, and American Law* (Ithaca: Cornell University Press, 2006)
Molesworth, William, ed., *The English Works of Thomas Hobbes of Malmesbury*, vol. III: Leviathan (London: John Bohn, 1839–45).
Morris, Christopher, "Moral Standing and Rational-Choice Contractarianism" in Peter Vallentyne, ed., *Contractarianism and Rational Choice: Essays on David Gauthier's Morals by Agreement* (New York: Cambridge University Press, 1991), at 76–95.
Mosoff, Judith, "Is the Human Rights Paradigm 'Able' to Include Disability: Who's In – Who Wins – What – Why" (2000) 26:1 *Queen's LJ* 225.
Murdoch, Iris, *The Sovereignty of Good* (London: Routledge & Kegan Paul, 1970).
Nagel, Thomas, *The View from Nowhere* (New York: Oxford University Press, 1986).
Neal, Patrick, *Liberalism and Its Discontents* (Washington Square: New York University Press, 1999).
Nedelsky, Jennifer, *Law's Relations: A Relational Theory of Self, Autonomy and Law* (Oxford: Oxford University Press, 2011).
Noddings, Nel, *Caring: A Feminine Approach to Ethics & Moral Education* (Berkeley: University of California Press, 1984).
Nozick, Robert, *Philosophical Explanations* (Cambridge: Harvard University Press, 1981).
Nussbaum, Martha, "Beyond the Social Contract: Toward Global Justice," Tanner Lectures on Human Values (Canberra, November 2002 and Cambridge, March 2003), tannerlectures.utah.edu/lectures/documents/volume24/nussbaum_2003.pdf.

Nussbaum, Martha, *Frontiers of Justice: Disability, Nationality, Species Membership* (Cambridge: Harvard University Press, 2006).
Okin, Susan Moller, *Justice, Gender, and the Family* (New York: Basic Books, 1989).
Oliver, Michael, *The Politics of Disablement* (London: Macmillan, 1990).
O'Neill, Onora, *Autonomy and Trust in Bioethics* (Cambridge: Cambridge University Press, 2002).
Ozon, François, *Potiche* (France: Mandarin Cinéma, 2010).
Paris, Joel, "Preface" in Joel Paris and James Phillips, eds., *Making the DSM-5: Concepts and Controversies* (New York: Springer, 2013), at v–vi.
Pateman, Carole, *The Sexual Contract* (Stanford: Stanford University Press, 1988).
Perlin, Michael L., *The Hidden Prejudice: Mental Disability on Trial* (Washington, DC: American Psychological Association, 2000).
Pfeiffer, David, "The Conceptualization of Disability" in Sharon N. Barnartt and Barbara M. Altman, eds., *Exploring Theories and Expanding Methodologies: Where We Are and Where We Need to Go* (Research in Social Science and Disability, vol. 2) (Bingley: Emerald Group Publishing, 2001), at 29–52.
Pothier, Dianne and Richard Devlin, eds., *Critical Disability Theory* (Vancouver: University of British Columbia Press, 2014).
Rachels, James, *Created from Animals: The Moral Implications of Darwinism* (Oxford: Oxford University Press, 1990).
Rawls, John, "Kantian Constructivism in Moral Theory" (1980) 77:9 *J Phil* 515.
Rawls, John, *Collected Papers*, ed. Samuel Freeman (Cambridge: Harvard University Press, 1999).
Rawls, John, *A Theory of Justice*, rev. ed. (Cambridge: Harvard University Press, 1999).
Rawls, John, *Justice as Fairness: A Restatement*, ed. Erin Kelly (Cambridge: Harvard University Press, 2001).
Rawls, John, *Political Liberalism*, expand. ed. (New York: Columbia University Press, 2005).
Raz, Joseph, *Value, Respect, and Attachment* (Cambridge: Cambridge University Press, 2001).
Regan, Tom, *The Case for Animal Rights* (Berkeley: Berkeley University Press, 1983).
Richardson, Henry, "Rawlsian Social-Contract Theory and the Severely Disabled" (2006) 10:4 *J Ethics* 419.
Richardson, Janice, "On Not Making Ourselves the Prey of Others: Jean Hampton's Feminist Contractarianism" (2007) 15:1 *Fem Legal Stud* 33.
Rohrer, Judy, "Ableism" in Susan Burch, ed., *Encyclopedia of American Disability History*, vol. 1 (New York: Facts On File, 2009), at 1–3.
Rounsaville, B. J., et al., "Basic Nomenclature Issues for DSM-V" in David J. Kupfer, Michael B. First, and Darrel A. Regier, eds., *A Research Agenda for DSM-V* (Washington, DC: American Psychiatric Association, 2002), at 1–29.
Sample, Ruth, "Why Feminist Contractarianism?" (2002) 33:2 *J Soc Phil* 257.
Sandel, Michael, "The Procedural Republic and the Unencumbered Self" (1984) 12:1 *Political Theory* 81.
Sandel, Michael, "What Money Shouldn't Buy" (2003) 5:2 *Hedgehog Review* 77–97.
Scanlon, Thomas, *What We Owe to Each Other* (Cambridge: Harvard University Press, 1998).
Schalock, Robert L. et al., *Intellectual Disability: Definition, Classification, and Systems of Supports*, 11th ed. (Washington, DC: AAIDD, 2009)
Scheffler, Samuel, *Boundaries and Allegiances: Problems of Justice and Responsibility in Liberal Thought* (New York: Oxford University Press, 2003).
Schmitt, Carl, *The Concept of the Political*, expand. ed. (Chicago: University of Chicago Press, 2007).

Schneider, Richard D. and Hy Bloom, *Law and Mental Disorder: A Comprehensive and Practical Approach* (Toronto: Irwin Law, 2013).
Silvers, Anita, "Reconciling Equality to Difference: Caring (F)or Justice for People with Disabilities" (1995) 10:1 *Hypatia* 30.
Silvers, Anita, "Formal Justice" in Anita Silvers, David Wasserman, and Mary Mahowald, *Disability, Difference, Discrimination* (Lanham, MD: Rowman & Littlefield, 1998), at 13–145.
Silvers, Anita, "On the Possibility and Desirability of Constructing a Neutral Conception of Disability" (2003) 24:6 *Theoretical Medicine & Bioethics* 471.
Silvers, Anita, "No Talent? Beyond the Worst Off! A Diverse Theory of Justice for Disability" in Kimberley Brownlee and Adam Cureton, eds., *Disability and Disadvantage* (Oxford: Oxford University Press, 2009), at 163–99.
Silvers, Anita, "Moral Status: What a Bad Idea!" (2012) 56:11 *J Intellectual Disability Research* 1014.
Silvers, Anita and Michael Ashley Stein, "Disability and the Social Contract," Book Review of *Frontiers of Justice: Disability, Nationality, Species Membership* (2007) 74:4 *U Chicago L Rev* 1615 at 1620.
Silvers, Anita, David Wasserman, and Mary Mahowald, "Introduction" in Anita Silvers, David Wasserman, and Mary Mahowald, *Disability, Difference, Discrimination* (Lanham, MD: Rowman & Littlefield, 1998).
Simmons, A. J., *Moral Principles and Political Obligations* (Princeton: Princeton University Press, 1979).
Singer, Peter, *Unsanctifying Human Life: Essays on Ethics*, ed. Helga Kuhse (Oxford: Blackwell, 2002).
Singer, Peter, "Speciesism and Moral Status" (2009) 40:3–4 *Metaphilosophy* 567 at 568.
Singer, Peter, *Practical Ethics*, 3rd ed. (New York: Cambridge University Press, 2011).
Slote, Michael, *The Ethics of Care and Empathy* (London: Routledge, 2007).
Slote, Michael, *Moral Sentimentalism* (Oxford: Oxford University Press, 2010).
Slote, Michael, *From Enlightenment to Receptivity: Rethinking Our Values* (New York: Oxford University Press, 2013).
Smith, Christian, *Moral, Believing Animals: Human Personhood and Culture* (Oxford: Oxford University Press, 2003).
Snow, Nancy E., "Iris Murdoch's Notion of a Loving Gaze" (2007) 39:3–4 *J Value Inquiry* 487.
Southwood, Nicholas, *Contractualism and the Foundations of Morality* (Oxford: Oxford University Press, 2010).
Stark, Cynthia, "How to Include the Severely Disabled in a Contractarian Theory of Justice" (2007) 15:2 *J Political Phil* 127.
Stark, Cynthia, "Respecting Human Dignity: Contract versus Capabilities" in Eva Feder Kittay and Licia Carlson, eds., *Cognitive Disability and Its Challenge to Moral Philosophy* (Malden, MA: Wiley-Blackwell, 2010), 111.
Stoljar, Natalie and Kristin Voigt, *Autonomy and Equality: Relational Approaches* (in press).
Tassé, Marc J., Ruth Luckasson, and Margaret Nygren, "AAIDD Proposed Recommendations for ICD-11 and the Condition Previously Known as Mental Retardation" (2013) 51:2 *Intellectual and Developmental Disabilities* 127.
Taylor, Charles, *Philosophy and the Human Sciences: Philosophical Papers*, vol. 2 (Cambridge: Cambridge University Press, 1985).
Taylor, Sunaura, *Beasts of Burden: Animal and Disability Liberation* (New York: The New Press, 2017).

Teichman, Jenny, "The Definition of Person" (1985) 60:232 *Philosophy* 175.
Teichman, Jenny, "The False Philosophy of Peter Singer," *The New Criterion* 2:8 (April 1993), www.newcriterion.com/issues/1993/4/the-false-philosophy-of-peter-singer.
Teichman, Jenny, *Social Ethics: A Student's Guide* (Oxford: Blackwell, 1996).
Tremain, Shelley, "On the Government of Disability" (2001) 27:4 *Soc Theory & Prac* 617.
Tully, James, *Public Philosophy in a New Key: Volume 1, Democracy and Civic Freedom* (Cambridge: Cambridge University Press, 2009).
Vehmas, Simo, "Discriminative Assumptions of Utilitarian Bioethics Regarding Individuals with Intellectual Disabilities" (1999) 14:1 *Disability & Society* 37.
Velleman, David J., "Love as a Moral Emotion" (1999) 109:2 *Ethics* 338.
Velleman, David J., "A Right to Self-Termination?" (1999) 109:3 *Ethics* 606.
Vorhaus, John, *Valuing Profoundly Disabled People: Fellowship, Community and Ties of Birth* (New York: Routledge, 2018).
Waldron, Jeremy, "John Rawls and the Social Minimum" (1986) 3:1 *J Appl Phil* 21.
Walvisch, Jamie, "Defining 'Mental Disorder' in Legal Contexts" (2017) 52 *Int'l JL & Psychiatry* 7.
Walzer, Michael, *Just and Unjust Wars: A Moral Argument with Historical Illustrations* (New York: Basic Books, 1977).
Warren, Mary A., *Moral Status: Obligations to Persons and Other Living Things* (Oxford: Oxford University Press, 2000).
Wasserman, David, et al., "Cognitive Disability and Moral Status," *The Stanford Encyclopedia of Philosophy* (August 2017), plato.stanford.edu/entries/cognitive-disability/.
Wasserman, David and Adam Cureton, eds., *The Oxford Handbook of Philosophy and Disability* (New York: Oxford University Press, 2019).
Wasserman, David and Jeff McMahan, "Cognitive Surrogacy, Assisted Participation, and Moral Status" in Rosamond Rhodes, Margaret P. Battin, and Anita Silvers, eds., *Medicine and Social Justice: Essays on the Distribution of Health Care*, 2nd ed. (New York: Oxford University Press, 2012), 325.
Williams, Bernard, "The Human Prejudice" in *Philosophy as a Humanistic Discipline* (Princeton: Princeton University Press, 2009).
Wong, David, "Chinese Ethics," *The Stanford Encyclopedia of Philosophy* (September 2018), plato.stanford.edu/archives/fall2018/entries/ethics-chinese/.
Wong, Sophia Isako, "Duties of Justice to Citizens with Cognitive Disabilities" in Eva Feder Kittay and Licia Carlson, eds., *Cognitive Disability and Its Challenge to Moral Philosophy* (Malden, MA: Wiley-Blackwell, 2010), 127.
Woolf, Virginia, "Professions for Women" in *The Death of the Moth and Other Essays* (London: Hogarth Press, 1942).
Young, Bruce, *Hotel California* (Vancouver: Good Earth, 1979).
Young, Iris Marion, *Justice and the Politics of Difference* (Princeton, NJ: Princeton University Press, 1990).
Young, Iris Marion, "Responsibility and Global Justice: A Social Connection Model" (2006) 23:1 *Social Phil & Pol'y* 102.
Young, Iris Marion, *Responsibility for Justice* (New York: Oxford University Press, 2011).
Zarka, Yves Charles, *La décision métaphysique de Hobbes: conditions de la politique* (Paris: J Vrin, 1987).
Zarka, Yves Charles, *Hobbes and Modern Political Thought*, trans. James Griffith (Edinburgh: Edinburgh University Press, 2016).

LEGISLATION

An Act to Ensure a Barrier-Free Canada, RSC 2019, c 10.
Convention on the Rights of Persons with Disabilities, March 30, 2007, 2515 UNTS 3 (entered into force May 3, 2008).
US Const art I, § 2, cl 3 (1788).

JURISPRUDENCE

Johns-Manville Canada Inc v. John Carlo Ltd, [1980] OJ No 3084, 113 DLR (3d) 686.
Louth v. Diprose, (1992) 175 CLR 621 (High Court of Australia).
Re Schebsman, [1994] Ch 83 (CA).
Reference re: Meaning of the Word "Persons" in s 24 of the BNA Act, [1928] SCR 276.

Index

access, 8, 15, 47, 132, 177
accessibility, 134
accommodation, 3, 17, 20, 48, 50, 54, 56, 58, 63, 74, 131, 134, 161, 215
advantage, 15, 75, 79, 102, 137, 164, 177, 189, 197, 245, *See also* bargaining, mutual advantage, *See also* disadvantage
　mutual, 36–37, 50, 64–66, 68, 73–77, 126, 150, 153, 189, 194, 196, 206, 220, 296
affection, 198, 222, 243–44, 246, 248–49, 253, 255, 259–60
agency, 14, 19, 21, 35–36, 38, 44, 146, 148, 153, 155, 171, 173, 280, 285
alienation, 7, 102, 132
American Association on Intellectual and Developmental Disabilities, 11, 18
American Psychiatric Association, 10, 18
Americans with Disabilities Act, 47
amorality, 66, 69, 76
Anderson, Elizabeth, 236, 248
animals, 29, 40, 42, 45–46, 51, 115, 119–21, 152, 155, 165, 177, 179–81, 184–85, 195, 210, 252
Appiah, Anthony, 146, 210
Aristotle, 267, 295
authorship, 4, 35, 145–46, 158, 160–61, 165
autonomy, 3–4, 18–19, 21, 30, 33, 35–36, 38, 51, 100–1, 103, 113, 128, 130, 135, 140–41, 143, 146, 148–49, 155–59, 166, 169, 173–74, 183–84, 207, 215, 227, 234, 236, 249, 260, 269, 271, 277, 279–80, 282–83, 286–87, 289–90, 293–95
　relational, 146–47
average, 13, 39, 44, 121, 133, 136–37, 265

babies, 20, 40, 43, 80, 156, 179, 222–24, 236, 245, 263, 265, 274, *See also* children
Baier, Annette, 85–86, 89, 92, 107, 271, 288–89, 291

bargaining, 36, 57, 68, 71–72, 75, 78, 83, 87, 89, 94, 96–105, 110, 126, 166, 171, 175, 216, 222, 226, 228–29, 231, 233, 238, 240–43, 247–48, 255, 257, 262–63, 265, 273, 287, 296, *See also* capacity, to bargain, *See also* power, bargaining; mutual advantage, 82, 268, 277, *See also* advantage, mutual
　self-interested, 62, 78, 100–1, 104, 167, 261, 264
　trust and, 99–100, 104
Barry, Brian, 213
Becker, Lawrence, 29, 31, 50, 64–69, 71–77, 81
behavior, 15, 43, 91–92, 95, 97, 105, 115, 121–23, 165, 221, 228, 230, 235, 242, 252–53, 261, 284
benevolence, 170, 205
biology, 9, 48, 58, 134, 274
Buchanan, Allen, 37
burden, 40, 51, 66, 74, 98, 127, 131–33, 137, 141, 193, 208, 218, 245, 296
Byrne, Peter, 44, 275

Callicott, J. Baird, 76
capacity, 3, 6, 12–14, 17–20, 35–36, 39–41, 64, 77, 101, 116, 124, 128, 136, 138, 143, 145, 148, 153, 157–61, 167, 174, 179, 184, 194–96, 200, 202, 204, 214, 223, 233, 257, 261, 265, 279, 289, 292, 294–95
　to bargain, 36, 82, 98, 101, 103, 172, 216
　cognitive, 12, 17, 19, 30, 39, 43, 46, 83, 119, 124, 157, 171–72, 274
　to consent, 30, 173, 216, 225, 266, 269, 287
　contractual, 8, 13–14, 18, 23, 29, 34, 36, 49–50, 123, 136, 151, 160, 163, 167, 170, 172, 203–4, 273–74
　to contribute, 75
　to cooperate, 21, 130–31, 144
　to engage, 149, 151–52, 154, 156, 290

307

capacity (cont.)
  expectations of, 13
  to have a conception of justice, 191
  to have a conception of the good, 18, 38, 128, 130, 145, 149, 160, 191, 195, 197
  intellectual, 17, 35, 44, 82–83
  legal, 35, 48
  mental, 20, 40
  moral, 42, 83, 170–71, 270, 288
  to participate, 119, 128, 131, 169
  physical, 20, 46, 82–83, 171–72, 274
  for reason, 3–4
  relational, 15, 201
  to be rational, 35
  to reciprocate, 43, 144, 197
  to suffer, 269
  to trust, 50, 64, 83, 85, 87–89, 93, 115, 117–19, 121, 123, 126–27
capitalism, 6, 58, 86, 273
care, 12, 44, 48, 52, 54, 60, 63, 66–70, 72, 79, 81, 87, 101, 104, 107, 116, 121–23, 125–27, 130, 134–36, 139–43, 152, 155–57, 159–60, 164, 176, 179–80, 182, 184, 189, 198, 200, 212, 217, 219, 221–22, 226, 238, 243, 246–47, 253–54, 256–60, 262, 269, 274, 282, 289–90, 292–95
  burden of, 245
  duty to, 141, 152, 247
  ethics. See ethics, care
  giving, 43, 65, 67, 71–72, 75, 92, 109, 116, 127, 139, 142, 154, 156, 189, 219, 223, 231, 247, 250, 253, 259, 287, 290
  health, 3, 48, 59, 212
  industry, 59
  justice and. See justice, care and
  object of, 135
  relations of, 41, 59, 71–73, 91–92, 108, 151, 154–55, 219, 253, 259, 276, 287–88, 290, 292–93, 295
  roles, 59–60
  trust and, 89, 94, 152
  work, 44, 59–60, 65, 102, 218, 247
caste, 41, 56, 81
charity, 2, 6–7, 33, 37–38, 49, 56, 140, 142, 168, 206, 220, 269
children, 20, 40, 42, 56, 70, 79, 98, 102, 105, 108, 112, 115, 156, 174, 178–79, 186, 194, 200, 209, 212, 218–19, 221, 223, 230, 238, 242, 244–45, 247, 250, 257, 261–62, 267, 289, 291, See also status, of children; babies
citizenship, 2, 14, 42, 46, 48, 51, 71, 123, 128–29, 131, 133, 148–49, 163, 165, 169–70, 172, 186, 188–89, 191, 197, 201, 203–4, 209–11, 214–15, 275, 282, See also dis-citizenship
  active, 74, 128, 133, 161, 173, 177, 186, 204
  passive, 51, 128–29, 148, 150–52, 163, 165, 168, 170, 173–74, 177, 181, 186–87, 190, 204, 214
civil rights movement, 70
Cohen, Andrew, 178–79, 187, 214
collaboration, 51, 88, 140, 147–48, 156, 158, 161
collectivism, 28, 42, 50, 54, 85, 131, 143, 146, 176
communication, 10–11, 14–15, 151, 154
communitarianism, 147, 233, 283–84
community, 6–7, 11, 19, 39, 44, 48, 83, 85–86, 88, 95, 102, 104, 114, 116, 118–21, 123, 126, 187, 201, 203, 231, 233, 248, 267, 276, 282–83, 285, 289
  contracting, 77, 104, 167
  disability, 47
  ethical, 83–84, 117–18, 121, 123–25, 127, 130, 228, 255
  hierarchy and, 81
  legal, 186
  medical, 18
  moral, 9, 38, 42, 46, 152, 166, 181, 183–84, 195
  notional, 183
  political, 9, 38, 42, 49, 65, 68, 72, 76, 129, 158, 166, 171, 173, 186, 196, 200, 214
compensation, 6, 55, 130–36, 138, 140–41, 157, 174, 176, 206, 213, 240–41, 243, 245, 274, See also justice, compensation and
concern, 5, 22, 24, 32, 41, 52, 60, 73, 96–103, 107, 112–13, 119, 121, 123, 127, 133, 139, 158, 162, 170, 232, 250–51, 261, 264, 268, 271, 275, 278, 281, 287–89, 293, 295
  other-regarding, 52, 54, 60, 70, 84, 93, 97–98, 100, 102–3, 105, 107–10, 114, 122–23, 126, 135, 200–1, 216–17, 226–27, 235, 237, 243, 247–49, 251, 253, 258–59, 269–70, 287, 290
  self-regarding, 84, 87, 102, 112, 228, 231, 233, 240–41, 254, 260, 270
Confucianism, 279–80, 286, See also ethics, Confucian, See also virtue, Confucian
consent, 167, 216, 225, 233, 238, 249, 255, 260, 263–64, 266, 270, See also capacity, to consent
contractarianism, 1, 24–27, 29, 32–37, 39, 49–50, 52–53, 55–57, 59–62, 64–66, 68, 71–77, 79–82, 87–90, 92–93, 95–96, 100, 103, 106, 110, 115–17, 119–21, 123–25, 150, 152–56, 162, 164, 166–67, 178–80, 187, 214, 216, 220–27, 229–30, 232–33, 235–45, 247, 250–51, 253, 255–57, 261–62, 264–67, 270, 289
  feminist, 52, 217–20, 223, 225, 228–29, 231–33, 235, 237–40, 245, 248, 250, 255–57, 259–60, 270–72
  generic, 58–59, 61, 63–64, 66–67, 71, 74
  Hobbesian, 36, 52, 58, 71, 79, 223–24, 234, 258, 263–64
  inclusivist, 62, 64, 78–79, 81
  Kantian, 37, 234, 259, 265, 268

moralized, 61–62, 68, 79
  rule, 49
contractualism, 1, 34–36, 38–39, 50–51, 64, 71, 80, 87, 104, 131, 136, 144–45, 148–53, 155–58, 160–61, 163–64, 166–68, 179–81, 183, 185, 187–88, 190, 196, 202, 204–7, 210, 213–14, 216, 229, 265–66, 289
  Kantian, 52, 152, 166, 224, 234
  Rawlsian, 154, 187, 189, 202–3, 205–6, 208, 210–13
  rule, 150
contribution, 7, 50–51, 54, 56–57, 63–64, 78–80, 83, 122, 136, 150–54, 163, 166, 172, 197, 203, 205, 209, 213, 217, 241, 284, 296
  active, 59, 63, 132–33
  capacity and. *See* capacity, to contribute
  contractual, 19, 23, 50
  cooperative, 149
  passive, 59, 63
  potential, 54
  reciprocal, 163, 265
  social, 7, 20, 28, 31, 59, 118, 128, 130, 133
cooperation, 21, 28, 30, 38, 83, 85, 88, 91, 94, 100–1, 103–4, 119, 130–32, 140, 150–51, 153–54, 156, 163, 189, 193–94, 196–97, 201–2, 204, 206, 208, 210–13, 215, 222, 276
  instrumental, 265
  non-, 204, 206, 208, 210, 212
  social, 2, 91, 105–6, 109, 122, 131, 145, 149–51, 157, 189, 192–97, 201, 208, 216
cooperative venture, 33, 49, 51, 89, 91, 93, 109, 118–19, 153, 155, 189, 194, 196–97, 206, 271
Cureton, Adam, 51, 176, 187, 191–92, 194, 197–99, 203, 213

Darwall, Stephen, 34, 37
dependency, 12–13, 21, 27, 30, 32, 41, 52–54, 59, 67, 70, 73, 83, 85, 90, 96, 105, 114, 118, 122–23, 131, 135–36, 141, 143, 146–47, 156, 159, 189, 193, 196, 200, 203, 274, 277, 287, 290, 293, 295
derivativeness, 37, 49–50, 64, 71, 75, 77, 93, 118–20, 151–52, 168, 170, 274–75, *See also* status, derivative, value, derivative, value, nonderivative
devotion, 112, 129, 198, 219, 240, 250, 253, 256, 261–62, 264
Diagnostic and Statistical Manual of Mental Disorders, 10–12, 15–18
Diamond, Cora, 165
dignity, 22, 25, 35–36, 60, 71, 76, 153, 169, 204, 224, 240, 259, 274, 287
Dimock, Susan, 43, 96, 217, 219, 221–23, 225–31, 233, 236, 238–39, 242–44, 247–49, 251, 253, 255–57, 263–64, 267–68, 270
disadvantage, 132, 137, 174, 189, 285

dis-citizenship, 48, 276
discrimination, 5, 20, 47–48, 56, 58, 62, 193
distribution, 26, 29, 47, 56, 130–34, 137–40, 142, 188, 194, 211–12, 218, 220, 239–40, 244–46, *See also* redistribution, *See also* justice, distributive;
Dumas, Alexandre, 97
Dworkin, Ronald, 132

egalitarianism, 193, 212
  relational, 133, 281
empathy, 15, 32, 52, 70, 96, 98, 139, 157, 181, 201, 230, 252, 282, 288, 291–92
entitlement, 7, 19, 22, 24, 26–27, 44–45, 76, 135–36, 139, 142, 162, 176, 190, 200, 208–9, 211, 228, 245, 267, 270
epistemology, 13, 15, 55, 92, 173–75, 280, 292, 295
equality, 1, 25–26, 29–30, 35–36, 62, 71, 133, 142, 150, 170–71, 194–95, 208, 255, 275, 281, 286
  natural, 170, 260
  physical, 171
  political, 171
ethics, 1, 17, 19–20, 34, 37, 44, 48, 52, 56, 83–84, 100, 117–18, 121, 123–25, 127, 130, 146, 156–57, 165, 169, 222, 228, 255, 267, 280–81, 295
  animal, 45–46
  bio-, 21, 23, 42, 135, 281
  care, 32, 45, 52, 136, 139, 152, 160, 218, 234, 246–47, 276, 282, 288, 290–91
  Confucian, 279, 286
  Hobbesian, 36, 222
  of justice, 218
  Kantian, 181
  nurturing, 230
  pluralistic, 169
  professional, 284
  Rawlsian, 199
  relational, 283–84
  role, 279–80, 284–85, 287–88
  social, 52
  virtue, 279–80, 288
eugenics, 47, 78
exclusion, 2–5, 10, 17, 21, 29–31, 35, 38, 48, 62, 64, 68, 75, 81–82, 92, 135, 142, 189, 193–95, 200, 208, 216, 223–24, 240, 243, 245, *See* alienation, *See* exclusionism
  professional, 61
  social, 7, 203
  structural, 204
exclusionism, 29, 39, 43, 134
exclusivism, 30, 131, 157

exploitation, 38, 45, 50, 52, 86, 98, 101–2, 109, 118, 121, 173, 194, 217, 219, 221–23, 225–27, 232–33, 235–38, 240, 242–44, 246–47, 253–57, 259–60, 262–63, 269–70, See also justice, exploitation and
expression, 11, 14, 23, 34–35, 112–13, 115, 132, 136–37, 142, 144, 148, 158, 160–61, 164, 174, 183, 187, 246, 269

fairness, 4–6, 24, 26, 30–31, 36, 55, 74, 76, 96, 105, 108, 116, 118–19, 124, 133–34, 142, 149, 154, 156, 168, 171, 173–74, 189, 193, 195–97, 200, 206–8, 211, 217, 220, 223, 227, 234–35, 239, 241–42, 245, 248–50, 258, 263, 266, 268, 270–71, 277, 284, 287, See also justice, fairness and
faith
  bad, 15, 100
  good, 98, 193, 255
family, 14, 43, 81, 92, 98, 113–14, 139, 151, 154, 209, 240, 247–48, 254, 262, 292, 294–95
feminism, 43, 52, 99, 142, 146, 217–18, 238, 246, 251, 271, 274, 280–81, 286–89, See also contractarianism, feminist, See also justice, feminist
fiduciary, 52, 76, 210, 276, 290, 293
Finnis, John, 169, 181
Francis, Leslie, 50, 57, 75, 77, 82–95, 97, 100, 103–6, 108–10, 113–19, 121–24, 126–29, 131, 141, 143–49, 152, 156–58, 160, 175–76
friendliness, 104
friendship, 15, 97, 108, 113–14, 122, 127, 139, 147, 154–55, 220–21, 223, 226, 231, 244, 247, 250, 252–53, 257, 271

Gauthier, David, 1, 42, 63, 80–81, 163, 220, 240
gender, 9, 12, 99, 189, 218, 238, 281
Good Samaritan, 222, 235, 256, 259–60
good, conception of, 18, 31, 33, 38, 50, 59, 66, 128, 131, 144–48, 158, 160–61, 168, 195–96, 198–99, 214, See also capacity, to have a conception of the good
Grimké, Sarah, 142

Hampton, Jean, 37, 43, 57, 217–19, 221–33, 235–36, 238–39, 242–49, 253–54, 256–57, 260, 262–63, 265–66, 268, 270
Hartley, Christie, 87, 145, 149–56, 204
Held, Virginia, 274, 291–92
Hobbes, Thomas, 1, 4, 25, 32, 36, 52, 54, 58, 60, 66–67, 69, 71, 79, 81, 83, 96, 100, 106, 114, 123, 167–68, 170, 219, 222–24, 234, 247, 258, 260, 263–64, 266, 268, 270
  Leviathan, 170

human exceptionalism, 21, 32, 39, 45–46, 284
humanism, 32–33, 48, 295

identity, 9, 20, 29, 44, 59, 98, 136, 146, 158, 169, 202, 242, 262, 278, 281, 289
  politics, 9
impartiality, 31, 33, 37, 39, 44, 55, 64, 188, 190, 237, 246, 285, 289, 294
incapacity, 15
inclusion, 5, 17, 21, 49–50, 60–61, 63, 84, 104–6, 115–16, 118, 123, 125, 133–34, 136, 150, 194, 196, 211, 280
inclusivism, 24, 53, 58, 61–63, 74, 79–81, 88–89, 145, 154, 156, 274
independence, 10–11, 14, 72, 83, 144–45, 147, 153, 158, 174, 274, 277, 280, 294
individualism, 4, 6, 17, 75, 89, 238, 279–80, 283, 285
inequality, 10, 48, 75, 223, 260, 264–65, 275, See equality
inequity, 218
infants. See babies
injustice, 76, 133, 194, 217, 223, 226, 232, 277, 287
instrumentality, 36, 50, 57–59, 66, 71–72, 88, 92–95, 101, 103, 106, 118, 125–26, 152–53, 165, 180, 216, 224, 235, 240, 249, 258, 260, 264, 269, 285, See also value, instrumental, See also value, noninstrumental, See also cooperation, instrumental
integrationism, 2, 5–7, 18–21, 29–30, 34, 130–31, 134, 190–91
interdependency, 281, 286
isolation, 6, 16, 30, 40, 47, 59, 104, 132–33, 135, 148, 183

justice, 18, 24, 30–31, 33, 36–37, 52, 54, 56, 61, 66–69, 73–74, 81, 84, 87, 90, 105, 115–16, 131, 133, 140, 144, 148, 197, 218, 224, 233, 245, 280, 293
  care and, 33, 158, 291
  compensation and, 135, 141
  conditions of, 194
  contractarian, 90, 93, 121
  contractual, 49–51, 104, 118, 121, 144, 149, 152, 157, 167, 188, 203, 213, 273
  cooperative, 153–54, 195
  distributive, 43, 132–34, 189, 191–92, 206, 221, 223, 232, 244–46, See also distribution, See also redistribution
  duties of, 3, 24, 85, 117, 127, 136, 141, 144, 152, 190–91, 210, 269
  exploitation and, 237
  fairness and, 2, 170, 188–89, 191–92, 194, 196, 199, 201, 206–7, 210
  feminist, 246, 271, 281

inclusivist, 156
integrative, 132, 141
liberal, 69, 128, 245
  love and, 221
  morality and. *See* morality, justice and
  object of, 245
  obligation of, 56
  political, 2, 192–93, 199–201, 203
  principles of, 35–36, 55–56, 65, 84, 90, 136, 149–50, 169, 188–89, 191, 194–96, 198–200, 203, 207, 211–13
  punitive, 192
  Rawlsian, 166, 169–70, 176, 188, 190–93, 195–96, 209, 213
  relational, 240
  rules of, 176
  social, 19, 29, 56, 67–68, 133, 192, 196
  status and, 170
  subject of, 3, 25, 30, 36, 38, 57, 71, 87, 115, 118–19, 122, 128, 131, 136–37, 145, 149–50, 153, 160, 167–68, 196, 208, 213, 273, 282, 285, 294–95
  talent and, 130, 134, 137–40
  theory of, 31–32, 36–37, 39, 52, 56, 58, 60, 64, 69, 76–77, 90, 92, 116, 120, 128, 131, 134–35, 145, 157, 160, 194, 207, 210, 291
  trust and, 50, 77, 84–88, 92, 117, 121, 129–30

Kant, Immanuel, 1, 3, 25, 35–36, 38, 52, 71, 120, 145, 149, 151–55, 165–67, 169–71, 173, 177, 180–86, 204–5, 214, 223–24, 229, 233–34, 259, 263, 265–66, 268, 280
  categorical imperative, 183
Kinghorn, Warren, 16
Kittay, Eva, 28, 63, 81, 141–42, 152, 175, 189, 194, 203, 274, 282
Korsgaard, Christine, 51, 145, 149, 167, 173, 177–87, 205, 214

labeling, 133
labor, 6, 14, 133
language, 8, 15–16, 30, 67
  disability-first, 8
  normative, 280
  person-first, 8–9
law, 3–5, 12, 19–20, 29–30, 35, 46–48, 59, 68, 83, 86, 94, 126, 143, 154, 160, 183, 189, 208, 245, 277, 281, 292, 294, *See also* status, legal, *See also* capacity, legal, *See also* community, legal; moral, 35, 166, 171, 183
  rational, 166
  reform, 3
  rule of, 258
  universal, 183

liberalism, 1, 4, 19–20, 29–30, 32, 46, 81, 128–29, 136, 141, 143, 145, 172, 226, 268, 270, 275, 278, 280, 282, *See also* value, liberal, *See also* justice, liberal
love, 37, 41, 44, 65–66, 70–72, 95, 112, 122, 139, 154–55, 221, 224, 226, 237, 245–46, 250, 254, 256–57, 261–63, 288, 295, *See also* justice, love and, See also value, of love
Luhmann, Niklas, 86

marginalization, 5, 13, 20, 45, 62, 79, 81, 133, 278, 288, 294
masculinity, 99, 280, 282, 287
Mbembe, Achille, 4
McMahan, Jeff, 39–40, 42, 157, 160–61
membership, 9, 38–39, 41–42, 44–45, 57, 61–62, 67, 72, 74, 77, 79–80, 87, 104, 114, 117–18, 123, 125, 129, 136, 149, 152, 156, 161, 166, 175, 193, 195–96, 203, 210–11, 215, 217, 255, 282, 285
  simpliciter, 201, 203, 214–15
metaphysics, 4, 21, 37, 130, 146–47, 173, 177–78, 180–81, 187, 214, 233, 236, 242, 255, 265, 268, 280, 283, *See also* value, metaphysics of
Mills, Charles, 6, 29–30
Minow, Martha, 132
misfortune, 56, 134, 192
model of disability
  medical, 10, 12, 15
  social, 8, 58, 137, 277
morality, 2, 9, 37, 40–41, 43, 49, 52, 92, 179, 186, 216–17, 219–20, 222–25, 227, 229, 232, 234–35, 237, 239, 247–50, 253, 256, 258, 260, 264–65, 267, 269–71, 275–76, 278, 282, 284, 288–94, 296
  justice and, 2–3, 5, 31–32, 35, 37, 39, 43, 50, 73–74, 141, 160, 171, 216–17, 220, 222–23, 227, 229, 232, 237, 240, 261, 267–68, 271, 274, 276, 280, 285, 295
  relational, 287–88, 290–91, 294–95
  role, 284, 289
motherhood, 43, 112–14, 222–23, 229, 234, 236, 247, 250, 254–55, 267, 274, 291
Murdoch, Iris, 157, 295

Nazism, 42, 45, 202
neutrality, 12–13, 36, 57, 131, 134, 169
  moral, 223–24, 244, 268–70
Noddings, Nel, 290, 292
normalcy, 2, 9, 13–14, 30, 38, 49, 133, 137, 154, 174, 192, 195, 204, 211, 215
normalization, 6, 20, 33, 51, 61–62, 74, 77, 134, 136, 274, 276, 293–94
normativity, 1, 3, 10, 13, 15, 18, 20, 22, 25, 34, 41, 43, 45, 48, 57, 60, 76, 88, 91–92, 96–97, 101, 122,

127, 146, 156, 158, 162, 167, 173, 177, 179, 181–85, 188, 196, 201, 203, 216, 222–24, 230, 233, 237, 239, 241, 244, 250, 252, 254–56, 265, 267–68, 270–71, 276, 279–80, 293, 295
nurture, 50, 75, 134–35, 219, 223, 250, 287, 292, *See also* ethics, nurturing
Nussbaum, Martha, 28, 63, 87, 117, 126, 144, 147, 149, 163, 169–70, 173, 175, 181, 190, 193, 195–96, 302

obligation, 2–3, 7, 22–24, 27, 41, 54, 56, 74, 94, 97, 101, 106, 108, 112, 117, 123, 141, 144–45, 148, 179, 181, 186, 190–91, 203, 209–10, 217, 231, 249, 252, 255, 261, 268, 270, 276, 284–85, 293–95
Okin, Susan Moller, 289
opportunism, 50, 61, 66, 90, 94, 101–2, 107, 115, 228
opportunity, 34, 131–33, 142, 208, 252
oppression, 5, 7, 9, 13, 17, 29, 31, 45, 47, 277, 280–81, 284–86
outlier, 9, 31, 56, 62, 64, 82, 84, 89, 118–19, 121, 124, 128, 134, 159, 224, 264–65, 267
Ozon, François, 99

participation, 3, 11, 28, 33, 50, 63–64, 136, 150–51, 157, 163–64, 168, 173, 176, 196, 198, 206, 210, 276, 290, 293, *See also* capacity, to participate
political, 17, 160, 169
social, 10, 133
Pateman, Carole, 6, 29–30
personhood, 4, 8–9, 14, 25, 44, 46, 48, 153, 194, 224–25, 232–33, 236, 242, 246, 249, 269, 271, 281, 285
contractarian conception, 232–33, 235, 241–42, 244, 248, 256
feminist conception, 232, 239, 244, 248
Kantian conception, 263, 266
pessimism, 69, 77
pity, 7, 49, 139, 174, 258
pluralism, 24, 32, 52, 92, 109, 141, 144, 160, 194, 231, 272, 287, 289, 291–95, *See also* ethics, pluralistic
relational, 289, 292
politics, 1–8, 12, 21, 23, 37, 83, 100, 105, 136, 143, 161, 165, 169, 171, 176, 199, 201, 207, 210, 280, 294, *See also* justice, political, *See also* identity, politics, *See also* community, political, *See also* status, political, *See also* power, political, *See also* participation, political, *See also* equality, political, *See also* rights, political
liberal, 32, 129, 141, 172, *See also* liberalism
philosophy of. *See* politics, theory of
theory of, 1, 14, 19, 21, 30, 34, 46, 49, 67, 69, 140, 147, 192, 273–74, 276–77, 283–84, 294

potentiality, 20–21, 35, 54, 63, 122, 131, 154, 157, 203, 252
power, 4–6, 15–16, 19, 21, 36, 43, 55, 65–66, 68, 70, 72, 74–75, 89, 94, 101, 107, 120, 133, 144–45, 171, 193, 207, 223, 260, 267–68, 285
bargaining, 225, 245, 266
constitutional, 207
dynamics of, 55
equality of, 36, 265
moral, 144–45, 148–49, 153, 171, 191, 197–98, 201, 208
physical and mental, 195–96
political, 34–35
state, 174
pragmatism, 26, 57, 69, 116, 129, 192–93
praise, 221, 248, 262
prejudice, 5, 15, 42, 47, 51, 58, 61–62, 120–21, 130, 132, 136, 141–42, 146, 276
preservationism, 11, 20–21, 41, 43–46, 48
production, 6, 28, 56, 62–63, 131, 203, 206, 274, *See also* productivity
productivity, 14, 28, 30, 48, 55, 62–63, 74, 78–79, 81, 100, 117, 135, 140, 212, 274, 279, *See also* production
profitability, 16, 54–55, 57–58, 61–62, 66, 68, 74, 76–80, 95, 105, 194, 229, 256, 269
profitable contractor, 57, 64, *See also* unprofitable contractor
prosthesis, 51, 129, 149, 157–58, 160–61

race, 9, 16, 281
racism, 42, 46
rationality, 1, 18–19, 34–36, 38, 51, 53, 61, 65–67, 69, 71, 73, 87, 92, 94, 96, 100–3, 107, 114, 116, 123, 144, 154, 161, 166–67, 169, 173, 177, 180–86, 188, 197–98, 200–1, 205, 207–8, 228, 238, 243, 264, 274, 279, 282, 287, 295, *See also* capacity, to be rational
Rawls, John, 1–2, 24, 28–29, 31–32, 37–38, 42, 51, 63, 66–67, 87, 129, 144–54, 164, 166, 168–69, 171, 176, 187–98, 200–8, 210–13, 224, 233, 240, 245, 268, 278, 280, 282, 289
original position, 51, 170, 176, 188–91, 197–203, 206, 211–13
reciprocity, 1, 28, 30, 37–38, 43–44, 50, 64–66, 68, 73–75, 85, 87, 118, 131, 135–36, 141, 144, 150–51, 154, 187, 189, 196–97, 200, 206, 211, 213–15, 222, 232, 251, 263, 265, 270, *See also* capacity, to reciprocate, *See also* contribution, reciprocal
redistribution, 24, 130–34, 138–39, 200, 245–46, *See also* distribution, *See also* status, redistribution and
reductionism, 8, 13, 103, 136, 140, 143, 215, 227, 279, 286–87

Regan, Tom, 165
rehabilitation, 66, 74, 81, 281
relation, 14–15, 23, 41, 43, 46, 50, 52, 66, 73–76, 81, 84, 89–91, 94–95, 99, 105, 109, 113–14, 120–22, 131, 136, 141, 146, 150–55, 200, 209, 216–17, 219–33, 239–42, 244, 247–51, 253–58, 261–63, 265, 269, 271, 276, 278, 281–86, 289–90, 293, 295, *See also* trust, relations of, *See also* autonomy, relational, *See also* care, relations of, *See also* ethics, relational
   contractual, 31, 33, 79, 88, 92–93, 97, 105, 112, 150, 155, 163, 189, 201, 205, 229, 234, 239, 243, 255, 264–65, 270, 276, 288, 292, 294
   human, 5, 21, 33, 43, 57, 167, 183, 187, 223, 272, 291–92, 296
   interpersonal, 232, 267, 273
   intimate, 227–31, 237–39, 241, 244, 246, 249–51, 253, 255, 264, 268, 271
   moral, 44
   social, 39, 42, 59, 75, 92, 133, 146, 277, 281
relationship. *See* relation
reliability, 90, 94, 102, 115, 118, 123, 126
reparation, 245, 269
respect, 5, 22, 24, 30, 35–38, 41, 44, 52, 62, 87, 96–97, 99, 101, 103, 108, 113, 117, 133, 135, 137, 139–41, 149–55, 158, 160, 166, 171–73, 183–84, 187, 190, 203, 208, 216, 224, 229, 231, 237–38, 242–43, 247, 257, 260–61, 268, 270, 280–81, 287, 293–94
responsibility, 9, 15, 95, 98, 144–45, 148, 218, 284, 286
revisionism, 3, 6, 39, 41–43, 45–46, 196, 202–3
Richardson, Henry, 213
Richardson, Janice, 262
rights, 5, 26, 29, 186, 209–11, 258, 281
   basic, 206, 209
   citizens', 26, 207
   civil, 70
   of contractor, 27, 154
   denial of, 48
   disability, 47
   discourse, 45
   equal, 5, 132, 168, 211
   fundamental, 27
   human, 5, 27, 285
   individual, 76, 148
   to life, 17, 40, 48
   minority, 20, 294
   moral, 22, 25–27, 164, 181
   natural, 170
   political, 181
   social contract and, 62, 69
   violation of, 5
romance, 113, 262

Sandel, Michael, 233, 236, 278, 282
Scanlon, Thomas, 1, 187, 251
Scheffler, Samuel, 284
self-authentication, 145, 165, 177, 184
self-interest, 23–24, 36–38, 50, 52–55, 57, 60, 62, 65–66, 68–70, 73, 76, 78–81, 84, 87, 89–90, 93–95, 97, 99–106, 110, 113, 119, 123, 126, 152, 155, 166, 172, 189, 216–17, 220, 225, 228, 231, 233, 236, 238–39, 243, 249, 254, 258–61, 264–66, 268, 279, 288–89
self-origination, 144–46, 148
sentimentalism, 32–33, 282
Silvers, Anita, 29, 50, 57, 63, 75, 77, 82–92, 94–95, 97, 100, 103–6, 108–10, 113–14, 116–19, 121–24, 126–42, 144–48, 150, 152, 156–58, 160, 174–76
Singer, Peter, 39–40, 42, 177
Slote, Michael, 139, 282, 287–88, 291–92
social order, 7, 70, 78, 193
social scripts, 129, 146, 148, 282, 286, 289, 295
Southwood, Nicholas, 147, 173, 187, 203
speciesism, 21, 41, 45–46, 175, 202, 285
stability, 23, 66, 68–71, 75, 88, 91, 93, 100, 103–4, 270
Stark, Cynthia, 51, 151, 170, 187, 203–8, 210–13
state of nature, 57, 80, 194
   Hobbesian, 54, 79
status, xiii, xv, 2–3, 5, 7, 10, 18–20, 22–24, 26–27, 32, 40, 46, 49, 57, 61, 83, 125–26, 138, 164, 170, 176, 178, 183, 185–86, 190, 201–2, 214
   contingent, 49–50, 60, 73, 79, 163, 177, 184–85, 203–4, 214, 274–75
   derivative, 65, 71–73, 120, 155, 177, 180, 274–75, *See* status, contingent
   direct, 72, 123, 169
   equality and, 170–72, 275
   indirect, 72, 123
   legal, 29
   moral, 3, 5, 18–20, 22–24, 27, 29, 31–33, 37–39, 41–42, 51, 53, 71, 76, 121, 126, 143, 156, 158, 161, 165–69, 171, 180, 190, 209, 214, 276, 293
   moral, robust, xiv–xv, 2–3, 5, 10, 12, 19–20, 22–24, 26–33, 36, 38–39, 41, 43, 45–46, 49–52, 57, 62–64, 71, 77, 79, 82, 88, 92–93, 106, 109, 117–18, 123–24, 126, 128, 133, 136, 143, 149–50, 156, 158, 160, 163–68, 170, 172, 174, 178, 180–81, 185, 187, 190, 195, 202, 204, 209–10, 212, 273–76, 290, 292–93, 295
   of animals, 120, 179
   of children, 179
   normative, 201
   political, 27, 29, 31, 33, 36, 39, 50, 143, 171, 181, 214, 276
   redistribution and, 138
   relational, 293

status (cont.)
  robust, 72–73, 76
  second-rate, 173–75, 177, 206, 275
  special, 28, 143, 168
  superior, 292
  trust-based, 117–18, 121, 123–24, 126
Steinbeck, John, 127
subjecthood, 4–5, 8, 20, 29, 37, 129, 141, 144, 146, 149–50, 152, 156, 166, 183, 194, 277, 279–80, *See also* justice, subject of
surrogacy, 234, 236
  cognitive, 157

talent, 14, 50, 54, 58, 63, 128, 130–42, 161, 200, 245, *See also* justice, talent and
Taylor, Charles, 148, 280
Thrasymachus, 66, 68
transaction, 36, 38, 50, 73–74, 94, 100, 102
trust, 50, 57, 63, 75, 83–86, 88–92, 94–95, 104–9, 112, 114, 116–24, 126, 152, 238, 258–59, *See also* capacity, to trust
  climate of, 50, 64, 87–88, 90, 106, 118, 120–22, 127, 152
  culture of, 83, 85, 87, 90, 105, 111, 116–17, 121, 124–25, 127
  Hobbesian, 106
  justice and. *See* justice, trust and
  mutual, 151
  nature of, 50, 88, 106
  other-regarding, 50, 83, 88–89, 92–93, 95, 100, 102–5, 107, 109–14, 117, 122, 124, 126–27
  relations of, 84, 90, 92–93, 108–9, 111, 114–16, 119–21, 126–27
  self-regarding, 50, 89, 92–96, 99–100, 104–5, 108, 111
  social, 130
  value of, 86
trusteeship, 84, 87, 147–48, 157–58, 160–61, 167, 169–70, 172, 174–77, 188, 198, 202, 253, 290

United Nations *Convention on the Rights of Persons with Disabilities*, 3, 164
unprofitable contractor, 54–58, 77, *See also* profitable contractor
usefulness, 58, 131, 152, 167
utilitarianism, 40–42, 139, 279
utility, 222, 243, 252, 264

value, 15, 19, 34–36, 45, 57, 74, 95–96, 116, 121, 127, 135, 146, 148, 153, 158, 160, 167, 173, 179, 182, 184, 206, 220–21, 229, 232, 252, 255, 264–65, 268, 274, 289, 295
  conferring, 180, 183–84
  contingent, 59, 117, 151
  derivative, 26, 72, 93, 117, 153, 155, 277
  instrumental, 26, 167, 224, 251, 264
  intrinsic, 13, 21, 25–26, 57, 86, 122, 153, 165, 174, 177, 180–83, 185–86, 205, 209, 214, 224, 233–34, 243, 251, 264–68
  judgments, 17, 47
  lesser, 39, 174, 275
  liberal, 1, 30, 129, 226, 281, 290
  of life, 47, 182, 261
  of love, 262–63
  market, 140
  metaphysics of, 181, 183
  moral, 21, 43, 180–81, 221–22, 233, 250, 256, 259, 266–68
  neutral, 12
  nonderivative, 24, 26, 145, 165
  noninstrumental, 233–34, 260, 264–67
  ontological, 169
  realism, 181
  of relations, 152–54, 221–22, 227, 233, 250, 252, 264, 287, 290, 293
  shared, 199, 201
veil of ignorance, 55–56, 170, 190
  Rawlsian, 188, 190, 200, 202, 207
virtue, 56, 87, 102, 105, 107, 109, 121, 139, 199, 218, 229, 237, 246, 250, 257, 274, 279, 285–86, 288, 295, *See also* ethics, virtue
  Confucian, 280
  democratic, 27
  philosophical, 77
  social, 31
vulnerability, 20–21, 27, 30, 32, 45, 50–53, 59–60, 67, 69, 78–79, 83, 85, 89, 92, 94, 96, 106–7, 109, 114, 118, 120–21, 123–24, 126, 131, 135, 141, 144, 156–57, 160, 168, 194–96, 200, 202, 227, 239, 257, 260–61, 269, 274, 277, 285, 287, 290, 293–94, 296

Walzer, Michael, 261
Warren, Mary A., 76
Wasserman, David, 132, 157, 160–61
worth, 21, 32, 36, 57, 73, 98, 152, 166, 174, 180, 182, 221, 223, 234, 240, 244, 260, 270, 279, 282, *See also* value
  human, 224, 233, 248, 268
  moral, 35, 51
  public, 36, 60

Young, Iris Marion, 133, 277